Fela

The Life & Times
of an African
Musical Icon

Fela

The Life & Times
of an African
Musical Icon

Michael E. Veal

Temple University Press
Philadelphia

Temple University Press, Philadelphia 19122
Copyright © 2000 by Temple University
All rights reserved
Published 2000
Printed in the United States of America

Library of Congress Cataloging-in-Publication Data
Veal, Michael E., 1963–
    Fela: the life and times of an African musical icon / Michael E. Veal.
      p. cm.
    Includes bibliographical references and index.
    ISBN 1-56639-764-2 (alk. paper) – ISBN 1-56639-765-0 (paper: alk. paper)
      1. Fela, 1938–[1997] 2. Musicians–Nigeria–Biography. 3. Afrobeat–
    History and criticism.
    I. Title.

    ML410.F2955 V43 2000
    781.63'092–dc21
    [B]   99-051605

ISBN 13: 978-1-56639-765-0 (paper : alk. paper)

112907P

There are some artists who, given the nature of their energies and the tug of their involvements, embody the tempers of an era. Their stories as enfants terribles run both at tangents to and roughly parallel with the turbulences of a miasmic generation. Because they grew up with the upheavals, affecting and being strongly affected by them, their stories form a kind of commentary on a period and provide a kind of understanding of its spirit. They personify controversy of one sort or another and they are part of the popular imagination in such a way that inspire tangles of legends.

—BEN OKRI, *"Living Legend"*

Artists are here to disturb the peace.

— *JAMES BALDWIN,*
Conversations with
James Baldwin

Contents

Photographs follow pages 75 and 220

Acknowledgments

I would like to acknowledge the following people without whom the completion of this book would have been impossible: Fela Anikulapo-Kuti for sharing his hospitality, his time, and the use of his alto saxophone; Dr. Gage Averill, for his long-standing support and encouragement; my parents, Henry and Yvonnecris Veal, for their lifelong support and encouragement; my godmother, Eula Mae Tyson, for her support and encouragement; and all the members of the Veal, Coleman, Smith, and Tyson families for their love and support.

At Wesleyan University, where I completed the first draft of this book as a master's thesis in ethnomusicology, I would like to thank Mark Slobin and Robert Rosenthal, as well as other professors who offered suggestions or helped in other ways: Indira Karamcheti, Peter Kilby, Peter Mark, and Karen Smyers. I would especially like to thank Dr. Su Zheng of the Music Department and Robert Lancefield of Davison Art Center for the time they devoted to reading and discussing my work. I would also like to thank Professor Abraham Adzenyah, Anthony Braxton, Eric Charry, and Jay Hoggard for their support and encouragement. The completion of this work was aided immeasurably by the kindness of several Wesleyan staff members: Allison Insall, Barbara Schukoske, and Beth Labriola of the Office of Graduate Student Services, Hope Hancock of the Music Department, Diane Kelly and Randy Wilson of Olin Library, Benjiman Jackson of Academic Computing, and Kate Wolfe of the Interlibrary Loan Office.

I would like to give a shout to my friends who have shared or endured my music obsession for decades: Marilyn Barnwell, Richard Ehrman, Yomi Gbolagunte, Peter and Jennifer Hadley, Trevor Holder, Arthur Jafa, Suzu and Shamballa Kawamoto, Tim "Groove Maneuvers" Kinley, Emily Laber, Steve Lantner, Mirjana Lausevic, Ingi-Mai Loorand, Rachael Miller, Rebecca Miller, Julius Ndimbie, Jon Shub, John Sims, Tony Sims, Ivan Smith, Preston Smith, Sharan Strange, Greg Tate, and Santi White. I would also like to acknowledge Olakunle Tejuoso and family, Wale Oki, and the staff of The Jazz Hole and the *Glendora Review*. Finally, I would like to thank Franya Berkman for her unconditional love, support, and companionship during the arduous months of completing this manuscript.

I would like to remember the following family members and friends who passed away during the writing of this book, and whom I will dearly miss: Mrs. Julia Coleman and Mr. Tony Coleman; Mr. Percell Smith, Jr.; Mrs. Gladys Bolden and Mr. Earl Bolden, Sr.; Ms. Rosa Veal; Mr. Raleigh B. Smith; Mrs. Mollie B. Smith; Mr. Calvin Brooks, Sr.; Mrs. Reggie Ann White; Mrs. Roger Mae Evans; Mrs. Estella Garrison; Dr. William M. Hewlett; Mr. Aurelius King; Mr. Alfred Sims, Sr.; Mr. Edward Blackwell; and Mr. Michael Malone.

I would like to acknowledge my musical friends and colleagues in New York City, Middletown, Boston, and elsewhere: Abraham Adzenyah's *New Talking Drums;* Gbenga Awoleye; *Afrophysics Research; Aqua Ife;* Idrissou Badarou; Chilly Mark Bader; Flip Barnes; Black Rock Coalition; Charles Blass; *Bula Matadi; Dub Culture;* Thomas Sayers Ellis; Los Afortunados; Tristra Newyear; *Pandemonium;* Anthony "Topi" Peterson; Mikke Ringquist; Felix "Quinto Kidd" Sanabria; Elizabeth Sayre; Toby Sims; Gustavo Vaz Da Costa; and *Zabe I Babe.*

I would like to thank the following people who graciously allowed their photographs or other work to be used in this book: Adrian Boot, Dr. John Collins, Toshiya Endo (http://biochem.chem.nagoya-u.ac.jp/~endo/africa.html), Andrew Frankel, *The Glendora Review,* Juliet Highet, Cheryl Johnson-Odim, Miki Kagami, Alan Leeds, Sandra Isadore McLeish, Leni Sinclair, C. C. Smith, and the Estate of Fela Anikulapo-Kuti.

I would like to acknowledge the fellowship support of Five Colleges, Inc., and the Music Department of Mount Holyoke College (Kathryn Ananda-Owens, Allen Bonde, Michelle Dempsey, Robert Eisenstein, Adrienne Greenbaum, Tim Johnson, Linda Laderach, Louise Litterick, Larry Schipull, and Gary Steigerwalt). I would also like to acknowledge other members of the MHC faculty and staff, including Awam Ampka, Lucas Wilson, Teena Johnson-Smith, Dan Czitrum, and Dean of Faculty Peter Berek. Finally, I would like to acknowledge my colleagues in the Department of Music at Yale University: Kathryn Alexander, David Clampitt, Gregory Dubinsky, Allen Forte, Michael Friedmann, John Halle, James Hepokoski, Robert Holzer, Patrick McCreless, Carole Morgan, Robert Morgan, Kristina Muxfeldt, Leon Plantinga, Ellen Rosand, Ramon Satyendra, Willie Strong, Matthew Suttor, and Craig Wright.

I would also like to thank the following for their invaluable assistance.

In Nigeria: Mrs. D. B. Gbolagunte and family; Wale Olaoye; "Mr. T" and Monsuro Adams of the Fela Musik Library, Ikeja; Dr. Beko Ransome-Kuti; Seun Anikulapo-Kuti; and especially the following members of the Egypt 80 Band and Kalakuta Organization: Yinusa Akinibosun ("Y.S."); Lekan Animashaun ("Baba Ani"); Boto; Rilwan Fagbemi ("Showboy"); Benjamin Ijagun; Durotimi Ikujenyu ("Duro"); Dede Mabiaku; Soji Odukogbe; Oghene; Femi Bankole Osunla ("Femi Foto"); Wale Toriola; and Kehinde Umokoro.

In the United States: Jay Babcock; Jennifer Ballantyne; Andy Breslau; Mike Akubude; Melissa Da; Pascal Imbert; Oluko Imo; Amy Ingram; Aaron Mulvany; Cyrille Nnakoum; Barbara Oplinger; David Sommerstein; Roger Steffens; Robert Teagan; Kaoru Tokumasu; Donatus Ugonabo; Deborah Wong; and Chris Zingg and Mark Henderson of *In Your Ear Records,* Boston and Providence. I would like to thank Doris Braendel and Jennifer French of Temple University Press and David Updike for the enthusiasm with which they have guided this manuscript through the publication process.

Finally, I would like to dedicate this book to two people. First, to the memory of Fela Anikulapo-Kuti, who, despite it all, left a model of artistic brilliance, fun, and social commitment for all musicians to aspire to. Second, to Tahmima Anam, the best friend a person could ever have.

English is the official language in Nigeria, spoken alongside hundreds of indigenous languages and dialects. Pidgin English, a fusion of English words and African syntactic structure, is also widely spoken in the major cities. Fela sings and speaks in three voices throughout this book—Yoruba, standard English, and pidgin English—and these are heavily infused with African-American jargon and continuously evolving Lagos slang. In every instance, I have reproduced Fela's voice as spoken. While certain passages may initially prove difficult for the Western reader, the main ideas are clear and I have provided standard English translations for particularly difficult sections. Song lyrics are reproduced with Fela's original and my translation side by side.

For the purposes of foreshadowing events or providing Fela's running commentary on various public events as they unfolded, I have excerpted his comments from "Chief Priest Say," the classified column he ran in various Lagos newspapers during the 1970s and 1980s, at various points throughout the text.

The Life & Times
of an African
Musical Icon

Introduction: "Abami Eda"

REPORTER: *A Nigerian senator just told me:* "*If even only 5000 Nigerians started imitating Fela, it would soon be very chaotic here!*"

FELA: *No, it would be a revolution!*

Quoted in MOORE AND KAMARA 1981

The date: a humid weekend night in the early 1990s. The scene: outside the Afrika Shrine nightclub in Ikeja, Lagos, Nigeria, home base of the legendary Nigerian musician Fela Anikulapo-Kuti and his thirty-piece orchestra, Egypt 80. Even though the ubiquitous, machine gun–toting soldiers of the Nigerian army have a well-deserved reputation for making the lives of ordinary civilians miserable, they are decidedly peripheral to tonight's scenario. The Shrine is understood to be Fela's autonomous zone, where his own anarchic, hedonistic law prevails.

The atmosphere is festive as the audience enters, a mixture of students, activists, rebels, criminals, music lovers, and even politicians, policemen, and soldiers arriving incognito. They make their way through the sea of traders hawking their goods by candlelight—snacks, drinks, cigarettes, and marijuana—as the sound of the Egypt 80 spills from inside the open-air club. After purchasing a ticket and being frisked for weapons at the doorway, audience members enter the interior of the Shrine, a semi-enclosed countercultural carnival of funky, political music, pot smoking, mysticism, and provocative dancing. Four fishnet-draped go-go cages, each containing a loosely clad female dancer grinding languorously, rise out of the smoky haze. A neon light in the shape of the African continent casts its red glow over the stage. In addition to more food, drink, and marijuana vendors, the rear of the club houses an actual shrine—a large altar containing religious objects and photos of Fela's Pan-Africanist political heroes, including Malcolm X, Marcus Garvey, Kwame Nkrumah, and Sekou Toure, and his late mother, Mrs. Funmilayo Anikulapo-Kuti.

The Egypt 80 band has been playing since midnight, warming up the crowd with classics from Fela's older recorded repertoire, such as "Trouble Sleep" (1972), "Why Blackman Dey Suffer" (1972), "Lady" (1972), "Water No Get Enemy" (1975), "Opposite People" (1975), "Sorrow, Tears and Blood" (1977), "Dog Eat Dog" (1977), "Beasts of No Nation" (1986), and bandleader/baritone saxophonist Lekan Animashaun's "Serere (Do Right)." The band is awaiting Fela's arrival, so these songs are sung by various band members, including Animashaun (known around the Shrine as "Baba Ani"), second baritone saxophonist Rilwan Fagbemi (known as "Showboy"), Fela's ten-year-old son Seun, and artist/musician Dede Mabiaku, whom Fela often referred to as his "adopted son."

Fela, the "Chief Priest of Shrine," finally arrives with his retinue around 2 A.M., to tumultuous applause. Dressed tonight in a tight purple jumpsuit stitched with traditional Yoruba symbols and shapes, he makes his way through the crowd to the stage and salutes his audience with the clenched-fist black power salute. He steps up to the mike and pauses, surveying the crowd with mischievous eyes while taking intermittent puffs from a flashlight-sized joint in his hand. Finally he speaks:

> Everybody say ye-ye!

The crowd roars in response, and Fela segues directly into the profane, no-holds-barred criticism of the country's leaders he has offered his audiences for the past two decades:

> Bro's and sisters, if you want to know how corrupt this country is, that word "corruption" has lost its meaning here!

Fela arches his eyebrows, thrusts his chest and stomach out, and marches around the stage in imitation of the arrogant and obese *ogas* (literally "bosses"), men of importance who parade their wealth around Lagos in the midst of suffering:

> "Yeah, I'm *corrupt,* man!"

The crowd bursts into laughter, and Fela continues his monologue:

> In fact, corruption has even become a *title* in this country! In Germany, they have *President* Kohl. In America, they have *President* Bush. In England they have *Prime Minister* Major. Here in Nigeria, we have *Corrupted* Babangida!

At the mention of their president, the audience shouts in deafening unison "Ole!" (Yoruba for "thief"). Fela switches into pidgin English and recounts an incident in which the president was snubbed by French president François Mitterand during a recent state visit:

When Corrupted Babangida go for France, Mitterand no wan meet am. He go dey send a cultural minister. He go say Nigeria be nation of thieves. The man was disgraced. When he came back, the fucking army was kicking ass all over Nigeria! Na how many students dem kill fo' dat one?

The crowd roars in laughter and approval, the Shrine now rocking like a revivalist church:

You see, bro's and sisters, I know dem. They are nothing but spirit beings. They are the same motherfuckers who sold Africans into slavery hundreds of years ago. In fact, the same spirit who controls Babangida controls Bush and Thatcher too. Everyone is here to play their same role again, and I want you all to know that tonight; Babangida, Obasanjo, Abiola, they have all been here before. That's why I call this time the era of "second slavery." They don't have to come here and take us by force—our leaders sell us up front. Everybody say ye-ye!

The audience shouts "ye-ye!" punctuated with cries of "yab dem!" (abuse them).

Bro's and sisters, I'm gonna play for you now, a thing we call M.A.S.S.—"Music Against Second Slavery."

Fela spins around and sternly surveys the orchestra members, who stare at him intently. Slowly, he begins to clap out the song's tempo to the band, wiggling his slender body to the rhythm. Though short in stature, he wields enormous authority onstage. A guitarist begins a serpentine single-note line, accompanied by a percussionist thumping out a thunderous rhythm atop an eight-foot traditional *gbedu* drum laid on its side. The audience indicates its growing excitement by yelling Fela's various nicknames in response: "Omo Iya Aje!" (son of a powerful woman [literally "witch"]), "Baba!" (father), "Abami Eda!" (strange one, or spirit being), "Chief Priest!" "Black President!" Fela raises his hands above his head and waves the percussionists and rhythm section in. Time itself seems to slowly shift along with the sticks and the *shekere* rattle, whose steady chirping frames an intricate tapestry of spacy rhythm. Stepping to his electric organ at center stage, Fela begins to improvise around the rhythm with greater and greater density. At the height of his solo, he waves in the ten-piece horn section, which enters dramatically, blaring the song's theme. With instrumental solos, featured dancers, and audience participation games, it will be another thirty minutes before Fela even begins to sing, but the audience is in delirious, swirling motion. Another night at the Afrika Shrine has begun.

Fela will perform from his arrival until dawn. This is partly in the tradition of Lagos nightlife, but it also results from more pragmatic considerations—Lagos is one of the world's most dangerous cities and travel is extremely ill-advised after dark. In keeping with his policy of only presenting unrecorded material in concert, Fela is playing a repertoire familiar only to regular attendants of the Shrine tonight.

"Chop and Clean Mouth Like Nothing Happened, Na New Name for Stealing" details the Nigerian economy's plundering by successive heads of state; "Country of Pain" bemoans the hardships of life in post–oil boom Nigeria; "Big Blind Country" uses the English blonde wigs worn by Nigerian judges and the hair straightening practiced by some African women as metaphors for the "artificial niceness" of the country's politicians; "Government of Crooks" details the siphoning of the country's oil wealth by corrupt politicians, bureaucrats, and soldiers; "Music Against Second Slavery" decries the impact of Islam on contemporary Nigerian politics and power relations; "Akunakuna, Senior Brother of Perambulator" criticizes government harassment of petty street traders and other participants in the country's informal economy; and "Pansa Pansa" is a defiant battle cry composed in the wake of the brutal 1977 army raid on Fela's Lagos compound, the "Kalakuta Republic."[1] Like most of his music since 1979, these are all lengthy, complex compositions, often lasting forty minutes or more.

On stage, Fela combines the autocratic bandleading style and dancing agility of James Brown, the mystical inclinations of Sun Ra, the polemicism of Malcolm X, and the harsh, insightful satire of Richard Pryor. Gliding gracefully around the stage in white face paint, which he says facilitates communication with the spirit world, he is not above interrupting the performance to harangue musicians, sound technicians, or audiences. However, the Egypt 80 band is in top form tonight, executing Fela's music with energy, clarity, and whiplash precision. On up-tempo numbers like "Government of Crooks" or "Country of Pain," Fela and the band play with an intensity that thoroughly possesses the Shrine audience. On slower, mid-tempo numbers like "Chop and Clean Mouth . . . ," Fela's highlife and funk roots are evident in the easy rhythmic flow of the percussion section; the chopping, stuttering guitars; and the blaring, syncopated horns. Above it all, Fela alternately jokes with the audience and spits out his political lyrics in angry, declamatory phrases darting between the shrill voices of the six-member female chorus and the guttural, baritone punctuations of the horn section. On "Government of Crooks," he sings about the government's complicity in the despoliation of southeastern Ogoniland by foreign oil companies, a state of affairs that had recently culminated in the state execution of Ogoni activist/playwright Ken Saro-Wiwa:

All of us know our country	All of us know our country
Plenty-plenty oil-e dey	There is plenty oil
Plenty things dey for Africa	Plenty resources in Africa
Petroleum is one of them	Petroleum is one of them
All di places that get di oil-o	All the places where oil lies
Now oil pollution for di place	Are spoiled with pollution
All the farms done soak with oil-o	The farms are soaked by oil leaks
All the villages don catch disease	The villages are rife with disease
Money done spoil di oil area	Money has ruined the oil areas
But some people inside government	But some people in government

Dem don become billionaires	Have become billionaires
Billionaires on top of oil-o	From oil wealth
and underhanded crookedness . . .	and underhanded crookedness . . .

On "Movement Against Second Slavery," he takes his most insulting potshots at the country's military government while subtly reprising his famous song "Zombie," which precipitated a brutal military attack on his compound fifteen years earlier:

FELA: Now come look our president	*FELA:* Now, look at our president
CHORUS: Zombie! (repeats after every line)	*CHORUS:* Zombie!
FELA: Na soldier, him be president	*FELA:* A soldier is president
He say he want to travel	He says he wants to travel
Travel on a state visit to France	Travel on a state visit to France
Na so him go,	And so he went,
He go Paris-o	He went to Paris
And when he reach there nko	And when he reached his destination
Na ordinary minister meet am	He was met by an ordinary minister
White man go dey tell-e dem:	The white man told him:
"We don tire for soldier	"We are tired of soldiers
Soldier cannot be president	A soldier cannot be president
It just be like robbery"	It's just like armed robbery"
Like armed robber come meet you for house	Like an armed robber coming to your house
The armed robber come take over your house—	The armed robber will take over your house—
Chop all your food	Eat all your food
Fuck all your wives	Fuck all your wives
Take all your money	Take all your money
Hen! Na so soldier government be-o . . .	Hmm! This is what a military government means . . .

Reflecting Fela's feeling that his music was as much for education as it was for dancing and entertainment, the Shrine audience enjoyed the music in various ways. Tuesday night audiences tended toward reflection; while some danced singly or in pairs, most enjoyed the music from their seats, listening intently to Fela's lyrics and freely offering responses or rebuttals to his comments. On these nights, the smell of Indian hemp mixed with the pulse of the hypnotic afrobeat in the thick tropical air, and the Shrine took on the ambience of a psychedelic town meeting held in a dance hall. Friday was mainly a dance night, with the house packed and people on their feet from the time Egypt 80 took the stage until dawn—laughing, cheering, and singing along with Fela's every line. Saturday—when Fela presented his "Comprehensive Show" complete with the Egypt 80 dancers and an enormous, ritual conical "cigar" presumably filled with marijuana and various native herbs—was also mainly a dance night, with the most diverse audience of the week; listeners traveled from all over Lagos and beyond to enjoy the music. For some attendees, a visit to the Shrine, with its marijuana smoking, go-go dancers, and antigovernment lyrics, was an act of social rebellion in itself. Others came to engage, examine, or debate Fela's political philosophy. Still other visitors were content merely to enjoy the music, irrespective of its political sentiments. Each show concluded at dawn with Fela pausing before the shrine in the rear of the building. With intense flames leaping into the air, the "Chief Priest of Shrine" paused—flanked by two young male attendants—to salute his ancestors and Pan-Africanist heroes, before returning home as the rest of Lagos awakened with the dawn.

This book represents the fruition of more than ten years of critical and recreational listening, musical performance, academic research, traveling, and collecting. My interest in Fela dates to 1983, when I was introduced to his music by a fellow musician while a jazz composition and arranging student at the Berklee College of Music in Boston. Having grown up in an environment in which I was surrounded by various genres of African-American music, I was immediately struck by Fela's music because it seemed to recontextualize and extend musical ideas which were meaningful to me. In Fela's music, I recognized unmistakable echoes of diasporic African musical innovators and styles: James Brown, John Coltrane, modal jazz, big-band jazz, funk, rhythm-and-blues, and salsa. At the same time, I recognized an overall spirit and use of many musical devices I associated with West African music: tightly woven rhythm patterns, vocal chants, call-and-response choruses, and an overall percussive approach to articulation, among others. Compositionally, I admired Fela's ability to compose a seemingly endless series of complex, catchy groove patterns, chorus lines, and horn riffs. Compositions rarely clocked in at less than fifteen minutes, with sections allotted for scored ensemble passages, jazz-styled solo improvisations, choral singing, and the vocal song proper, which itself comprised a number of movements. In his fashioning of a long-form highlife-funk-jazz fusion called "afrobeat," he had countered the commercialism dictating that songs be restricted to three-minute formats that were, in cultural context, insufficient for satisfying dancing or reflective listening. More generally, I was inspired by the way Fela had refashioned many conventions of recent African-American music within a West African cultural context, and by the awareness of Pan-African identity and musical practice that implicitly underlay this process.

Of course, no introduction to the world of Fela would be complete without the mythology that inevitably accompanies the music: the musician who created his own countercultural enclave in the heart of Lagos, married twenty-seven women in one day, made a career of criticizing his country's leaders in song, survived numerous attacks by the Nigerian authorities (and whose mother died as a result of one such attack), publicly smoked marijuana in a country where people are sentenced to lengthy prison terms for the most minor of such infractions, and was regarded by his fellow Nigerians as both a singularly courageous hero and Public Menace No. 1.

My continuing study of Fela's music eventually led to an opportunity to participate in his music. I met Fela in New York City in the autumn of 1986, during his first major American tour, following his much-publicized eighteen-month imprisonment in Nigeria on currency smuggling charges. During his next three American tours, in the summers of 1989, 1990, and 1991, I played out with his group as a guest soloist on saxophone whenever they visited the New York area. Finally, during the spring of 1992, I made a trip to Lagos. In what amounted to an intensive "master class," I made several visits to Fela's three-story residence located in the Ikeja section of the city. During these visits, Fela gave me further insight into his compositional method by playing me recordings of his unreleased music and showing me his scores. I also played as a saxophonist with Fela and his Egypt 80 band at the Afrika Shrine, located on Pepple Street a block away from the Ikeja bus roundabout.

While the sound of afrobeat was clearly distinguishable from other popular Nigerian genres, it required a visit to Lagos to fully understand the subcultural distance at which Fela operated from the dominant culture surrounding him. On the streets of densely populated Lagos, the distinctive culture of urban West Africa is immediately evident in the flowing, colorful traditional attire, bustling outdoor markets, ubiquitous music, and endless stream of street traders and merchants haggling in melodious local tongues. With the beat of Nigerian music pouring from every other storefront, the relentless beating sun, and the aggressively melodious patter, the intensity of Lagos gives one the impression that everything is vibrating to an underlying rhythm, a kaleidoscopic, spontaneously orchestrated urban African sensory overload.

Equally evident against this colorful backdrop is the staggering, inescapable poverty and desperation of Lagos. Extending outward in nearly every direction from the modern business center on Lagos Island is a sea of corrugated metal-roofed shacks and wooden shanties, populated mostly by rural migrants forced from their village homes into the city by a neglected agricultural sector and dreams of big city money. The streets are lined with acrid, open sewers festering in the tropical heat. The population density and scale of poverty is virtually unimaginable for a Westerner. A drive across town can take hours as the driver laboriously negotiates the "go-slow"—the incessant crush of humans and vehicles amassed on every thoroughfare. Passengers dangle precariously from the outsides of public buses packed far beyond capacity and tottering with their loads. Children of all ages dart perilously across streets, avenues, freeways, and highways, hoping to sell their petty goods to any passenger whose car slows down enough for a quick transaction. Occasionally, a foreign-manufactured luxury vehicle makes its way through this morass, its passengers resplendent in traditional robes or fashionable Western attire. This and other signs indicate the opulence enjoyed by the city's elite classes, who live in the more upscale areas such as Victoria Island and Ikoyi. Although there are middle-class areas such as Surulere and Ikeja, the city is dominated mainly by two elements—the millions of urban poor living in squalor, and the menacing, machine gun–wielding soldiers of the Lagos police and

Nigerian army who have held power, with brief interruptions, since independence in 1960.

The postcolonial mix of architectural styles in Lagos—glass-and-steel modern, Victorian English, Portuguese, corrugated iron-roofed shanties, and walled compounds—bespeaks a history of turbulent, sometimes violent cultural contact and social transformation, and a contemporary culture constructed by patchwork collage. Similarly, the icons and symbols of Christianity and Islam, evidence of Africa's historical interaction with European and Middle Eastern cultures, are ubiquitous. The Christian influence is reflected in the scriptural quotes and slogans that abound on nearly every type of surface including public buses, billboards, and buildings. Numerous churches represent a variety of denominations, including Anglican, Roman Catholic, Baptist, Pentecostal, and the more indigenized sects of Aladura, Seraphim, and Cherubim. The sound of *juju* music, with its stylistic foundation of Christian hymns and indigenous percussion, is encountered at nearly every turn.

The influence of Islam is less immediately evident, but the foreign visitor will find ample evidence of its growing prominence in Nigeria. Rows of private mosques have been constructed on the properties of Lagos Island's wealthiest Muslim businessmen, and tremulous prayer calls periodically soar above the city noise from distorted public loudspeakers. Aside from a visit to the northern region of the country, however, the most immediate evidence of Islam's influence is the *fuji* music blaring from stores, portable tape players, and bootleg cassette stalls. With its Koranic verses, nasalized melismatic singing, and virtuoso traditional drumming, fuji borrows from Middle Eastern musical techniques to create a powerful African pop music hybrid.

Confronted with the spectacle of modern Lagos, any Western visitor sympathetic to black African culture must wonder whether they are witnessing a radically alternative civil and social structure—an unbridled, distinctly African intelligence, which (despite Negritude and Afrocentrism) is not yet completely articulated. Or, on a more apocalyptic note, they may wonder if they are witnessing the degraded disorganization of a postcolonial society skirting the abyss of complete civil, social, and infrastructural collapse. The truth seems to lie somewhere in between. On the one hand, this chaotic energy reflects an endlessly mutable and traditionally rooted form of creativity that has endowed urban African cultures with an extremely high level of adaptability, leading to a profusion of new social and cultural forms. In some respects at least, the breakdown of traditional forms has led to new possibilities within the current disorder. On the other hand, the breakdown of traditional social structures, coupled with the realities of gross inequality, overpopulation, corruption, ethnic tension, religious conflict, and environmental stress, points to an impending crisis of epic proportions.

The twenty-minute journey along Ikorodu Road and Obafemi Awolowo Way from the center of Lagos into the outlying area of Ikeja takes the visitor past walled compounds, banks, hotels, nightclubs, and an endless row of palm trees swaying in the humid tropical breeze. Ikeja is known for its hotels, clubs, and street traders, and its active nightlife continues despite frequent power outages and the country's recent economic and political hardships. Traffic grinds to a virtual standstill as one approaches the Ikeja bus stop, a bustling maelstrom of pedestrians, street traders, buses, taxis, and motorists attempting to make their way under the relentless midday sun. It is the energy of this inner-city chaos that infuses Fela's music. Approaching the intersection, the visitor will gradually be able to differentiate the blaring, discordant strains of Fela's horn section from the surrounding noise. The recorded afrobeat music is coming from Mr. T's Fela Musik Library, a record store devoted exclusively to Fela's music. From here it is a short walk to both the Afrika Shrine and Fela's house, known as "Kalakuta," on nearby Gbemisola Street.

This was actually Fela's second Afrika Shrine. The original club, located in the Empire Hotel in Surulere, was permanently closed by the government in 1977. And Fela's final Ikeja residence was not the Kalakuta of legend, located at Mosholashi Junction in Surulere, which was set ablaze by irate soldiers in 1977 and completely razed the following year. Gbemisola is an upper-middle-class Ikeja street, lined with private houses and apartment buildings. Apart from the huge poster of Fela on the front of the house, his residence blended easily into the neighborhood—a far cry from the old Kalakuta, which dominated the surrounding neighborhood and spawned its own subculture. Still, the Gbemisola house operated according to the same communal structure as Fela's earlier residence.

When I visited Fela there in 1992, the first floor housed the thirty or so female dancers and chorus singers of the Egypt 80 band, as well as other senior members of the Kalakuta Organization. In addition to Fela's bedroom, the second level was occupied mostly by young men who served a variety of functions in Kalakuta, and who could often be found lounging on mats spread over the carpeted sitting-room floor, which doubled as sleeping mats. The centerpieces of the sparsely furnished sitting room were an old upright piano and a painting of Fela's mother. The third floor of the house was occupied by Fela's remaining wives from his 1978 communal marriage, as well as his two youngest children: his son Seun (then ten) and his daughter Motunrayo (then twelve). The house was a beehive of activity. Its mostly young occupants variously ran errands, performed household tasks, or sat chatting and smoking cigarettes or marijuana. The house members were generally very friendly; though various arguments spontaneously erupted among them, these evaporated equally suddenly, usually just as they seemed to hover on the brink of a deathly confrontation.

One trait that distinguished Fela in the sphere of musical celebrities was his unusual accessibility. On my first visit to his house in 1992, my friends and I arrived well after 10 P.M. during a power outage. We had to wait in the darkness of the Kalakuta sitting room for about an hour until the lights came back on, but Fela emerged shortly thereafter in his usual attire of bikini briefs. After a long chat, the entire party relocated to his bedroom. It was here that we encountered Fela in his most frequent offstage mode—reclining with ever-present joint in hand and chatting on various topics from the mundane to the mystical, while house members filtered in and out.

Fela performed at the Shrine three nights a week—Tuesday, Friday, and Saturday. During my stay, his popularity in Lagos was still quite high, despite the long lapses between his record releases, the Nigerian public's general lack of familiarity with his most recent music, and the fact that he had begun to cancel the occasional show due to ill health. The Tuesday shows were well attended, and the Shrine was filled to capacity for the Friday and Saturday shows. Besides being his nightclub and musical home base, the Afrika Shrine functioned as a ritual space in which Fela could actualize his spiritual beliefs and channel this spiritual energy into his artistic creativity. His beliefs represented a variation on traditional Yoruba ancestor worship in which the deities were both traditional Yoruba entities and more recent historical figures of deep personal significance. While this was a highly personalized variation on traditional belief, it did conform in the broadest sense to the historical development of the Yoruba religion, in which deities are considered mythologized representations of actual historical figures.[2]

In the Judeo-Christian cultures of the West, religious activity is often seen as a contemplative, devotional, or service activity centered around a single, all-powerful supreme being. In Fela's variation on traditional spirituality, a different quality was strongly apparent. In his 1982 autobiography Fela discusses his initial involvement in traditional African mysticism as primarily motivated by a need to repel the increasing episodes of government violence directed toward him and his followers.[3] Witnessing him saluting in front of the Shrine's altar, fists raised and eyes ablaze with defiance, flashbacks of government brutality—1974, 1977, 1981, 1989—seemed to linger in the flickering flames, invoking the sense of constant risk and danger that infused his art and life over three decades of continuously courting violent censure. A maverick spirit on even the most esoteric levels, Fela appealed to his personal pantheon of archaic and contemporary deities for political empowerment, psychic renewal, and physical protection, regenerating his community's psychic energy through music and ritualized revisitations of past personal terrors directed toward them. In a heavily militarized society that harbors many beliefs in complex supernatural forces, Fela's manipulation of this type of energy seems to have both protected him and provoked his most vicious enemies.

By his death at age 58 from AIDS-related complications in 1997, Fela had become something of a Nigerian institution, despite the disdain many held for his lifestyle and consistent antagonism of the country's rulers. Even in light of the widespread popularity of fuji, afrobeat could still be heard blaring from storefront shops and portable tape players throughout Lagos, and listeners who abhorred the man likened the refinement, restraint, and grace of his later music to "old, fine wine" when heard against the ever-present, frantic backdrop of fuji. Even Fela's day-to-day relationship with his longtime nemeses—Lagos police and Nigerian army soldiers—seemed relatively stable, having apparently settled into an uneasy truce after two decades of active hostility. Until the last year or so of his life, the red-light activity at the Shrine seemed largely tolerated, and audiences were generally free from fear of the police raids that were so frequent during the 1970s and 1980s. Late one night en route from Fela's house to the Shrine, the loose caravan of vehicles in which we rode was halted by soldiers—a sign of potential trouble. Upon recognizing the occupant, however, the soldiers waved the caravan past with clenched-fist salutes and shouts of "baba!" ("father") and "Black President!" The remarkable fact that such a well-known political dissident continued to flourish after three decades of subversive activity was likely a reflection of the (grudging to adoring) affection many Nigerians held for Fela, as well as the social marginality accorded to many musicians throughout West Africa. Fela alluded to this in

1977: "[The government and elites] think I'm crazy. If I were a respectable professor at a university saying these things, that would be something different. But to them, I'm just a musician, a crazy artist saying a lot of crazy things."[4]

It was this volatile mix of personal ingredients—charisma, musical talent, maverick lifestyle, populist ideology, and persistence in the face of persecution—that combined to make Fela a legend throughout Africa and the world. Celebrated during the 1970s as a musical innovator and a spokesperson for the continent's oppressed masses, he enjoyed worldwide celebrity during the 1980s, and was recognized in the 1990s as a major pioneer and elder statesman of African music.

Situated between a musical study and an ethnography, my semi-biographical narrative of Fela's life operates on three levels. First, I analyze Fela the musician, in his various roles as composer/arranger, bandleader, vocalist, and instrumentalist. In so doing, I survey his various musical influences, provide a continuous stylistic analysis that charts the development of his art throughout his career, and discuss concurrent trends in related musical genres. Second, I analyze Fela the social figure and the way his roles as political musician, derisive social/political critic, heir to a family protest tradition, social maverick, and creator of a distinct artistic subculture shaped his analysis and articulation of the major social, political, and cultural themes of his time in Nigeria. Third, I analyze Fela's work within two wider spheres: post-colonial Africa, and a dynamic of cross-cultural influence operating between Africa and cultures of the African diaspora.

Fela as Musician

Fela's body of musical work stands as one of the most original in contemporary Africa, a fusion of musical styles from around the world. Around 1970, he single-handedly developed and popularized an innovative musical genre which he named "afrobeat." A simplified musical definition of afrobeat might describe it as a heavily politicized, African-American influenced variant of the Nigerian dance-band highlife tradition, or, conversely, as a "re-Africanized" form of African-American funk music. In either case, it is a fusion of stylistic elements drawn both from Fela's native popular and traditional musical culture, and from African-American popular styles, with heavy overtones of Afro-Latin music and modal jazz.

Dance-band highlife, a West African ballroom style fusing big-band jazz horn sections, adapted indigenous folk songs, and Afro-Caribbean styles such as calypso and salsa, was developed by musicians such as E. T. Mensah in Ghana and Bobby Benson in Nigeria during the 1950s and was strongly associated with the nationalist, Anglophile elite. Funk music, developed primarily by James Brown during the late 1960s, is an African-American popular style that placed Brown's impassioned, gospel-derived vocals over jazzy horn arrangements and a highly syncopated, percussive rhythmic scheme (derived in part from Afro-Cuban music) similar to those found in traditional West African music. In the late 1960s, funk music was implicitly associated with an African-American rediscovery of African cultural roots as well as the political currents of the day, such as the black power movement. At the same time, the funk music of James Brown in particular was extremely popular and influential throughout West Africa.

With more than eighty albums containing about 150 songs (and a wealth of unrecorded or unreleased material), Fela's output rivals that of other prolific African music giants such as King Sunny Ade and Franco. His work was informed by the art music, traditional music, and popular music of West Africa; the art music and popular music of the African diaspora; and—indirectly—the art music of Western Europe. Specific musicians whose influence is strongly felt in Fela's music include James Brown (U.S., b. 1930), John Coltrane (U.S., 1926–1967), Ambrose Campbell (Nigeria, b. 1920s), a number of West African highlife bandleader/composers including E. T. Mensah (Ghana, 1919–1996) and Victor Olaiya (Nigeria, b. 1920s), and a number of neotraditional Yoruba musicians such as *apala* singers Haruna Ishola (Nigeria, d. 1983) and Ayinla Omowura (Nigeria, d. 1982).

As a member of the Yoruba ethnic group of southwestern Nigeria, Fela was heir to a long tradition of artistic innovation. The Yoruba are especially renowned worldwide for their creativity in the sonic, visual, and plastic arts. Modern Yoruba musicians such as Fela, King Sunny Ade, and Sikiru Ayinde Barrister are internationally recognized, as are modern visual artists such as Jimo Buraimoh and Twins Seven-Seven. The naturalistic bronze and terra-cotta portrait sculptures produced during the classical period of Ife (A.D. 1000–1400), the colorful beaded robes, vests, and crowns of Yoruba royalty, and the devotional wood carvings of various religious cults are among the most treasured objects of world art.[5] This rich, expressive culture developed as a result of three primary factors. First, the historically urban organization of the Yoruba, who claim the earliest urban settlements in West Africa,[6] was conducive to rapid and intense creative ferment. Second, their geographic location as a historical crossroads for trading activity between Europe, Africa, and the Middle East provided the Yoruba extensive cultural contact that enabled them to become masters at *syncretism*— the borrowing, refashioning, and integration of foreign cultural forms into their own cultural framework. Third, within their sociopolitical structure and tradition of divine kingship, the arts were strongly encouraged and patronized by traditional rulers.

Lagos, the modern Nigerian capital established during the colonial era, is a predominately Yoruba city, as well as a major West African port.[7] The syncretic Yoruba urban tradition, combined with the international cultural exposure and rapid development that have characterized Lagos during the colonial and postcolonial eras, has made the city the focus of successive waves of major musical innovation that continue to the present. This process has drawn on local, regional, and international styles of diverse origins, including West African, Western European, European-American, African-American, Afro-Caribbean, and Middle Eastern styles. It was in this fertile arena of creativity that Fela developed his afrobeat style from the remnants of dance-band highlife in the late 1960s, during a period in which the influence of African-American rhythm-and-blues music was particularly pervasive. Taking account of popular styles while directly addressing the new postcolonial African reality, Fela's afrobeat represented in the most immediate sense a transformation of highlife via a transmutation of funk. Thus, like the other dominant Yoruba popular styles such as juju, fuji, and apala, Fela's afrobeat style fits into a broader historical pattern of dynamic Yoruba innovation, urban creative hybridization, and cross-cultural synthesis.[8]

Fela's age, class background, and British collegiate musical training also place him on the periphery of a tradition of Nigerian art music composers such as Samuel Akpabot (b. 1931), Ayo Bankole (1935–1976), Lazarus Ekueme (b. 1936), Akin Euba (b. 1935), Adams Fiberesimi (b. 1936), and Okechukwu Ndubuisi (b. 1936).[9] Utilizing their formal knowledge of Western music in the contexts of late colonial-era nationalism and postcolonial nationhood, these composers generally conform to the reflective functions of European art music, while deriving source material from local African folk traditions.[10] In this sense they are similar to European composers such as Béla Bartók (1881–1945) and Antonin Dvorák (1841–1904) in the implicitly nationalist agenda that underlay their work. The adaptation of local folk materials to a Western European compositional model was largely motivated by the modernist project of channeling ethnic identity toward a new allegiance to European-styled nation-states, with their attendant aesthetic forms and cultural institutions. Fela worked partly within this tradition through-out his career, but it can be seen particularly in his post-1979 work, when he began to entertain serious political aspirations while simultaneously fashioning himself as a "composer" and referring to his music as "classical African music." He had, in some ways, quite a westernized conception of the composition, which differs from more fluid conceptions held by traditional musicians. He was also more exacting in his application of Western musical theory than most of his Nigerian popular music contemporaries, for whom music is mainly transmitted by oral channels. Thus, Fela's work can also be regarded partly as "composition" in the Western sense of the term.

Yet for all his formal training and conscious manipulation of the compositional process, Fela steered clear of the setting and goals of art music. Although he referred to his music as "classical" and often downplayed its danceability, it operated firmly within the sphere of popular music. Its performance venue was not the symphony hall, chamber parlor, or recital hall, but the nightclub, arena, stadium, radio, phonograph, and discotheque. Unlike most art musics, it was not sustained by the patronage of the ruling classes, with whom Fela maintained a consistently antagonistic relationship; nor does it aspire to the functional goal of pure aesthetic contemplation. Afrobeat belongs—alongside reggae, rap, salsa, funk, calypso, souk-ous, juju, and mbaquanga—as one of the premier Afrocentric popular dance gen-res of the post–World War II era.

Fela as Social Figure

Fela was the eye-opener for a lot of us—this man had a message. . . . In the 1970s, Fela would be in the Shrine with books spread out for all the university students, telling them: "You don't know anything, go and read

this book . . ." He was a force for us. Where else could we get this knowledge? There were no books to read, if you're not in the right discipline, you wouldn't know. But you go to the Shrine, listen to the records, and there's a message there.
                    OLAKUNLE TEJUOSO, *interview with author, December* 1992

As much as it conformed to historical patterns of Yoruba creative ferment, Fela's work differed significantly from other modern Yoruba genres in several crucial ways. First, his work cannot be analyzed from exclusively within the Yoruba tradition. Initially a Christian member of the consolidating Nigerian pan-ethnic bourgeoisie (a class position from which he later dissented), his identity was molded more along class than ethnic lines. In recounting his youth, Fela noted his parents' disdain for traditional Yoruba beliefs and ceremonies, and both parents were involved in professional activities that took them far beyond the local sphere. Having learned Western art music from an early age, it was natural that Fela would gravitate toward highlife music at the outset of his career. Not only was it the popular dance music of the day, but it required a practical knowledge of Western music, and it was a cosmopolitan, pan-ethnic style that operated largely independently of traditional ethnic social networks. While Fela subsequently strove to ground his art in more traditionally African conceptions of social function, his highlife-era roots remain clear in the conception and instrumentation of his band, its multiethnic membership, and the Pan-African orientation of his song lyrics.

Second, most popular Yoruba styles have historically been developed by two or more practitioners over a period of decades, with innovation occurring as a natural product of their competition.[11] Thus, the development of modern juju has largely been dominated by Chief Ebenezer Obey and King Sunny Ade; fuji by Sikiru Ayinde Barrister, Wasiu Ayinde Barrister, and Ayinla Kollington; apala by Haruna Ishola and Ayinla Omowura. However, Fela alone was responsible for the development of afrobeat. Although other composers—most notably Sunny Ade and Sonny Okosuns—have integrated components of the style into their music, afrobeat is indelibly associated with Fela in its instrumental sound, textual content, and social function.[12]

A third distinction is the most significant. Juju, fuji, and apala music are all deeply rooted in both traditional rural culture and the modern urban Yoruba elite and are heavily dependent on both networks as sources of patronage. The common West African custom of praise singing is integral to this relationship, and both commercial recordings and live performances in these genres typically include a number of songs in praise of traditional rulers, government officials, successful businessmen, and other respected members of the community. This is merely a modern variation of traditional social practice, in which musicians were usually in the employ of political rulers. In live performance, talented praise singers are rewarded with "spraying," a common West African gesture of appreciation in which currency is pasted onto the perspiring forehead of the praise-singing musician. Spraying serves two purposes—it confers appreciation and financial remuneration upon the recipient musician, while demonstrating the wealth, importance, and prestige of the patron. Thus the praise-singing musician functions as an important mediator and validator of social and economic status.

Situated as they are in close proximity to traditional and modern institutions of political power, these styles often express sentiments that indirectly legitimize and reinforce the material inequalities in contemporary Nigerian society by referencing modern power dynamics in the context of traditional Yoruba values.[13] This close relationship between music making and institutions of power—generally encompassing both praise singing and reciprocal financial patronage—is nearly universal throughout sub-Saharan Africa and conditions the production and reception of music on a variety of levels.

While praise singing is essential to much music making, direct criticism is almost never employed, unless it is directed toward rival musicians. Lyrics are more likely to employ oblique or elliptical references and admonishments that are themselves often heavily couched in proverbs and aphorisms drawn from traditional poetry and subject to widely varying interpretations. Despite this tendency, it should come as no surprise that a cultural area with such a strong tradition of praising activity should have an opposing or mediating tradition. Operating as a powerful undercurrent—with examples ranging from subtle to explicit, traditional to modern—is a highly refined tradition of criticism, mockery, derision, satire, and irreverence. It is in this light that Fela's afrobeat differs sharply from other African musical genres. From its conception in 1970, Fela conceived of afrobeat as a vehicle for explicit social and political criticism.

From the stages of his Afrika Shrine nightclubs in the working-class areas of Lagos, Fela used his music to present uncharacteristically blunt satires and vilifications of the forces he identified as agents of cultural imperialism, social degradation, political oppression, and economic domination. He ridiculed sociocultural ideas and practices that reflected, in his eyes, the compromise or rejection of what he considered an "essential" African cultural identity. In this category are songs such as "Yellow Fever" (1976), criticizing the practice of skin bleaching, and "Gentleman" (1973), lampooning the "colonial" African personality and presenting his image of an "authentic" African. He commented frequently on the disruptive effects of rapid urbanization in Africa in songs like "Confusion" (1975), "You No Go Die . . . Unless" (1971), and "Go Slow" (1972), which satirize the infrastructural chaos of modern Nigeria. Fela also scandalized Nigerian audiences with his blunt depictions of intimate or even illegal activities: in "Na Poi" (1972) he presented a how-to sex manual set to music, while he celebrated his love of marijuana in the unrecorded "Nigerian Natural Grass" (1977).

Starting in 1974, Fela's hedonistic, rock-star lifestyle, influence among youth, and outspoken criticism led to his being harassed by Nigeria's law-enforcement authorities, spurned by the country's elite classes, and discredited by its official media. During this time, he increasingly focused his attacks on more specific targets: the Nigerian police and military, multinational corporations operating in Nigeria and the Nigerian comprador elite who staff them, corrupt bureaucrats and politicians, and clergy of the "foreign" religions of Christianity and Islam.[14] In this category are songs such as "Alagbon Close" (1974), questioning the authority of police and soldiers; "International Thief Thief" (1981), vilifying multinational corporations; "Authority Stealing" (1982), detailing government corruption and white-collar theft; and "Perambulator" (1983), a lampoon of ineffectual bureaucrats. Over his intoxicating instrumental brew of highlife, James Brown–style funk, and modal jazz, Fela attacked all of these targets with his trademark mixture of derisive humor, outrage, irony, satire, blunt criticism, and revolutionary fervor. He also attempted to move beyond the strictly musical arena into actual involvement in Nigerian politics. Besides being a consistent rallying point for student unrest and radical activism, Fela briefly formed his own Movement of the People political party and twice attempted to run for the Nigerian presidency (in 1979 and 1983), although his candidacy was disqualified by electoral commissions on both occasions.

Fela's political identity, which was enabled by his upper-middle-class background, was a fusion of ideologies from around the African diaspora and beyond. On one level, he was heir to a local tradition of ethnic pride and political struggle associated with his native Egba, a subgroup of the Yoruba, and their hometown of Abeokuta.[15] His youth afforded him a close proximity to the anticolonial struggle of the 1940s and 1950s through his mother, an anticolonial women's rights activist with international socialist ties. Through her, he was also exposed to the Pan-African ideals of Ghanaian premier Kwame Nkrumah, her close associate. Later, during a 1969 trip to the United States, he was exposed to the African-American ideologies and exponents of black power, black nationalism, African pride, and modern jazz, as well as the intertwining of political activism, drug use, and sexual freedom that characterized the American counterculture of the 1960s. These experiences were crucial in the formation of his musical, personal, and ideological outlook and, ironically, in clarifying his sense of an "African" identity. He returned to Nigeria in 1970 committed to using his music as a "weapon" against the continuing exploitation of the African masses by native and foreign interests, and to living his life as an "authentic" African personality, speaking out against the forces of cultural imperialism and rejecting the vestiges of Western colonial culture. Accordingly, he steadfastly avoided praise singing in his music, denigrating praise-singing musicians as "beggars."

Fela was also the creator of a subculture in Lagos in the 1970s that was unique in its juxtaposition of anarchy and authority and radical in its social nonconformity. Fela's frequent seminude public appearances, his high-profile use of marijuana, his harem of women, his inner-city commune of the socially marginalized, and his general profile as public mischief maker were unprecedented in West African societies. If his experience of the American counterculture was the catalyst for his own vision of an African counterculture, this vision, when transplanted into Africa, also conformed to an existing social stereotype of what might be called the "palmwine" image of musicians as social deviants given to drunkenness, womanizing, and general irresponsibility.[16] This behavior stands in stark contrast to most other African musicians, who strengthen their ties to power and respectability through religious, political, entrepreneurial, or patronage associations. It marked Fela as a unique and maverick personality, but it also left him especially vulnerable to state-sponsored harassment.

In the interest of self-preservation, African creative artists who have taken (or been afforded) the liberty of outspoken criticism and radical deviation from social norms have usually operated at a social and physical remove from their native societies, where respect, etiquette, and decorum are generally maintained at all costs. Traditionally, this may have taken the form of social and physical marginality (as in the case of certain classes of Senegambian griots who maintain a nomadic lifestyle); today, it might mean temporary or permanent exile (as with the recent exile of novelist/playwright Wole Soyinka). However, Fela stubbornly continued to reside in Nigeria, regardless of the personal or professional consequences, leaving only for the occasional foreign concert tour or recording session.

In a tradition-conscious society that has, since independence, been governed by a series of authoritarian, sometimes brutal military regimes, Fela's unconventional lifestyle and oppositional political stance cost him dearly, and any acknowledgment of him as a popular musician must be qualified by an appraisal of the struggles created by his thoroughly political brand of popular music. Frequent harassment by the Nigerian government denied Fela the opulent "high life" enjoyed by Western entertainers of comparable popularity, even during the financial peak of his career in the 1970s. And while he was lionized by Nigeria's intellectuals, inner-city youth, and university students, he was largely dismissed by traditional rural Yoruba and the urban Yoruba elite. He was reportedly arrested, detained, framed, and imprisoned more times than any other Nigerian in history by successive governments attempting to muzzle him at home and abroad. His residences were frequently attacked and occasionally destroyed by soldiers of the Nigerian army, and he was beaten nearly to death on a number of occasions. Serious and even mortal harm was visited upon members of his family and household. However, Fela responded to each attack with a renewed determination to speak and sing his message without compromise. He was also able to use his victimization to fuel his image as a popular hero and champion of the people; his album jackets often displayed wounds inflicted during attacks by the authorities. It was after his April 1986 release from a politically motivated prison term that his legions of fans nicknamed him "Abami Eda"—Yoruba for "strange one" or "spirit being"—in acknowledgment of his indomitable spirit and successive phases of musical innovation with his Afrika 70 and Egypt 80 bands. He had taken the modern highlife tradition and infused it with the traditional role of truth-sayer, social critic, and jester.

Karin Barber has suggested that "from an emergent social class comes emergent popular artistic forms."[17] Fela's ascendance as a cultural hero in the 1970s coincided with the maturing of a generation of Nigerians who had grown up under independent African rule, but who had become disillusioned by civil war, military rule, gross disparities of wealth, and conspicuous consumption by the elite. Comprised of inner-city youths, the unemployed, university students, and others from a wide variety of ethnic, professional, and class backgrounds, his audience was more diverse than those of most African styles in which musical taste is inextricably bound with ethnicity and socioeconomic status. He accomplished this largely by singing his songs in pidgin English, the lingua franca of Anglophone Africa, understood by millions of listeners across national, class, and ethnic boundaries. As a result, afrobeat is able to penetrate the common experience of many Africans—simultaneously articulating the frustration of an entrenched urban underclass, the black pride ideals of university students, and the disenchantment of marginalized intelligentsia and cultural producers who reject elite values. This ability to impact various sectors of the society accounts for much of Fela's wide influence, as well as the drastic reprisals his work provoked.

Fela in Postcolonial Africa and the African Diaspora

The notion of "tradition" in Africa has become highly charged as a result of the massive disruptions wrought by slavery and colonialism. In this atmosphere, musicians have been important negotiators of tradition and modernity. Fela embodied many of the complexities and contradictions of the postcolonial African condition during a period of intense negotiations between contested notions of "traditional" and "modern," "black" and "white," and "Africa" and "the West." These contradictions manifested themselves in various ways within Fela's stated ideology. On the one hand, his insistence on male superiority, his championing of despots such as Uganda's Idi Amin, his essentialist conception of African identity, and his romanticized conception of the precolonial African past seemed detrimental to his ultimate goal of African progress. On the other hand, his belief in transnational African unity, his fearless running critiques of corrupt and dictatorial regimes, and the political orientation of his popular art all contained critiques crucial to the survival of healthy African societies into the twenty-first century. Thus, Fela's contradictions encapsulated many of the critical issues involved in postcolonial Africa's transition from past to future just as his courage encapsulated many of its struggles.

The Ransome-Kuti Family

Besides fitting into various West African traditions, Fela's mode of expression reflected a family tradition most obvious in the lives and work of his parents. I identify his work as a fusion of two main parental tendencies. First is the tendency toward social activism and derisive criticism typified by his mother, Mrs. Funmilayo Thomas Ransome-Kuti (1900–1978), an anticolonial women's rights activist with a strong antiauthoritarian streak. As a political personality, Fela's primary role model was his mother. From her he probably internalized an antagonism toward authority, a distrust of the Nigerian ruling classes, and a derisive wit, along with an early exposure to Marxist rhetoric, Nigerian nationalism, and the ideology of Pan-Africanism. The Marxist influence provided a blueprint for his use of art as a means of shaping political consciousness; the nationalist influence led Fela to use his art to uplift his nation; and the Pan-Africanist influence led him to define his art within a theoretically unified Afro-Atlantic cultural sphere. This basic model was later enriched by his experience of African-American nationalism and black power during the 1960s. The African-American cultural-nationalist model inspired him to elaborate his political philosophy in an uncharacteristically (for Africa) oppositional fashion, probably derived from the racially polarized rhetoric of the African-American civil rights struggle.[18]

The other strong element in Fela's work was a tendency towards authoritarianism, education, and musical talent. In this, he belonged to a paternal family tradition of accomplished musicians spanning four generations. His grandfather, the Reverend Josaiah J. Canon Ransome-Kuti (1855–1930), was a pioneer of Christian music in Yorubaland, recording a series of records for the British company EMI in the early 1920s featuring Christian hymns sung in the Yoruba language. He was later the subject of *The Singing Minister of Nigeria,* a biography by Isaac Delano. Fela's father, the Reverend Israel Oludotun Ransome-Kuti (1900–1955), was a prominent educator and school principal who taught daily classes in Western music and was a well-known song composer. This tradition continues in Fela's oldest son, Femi (b. 1960), a multi-instrumentalist who has established himself as a popular bandleader in Nigeria following a period of apprenticeship in his father's band, as well as his younger son Seun Anikulapo-Kuti (b. 1982), who performed with his father's band in Nigeria and on international tours and has led Egypt 80 since Fela's death in 1997. It also continued in Fela's late niece Frances Kuboye (daughter of his sister Dolupo), a well-known jazz vocalist who operated the Lagos nightclub Jazz 38 along with her husband, Tunde Kuboye.

Although these two primary tendencies occasionally overlapped in the lives of his parents—his father was also an anticolonialist who had periodic brushes with colonial authorities, and his mother was a strict authoritarian who had briefly studied music in her youth—they are generally stable points of departure in the analysis of Fela's life and work. The harmonious elements of these occasionally contrasting tendencies found their expression in the potency of his highly refined political music, while the less easily reconcilable elements often found their expression in his ideological contradictions as well as the anarchic style of his personal life and domestic environment. Ultimately, the family influence was crucial, providing Fela with an early foundation in Western music, a collegiate musical education in England, and an early exposure to politics—allowing him to advance beyond strictly local perceptions of musical style, content, and function, as well as the economically conditioned options available to traditional musicians of less privileged backgrounds. But despite all of these distinguishing factors, Fela is a solid product of Yoruba history, and his personal story is inextricably intertwined with the history of postcolonial Nigeria.

Abeokuta
(1938–1957)

Nigeria is located on the Bight of Benin in West Africa and bordered by the nations of Chad in the north, Benin in the west, Cameroun in the southeast, and by the Atlantic Ocean in the southwest. The country covers 356,669 square miles and contains approximately 100 million people encompassing roughly 250 ethnic groups and subgroups. These various cultures may be divided into three main geographic configurations. The northern region, comprised mainly of open savannah and low grasslands bordering on the Sahara desert, is predominately Muslim and is largely defined by the Hausa ethnic group, though it is also home to the Kanuri and Fulani peoples. The country's middle region is marked by rougher, mountainous terrain and is home to the Nupe, Igala, Tiv, and Idoma peoples. The densely forested southern region, stretching to the Atlantic coast, is heavily Christian and home to the Yoruba, Igbo, Ibibio, Efik, and Edo, with the Igbo (in the southeast) and the Yoruba (in the southwest) most populous. The strong presence of Islam in northern Nigeria reflects centuries of interaction with the Islamic cultures of northern and northeastern Africa and the Middle East by way of trans-Sahara trade routes. Christianity's equally strong presence in the south reflects historical interaction with the Christian cultures of Western Europe by way of the Atlantic Ocean. Throughout the country, but particularly in the southern and middle regions, there also remain numerous adherents of the traditional indigenous religions.

The Berlin West Africa Conference of 1885, generally regarded as the formal beginning of European colonialism in West Africa, settled territorial disputes between competing European powers by formalizing each nation's "sphere of influence" and drawing corresponding territorial boundaries. Most modern African nation-states demonstrate the disruptive effect this had on traditional cultures. Previously autonomous and occasionally antagonistic ethnic groups found themselves forcibly combined into single political entities, while other groups saw their members divided between one or more newly created "nations" by arbitrarily drawn national borders. The Yoruba, who number approximately 20 million, are found primarily in southwestern Nigeria and, to a lesser extent, the northeastern region of the neighboring Republic of Benin (formerly Dahomey), which borders Nigeria on the west. Further west, a small number of Yoruba also inhabit Togo, the coastal nation that lies between the Republic of Benin and Ghana.

Though predominately farmers, Yoruba have also lived in large urban settlements since around A.D. 1000, and these are among the largest and oldest cities in West Africa.[1] The Yoruba are also noted for their complex system of religious belief consisting of a supreme being, Olodumare, and a host of intermediary deities known as *orishas*.[2] Connected with this is an ancestrally based, quasidivine kingship tradition, which is served by an extensive system of royal and religious art patronage and production encompassing music, dance, masquerading, sculpture, and a variety of oral arts.

The current cultural meaning of the term *Yoruba* is relatively recent. Prior to the late nineteenth century, the various subgroups inhabiting this area—known as Egba, Ife, Oyo, Ijebu, Egbado, Ekiti, Ketu, Nago, Ijesha, Igbomina, Owo, Ondo, Shabe, Dassa, and Lagos—might more accurately have been described as a group of autonomous kingdoms united more by similar sociopolitical organization, common language, and common cultural practices than by any broad, shared sense of ethnicity.[3] In earlier times, these kingdoms were also united in their recognition of the city of Ile-Ife, located in the center of the Yoruba territory, as a common cultural and spiritual center, and by their economic and political allegiance to the central military kingdom of Old Oyo, located in the northeastern region of the Yorubaland near the Niger River. Since approximately 1200, they had been ruled by Oyo in what might be described as a federation of tributary kingdoms, with other non-Yoruba-speaking peoples—Nupe, historical Benin,[4] and Abomey—also paying tribute. By the end of the eighteenth century, however, this federation was rapidly disintegrating due to internal and external factors.

Resentful of their historically subordinate relationship to Oyo, a number of Yoruba subgroups began asserting their independence starting in the late eighteenth century, dividing the federation internally and leaving it vulnerable to attack by hostile neighbors. Of these groups, the Egba—concentrated in a region of southern Yorubaland—were the first to secede, in 1780.

Concurrent with this period of widespread secession, Yorubaland was faced with military aggression from other sources. Having united under the Muslim leader Shehu Usman Dan Fodio (d. 1817) at the beginning of the nineteenth century, crusading Hausa and Fulani Muslims exerted pressure from the north, penetrating as far as the northern Yoruba town of Ilorin in their attempt to spread Islam by force southward to the Atlantic coast. Southwestern Yorubaland endured attacks across the western frontier from the formerly tributary kingdom of Abomey, which was attempting to turn the internal strife among the Yoruba to its advantage. Meanwhile, European merchants, missionaries, and soldiers were gradually advancing northward from the Atlantic, laying the foundations for later colonization. The Portuguese had been the first Europeans to establish contact, in the late fifteenth century. By the seventeenth century, France, Spain, Sweden, England, and Holland were competing for influence in the area.

The combination of these external and internal pressures plunged Yorubaland into a protracted period of civil chaos and internecine warfare lasting through the beginning of the twentieth century. The Egba were among the southern Yoruba most affected by this state of affairs. Caught among fleeing refugees from the north, slave-raiding coastal kingdoms in the south, hostile Dahomeans in the west, and antagonistic local Yoruba subgroups, the Egba had abandoned their historic settlements, scattering among non-Egba towns throughout southern Yorubaland. Eventually reunited under the military leader Sodeke (d.1844), they settled and founded the town of Abeokuta in 1830, approximately sixty miles north of the port city and future capital of Lagos (formerly Eko).

Because of this precarious situation–exacerbated by increasing Egba participation in the trans-Atlantic slave trade–the leaders of Abeokuta were eager to establish preferential relations with the British, who had emerged as the dominant European presence, largely concentrated in the coastal port city of Lagos. Simultaneously mediating and exploiting the internal tensions among the Yoruba, the British played a crucial role in the restoration of peace throughout the region, while their peacemaking activities provided a convenient pretext for the establishment of regional economic influence and political control that would culminate in colonization.[5] Cordial relations with the British would enable Abeokuta to obtain not only Western arms for protection, but also Western knowledge, which was becoming increasingly essential in this period of developing cross-cultural contact. In 1841, Sodeke extended an invitation to the British to establish mission schools in Abeokuta, the first in the Yoruba hinterland.[6] Following the first British attempts to abolish slavery in 1807, the town also became a center for returning Yoruba slaves repatriated in Sierra Leone and subsequently educated there in Christian mission schools.[7] This influx contributed greatly to Abeokuta's image as a modern center for both mission Christianity and Western education.

However, the Egba did not universally convert to the cross. Fiercely proud and independent, they had managed to preserve their ethnic identity through a series of political crises that had torn other Yoruba groups asunder, and many of them remained staunch traditionalists, loyal to the various ancestral cults. A small but growing number of Egba also voluntarily converted to Islam, further diversifying the cultural life of the town. Abeokuta now contained westernized Christians, syncretic Muslims, and traditionalists. This diversity, combined with the presence of an emergent Western-educated elite, transformed Abeokuta, with a population of approximately 500,000 in 1940,[8] into the most dynamic and progressive Yoruba city. It was also the most politically volatile. A newspaper editorial from 1946 opined: "Egba politics is highly combustible. It is by far and away the most explosive in Nigeria. Like enteric fever, political unrest in Abeokuta oscillates and scintillates. The pendulum is never at rest. The temperature is almost always at boiling point."[9]

The complex interaction between these competing belief systems and their sociopolitical implications–Christianity as a new means of spiritual, political, and educational empowerment in the face of approaching modernity; Islam as a relatively indigenous renunciation of the more extreme "pagan" beliefs; and complete loyalty to the ancestral cults and their related institutions—encapsulated the challenges facing many African societies at the dawn of the twentieth century. Among the Yoruba, the citizens of Abeokuta were to play an important role in confronting these challenges.[10]

This was the Abeokuta into which Olufela Olusegun Oludotun Ransome-Kuti was born on October 15, 1938. Fela, as he became known, was the fourth of five children born to the Reverend Israel Oludotun Ransome-Kuti (1900–1955) and Funmilayo Thomas Ransome-Kuti (1900–1978).[11] Although not affluent in the modern sense, the Ransome-Kutis were solidly upper middle class and were among the most respected Abeokuta families. In many ways, they were a model colonial family. Second-generation Christians, they lived in a large, self-sufficient compound in the town's Kemta district. The Ransome-Kuti family raised its own livestock and were for a long time the only family in Abeokuta to own an automobile.[12]

Reverend Israel Oludotun Ransome-Kuti (or "Daudu," as he was commonly known) was an Anglican pastor, prominent educator, union activist, and the first president of the Nigerian Union of Teachers. One of the first graduates of Abeokuta Grammar School, Reverend Ransome-Kuti attended Fourah Bay College in Freetown, Sierra Leone. Upon his return to Nigeria in 1925, he married Funmilayo Abigail Thomas, one of the first graduates of Abeokuta Girl's School. Shortly thereafter, the couple moved to the nearby Yoruba town of Ijebu-Ode, where Reverend Ransome-Kuti was principal of Ijebu-Ode Grammar School until 1932. A member of the pre-independence Elliott Commission for the Institutionalisation of University Education in Nigeria, he is recognized as one of the founders of higher education in Nigeria.

Frances Abigail Olufunmilayo Thomas Ransome-Kuti (commonly known as Funmilayo or by her nickname, "Beere") was an internationally recognized women's rights activist. A champion of female suffrage and the founder of the Nigerian Women's Union, she was an important player in the movement for Nigerian independence and a confidante of independent Ghana's first president, Kwame Nkrumah. Funmilayo Ransome-Kuti was also reportedly the first Nigerian woman to drive an automobile. More significantly, she was the first African woman to visit China, the U.S.S.R., Poland, Bulgaria, Hungary, Yugoslavia, and East Germany during the Cold War.

Fela's siblings—all of whom were educated abroad—have continued this family tradition of leadership and achievement in their chosen professions. His older sister, Dolupo (b. 1926), was a respected head nurse in a number of private hospitals in Lagos before her retirement in 1974. His older brother, Olikoye (b. 1928), was professor of pediatrics at Lagos University Teaching Hospital before being appointed national Minister of Health by President Ibrahim Babangida, in whose administration he served from 1985 to 1993. Dr. Ransome-Kuti has been the recipient of several prestigious medical awards, including awards from the World Health Organization and the United Nations. At the time of this writing, he is working with the World Health Organization in Washington, D.C. Fela's younger brother, Bekolari (b. 1940), is also a physician and is former secretary-general of the Nigerian Medical Association. Widely acknowledged as the leader of young radical doctors in Nigeria, "Dr. Beko"—as he is widely known—served six months in prison in 1985 for his outspoken criticism of the medical policies of President Mohammedu Buhari. As the chairman of the Campaign For Democracy, he has also spent time in prison since 1993 for his outspoken criticisms of the Babangida, Shonekan, and Abacha regimes. In 1995, Dr. Ransome-Kuti was given a fifteen-year prison sentence for his involvement in an alleged coup plot, which has been widely dismissed by domestic and international observers as a fabricated pretext for the silencing of dissident voices. He was released in 1998 following another change of government.

Members of Fela's extended family have also become prominent Nigerians, most notably his first cousin, the poet, novelist, and playwright Wole Soyinka. Soyinka, the 1985 Nobel laureate in literature, often spent his holidays at the Ransome-Kuti family compound.[13] Fela remembered that "Wole and I were very close as children. He was a bit older than I but not too old, at Abeokuta. But our association was only when he came on holidays."[14] As college students in London, the two would later share an apartment and collaborate on politically charged dramatic productions. Soyinka's brother Femi is also one of the country's foremost physicians and, along with Fela's brother Olikoye, is in the forefront of the campaign to stem the AIDS epidemic in West Africa.

> *I always stole my mother's money. She had a school, so I had a lot of money to steal from her. The more she beat me, the more I stole. Anytime she caught me she must beat the shit out of me but next time I have a chance, I would steal it. So, I stole till I left school from my mother. I came out still not to be a thief.*
>
> FELA *quoted in* ALEGBE AND OJUDU 1988a

Most people who knew Fela as a youth describe him as a well-mannered, respectful young man with a mischievous, playful streak that endeared him to elders and peers alike. Femi Oyewole, Fela's former teacher in Abeokuta, remembered him as "a rascal that everybody loved, and couldn't help loving."[15] His parents, however, were worried by what they perceived as their son's "restlessness." Reverend Ransome-Kuti reportedly saw in Fela his own image—both in musical talent and in stubbornness—and sought to nurture the former tendency while curtailing the latter. As Fela grew, many would compare his personality alternately to those of his paternal great-grandfather, Likoye, and his paternal great-uncle, Sogbeyinde. The former was remembered by Isaac Delano as "one of Egba's greatest diplomats, a weaver by trade whose hobbies were singing and dancing,"[16] and the latter as "a great drummer and dancer who suffered the penalty of his many crimes in accordance with native laws and customs."[17] Delano went on to remark, "We cannot help comparing these two brothers. One a diplomat, valiant soldier and musician, and the other a town dweller and a star in social circles; one a sober and gentle man, and the other a wild and wicked ruffian who had no respect for his home and family."[18]

The Ransome-Kuti parents sought to contain these latent tendencies, primarily by means of strict discipline and frequent punishment. Fela's childhood recollections thus tended to center around four themes: his budding musical talent, his harsh upbringing at the hands of his parents, the stubborn pride that characterized their personalities, and their tendency toward activism and challenging authority. These recollections were marked by both admiration and exasperation, with music and the excitement surrounding his parents' activism providing the high moments of an otherwise stilted childhood. Professionally and as parents, the Ransome-Kutis were known to be strict disciplinarians. Fela recalled:

> We were all not too close to our parents very much, especially my father. My parents treated us more like boarding-house students than their children, whom we all are. . . . Everytime I always get beating for either doing this thing wrong or the other thing wrong. . . . It got to a point where everyone of us was always afraid at the slightest sight of them because you don't know what wrong you are going to do next, before they descend on you.[19]

As both a student in his father's school and at home, Fela recalled receiving the harshest chastisements of all the children, owing to his mischievous streak:

> My father was so strange! He was strict, but he was also interesting because he was always jovial. . . . I always wondered how a man who looked so jovial could be so fucking cold when he would flog you. . . . My mother wasn't any better than my father . . . she beat the hell outta me, man! My mother was the most wicked woman in life when it came to beating. . . . My teachers, too. Oh yes, they kicked my ass almost everyday, man![20]

He would eventually attribute this harshness to the colonial influence of the British educational system, with its emphasis on corporal punishment.

"Daudu"

As principal of Abeokuta Grammar School, Reverend Ransome-Kuti occupied a unique position. Unlike the other schools in the area, which had been built by either British missionaries or the British government, Abeokuta Grammar School had been built by the residents of the town through the Abeokuta District Council. The school was thus a source of local pride and subtle resistance against the colonial authorities. Reverend Ransome-Kuti shared this sense of pride, having been one of the school's first graduates. He was determined to maintain the school's standard of excellence, while developing a solid reputation as a no-nonsense disciplinarian. Fela remembered that the school became known "because of my father's ability to control all the rascal students regarded as beyond control."[21]

He told Carlos Moore, "The students were terrified of him. Whenever they heard the words "Oga mbo" ["principal is coming"], there was a stampede. The whole place would become pandemonium-o, with everyone trying to find their own place to avoid the beatings."[22]

In light of his stern character, one surprising trait that distinguished Reverend Ransome-Kuti was his refined aesthetic sense. For example, he was a lover of flowers, and Abeokuta Grammar School was known to have the prettiest, best-maintained flower gardens in Abeokuta. More significantly, Reverend Ransome-Kuti also loved music; he composed the Abeokuta anthem, and taught daily music classes at his school.

There was a tradition of musical talent in the Ransome-Kuti family. Fela's paternal grandfather, the Reverend Canon Josiah J. Ransome-Kuti was an Anglican pastor, a pioneer of the Christian church in Yorubaland. It was through his encounter with British missionaries that Christianity entered the Ransome-Kuti family, as well as the English name "Ransome," which he apparently took in honor of the British missionary who baptized him.[23] The senior Reverend Ransome-Kuti was a composer of religious hymns and also one of the first West Africans to have his music commercially recorded. During a 1925 trip to London, he recorded a series of 78-rpm religious discs sung in Yoruba for the EMI Zonophone label.[24]

Although Fela's father did not make music a profession, he did consider Western musical training an important part of education. This was a common sentiment among colonial West African families, although most frowned upon it as a career choice, since musicians in traditional culture were generally regarded as scarcely more than beggars. It was, however, an important sign of worldliness and Western acculturation, and many Africans cultivated an aesthetic appreciation of the various genres of Western art music during the colonial period.

Reverend Ransome-Kuti's daily music classes were conducted in the same strict manner as the rest of the curriculum:

> To show you how seriously he took his music lessons, my father had three different styles of beatings for offending students. One be "Touch your toe" . . . anybody whey him tell so, make that person know say my father go beat the shit out of him yansh [behind]. . . . Another one be say if him dey for jovial mood he will say make you push your yansh out behind you. He calls it "Yoo booli." If you no "yoo booli" him go beat your back-bend by force. Third style whey him dey take beat people be "Suu'ke" ["hunch your back"]. These are his special ways of dealing with students who didn't sing the tonic solfege correctly.[25]

Wole Soyinka, an intermittent visitor to Abeokuta Grammar, concurs:

> Daudu was manic in his treatment of music. . . . His ears picked up unerringly the source of a wrong sound. I was mystified however by his failure to simply weed out those who were obviously tone-deaf. Instead, he picked out the offending row, or class, and caned them after a faulty per-

formance. . . . [His] solution was very simple. . . . The school was required to sing; any portion of it which could not sing well had to be punished.[26]

The rich cultural life of Abeokuta also provided Fela many opportunities to experience a variety of traditional Yoruba performing arts. There were masquerades such as the Egungun and Gelede ceremonies, found throughout Yorubaland. The Egungun masquerades, concerned with the appeasement of deceased ancestors, are also considered occasions for the reincarnation of these ancestors in the form of the masked dancers or "spirits," as they are known. Gelede masquerades serve to placate both female elders and female divinities, the former of which are thought to possess supernatural powers affecting the fertility of the community as a whole. The musicians who accompany the masquerades are generally drawn from traditional lineages, and their ensembles use an array of traditional instruments. Egungun musicians rely on the hourglass-shaped, variable-pitched tension drums known as *dundun* (called "talking drums" because of their ability to imitate the tonal contours of the spoken Yoruba language), while Gelede musicians use a set of fixed-pitch drums known as *osoro*.[27] Very few traditional Yoruba activities took place without the accompaniment of some kind of music—even meetings of the various secret and civic societies such as the Ogboni all had their own accompanying drums, sounded at meeting times or to summon attention for public announcements.[28]

There were ample opportunities for enjoying popular musical as well. Abeokuta is recognized as a center of both sakara and apala music—two popular neotraditional styles performed mainly by Muslim Yoruba, but widely enjoyed across religious lines. As popular styles rooted in traditional musical practices, both feature proverbs, praise lyrics, and the nasalized, melismatic vocals of Islamic music laid over a variety of traditional percussion instruments. Popularized by the late Yusuf Olatunji (d. 1986), sakara music is built around the flat, variable-pitch drum of the same name, and the solemn-sounding *goje,* a bowed fiddle borrowed from the neighboring Hausa. The best-known apala musician is the late Haruna Ishola (d. 1983), who synthesized a dance music built around the dundun lead talking drum and the *agidigbo* bass thumb piano. A number of leading musicians made their homes in Abeokuta, including Olatunji and the late apala musician Ayinla Omowura (d. 1983). Unlike the musicians accompanying traditional ceremonies like Egungun and Gelede, the popular apala and sakara musicians were not necessarily born into traditional musicians' lineages. Nevertheless, they were integrally connected with traditional social life and its institutions. As Christians, however, the Ransome-Kuti family seems to have participated only marginally in the town's traditional culture.

Under his father's tutelage at Abeokuta Grammar, Fela excelled at his lessons in Western music and distinguished himself as a musician at an early age, occasionally being called upon to entertain his parents and their guests at the family piano by the time he was eight years old.[29] Femi Olodomosi, a classmate, recalls that Fela was also playing from written music by this time.[30] Years later when Fela was a well-known musician, many would note the traces of his father's conducting style in his stage manner.[31]

Regardless of his aesthetic appreciation of Western music and his embrace of Western educational and cultural values, Reverend Ransome-Kuti viewed Western education primarily as a means of empowerment against colonialism, and his aesthetic appreciation did not extend to appreciation of the British presence in Abeokuta.[32] In his efforts to maintain the independent and autonomous status of Abeokuta Grammar, for instance, he frequently clashed with the authorities, once physically attacking a colonial inspector who insisted upon inspecting the premises. On another occasion, he had a physical confrontation with a colonial soldier when he refused to remove his hat in obeisance to the British flag.[33]

> **Chief Priest Say:**
> Tell the man with the gun that the people who teach our people fear, render the whole country defenseless.

Like musical talent, stubbornness ran in the Ransome-Kuti family. As a first-generation Christian, the Reverend J. J. Canon often faced staunch, and sometimes violent, opposition from Yoruba traditionalists. On one occasion he was even beaten and left for dead by traditionalists who opposed his efforts to spread the cross throughout Yorubaland.[34]

J. J. Canon's stubbornness sometimes assumed mythical proportions, as Soyinka recalled:

> One frightening experience occurred in one of the villages in Ijebu. He had been warned not to preach on a particular day, which was the day for an Egungun outing, but he persisted and held a service. The Egungun procession passed while the service was in progress and, using his ancestral voice, called on the preacher to stop at once, disperse his people, and come out and pay obeisance. Rev. J. J. ignored him. The Egungun then left, taking his followers with him but, on passing the main door, he tapped on it with his wand, three times. Hardly had the last member of his procession left the church premises than the building collapsed. The walls simply fell down and the roof disintegrated. Miraculously however, the walls fell outwards while the roof supports fell among the aisles or flew outwards—anywhere but on the congregation itself. Rev. J. J. calmed the worshippers, paused in his preaching to render a thanksgiving prayer, then continued his sermon.[35]

"Béère"

The two Reverends Ransome-Kuti were not the only members of Fela's immediate family given to challenging authority. His mother, Funmilayo Ransome-Kuti, won the hearts of Nigerian women during the pre-independence period through her fight against sexist exploitation in traditional, colonial, and national institutions.

A 1951 portrait of the Ransome-Kuti family in *West Africa* magazine described Funmilayo this way:

> In a land where women are accustomed to bend the knee to the all-powerful male, and regard servitude as their rightful status, Mrs. Ransome-Kuti is a refreshing personality in her own right. About her was an air of authority, a compelling manner not common with Nigerian women; she had the look of one whose "decision is final." It is the independent outlook of Mrs. Kuti that first impresses the visitor; for once he finds himself confronted with a woman in Nigeria who has to be assessed on her own merits . . . a resolute, tenacious woman who has made even rulers totter.[36]

Like her husband, Funmilayo Ransome-Kuti combined charismatic public activism with harsh discipline in the home, and Fela's reminiscences betray a mixture of dread and admiration:

> I don't think anybody kicked my ass as much as my mother. But I dug her. I liked to hear her talk, discuss. . . . I vaguely remember when she started getting into politics . . . because when she was running around doing politics she didn't have time to flog me. The more she got into politics the less time she had to beat me. So I, too, began liking politics. . . . That was when I began getting close to her.[37]

The daughter of educated Christian parents, Funmilayo was among the first graduates of Abeokuta Girl's School (at which she also taught from 1922) and for a brief period of her youth lived in England, where she studied elocution, domestic science, and music.[38] An eloquent and expressive orator who, like her husband, delighted in antagonizing and even physically confronting the colonial authorities, she was known for her courage, fiery personality, incisive wit, and flair for the dramatic.

Although her education gave her class mobility, Funmilayo maintained a strong sense of community service, grounded in her Christian service background with its strong emphasis on moral and social uplift. This translated into a political ideology that was highly effective for mobilizing women across class and ethnic divisions. Her commitment to the advancement of Nigerian women began during the family's stay in the town of Ijebu-Ode, where she opened a nursery school and organized literacy classes for the local market women. She continued these efforts upon the family's return to Abeokuta in 1932, and it was here that she would have her most dramatic impact.

Abeokuta's volatile political climate resulted mainly from the historical restlessness of the Egba people and the way in which colonial rule had been implemented in the area. The British Sole Native Authority (SNA) system granted unprecedented power to the town's traditional ruler, the Alake, while sweeping aside the other indigenous political institutions that traditionally exerted a moderating effect on his power.

As the first British-educated Alake in Abeokuta, The Oba Alake Ademola II had been the target of mass protests since his assumption of the throne in 1920. He was accused of flagrant abuses of power, and of collusion with colonial authorities and business interests. Animosity toward the Alake was particularly intense on the part of the town's market women, who were deprived of their traditional political influence and economic power through the male-dominated political institutions imposed by the British colonizers. The new concentration of male power also led to particularly humiliating forms of harassment. Women were often forced by tax collectors to strip naked so that their age—and thus their obligation to pay taxes—could be verified. It was women, in fact, who bore the brunt of the heavy taxes levied on the people of Abeokuta.[39]

> **Chief Priest Say:**
> Let us laugh at our traditional rulers of Nigeria: William of Ila, Peter of Ijesha-land, Gabriel of Akure, Robert of Ondo, Daniel of Ibadan, Solomon of Benin, Douglas of Opobo, Josef of Ilawe, Mustapha of Borno, Abubakar of Sokoto, Abdul-Limid of Oyo, Jimoh of Ogbomosho, Idrisu of Zaria, Usman of Katsina, etc. When we don sell all our birthrights to Europe finish, how we no go hungry?

By the mid-1940s, the stage was set for the emergence of Funmilayo Ransome-Kuti. An articulate and witty orator, she expressed her contempt of the colonial authorities by speaking to them in Yoruba at public meetings and insisting on having their English replies translated into Yoruba. She was courageous in the face of coercive authority, and on one occasion had a widely publicized physical confrontation with a British District Officer.[40] Thus, the charismatic Mrs. Ransome-Kuti had the ability to galvanize the mass support of Abeokuta's women.

Fela was nine years old in 1947, when his mother organized the first in a series of legendary protest demonstrations against the colonial government and traditional rulership on behalf of the town's market women. These demonstrations, which involved more than ten thousand local women and brought Abeokuta to a standstill on several occasions, were unprecedented displays of female solidarity in Nigeria. The *Daily Service* reported that "the whole of Abeokuta was shaken to its foundation,"[41] while the *West African Pilot* reported:

> One of the greatest crises in Egbaland has been reached in the present agitation of Egba women against the payment of poll tax. . . . Thousands of women of Egbaland, including those in the neighboring districts, assembled themselves at the Afin where they stayed for two days. They kept a vigil throughout two nights, singing, dancing, and making all sorts of weird gestures around the palace . . . all the titled chiefs and councillors had to take shelter in their houses for fear of their lives. . . . Throughout Wednesday, [the women] could be seen parading on principal streets of Egbaland singing songs of praises to their leader, Mrs. Funmi Kuti.[42]

In 1948, the agitation against the Alake reached a boiling point when he announced his plans to increase the amount of taxation on the women's market earnings, despite the recent protests. In response, Mrs. Ransome-Kuti organized a demonstration even larger than the first—making her a national hero of Nigerian women and an important political player in Nigeria's nationalist movement. In the process, she also inspired her son's later reliance on similar civil disobedience tactics to achieve his aims.

> Oh, those were fantastic times-o! My mother succeeded in dethroning this pseudo-king, the Alake. . . . Everybody hated the Alake . . . my mother said, "Let's all go and take over the entire house." About 50,000 women went, with my mother at the head. They went and slept there in the yard of his house. The Alake was surrounded by 50,000 women. . . . He fled to Oshogbo . . . she chased him into exile. And the Alake stayed in Oshogbo for three years.[43]

Throughout the protest, the market women staged mock sacrifices and directed funeral dirges at the Alake. Music played an important role in this demonstration, as the assembled sang a number of explicitly abusive songs. Deriding the Alake as possessing the "penis of a poison rat," the lyrics reflect the overall spirit of the rallies:

> O you men, vagina's head will seek vengeance;
> You men, vagina's head shall seek vengeance
> Even if it is one penny.
> If it is only a penny Ademola, we are not paying tax in Egbaland
> If even it is one penny

and:

> Ademola Ojibosho
> Big Man with a big ulcer
> Your behaviour is deplorable;
> Alake is a thief
> Council members thieves;
> Anyone who does not know Kuti will get into trouble;
> White man, you will not get to your country safely;
> You and the Alake will not die an honorable death.[44]

The ideas expressed in these songs represent a complete inversion of the types of sentiments usually directed toward traditional rulers in praise lyrics, which praise the physical grace, presence, and integrity of the ruler and appeal to the orishas for his travels to be safely undertaken. While the ridicule of male sexual prowess and physical appearance by women is a traditional defensive rhetorical strategy,[45] these verses are unusually direct and explicit in their ridicule of the Alake.

The coalition of women mobilized in Abeokuta formed the foundation of the Nigerian Women's Union (NWU), a national organization founded by Mrs. Ransome-Kuti in 1949.[46] She gained international recognition for her work, and in 1949, the NWU became affiliated with the Women's International Democratic Foundation (WIDF), an international socialist women's organization. She was subsequently elected vice-president of the WIDF in 1953, and it was in this capacity that she visited Bulgaria and Hungary (1953 and 1961), Peking (1956), and Moscow (1956 and 1961), becoming the first African woman to travel to the "Iron Curtain" countries, and to meet Chairman Mao Tse-tung.[47] However, Mrs. Ransome-Kuti's activities with the WIDF were sharply criticized by the Nigerian and British governments, which frowned upon her repeated visits to Communist countries. She was denied an entry visa to the United States during the 1950s as a result of her previous travel, as well as her correspondence with politically outspoken public figures such as the African-American actor/activist Paul Robeson. In 1957 the Balewa government confiscated her passport, which was not reissued until 1961. Undeterred, she intensified her domestic focus, utilizing the now internationally affiliated NWU as the power base for her next political objective—universal suffrage for all Nigerian women. She was successful in this also; Nigerian women cast their votes in the first general elections in 1959.

Funmilayo Ransome-Kuti was also a close associate of independent Ghana's first president, Dr. Kwame Nkrumah. Nkrumah drew on his study of Pan-Africanism and Marxism, and his firsthand experience of the African-American civil rights struggle, to become the first African leader to guide his country to independence from a European colonial power, in 1957.[48] The philosophy of Pan-Africanism, stressing political unity between all people of African descent, was the cornerstone of Nkrumah's ideology, and he enjoyed enormous popularity throughout the African continent and the African diaspora, and especially among African youth and students. Fela recalls meeting him in 1957:

> At that time he would come now and then to Lagos in his yacht on holidays. . . . Nkrumah told my mother he didn't want to see anybody; that he hadn't come for any official visit. . . . But he had sent a message to my mother, saying that he wanted to see her. When she got there they started joking. My mother said teasingly: "Ah, you come to Nigeria and you don't want to see your brothers here." "I don't deal with corrupt people," he answered. My mother looked at him and smiled. Nkrumah went on: "They are slaves to the people in England. You know that." He was smiling while saying it. Man, he was so cool.[49]

The years leading to Nigerian independence were turbulent, as the country's three main administrative regions vied for control of the impending government. Three parties dominated the political landscape, and while each purported to be a national party, each was ultimately identified with one of the three major ethnic groups and geographic regions. The Northern People's Congress (NPC), led by the Sarduana of Sokoto, represented the Northern Region, dominated by the Hausa.

The Action Group (AG), led by Obafemi Awolowo, represented the interests of the southwest region, dominated by the Yoruba. Funmilayo Ransome-Kuti was affiliated with Dr. Nnamdi Azikiwe (or "Zik," as he was popularly known) and his National Council of Nigerian Citizens (NCNC).

Ethnically Igbo, Dr. Azikiwe enjoyed nationwide popularity and, of all the candidates, had most managed to transcend the climate of regionalism and ethnic rivalry as independence approached. He enjoyed broad, pan-ethnic support from students, including Fela, who has cited him as an important early political influence.[50] Ultimately, however, Azikiwe's NCNC, like its rivals, came to be identified with a particular region and group—the Igbo of the southeast region. The fiercely independent Mrs. Ransome-Kuti soon left the NCNC as a result of a dispute with Azikiwe and what she termed his "authoritarian" leadership of the organization.[51]

In recognition of her efforts on behalf of Nigerian women and her "noble activities for many years in promoting friendship and mutual cooperation between Nigerian and Soviet peoples,"[52] Mrs. Ransome-Kuti was awarded the Lenin Peace Prize in 1970. Though she remained active in politics until her death in 1978, she became increasingly alienated from Nigerian politics. Her public profile declined somewhat during the years following independence, largely due to the succession of military regimes that outlawed political parties, confiscated passports, and banned other political activity. Her radical feminism, hostility to authoritarian leadership in any form, and unshakeable faith in the "common" people, resulted in a political philosophy often bordering on anarchism.[53] She was also disgusted at the gradual degeneration of national politics into competing ethnic interests, as well as the systematic exclusion of women from positions of power. Finally, she distrusted any hint of collusion between traditional rulers and foreign business interests. She summed up her career as an activist in a 1968 interview. After declaring, "This is not a man's world; it is a world belonging to all of us," she told Sola Odunfa: "I was not a politician. . . . If you call bribetaking politics, that is nonsense. I work only to defend the rights of the common people. I will never be a politician."[54]

Funmilayo Ransome-Kuti's experiences were crucial to Fela's development,[55] as his political environment already reflected an internationalist perspective. Emerging in a historical period of disseminating ideologies in which China and the Soviet-bloc powers were competing for influence in the newly independent African states, Funmilayo Ransome-Kuti was strongly influenced by Marxist rhetoric and drew parallels between the political struggles of nonwhite cultures around the world.[56] Likewise, Nkrumah's philosophy was rooted in Marxist rhetoric and the proto-Pan-Africanism of Jamaican Marcus Garvey. These were Fela's ideological foundations.

Fela was something else when I first met him. Outwardly, he looked like a nice, clean boy. A perfect square. But inside he was a ruffian, man. And I knew it. . . . I told many guys, "This boy, he's a ruffian. He doesn't even know how to talk to people. You just wait. We'll see what this guy

*can do." And it was true. Even my family didn't like Fela and didn't
want me associating with him.*

J. K. BRAIMAH *quoted in* MOORE 1982:55

Upon completing his primary schooling at Abeokuta Grammar in 1953, Fela
began secondary school. Now free, at least during the daytime, from his father's
constant supervision, another side of his personality gradually began to emerge.
He developed a reputation in school as a prankster, and some of his pranks, such
as his "disobedience club," were clearly a reaction against the strictures of his
upbringing.[57]

Two important events occurred during Fela's four years in secondary school.
The most significant was the death of his father. Reverend Ransome-Kuti had been
diagnosed with prostate cancer in 1954, and he succumbed to the illness in April
1955, when Fela was seventeen. "When my father died, I did not really feel his
absence because he was goddamn too strict with the students and his children
inclusive, to me at the time (despite the fact that I cried) I was almost thanking God
that the man died—at least if not for anything I will have peace."[58]

The second significant development of Fela's secondary school years was his
friendship with "J.K." Braimah, a friendship that endured for decades. A former student at the primary school in Ijebu-Ode (at which Reverend Ransome-Kuti had
served as principal), J.K. was familiar with the disciplinary tactics of Fela's father,
and this created a fraternal bond between the two boys. Beyond their classroom
experiences, however, the boys' lifestyles diverged. Where Fela was still subject to
the rules and regulations of his parents' home, J.K. was more of a free spirit, often
traveling to Lagos and singing with highlife bands. Fela admired his friend's spirit—
and aspired to his lifestyle. Apparently, neither Fela nor J.K. were particularly interested in schoolwork, and the musical nightlife of Lagos began to occupy the place
that academic studies held for their peers.

The 1950s are often called the "Golden Age" of Nigerian highlife, the culmination of four decades of creative ferment. The dominant style at the time, dance-
band highlife, is one of highlife's two occasionally overlapping stylistic branches.
The other branch, guitar-band highlife, developed during the early twentieth century from the guitar music played in coastal Liberia and disseminated to other
West African ports by Liberian Kru merchant sailors.[59] This style, which is associated with Nigeria's eastern region, flourishes today in the acoustic palmwine style
and in modern ensembles that have adapted the finger-picked palmwine technique to the electric guitar.

Dance-band highlife developed primarily in Lagos and has its roots in the
British-styled pan-ethnic marching brass bands that developed in Anglophone
West African port cities like Lagos and Accra, Ghana, at the end of the nineteenth
century. Membership in these bands required technical proficiency on the European string, brass, and woodwind instruments, as well as the financial means of
obtaining them. These bands were thus associated with the upper classes, providing entertainment for the ballroom dances and private parlor affairs of the developing pan-ethnic West African bourgeoisie. In fact, the name "highlife" is generally

understood to have originally referred to the opulent upper-class social settings in which the music was performed.[60]

The early highlife bands specialized in various genres of Western European music, from light versions of concert music to ballroom selections such as waltzes, foxtrots, and two-steps. By the late 1940s, however, these groups had come under the influence of Afro-Cuban dance music, which spread rapidly throughout Africa with the help of recently established branches of European recording companies. These rumbas, mambos, and cha-chas—modern, cosmopolitan Afro-Latin recycling of African sounds—became very popular throughout sub-Saharan Africa and were also indirectly instrumental in the upper-class nationalist agitation that followed World War II. It was the immensely influential Ghanaian bandleader E. T. Mensah (1919–1996) who, aided by the versatile drummer Kofi Ghanaba (a.k.a. Guy Warren), developed modern dance-band highlife from a mixture of Afro-Carribean and indigenous elements. With his group The Tempos, Mensah raised the style to its peak popularity during the 1940s and 1950s.

Nigerian dance-band highlife developed rapidly in the wake of Mensah's Nigerian tours of the 1940s and 1950s, spearheaded by bandleader Bobby Benson (1920–1983) and his Jam Session Orchestra. Benson's group in turn spawned other important Nigerian highlife bandleaders such as Eddie Okonta, "Cardinal" Rex Lawson, Zeal Onyia, Chief Billy Friday, King Pagoe, and Victor Olaiya.

J. K. Braimah had lived in Ghana as a boy and knew many of the popular Ghanaian highlife songs. He was also a talented vocalist, associated with several of the leading Lagos highlife bands, including Victor Olaiya's Cool Cats. Singer, trumpeter, and bandleader Olaiya (b. 1920s) was known as the "Evil Genius of Highlife" and began his career playing ballroom music as a member of Benson's Orchestra. Inspired by E. T. Mensah's tours, Olaiya formed his own group and, like Benson, began fashioning a distinctly Nigerian highlife sound with a string of hit singles during the late 1950s and early 1960s such as "Omo Dudu," "Omele 'Dele," and "Sisi Jowo." J.K. introduced Fela to the Lagos music scene, and Fela's first professional musical experience was as a backing vocalist in Olaiya's band. Olaiya remembered that Fela joined the second-tier Cool Cats (the first band was already full) with a prior knowledge of music and a keen desire to learn trumpet. He called his protégé "very restless and a very big rascal. . . . I found traces of greatness in him . . . he had the tendency of going places musically."[61]

Fela's two final years in secondary school were spent enjoying his new freedom and the musical nightlife of Lagos, to the detriment of his academic studies. Upon his graduation in 1957, it was unclear which form of higher education or career preparation he would pursue. His older brother, Koye, and his older sister, Dolupo, had gone to England to pursue medicine and nursing, respectively. In the absence of any clear plans, Fela began working at the Ministry of Commerce and Industry in Lagos, while singing with Olaiya at night. The following year, his younger brother, Beko, also left for England to study medicine. Although Reverend Ransome-Kuti had desired medical careers for all of his sons, Fela's interests did not lie in this direction. In fact, aside from his obvious enthusiasm for music, his interests did not lie in any apparent direction.

[My parents] taught me music but they discouraged me from making it a profession. By the time I finished school, there was nothing I could study, nothing. My subjects were Religious Studies, English Literature, Yoruba, Biology, Physics, Chemistry, Arts. . . . When I left school I could not [enter school in] anything. I couldn't do law, I couldn't do shit and they were telling me I couldn't make music a profession in Nigeria. . . . I was just a Lagos boy. I wasn't going to do anything. My mother bought me a bicycle and I was satisfied and I was singing with the Cool Cats. England did not interest me.[62]

Worried that Fela would choose music as a profession, family and friends began suggesting careers they felt were most appropriate to his background, but it was ultimately Beko who raised the idea of music school in England. With Beko's help, Fela was able to convince his mother to send him to England's Trinity College of Music, with the understanding that he would not return home to Nigeria without a degree in hand. There are conflicting accounts of his initial intentions for the trip. Some suggest that he left Nigeria to attend medical school but switched to music school after his arrival in London, surprising and angering his parents in the process. One such profile reports that "in the late 1950's, Fela went to London to study medicine. . . . Captivated by Charlie Parker, he transferred to the London School of Music."[63] Another states: "In 1958, Fela finally managed to throw off the parental shackles by persuading them to send him to London to study to become a doctor. Once there, however, he promptly enrolled himself at Trinity College of Music."[64]

These accounts, attempting to recast Fela's early years in light of his later rebellious image, are not entirely accurate. Obviously, it was not possible to anger his "parents," as Reverend Ransome-Kuti had passed away in 1955. Fela himself was clear about both his intentions for the trip and his family's understanding of it: "Music was all I wanted to work at. And now that my father wasn't there, it was easier to persuade my mother to let me go and study music abroad."[65]

Funmilayo Ransome-Kuti's capitulation probably reflected three factors: the absence of Reverend Ransome-Kuti's dominant influence, her developing closeness with her son, and the fact that she already had three children preparing for more mainstream careers. New developments also led to a gradual change in attitudes toward musicians. Although musicians were often still regarded with derision, the colonial era had spawned a number of new performance contexts and opportunities for music as a viable professional career, and musicians were no longer limited to praise-singing or accompanying traditional ceremonies. The development of marching bands, patterned after British military bands, led to the formation of various ensembles utilizing Western and indigenous instruments. These bands found ready performance venues in the Western-styled nightclubs that had proliferated since the early part of the century, catering to the international population of the major port cities. Mission schools and churches offered opportunities for Western musical education, and provided the impetus for the development of Nigerian art music.

One of the most significant factors stimulating change was the growth of the recording industry throughout Africa. For some time, British recording companies like EMI and Decca had gradually expanded their activities throughout the region. Their first recordings, in the early part of the century, tended toward novelty items such as African renditions of famous speeches, religious hymns (such as the type recorded by Fela's grandfather), patriotic songs, or documents of traditional songs. During the late 1920s, they began to record popular music; the first recorded Ghanaian highlife song dates about 1927.[66]

By the 1950s highlife had become the most popular music throughout West Africa, and the recording industry was selling millions of records annually by highlife singers like Mensah, Benson, and Olaiya. Highlife singers were in a unique position to capitalize on the recording industry, as their music operated independently of both traditional ethnic contexts and Christian or Islamic religious contexts. Secular, pan-ethnic, and widely popular, highlife was largely aimed at urban middle- and upper-class record-buying audiences. It was with these musicians as his models that Fela departed Lagos for London in 1958, marking the beginning of the next major phase of his life.

Fela summarized his feelings about his childhood in 1986:

When I was young, when I saw the way other parents behaved to their children, I would regret being born to my parents; the way my father was kicking my ass, my mother's disciplinary actions, that was my first regret. Then as time went on and my knowledge increased, I knew that I had to have that training through those two people. So no regrets.[67]

Ultimately, Fela's identity was highly informed by his elite background. His parents had prepared their children to play important roles in an independent Nigeria, while establishing a family precedent of activism, notoriety, and professional achievement. All four children would eventually conform to this precedent and establish themselves at the forefronts of their chosen professions, and Fela would achieve distinction as a unique contributor to postcolonial Nigeria.

"Gentleman"
(1958–1970)

London (1958–1963)

Fela arrived in London in August 1958, expecting to enroll promptly at Trinity College of Music—but this was not so easily accomplished. The musical training he had received from his father at Abeokuta Grammar was not enough to help him pass the college's entrance examinations, and it was ultimately a gesture of good-will on the part of the principal that enabled him to enroll:

> When I got to London the principal of the college told me I was not fit to enter college. He said if I hadn't come from 5,000 miles away, he would have sent me back to my house. Because I came from 5,000 miles, he was going to ask me a question: "Why do you want to study music?" I said that was the only thing I could do. He said in that case he would admit me because most people in the college gave that answer to the question before they entered.[1]

Having been admitted, student Fela Ransome-Kuti joined the growing ranks of students arriving from Britain's far-flung colonies. There were a number of African students attending European music schools, with varying intentions. Some came with the clear intention of composing and performing Western art music. Such was the case with Nigeria's "Great Five" composers—Ayo Bankole, Fela Sowande, Adams Fiberesimi, Akin Euba, and Samuel Akpabot—as well as their counterparts elsewhere in Africa, including Solomon Mbabi-Katana and Anthony Okelo of Uganda and Ephraim Amu, Kwabena Nketia, and Ato Turkson of Ghana, all of whom were educated abroad.[2] These men can be considered Africa's first well-known art music composers in the European sense of the term,[3] shepherding a limited tradition of Western art music performance in Africa, with chamber groups, choirs, and even symphony orchestras active in major cities like Lagos and

Accra, supported and promoted by appreciation groups such as the Lagos Musical Society. However, there was another category of African music students who simply desired greater technical knowledge of the Western instruments and theory that were being digested and transformed into popular styles back home in Africa. Fela's activities during his college years indicate that he most likely went to London with the implicit intention of playing in jazz bands. This conforms to an established pattern among highlife musicians, who felt that experience in English or American jazz bands was the best means of developing advanced instrumental technique. A number of African music pioneers, including Zeal Onyia, Bobby Benson, Manu Dibango, and Guy Warren, spent formative periods studying and playing abroad.[4]

Emigration from Africa, Asia, and the Caribbean increased dramatically in the years following World War II, and postcolonial London became an important center of cross-cultural fertilization. This was especially true of the interaction between Africans and West Indians, culturally related by their African heritage, and politically related as former colonial subjects and members of the new British Commonwealth. They all brought their respective musics—calypso, highlife, ska, mambo, jazz—which could be heard at student parties and at clubs, for those willing to seek it out.

Fela's presence in the cross-cultural melting pot of London would accelerate his musical sophistication in a way Trinity alone could not, providing him easier access to styles that were difficult to obtain back home in Africa. "At that time they [the colonial government] only let us hear what they wanted us to hear. When you played the radio it was controlled by the government, and the white man played us what he wanted; so we didn't know anything about black music. In England I was exposed to all these things."[5]

In other respects, Fela's enrollment at Trinity parallels the experience of African-American musicians such as Miles Davis or Wynton Marsalis who, by virtue of their privileged class positions, were expected to attend elite Western art schools. Both Davis and Marsalis initially enrolled at New York's prestigious Juilliard School of Music, and both eventually aborted their studies to immerse themselves in the jazz music of their own cultural tradition. Fela similarly left Nigeria having promised his family that he would not return without a degree, but his extracurricular musical activities would ultimately delay his graduation. Like Davis and Marsalis, his primary interests lay in music that was transmitted under less formal circumstances outside of the Western academy. A compromise with his family, Fela's enrollment in Trinity was an attempt to apply a sheen of respectability to a profession largely at odds with the Ransome-Kuti family's social status.

Primarily a college specializing in the training of music teachers, Trinity divided its curriculum into two halves: theoretical and practical. The theoretical half encompassed composition, harmony, counterpoint, and Western music history, while the practical part focused on instrumental study. Although Fela's musical experience to that point included his childhood piano lessons and stint as backing vocalist with Victor Olaiya, he hoped to enter music school not as a pianist or vocalist, but as a trumpeter. It was not an unlikely choice, as the instrument was often featured in highlife bands of the time. In fact, most of the day's top highlife bandleaders, including E. T. Mensah, Cardinal Rex Lawson, and Fela's former employer Victor Olaiya, were trumpeters; Olaiya even had a popular hit at the time called "Trumpet Highlife." Fela also cited Louis Armstrong, who performed in West Africa in 1956, and Louis Prima as important early influences.[6]

His arrival in London coincided with the arrival of his friend J. K. Braimah, who had come to study law. Drawing on their experience in the Lagos highlife scene, the two decided to form a highlife group, which they initially named "Highlife Rakers" and later changed to "Koola Lobitos." Comprised in its most stable formation of eight Nigerian and two West Indian musicians, Koola Lobitos performed mainly on weekends, entertaining Nigerian and West Indian students in London. Information is sketchy regarding the specific personnel; drummer Bayo Martins was a member,[7] and Braimah remembered that he and Fela formed Koola Lobitos "with some West Indian guys. I played guitar and Fela played trumpet. . . . Wole Bucknor, who's now a high-ranking officer in the Nigerian Navy, was there with us. He was playing piano in the group."[8]

Later in his career, Fela would dismiss his band's name as inconsequential, but while "Koola" has no apparent meaning, "Lobitos" is Spanish for "little wolves." Regardless of any literal meaning, it is more likely that Fela was attempting to infuse his work with a Spanish aura to evoke the mood of the Latin-American musical styles that were exerting such a strong influence on African dance bands. This influence was evident on many levels and in many places throughout sub-Saharan Africa. In French-speaking Senegal, Cuban salsa was the crucial ingredient in the dance-band style known as *mbalax*. Further south, in Zaire and the Congo, the dance style that came to be known as *rhumba* took its name from the Afro-Cuban style of the same name, which was influential in its formation. This influence was also reflected in the images adopted by individual musicians. The popular Sierra Leonian singer Gerald Pine was so taken with Latin American music that he changed his name to the Spanish-sounding "Geraldo Pino." The newly christened Pino often gave his compositions Spanish-sounding titles such as "Oh Ye Charanga" and imitated the sound of the language in his lyrics, although they rarely had any literal meaning in Spanish.[9]

Jazz was another particularly potent influence on Fela during his London period. Like Afro-Cuban music, this diasporic style provided a different perspective on the musical encounter between Africa and Europe. It helped Fela clarify his aims as an African student of Western music and circumvent the assumption that he would continue his family's embrace of Western art music. In a 1989 interview, Fela commented on the role jazz played in his musical development: "I played a lot of jazz in the beginning of my career because it had cultural information that enriched my mind . . . Coltrane, Miles, Sonny Rollins, that era, because I found a heavy relationship between that music and my culture. . . . [Later], I used this knowledge to penetrate into the culture of my people."[10]

The various stylistic phases of jazz had a varied impact in Africa.[11] The most immediately influential were dance-oriented styles such as swing and big-band jazz, which were strong influences on popular African styles such as highlife. With the emergence of more abstract styles of jazz from the late 1940s, the role of jazz in the dance music of West Africa gradually diminished until it was largely symbolic, used to provide a variety of neotraditional and popular African idioms an international, cosmopolitan, or improvisational sheen. From this time, the term "jazz" tended to be used to throughout sub-Saharan Africa to denote two things. First, it often referred to any large dance music ensemble with Western instruments—especially a horn section—an association derived from American big-band jazz ensembles. Large dance orchestras such as Prince Nico Mbarga's Rocafil Jazz from Nigeria and Franco's T.P.O.K. Jazz from Zaire did not play jazz in the modern sense, but rather a variety of locally popular dance styles. Second, "jazz" was also often applied to any ensemble or genre in which improvisation played a major role; this designation covered a wide stylistic range, from Western-styled "pure" jazz combos to traditional or neotraditional drumming ensembles such as the neotraditional masquerade drumming genre in Sierra Leone known as "Mailo Jazz."[12]

In its "purer" or more modern forms such as bebop, hard bop, and "free jazz," jazz was a highly specialized taste cultivated by a small group of African music aficionados. These modern forms tended to be much less popular throughout Africa due to their strong emphasis on abstractions of meter and harmony, and their consequent unsuitability for social dancing and/or singing. In fact, those Africans who appreciated modern jazz frequently did so for improvisational spirit or sonorous qualities that they associated with their own traditional musics. Yomi Gbolagunte notes: "The ones who appreciate it enjoy the polyrhythms and the complexity; they recognize the method to the madness, and to them it's similar to traditional drumming with all the crazy rhythms . . . then again to other people, it's like taking a walk through the bush and whistling, and having nature respond."[13]

The reciprocal influence of African music on jazz of the late 1950s and early 1960s was equally important. Africa's independence struggles provided a source of political inspiration for African-Americans involved in the emerging civil rights movement. At the same time, Africa's conscious revitalization of its indigenous cultural traditions provided an affirming cultural perspective for people across the African diaspora. This awareness was reflected in the work of a number of leading jazz musicians such as Randy Weston, Art Blakey, Herbie Mann, and Donald Byrd, who integrated traditional West African instruments into their ensembles, titled their pieces with African names, and collaborated with African musicians such as Nigerian percussionists Babatunde Olatunji and Solomon Ilori.[14] In its spare, open harmonic structures, African music was clearly referenced in the modal jazz developed by Miles Davis and John Coltrane in the late 1950s, and it would later figure equally in the various approaches of avant-garde jazz musicians such as Coltrane, Archie Shepp, Sun Ra, Ornette Coleman, and Cecil Taylor.

Fela's take on jazz was initially rather conservative. While the dominant trends during his college years were hard bop and cool (which were gradually being supplanted by modal and avant-garde styles), his initial exposure was to the older, more commercial styles. It might strike some as ironic that the future "Black President" of African music would cite two Sicilian-American musicians as formative influences: "I had this single I was listening to all the time, Frank Sinatra's 'Mr.

Success.' . . . But the first guy who really got me was Louis Prima. Then I went to hear Louis Armstrong at a ballroom club in London and he knocked me out."[15]

Over time, Fela developed a broader range of influences: he listened intently to trumpeters Miles Davis, Lee Morgan, and Clifford Brown; pianists Red Garland, Wynton Kelly, and Herbie Hancock; and saxophonists Charlie Parker, John Coltrane, and Harold Land.[16] He immersed himself in London's nocturnal jazz scene, making the rounds of the then-popular clubs—Ronnie Scot's, the Marquee, the Flamingo, the Roaring 20's—and honing his craft by sitting in at nightly jam sessions. Inevitably, this education included a type of public ritual that has often been an aspiring jazz player's rite of passage. Fela recounted one such occasion to M. K. Idowu:

> It got to a point when I realized they were all making fun of me. . . . I kept blowing nonsense from my horn. . . .The more I tried to impress my audience, the worse for me. . . . Fortunately the man who took over from me was the late Joe Harriott. He did not allow the audience to laugh at me for too long, with the way he came to my rescue with his fantastic solo works.[17]

It was not surprising that Fela would share a stage with the Caribbean saxophonist Harriott. In his attempt to fuse modern jazz with Afro-Caribbean styles, Harriott was drawing on the two main styles that had influenced modern African music, and his fusion of high-art technique and folk dance rhythms was similar to the fusion that would later form the basis of Fela's work.

A complex term in itself, jazz as a sound would become a crucial ingredient in Fela's music, while the symbol of "jazz" would become a complicated and contested signifier later in his career.

In the cross-cultural environment of postcolonial London, Fela's political awareness grew simultaneously with his musical sophistication, although not at the same rate. While he had not yet become consciously politicized, Fela had a number of experiences in London that served as catalysts for a growing sense of culture and politics. For example, his experience of British racism awakened a sense of cultural difference:

> It was in England that I started to feel the awareness of having to be an African because for the first time when I came to England I started to feel "Oh wow. These white people don't like us too much." . . . This was my experience from having to rent rooms. . . . At that time you would read in the newspapers in England: "House for rent—no coloreds, no dogs." That annoyed me a lot. It annoyed many students.[18]

The continuing influence of Fela's mother was also a strong factor. Mrs. Ransome-Kuti's involvement with Communist organizations led to the confiscation of her passport by the Balewa government in 1957, and she was unable to visit her sons Fela and Beko during the early years of their study in London. In spite of this, she used her international connections to arrange a visit to East Berlin for Fela. This was the height of the Cold War, and the trip had a major impact on Fela's understanding of politics:

> My mother made arrangements for me to visit, of all places, East Berlin. At that time they had just put up the Berlin Wall. . . . It was said that if you went into communist countries, you would never come out. . . . I saw many Africans waiting to go on this tour too. Then I started to feel a bit comfortable . . . we all went sightseeing. I had the most beautiful time of my life those ten days I spent there. All the racist thing I experienced as a student in England wasn't there. Ten happy days. So I took a different view on that whole shit about communism . . . I was thrilled.[19]

By far the most important factor in Fela's emerging awareness was the political change sweeping the African continent. The late 1950s were a politically charged era for African students at home and abroad, and the Pan-African melting pot of late-colonial London reinforced the sense of cultural and political difference, as well as a sense of Pan-African solidarity. After decades of anticolonial agitation, nationalist independence movements were in full swing; beginning with Ghana in 1957, twenty-four African countries gained their political independence from European colonial powers during the five-year period in which Fela studied in England.[20] It was a time of optimism, high hopes, and charismatic nationalist leaders like Ghana's Kwame Nkrumah, Guinea's Sekou Toure, Senegal's Leopold Senghor, Kenya's Jomo Kenyatta, and the Congo's Patrice Lumumba. Nigeria's independence from the British came in October 1960, with Sir Tafawa Balewa as head of state. This new political reality was surely not lost on even the least politicized students. Despite his relative disinterest in world affairs, Fela acknowledged the effect that Nkrumah and the various African independence struggles had on African students in England: "I was 'jaiye-jaiye' [happy-go-lucky] man. I was just enjoying myself. Politics was not in my brain. I spent all my time playing music. But I always followed Nkrumah. . . . He was so respected. Anytime he came to London, they put him in the front page of the newspapers. . . . I was so proud of Nkrumah, all African students were proud of him."[21]

It was inevitable that the climate of the times would be reflected in Fela's earliest artistic experiments, and he evidently moved in at least relatively politicized circles. Koola Lobitos regularly played the rounds of expatriate African student organizations such as the Northern Nigeria People's Congress and the Ghana Union of Great Britain and Ireland, and they were also one of a number of African acts featured in an "African Freedom Day" concert at the Royal Festival Hall in 1962, which included Johnny Dankworth, the Ghana Cultural Society, and Ginger Johnson and his Highlife Rhythms Band.[22] Fela's cousin Wole Soyinka, also studying in London, became interested in jazz, which was just beginning to be used explicitly as a form of social protest. Even during his student years, Soyinka's art reflected strong political concerns, and in December 1959 he enlisted his cousin

Fela, along with Ambrose Campbell, as a musical accompanist for a series of dramatic productions protesting the French explosion of an atomic bomb in the Sahara Desert.[23]

Along with his musical and political growth, Fela's college years were also a time for social growth. According to Braimah, he initially exhibited the influence of his parents in his personality and social interactions,[24] but this began to change when the two shared an apartment and Fela suddenly enjoyed a social freedom he had previously been denied. Gradually, other facets of his personality emerged during his stay abroad. A fellow Trinity student recalled Fela as

> an extraordinary fellow in every sense. . . . Fela, clad always in some garish garb, was a most curious sight especially as, at that time, there were very few African or Caribbean students. A stunning extrovert, Fela regularly held court among the bedazzled students, whom he often left speechless and bemused. He was loud and jovial, and he seemed to regard the whole collegiate establishment as comical. The feeling was mutual.[25]

Fela recalled his approach to life at the time:

> I was always practicing with my trumpet so the landlady charged me extra for making noise, so I started to make extra noise. . . . The woman didn't like it at all . . . she decided to call the police. When [the policeman] saw that I was a black man, he just threw me straight into the police van. . . . I tried to yab [verbally abuse] him: "Foolish bastard, I am going to sue you, I am going to sue you for wrongful detention. . . . You won't wear that uniform for a very long time." They knew I was jiving. How can a person who cannot pay his rent be able to employ a lawyer?[26]

Apart from socializing, Fela's time in London seems to have been divided among studying, playing with Koola Lobitos, and investigating foreign musical styles. Toward the end of his stay, his life changed in another significant way: he married Remilekun (Remi) Taylor, a British woman of mixed Nigerian and African-American heritage, in 1961. Fela and Remi had three children in three years—Yeni (born 1961), Femi (born 1962), and Sola (born 1963), firmly rooting Fela in domestic family life. Whatever his and Remi's motivations may have been at the time, he later equated his participation in the institution of Western monogamous marriage with his "colonial mentality" and lack of cultural awareness. He said in 1988: "It was really colonial, inside a court. . . . Can you imagine me standing in front of a white man to get married? . . . The marriage was not in my mind, because I cried throughout. I cried throughout because I didn't want to marry in the first place. . . . I was crying, my mother joined me in the crying. We cried throughout the marriage."[27]

For her part, Remi acknowledged the open nature of their relationship from its early stages: "If we get into girlfriends, he always had them. He made me understand before I married him that he would always have them. . . . It didn't really bother me because he had you know, girlfriends outside. He never brought any woman to my house. . . . He always respected me."[28] Remi's account of Fela at this time, when compared with Braimah's early accounts, shows just how much he had changed during his stay in London. It also provides a context for understanding his later relationships with women.

With a family, a nascent musical career, and studies to complete, Fela's final years in London were busy ones. Not surprisingly, his involvement with jazz and highlife detracted from his studies at Trinity—especially his trumpet studies. Like many wind players in their formative stages, Fela experimented with a variety of mouthpieces in his search for a personal trumpet sound. This, as well as the lack of time devoted to his theory studies, had academic consequences for Fela—he failed to pass his theoretical exams on the first two of three attempts and had to struggle to pass the practicals. His graduation delayed by a year, he finished in 1963.

Having obtained his college degree and started a family, Fela was ready to return to Nigeria and begin his musical career in earnest. He would be able to draw on the accumulated musical knowledge gained during his time in London—highlife, Afro-Caribbean styles, jazz, and Western art music—and could choose to work either within one of these genres exclusively, or attempt to innovate and create a new, hybrid form.

Fela would also be working in a climate of intense political transformation and cultural self-examination. The late 1950s were an era of idealism and renewed optimism for former colonial subjects throughout Africa—especially for African students, both at home and abroad, who anticipated playing prominent roles in creating new postcolonial societies. Those in professions such as economics, law, engineering, medicine, and the sciences clearly would be crucial to the rebuilding of the infrastructures of societies shattered by colonialism. However, creative artists would also play a very important role in the symbolic process of cultural revitalization, often with substantial government support. Musicians and other creative artists throughout sub-Saharan Africa were essential in fostering a sense of national identity and cultural pride in the postcolonial era. In Guinea, President Sekou Toure banned the importation of foreign music and established a state-owned music label that recorded and promoted the country's top bands such as Syli Orchestra and Bembeya Jazz. These and other national bands sung the praises of the president, the new nation, and nationalist heroes, while developing international reputations as top highlife ensembles. Toure also pioneered the formation of national dance troupes, and Guinea's National Dance Troupe reigned as the top such national company for years. In Senegal, president, poet, and philosopher Leopold Senghor stimulated the existential search for an "authentic" African cultural identity and expression through his philosophy of "Negritude," expressed in both prose and policy.[29]

Nowhere was this process more apparent than in Nkrumah's Ghana. Under his policy of "Africanization," the new president strongly supported Ghanaian musicians, channeled resources into the arts, and proclaimed highlife the national music. Top highlife bands such as E. T. Mensah's Tempos, Stan Plange's Uhuru Dance Band,

and Jerry Hansen's Ramblers regularly accompanied the president abroad on state visits. Nkrumah was particularly committed in his support of the country's traditional arts. He established state schools for revitalizing and transmitting traditional music and for retraining highlife musicians in traditional idioms. In line with his Pan-African vision, Nkrumah also embraced jazz as a neo-African cultural form and welcomed people of the African diaspora to assist in the development of his new nation. A community of expatriate African-American artists and intellectuals, including Maya Angelou, Max Bond, and Julian Mayfield, thrived in Accra during the Nkrumah period.[30]

In Nigeria, however, such official arts sponsorship did not exist, so despite his admiration for Nkrumah, Fela would be thrown into a creative context driven more by commerce than ideology.

During this period, two older African musicians—in their mediation of foreign and local musical influences—foreshadowed the directions Fela's career would take during the 1960s and 1970s. Drummer and guitarist Ambrose Campbell (b.1923) began his musical career as a member of the Jolly Orchestra, a palmwine guitar band performing in Lagos during the 1930s. Campbell was a member of Lagos's Saro community, descended from former slaves repatriated in Sierra Leone and returned to Nigeria toward the end of the nineteenth century.[31] As such, he belonged to a class of educated, Christianized Africans who operated in the urban cultural space between indigenous African and European traditions. Ridiculed by other Africans for their embrace of European culture and paternalistically dismissed by European colonizers as "inauthentic" Africans, the Saros bore the brunt of social transformation. Nevertheless, their intermediate cultural position meant that they were crucial in the appropriation and translation of European cultural elements into African forms, a process important for the gradual reorientation of African culture in general.

While Campbell's Jolly Orchestra consisted of European stringed instruments like banjos, guitars, and mandolins, their music was largely constructed upon African musical principles, and a number of their early recordings "suggest strong identification with the interests of African wage workers."[32] This conscious reworking of European music into African forms continued throughout Campbell's career. In the late 1940s, he emigrated to London, where he formed the West African Swing Stars. The Swing Stars included musicians from Africa, the West Indies, and Europe, and as their name suggests, they offered a hybrid mixture of highlife with jazz overtones. From 1946, Campbell led the African Brothers Band as a conscious musical reaction to the African ballroom music of the war years. The African Brothers responded to the increasing trend toward westernized highlife and ballroom dancing by assembling a percussion-based ensemble lightly augmented with European string instruments, playing a repertoire comprised mainly of adapted traditional songs from around Nigeria (ironically, Campbell performed using a set of African drums borrowed from London museums).[33] Thus, throughout his career Campbell was one of the pioneers in the "Africanization" of highlife, a process in which Fela would later figure importantly.

Another musician whose career foreshadowed Fela's was the Ghanaian percussionist Kofi Ghanaba (b. 1923), previously known as Guy Warren. By the late 1930s, Warren had developed a national reputation as an accomplished percussionist in both jazz and traditional Ghanaian idioms. His unique configuration of talents resulted partly from travels in the United States, where he had been exposed to jazz drumming, and was bolstered by a 1948 trip to London, where he participated in jazz and Afro-Caribbean fusions as a member of Kenny Graham's Afro-Cubists. Upon his return to Ghana later that year, his knowledge of Afro-Caribbean idioms helped revolutionize the highlife sound of E. T. Mensah and the Tempos, with whom he had also played prior to his trip.

Warren made another trip to the United States during the 1950s, playing with jazz luminaries such as Duke Ellington and Charlie Parker. While jazz was his first love, during this second U.S. trip Warren began to cultivate a consciously African musical identity. He changed his name to Kofi Ghanaba, a name taken from the local Ga language. Desiring to express his jazz knowledge within his own cultural tradition, he also began to draw more consciously upon Ghanaian percussion traditions. In one notable experiment, he used a Ghanaian talking drum to improvise melodically over the chord changes of a jazz tune.[34] Like the Nigerian percussionist Babatunde Olatunji, Ghanaba helped introduce African percussion sounds to Americans in general, and to reintroduce them to African-Americans in particular. He was an important, if occasionally misunderstood, presence among African-American jazz musicians of the bebop era, as jazz percussionist Max Roach acknowledged. "Ghanaba was so far ahead of what we were doing [in the fifties] that none of us understood what he was saying—that in order for Afro-American music to be stronger, it must crossfertilise with its African origins. . . . Years later Black music in America has turned to Africa for inspiration and rejuvenation."[35]

Both Campbell and Ghanaba were important pioneers in the synthesis of a consciously "African" style of popular music; more specifically, both sought to infuse highlife and other westernized African musics with more traditional African elements.

As one of the first pan-ethnic, pan-national African popular styles, highlife music provided the soundtrack of political independence throughout West Africa, and it remains closely associated with the optimistic, halcyon days of the late colonial era and its politically active elites. This association would ultimately factor in both its historic significance and its commercial demise as the 1960s progressed. As one musician put it, highlife "was liked by people who took the English way; they were the first middle-class Ghanaians and Nigerians. There was a kind of snobbery in that the man who was in the dance bands felt himself nearer the white man, as he would put on hat, tie, and jacket and would be called to balls and formal occasions."[36]

While highlife musicians born during the 1920s, such as E. T. Mensah and Bobby Benson, laid the foundation for African popular music, Fela belonged to a distinct subgeneration of musicians born between 1930 and 1940. These musicians, such as Miriam Makeba (South Africa, b. 1932), Manu Dibango (Cameroun, b. 1933), Abdullah Ibrahim (a.k.a. "Dollar Brand," South Africa, b. 1934), Franco

(Zaire, b. 1938), Hugh Masekela (South Africa, b. 1939), and Tabu Ley Rochereau (Zaire, b. 1940), would benefit from the dissemination of the Western music industry, refashioning a variety of international and indigenous musical elements into distinct popular African styles that would gain them international reputations.

Twenty-four years old in the spring of 1963, Fela was returning to a Lagos in which highlife was the order of the day in popular music; jazz was the emergent cosmopolitan art music, technically dazzling in the Western sense, with audible African roots; and Western art music was an extremely specialized taste associated with the Europhile segment of the urban ruling elite. Naturally talented and versed in all three styles, Fela was determined to make a substantial contribution to Nigerian music and culture, and he returned to Nigeria confident of this success.

Lagos (1963–1969)

It is a little-known and highly ironic fact that shortly after Fela returned to Nigeria in 1963, he was persuaded by his mother and others close to the Ransome-Kuti family to apply for the post of Director of Music in the Nigerian Army. At the interview, which was also attended by Fela's friend and early manager Benson Idonije, it became obvious that Fela was not earnestly interested in the position and had only agreed to the interview to placate his family. He was thus not offered the position.[37] Soon afterward, however, he was hired as a staff producer for the Nigerian Broadcasting Company (NBC), again with Idonije as contact. Idonije, himself a member of the NBC staff, had been impressed by singles Fela had recorded in London and released on his own FRK label, calling them "beautiful progressive highlife, a revitalization of the conventional approach that was in vogue."[38]

The senior staff at NBC included prominent members of the Lagos Musical Society, and the network employed a number of prominent Nigerian musicians such as Ayo Bankole and Fela Sowande.[39] Fela's responsibilities at NBC included recording new local bands for broadcast and leading the new studio orchestra, which the station had agreed to provide. It was potentially an ideal situation for an aspiring musician, guaranteeing steady income, a reliable means through which he could work out his ideas, and familiarity with the work of diverse Nigerian musicians. However, the relationship between Fela and NBC soured in a matter of months. The station apparently failed to provide the studio orchestra and complained of Fela's chronic lateness. His superiors also frowned upon Fela's use of the position to record and promote his own jazz group, the Fela Ransome-Kuti Quintet, instead of the broader-based, middle-of-the-road presentation the network expected.[40] The original Fela Ransome-Kuti Quintet featured Fela on trumpet, Don Amechi on guitar, Emmanuel Ngomalio on bass, John Bull on drums, and Sid Moss on piano, and occasionally Igo Chico on tenor saxophone,[41] and a press announcement promised listeners that the group would provide a wide range of music including "Highlife, jazz, the Twist, the Madison, rock and roll, rumba, and what-have-you."[42] Instead, the band offered its audience jazz standards. Fela's agenda was clear: "My intention was to introduce jazz into Nigeria when I first came. . . . But I was so unsuccessful. People just refused to accept it."[43]

The popular music scene in Lagos at this time was dominated by highlife bands led by Victor Olaiya, "Cardinal" Rex Lawson, Eddie Okonta, Victor Uwaifo, Roy Chicago, Eric Akaeze, Charles Iwegbue, and others, performing at venues such as the Kakadu Club, the Lido Club, and the Empire Hotel.[44] Fela's goal of introducing modern jazz to Nigerian audiences presented a creative quandary, as recent styles such as bebop and modal jazz differed from the earlier jazz styles that had impacted African popular music. The high degree of rhythmic and harmonic abstraction of the newer styles was more suited to reflective listening than social dancing, and neither style was particularly popular in Africa. Fela's first attempts at playing jazz in Nigeria seemed doomed to commercial failure.

Koola Lobitos, Edition II

The combination of the unfulfilled orchestra arrangement, Fela's work habits, and his use of the position to promote his own professional interests ultimately led to his dismissal from NBC in 1965; he would henceforth generate his income solely through performing music. In the same year, however, he had assembled a new, larger band, which he again named Koola Lobitos. The new band comprised Fela on trumpet and occasionally piano, Tunde Williams and Eddie Aroyewu on trumpets, Isaac Olasugba on alto saxophone, Tex Becks and Christopher Uwaifor on tenor saxophones, Lekan Animashaun on baritone saxophone, Fred Lawal or Yinka Roberts on guitar, Tony Allen on drum set, Ojo Okeji on electric bass, and Easy Adio on congas.[45] Given the failure of his straight jazz quartet and the continued popularity of highlife, the success of the new Koola Lobitos depended on Fela's ability to wed his jazz aspirations to a local musical form agreeable to the Lagos highlife crowd. In fact, according to Fela, his mother had counseled him at this time to "start playing music your people understand, not jazz."[46] "Highlife-jazz" was the label he coined to describe his new musical fusion, indicating that the main stylistic and structural devices of Nigerian dance-band highlife would serve as a basic scheme onto which jazz elements—improvisation, more elaborate orchestration and more complex harmonic movement—would be integrated.

Essential to this new fusion was the drummer, Tony Allen. Allen and Fela met in 1964, while the former was the drummer for the Western Toppers Highlife Band. Prior to joining the Western Toppers, Allen had played with Victor Olaiya, Agu Norris and the Heatwaves, The Nigerian Messengers, and The Melody Angels. Fela was impressed by Allen's playing and asked him to join the NBC quartet, performing jazz on the weekly radio broadcasts. When Fela reformed Koola Lobitos the following year, he again offered Allen the drum chair. "He discovered me to be one of the best drummers in Lagos," Allen recalls. "So he started using me on his jazz program, with his intention of making a different band later, playing highlife-jazz."[47]

The association between Fela and Allen would last from 1965 to 1979 and would result in some of Nigeria's most innovative popular music. Allen brought a distinct jazz sensibility to Fela's compositions. His talent lay in his ability to utilize the stylistic vocabulary of jazz drumming—ride cymbal patterns, interjected tom-tom and bass drum accents ("bombs"), and independent coordination—within a highlife rhythmic scheme. He was especially adroit at blending his drum set playing with the soundstream of small percussion instruments found in the highlife ensemble, such as bells, shekeres, congas, bongos, and clefs.

Another charter member of Koola Lobitos was baritone saxophonist Lekan Animashaun, who joined the group in 1965 and remained with Fela for the rest of the latter's career, also serving as bandleader following the 1979 departure of Tony Allen.

The new group's maiden performances were enthusiastically received, and the Lobitos got an additional boost when they were hired to back Chubby Checker and Jamaican ska singer Millie (Millicent Small) of "My Boy Lollipop" fame on their respective Nigerian tours.[48] Fela's modern-jazz background brought a new flavor to Lagos highlife audiences, who were impressed with the complex arrangements and horn solos. Engaging the competitive rhetoric common in the Nigerian music scene, he spoke in 1965 of "revolutionizing" the highlife tradition with jazz elements: "People seem to be embracing the revolution enthusiastically. The young ones are chasing us all over the place and even the older set enjoys us a lot. I will tell them that a new dawn has broken for Nigerian highlife and we are all moving forward."[49]

The music recorded by Koola Lobitos between 1965 and 1969 can be roughly divided into three stylistic types, reflecting Fela's progressive attempts to assimilate and compete with the foreign styles that continued to influence African music as the decade progressed. The earliest songs conform to highlife conventions while introducing a number of jazz elements. The middle-period songs gradually reflect the growing influences of rhythm-and-blues and Afro-Latin styles, particularly Cuban salsa music. The later songs, composed during a period in which African-American rhythm-and-blues music had become the dominant popular style, show Fela attempting a more explicit fusion of highlife and rhythm-and-blues. In general, Koola Lobitos's style is distinguished from other Nigerian highlife of the time by its greater formal and harmonic complexity and its more strident mood. The band's blaring horns, aggressive jazz solos, and dense arrangements, as well as Tony Allen's jazzy propulsion, set them apart from other bands offering more lilting, melodious highlife sounds.

Thematically, these songs address a range of standard highlife topics—love songs, moral admonishments, mild praise songs, social commentaries, and traditionally inflected poetic songs—with moods ranging from the pedestrian to the philosophical. As the lyrics demonstrate, almost all of Fela's highlife is notable more for its instrumental rather than textual sophistication. Sung mostly in Yoruba, occasionally in English, and rarely in other West African languages,[50] the texts intermittently exhibit a fairly contrived traditionalist approach.

Four examples of Fela's approach to conventional highlife composition are "Bonfo," "Fere," "Onidodo," and "Eke." "Bonfo" (Short Skirt) is similar to much highlife of the period in its chord progression (a major key sequence alternating between tonic and dominant), up-tempo rhythm pattern, and bouncing, introductory horn theme. The text is sung in Yoruba:

Arabinrin, ese re ga	Young lady, your style is chic
Arabinrin, se bonfo ni	Lovely, it is "short skirt"
Ye o ma ba e lo	Yes, I'll go with you!
Se America ni	Even if you're America bound
Se Jamaica ni o . . .	Even if you're Jamaica bound . . .

"Fere" (alternately translatable as "Smooth Ride," "Magical Benevolence," or "Zoom") also contains a fairly typical highlife horn theme and major key chord progression over a lilting, mid-tempo rhythm pattern. An example of the possibilities of varied interpretation in many West African lyrics, "Fere" can be read both as an exhortation to the forces of destiny and as a celebration of the sensory pleasure of music (i.e., a celebration of music as a "ride"):

Gbe wa dele o	Carry us home, yeah
Gbegbe gbe wa lo'le o	Benevolence, carry us home
Ayi niwa o	The feeling is nice
Gbegbe gbe wa le' le . . .	Destiny, carry us home . . .

Over a rambling, up-tempo highlife rhythm and alternating tonic-dominant chord sequence, "Onidodo" (Fried Plantain Seller) describes the chaos that ensues when a Lagos street vendor exhausts his wares in the face of a hungry crowd:

Onidodo oni moin moin	The fried plantain and bean-cake seller
Nigba ti o ta o gbe 'gba kale	When he did not sell, he rested his cart
E wa woja ni Lafiaji!	Oh, you should have seen the fight in Lafiaji![51]

"Eke" (Deceit) is a virtual inversion of the topical themes for which Fela would later become famous. The horn theme is played in a major key, giving the song an upbeat, celebratory mood; the lyrics—concerning love, infidelity, and gossip—represent the type of concerns from which he would later completely distance himself in his songs:

Lo wa se se ore	Find a meaningful employment, my friend
Ko ye mura eke	Give up the spectre of deceit

Rani lati s'ooto	Endeavor to say the truth and live the truth
Ko ye mura eke	Give up the gossiping lifestyle
Eke ma npa ni o	Gossip destroys the person
Esan ma nbo o	Vengeance is coming
Itiju ni lati pofo	It's a shameful thing to not achieve
Fi mi sile baby	Leave me alone, baby
Asewo le ju o	Prostitution is hard to contain
Ayiri ni ko mo kan	It is a crazy guy who does not know right from wrong
Iku le ri yen o ke ya sa	It is good to run from him—he is "death"
Fa'ye mi sile o . . .	Leave my life alone . . .

Instrumentally, these songs conform to most stylistic norms of highlife music of the time. They also contain a number of stylistic departures that demonstrate how Fela integrated jazz elements. For example, the bridge of "Bonfo" utilizes an extended sequence of interpolated II-V7 chord patterns more complex than most highlife songs of the time, which tended to rely upon simpler progressions. "Bonfo" is also notable for the acoustic rhythm piano figure, which continues throughout the song, as well as for the piano solo during the middle section. This was a clear departure; for obvious reasons of size, portability, and climate, the acoustic piano was rarely used in Africa. Fela's introduction of it was most likely an attempt to apply his knowledge of Western music in a novel way; integration of new instruments into an ensemble was one of the most reliable means of building a reputation as an innovator in West African popular music.[52] "Fere" also contains acoustic piano, in an unaccompanied introduction to the song. Significantly, it also features Fela scat singing over the highlife rhythm during the song's fade, a clear borrowing from jazz. "Eke" is unique in the frantic chromatic exchange between the bass guitar and the horns in the song's introduction.

"Onidodo" is another composition that, while rooted in highlife conventions, is unique in some aspects of its arrangement, and it contains many of the devices that distinguish Fela's brand of highlife. The song is built on a standard twelve-bar form. After a brief, introductory horn statement, Fela enters along with the rhythm section, singing two verses over a declamatory, percussive horn riff. Fela's jazzy trumpet solo follows for a chorus, followed by a complex horn arrangement utilizing a number of stock big-band techniques, including soli writing, sectional call-and-response writing between trumpets and saxophones, and a fourteen-bar "shout" chorus.[53] Fela reenters following the horn interlude to sing the song's final verse, and the song fades out on a call-and-response vocal exchange between Fela and the chorus. This song gives the clearest picture of the compositional skills Fela acquired through his study of jazz and is the first well-defined example of his highlife style; virtually all of the compositions that followed adhered to a similar formal scheme.

By the mid-1960s, Fela was already relying on a fairly predetermined arranging style, and this approach would characterize most of his later work. The songs are usually introduced by a brief horn statement, without rhythm section accompaniment. Fela's vocal enters along with the rhythm section, singing one or two verses over a prominent, repeating horn riff. This is followed by a horn solo (accompanied by a background horn line), generally by Fela on trumpet or one of the saxophonists. A horn section interlude follows, written in soli or sectional call-and-response fashion, the second half of which is often accompanied by a second trumpet solo. Finally, Fela sings the final verse and the song fades on a repeating chorus figure or vamp.

As innovative as it may have been, the success of Koola Lobitos's self-consciously compositional highlife did not ultimately match the band's expectations. Conservative Lagos audiences found the music too busy, dense, and aggressive compared with the highlife styles to which they were accustomed. Interestingly, Fela was voted the top Nigerian "jazz" musician in a popular music magazine at this time, a characteristically West African double-sided compliment acknowledging at once the complexity of his music and its distance from accepted popular music tastes.[54]

Tony Allen confirmed this distance: "In five minutes we'd use about five different arrangements . . . it was far too complicated for the audience. They couldn't understand what was happening; except, possibly, the musically inclined who knew that the music was different from all the local things they'd been listening to. It was a bit like showing off."[55] A musician from a rival band remembers Koola Lobitos performances as sounding "like jazz-highlife-fusion. And the people couldn't relate to it because he had all these horns and all these arrangements, and it was all too much for the people to comprehend. . . . He was playing to empty houses while we were packing [them]."[56]

The general conservatism among highlife listeners was such that some were actually offended by the band's departure from highlife conventions. Their first LP on EMI sold poorly, confounding the company's Nigerian director and, in one account, infuriating its London distributor, who "had never in her entire sales life seen a merchandise this much spurned by African and most especially Nigerian record buyers."[57]

Although this was a difficult period for Fela and the Lobitos, it was notable for another development that was to have long-term significance for Fela—he began to smoke marijuana. Use of marijuana (commonly referred to in Nigeria as "Indian hemp" and in Lagos as *igbo*) was looked down upon as a degenerate habit, and Fela approached it with suspicion. Although he admitted enjoying the initial experience, he abstained thereafter and forbade his band members to smoke under penalty of dismissal. "I liked it when I smoked it in London. But my brother professor told me a long time ago that if I 'smoked' I would go crazy, so that is why I run away from it."[58] However, by 1966 his views had radically changed: "I used it a couple of times to relax. Then one night I went on stage stoned. Man, I used to just stand there stiff as a stick. My feet were glued to the floor. This night I started jumping, dancing, flying. The music poured out. From now on, I said, we all turn on."[59]

While its effect was not immediately apparent, marijuana would become a crucial catalyst in Fela's work, musically and symbolically. Gradually, he began to acquire an image as the young "rebel" of highlife. In one incident, for example, he is said to have blown his trumpet outside the house of veteran highlife star Cardinal Rex Lawson, to prove himself the better trumpeter. Although he was circumspect about his hemp smoking, he was acquiring a reputation in other areas: he was opinionated and outspoken in interviews, and he was known to have several girlfriends outside of his marriage. Above all, he was determined to transform highlife conventions.

By 1967, he felt the band might fare better by presenting its music in Ghana, where highlife's popularity was as high as ever. He visited the country to plan a prospective tour, and initially the "home of highlife" was all he expected and more. "I never see a country like that before, only in Europe. . . . Their nightlife was swimming with highlife music, the whole country was swinging so much that I said to myself that this is the right place to come and play."[60]

Returning to Lagos, Fela announced his plans to take Koola Lobitos on a Ghanaian tour. This first international outing was a prestigious undertaking, and Nigerian fans wondered how the Lobitos would fare against Ghana's internationally recognized "second-generation" highlife bands like Stan Plange's Uhuru Dance Band and Jerry Hansen's Ramblers. The initial shows in Accra (at hotel ballrooms such as the Pan-African and the Mayor) were well attended, although the audience dwindled somewhat at later shows. Still, the Lobitos were fairly popular in Ghana overall; the Uhuru Dance Band even added the Lobitos' song "Yese Yese" to their live set. The tour was organized by the Ghanaian promoter Faisal Helwani. "I talked to Fela about coming to Ghana. . . . He didn't have any amplification so when he came I also hired the equipment for him. I took him all over Ghana: Koforidua, Cape Coast, Swedru, Takoradi, Kumasi, Akim Oda, everywhere. . . . I promoted the record 'Yese Yese' and went into business with Fela. With Fela I never made any money, but Fela liked Ghana and kept coming."[61]

The rudimentary equipment on which Koola Lobitos performed was only one of the band's problems. Besides considerations of individual style, there were other large-scale factors affecting the popularity of highlife music in general during the mid-to-late 1960s. Paramount among these was the eruption of the Nigerian Civil War in 1967, the culmination of problems that had long simmered beneath the postcolonial euphoria since independence. While no longer a British colony, the country still suffered from inadequate infrastructure, a shortage of educated professionals, and a problematic constitution that did little to ameliorate regionalism, educational imbalances, and deep-seated ethnic rivalries. The first attempts at civilian government ended with the assassination of Sir Tafewa Balewa and other top officials in a military coup, and the country was increasingly plagued by regional and ethnic tensions as it lurched forward under the military regimes of Johnson Aguiyi-Ironsi and Yakubu Gowon.

These myriad problems culminated in the Nigerian Civil War, which lasted from 1967 to 1970. Commonly known as the Biafran war, the conflict was sparked when the predominately Igbo Eastern region of the country attempted—under the leadership of Colonel Odemegwu Ojukwu—to secede from the Federal Republic of Nigeria to form the independent nation of Biafra. In the resulting military crisis, which was precipitated by anti-Igbo pogroms waged around the country, Igbos returned to their southeastern homeland en masse. Many prominent highlife bands were led by or comprised of Igbo musicians, and their exodus left a void in the Lagos highlife scene which was never filled, and which ultimately fostered the growth of more specifically ethnic styles such as juju. Blackouts, conscriptions, and curfews also curtailed the country's nightlife during wartime.[62] To date, contemporary highlife music in Nigeria is most associated with the eastern, Igbo region.

The symbolic associations of highlife also began to change as the decade progressed. While it had been strongly associated with the drive towards independence in the 1950s, the style's upper-class, westernized associations led to a decrease in its popularity as more "authentically" African cultural symbols were sought to replace the older images of the colonial era. As noted by Charles Keil, highlife musicians operated in a particular sphere of the popular music scene, and certain key factors distinguished them from other local traditional and neotraditional musicians. They often relied on written music and used Western wind instruments, largely avoiding indigenous instruments with deep cultural significance such as talking drums. They also tended to wear European clothing, sing in English or pidgin English, perform in ethnically heterogeneous bands for varied audiences, and rely on salaries rather than cash donations from patrons.[63] By contrast, ethnically identified bands such as Yoruba juju bands tended to operate exclusively within well-defined ethnic spheres, economic networks, and stylistic norms. Although juju groups did use modern Western instruments such as electric guitars, these instruments were blended with a variety of traditional instruments, and it was juju groups, and not highlife groups, that were usually identified as more culturally "authentic."

When Fela, in an article discussing highlife's future, linked continued stylistic evolution to musical literacy, he was clearly operating from a different cultural and creative stance: "Highlife will not die. It will only take a new shape. . . . You will soon find that it will be a very great asset for Nigerian musicians to be able to read and write music. When it reaches that stage, you will see the wonderful brand of highlife they will be playing. I personally am on a crusade to rejuvenate the style."[64]

Soul Power

They're doing it on the moon y'all . . . in the jungle too.
                    CHARLES WRIGHT, *"Express Yourself"* (1970)

For me and many of my friends, to be liberated was to be exposed to more R&B songs and to be au courant of the latest exploits of Muhammad Ali, George Jackson, Angela Davis, Malcolm X, and Martin

Luther King, Jr. These were becoming an alternative cultural capital for the African youth—imparting to us new structures of feeling and enabling us to subvert the hegemony of Francité *after independence.*

MANTHIA DIAWARA (1992b)

Another factor eroding the popularity of highlife was the continued influence of foreign music. Congolese styles like rumba and soukous had been long popular across the continent, while emerging British rock-and-roll acts like the Beatles, the Kinks, and the Rolling Stones had a substantial impact on young African musicians. Nigerian singer/bandleader Sonny Okosuns, for example, began his career in the mid-1960s with a cover band playing material by the Beatles, the Rolling Stones, and Cliff Richard.[65] But by 1966–1967, the most popular foreign style throughout West Africa was the African-American "soul" music of performers such as James Brown, Wilson Pickett, Sam and Dave, Aretha Franklin, and Otis Redding. By the end of the decade, soul had even eclipsed the popularity of highlife and other local styles, with James Brown as the reigning favorite. There were important musical and symbolic reasons for Brown's dramatic impact throughout Africa, and, as with Afro-Caribbean music, these illustrate the cultural role of the African diaspora in the construction of modern Pan-African identity.

From 1964 (with the release of "Out of Sight") through the rest of the decade, Brown—along with his arrangers, Nat Jones, Alfred Ellis, David Matthews, and Fred Wesley—developed a synthesis of blues and gospel music flavored with jazz and Latin-styled arrangements and marked by an urban sensibility that came to be known as "funk." These musicians' use of musical techniques like hocketing (combining simple parts into complex structures), ensemble stratification (layered construction of parts), call-and-response, and the overall percussive articulation in early funk compositions such as "Cold Sweat," "Let Yourself Go," "There Was a Time," and "Get It Together" paralleled traditional approaches to ensemble structuring throughout West Africa.

John Chernoff explains Brown's popularity in Africa.

> James Brown is the most popular Afro-American musician in Africa partially because the rhythms in his arrangements are extremely open and stable, and his songs generally involve a bridge in which all the instruments change together and then return to their former relationships. To an African ear, James Brown times these changes extremely well as he and his band move through the transitions of a song, and his arrangements bear close comparison with African arrangements.[66]

Olly Wilson elaborates on this idea:

> The widespread popularity of James Brown throughout West Africa is a vivid testimony of the close relationship of Afro-American to African music. Brown's style is based upon an intensification of the most salient aspects of West African music, modified by the divergencies . . . charac-

teristic of Afro-American music and the peculiarities of Brown's individual musical personality. The result is a style which is consonant with traditional West African approaches and yet different enough to benefit from the advantages of novelty.[67]

The unique power of Brown's music from the late 1960s results, in one sense, from the novel way African-American elements were fused with other elements originating elsewhere in the African diaspora. Specifically, varying articulations of the generic West African timeline patterns that came to be known in the diaspora as "clave" are crucial to both funk and afrobeat because they provide the link between full- and half-time tempos that gives these musical styles much of their structural and dynamic tension.

Alfred "Pee Wee" Ellis, arranger of much of Brown's most innovative work, defined funk as developing from the interplay of African-American and Afro-Caribbean musical practices. It was as a result of Ellis's familiarity with Latin-jazz fusions that he introduced Afro-Cuban conga drums into Brown's ensemble, and the instrument played an integral role in many of Brown's most popular compositions of the late 1960s, including "There Was a Time," "Give It Up or Turnit Loose," "It's a New Day," and "Super Bad."[68] In particular, Ellis has cited the *montuno* section of salsa arrangements as central to the development of funk: "The 'jungle' feeling came from the drummers . . . and the bass patterns we were using and the monotone, the one-chord idea . . . sets up a *montuno* which is a vamp type thing, a Cuban thing which makes it mesmerizing. . . . We also brought it over here with us [from West Africa] you know, it came through the Baptist church."[69]

The consolidation of these diasporic African musical worlds functioned as a sonic analogue to the conscious reconstruction and reintegration of Africa as a cultural symbol into the African-American psyche. Brown's music—with its mixture of consciously emphasized West African structural characteristics and vocal sentiments of black empowerment (in songs such as "Say It Loud: I'm Black and I'm Proud" and "Soul Power") provided a cross-cultural blueprint for using funk as a medium for contestational, counterhegemonic messages. For African-Americans, this was an important psychic reintegration after centuries of forcibly suppressed Africanity. Brown's trademark vocal scream—an emotionally harrowing and stylistically unprecedented feature sonically analogous to Pharoah Sanders's or Albert Ayler's "new thing" saxophone squalls—began to emerge in his recordings around 1967, exactly simultaneous with the "Africanization" of his musical approach and the emerging pro-black sentiments in his lyrics. Thulani Davis remarked that Brown's music "was proof that black people were different. Rhythmically and tonally blacks had to be from somewhere else. Proof that Africa was really over there for those of us who had never seen it—it was in that voice."[70] The sociopolitical climate of the time infused soul music with an important symbolic resonance. During the 1960s, many musicians in Africa and throughout the African diaspora looked to traditional African models for creative and cultural inspiration, and to African-American models for stylistic innovation. In Africa, soul music was the latest example of West African musical elements being transmuted through the African-American experience and transformed by their encounter with Western technology, while retaining clearly identifiable African characteristics.

One example of this cross-fertilization was the "boogaloo" (also spelled "bugalu") dance craze of 1967, demonstrating the effect that diasporic reformulations of African traditions had on African music. Stylistically, the boogaloo was a conscious attempt by Latin musicians such as Ricardo Ray, Willie Rodriguez, and Johnny Colon to fuse elements of soul with Latin music, in order to attract both African-American and Latino listeners.[71] Ultimately however, the boogaloo is most remembered as a soul dance style. As was the trend, a host of soul performers subsequently released boogaloo songs, including James Brown, who mentioned the dance on his 1968 compendium of dance styles "There Was a Time." The boogaloo soon swept across West Africa, where—like the "Twist," "Lunar Walk," "Jerk," "Popcorn," and "Mashed Potatoes" before it—the dance was interpreted as a variation on traditional dances and invested with deep cultural and philosophical significance.[72] Nigerian music journalist Victor Dorgu, who was visiting the United States at this time, observed:

> The Boogaloo quickly reminds one of some exotic African dance steps and when I asked how come there was such a great similarity between it and some typical African dances, some of the Negroes said it had to be so because they were as a race fast seeking to identify themselves with Africa, the home of their ancestors. In fact there is so much similarity that when we had on some Nigerian music at a party in San Francisco, California, our American friends—white and black—were doing the boogaloo and I couldn't help joining.[73]

Like highlife during the late 1950s, soul music became an important cultural tool as postcolonial Africa began to dismantle the psychological legacy of the colonial era and define its role in the larger world culture. Africans watched the African-American civil rights struggles closely, and the assertive black pride sentiments expressed in songs such as Brown's "Say It Loud: I'm Black and I'm Proud" reinforced the postcolonial embrace of indigenous culture taking place throughout the continent.

Not all listeners welcomed the soul "invasion"; some saw it as an unabashedly destructive presence. A writer for the *Daily Times* wondered

> how on Earth a Nigerian . . . could condescend to "soul." . . . As the Nigerian James Browns wish us to believe, this soul thing is more than a dance. It is a fraternity, it is black smoothness, negroid rhythm . . . the lot. I ask you—what is negroid about soul? The black Africans [*sic*] in Brazil use African musical instruments and really sweat it out to Yemoja, the long-forgotten Yoruba goddess. . . . What the American Negroes are doing, and converting young Nigerians to, is a perversion of the African beat.[74]

J. K. Obatala, an expatriate African-American living in Ghana, took issue with the very term "soul," feeling it reflected—like "Negritude" and "African Personality" before it—a romanticized, uncritical black essentialism. In Obatala's analysis, the success of soul music among Africans was strongly dependent on a pervasive myth of African-American affluence; the music was, he thought, only rarely interpreted as a pro-active response against centuries of cultural oppression. Soul in this light essentially became what highlife had previously been—a hedonistic, ideologically ambiguous soundtrack to the elite African celebration and consolidation of its newfound presence in global and local economies, while also functioning as a symbolic first step toward American capitalism, facilitated by friendly black American faces and familiar neo-African sounds.[75]

In the case of Nigeria, the dramatic impact of American music must be at least partially considered in light of the fact that the country did not have a charismatic leader able to galvanize the ethnically diverse population, stress the importance of indigenous culture, implement programs to promote that culture, or regulate the influx of foreign cultural products. The situation was different in Toure's Guinea, in Tanzania under Julius Nyerere (who actually banned soul music and soul nightclubs from his country in 1969),[76] and especially in Nkrumah's Ghana.

Of course, Nkrumah had more substantial threats to deal with than the popular songs of African-Americans. Having single-mindedly pursued his vision of Pan-African unity during nine years in office, he had run progressively afoul of the Western powers. Nkrumah actively courted nationalist leaders from around Africa and the diaspora, and established bases in Ghana for training soldiers involved in the various African liberation movements. His international prestige was quite high in 1965 when he almost single-handedly engineered the expulsion of apartheid South Africa from the British Commonwealth of Nations. When, in the same year, he highlighted the inner workings of international capital in his highly publicized book *Neo-Colonialism: The Last Stage of Imperialism,* it brought down the full wrath of the U.S. government. The Americans withdrew $35 million in foreign aid virtually overnight and doubled the CIA presence in Accra (which included several African-Americans working to destabilize Nkrumah's government). A military coup followed shortly, while Nkrumah was in Hanoi at the invitation of President Ho Chi Minh. Nkrumah is remembered in Ghana as "the tree that was cut short," and it would take more than a quarter century for both his image as a leader and his dream of Pan-African unity to be resuscitated. Ghanaian president Jerry Rawlings erected a monument to Nkrumah in 1992 on the spot where the latter had proclaimed Ghana's independence in 1957, and the idea of a transnational alliance in Africa began to be discussed again in the 1990s, in light of the newly formed European Economic Community.[77]

Mr. Follow Follow

As popular as soul performers were, it was not until the beginning of the 1970s that they began performing in West Africa with any regularity.[78] Until that time, the task of reproducing rhythm-and-blues music in live performance fell to "copyright" bands. "Copyright" referred to the practice of West African bands playing music by Western performers. The term initially referred to the performance of a variety of Western genres, but by the end of the 1960s, it had become virtually synonymous with soul music as a result of soul's overwhelming popularity. Many of these copyright bands were former highlife bands who had been forced to add soul numbers to their repertoires to avoid losing their audiences.

Among the scores of copyright bands performing throughout West Africa, Sierra Leonian singer Geraldo Pino and his band, the Heartbreakers, were especially popular. Pino, whose earlier work was strongly influenced by Latin American music, had recently restyled his image after James Brown, and the Heartbreakers became enormously successful throughout West Africa, performing cover versions of Brown's hits of the time such as "Cold Sweat" and "Let Yourself Go." They were particularly popular in Nigeria, and Fela—who was considered an innovator despite his limited popularity—felt especially challenged by Pino's increasing presence and popularity in Lagos. However, even he admitted to being impressed by their performances, as he told Gary Stewart: "They were great, I must be frank with you. They copied James Brown throughin, throughout, every note, every style. And they had the equipment. . . . Before they came into my country, bands only used one microphone, at the time, a whole band. But they came in with five microphones, and the sound, and it's deep, you know. . . . So nobody wanted to hear anybody but the Heartbeats . . . they drove everybody out of the market."[79]

The Heartbeats' tremendous impact was due largely to the fact that Pino was the closest African audiences could get to experiencing James Brown in person. Having traveled abroad and witnessed Brown in performance, Pino had been able to assume much of Brown's stage persona. A Lagos review described his impact on West African audiences:

> If you haven't seen the great James Brown do his groovy stuff before, take heart—for there's plenty consolation in Geraldo Pino, who socks it to you a plenty. . . . Pino sets the pace—an inward emotional "fire" envelopes him; shuffles, shakes, and like a man possessed (with what else but soul!) rants a rhapsody that has his audience spellbound and shuffling unconsciously. [Pino] sweats and more sweats but suddenly, the "fire" within gets too much for him. He asks for a glassful of cold water, sips it down and wow! . . . he is at it again in the next minute![80]

Another copyright band, the Clusters, led by singer Joni Haastrup, was often paired in Lagos with Pino and the Heartbeats to create immensely popular double-bills, cutting into the Lobitos' audience. Haastrup, who was known as "Nigeria's Soul Brother Number One,"[81] remembers the Clusters' approach to copyright: "We were hot! We played everything and everybody. . . . We stayed as close to the original as possible. We made sure that when you heard it you thought you were hearing the record except that we had our own little innovations added to it."[82]

By 1968, the Lobitos had worked hard to consolidate their audience but found themselves rapidly losing ground to soul music. Attempting to carve a distinct space for his music, Fela arranged to take the band on a second tour of Ghana in 1968 only to find that the home of highlife, too, was thoroughly in the grip of the soul music craze. One local writer noted that "no reader of the Accra *Daily Graphic* . . . can be in doubt that the most important event in Ghana in recent weeks has been the 'Soul Contest' at the Labadi Pleasure Beach, at which Pepe Dynamite was crowned Soul Brother No. 1, beating formidable contenders such as Elvis J. Brown and James Brown, Jr. . . . The soul craze . . . now dominates the West African pop music nightclub scene (with highlife coming a poor second best)."[83] Fela also found that Pino was as popular in Ghana as he was in Nigeria. "One day in Accra we entered this club, Ringway Hotel. The place was packed man! Geraldo Pino was playing there. . . . The whole place was jumping. The music carried me away completely. . . . Can you understand my situation at the club that night? Needing to find a job myself, but enjoying the music so much that I even forgot I myself was a fucking musician. . . . After seeing this Pino, I knew I had to get my shit together. And quick!"[84]

It soon became clear that soul was not simply the latest in a series of musical fads. Rather, it was a long-term fascination that was transforming West African popular music. Arguably, this transformation did have positive effects on highlife. While the conventional style was fading, the most innovative highlife musicians were at the forefront of the effort to digest and reinterpret the stylistic alternatives offered by soul. Thus, the impact of soul was the catalyst for keen competition and innovation among the region's remaining highlife bands, such as Koola Lobitos, Ghana's Ramblers and Uhurus, and Benin's Black Santiagos, all of whom were faced with the choice of playing soul or developing a type of highlife capable of competing with the foreign style.[85]

The most significant result of this second Ghanaian tour, however, was Fela's coining of the term "afrobeat" for his music. "Soul music took over. James Brown's music, Otis Redding took over the whole continent, man. It was beautiful music though, I must agree. I said to myself I must compete with these people. I must find a name for my music, so I gave my music [the name] "afrobeat" to give it an identity."[86]

Upon his return to Nigeria, Fela informed the local music press of his new label. His statement pursued a clear middle path—asserting his individuality while distancing himself from both soul and the rapidly fading star of highlife. It was clear that he held loftier goals for his music than mere commercial popularity, and while he distanced himself from highlife, his comments recall the close connection between artistic expression and cultural pride characteristic of highlife musicians during the nationalist period: "*Highlife* is a loose term which has no reference to any concrete happening in actual life. And besides, my music is much stronger than what people are already used to as highlife music. . . . It is my desire to create a new trend worthy of emulation in the music scene of this country in particular and Africa in general, which will be a pride to the black race."[87]

Christopher Waterman has discussed the significance of naming a musical genre as a mark of distinction in Yoruba popular music and its role in boosting a performer's reputation, often irrespective of the actual degree of stylistic innovation involved.[88] Fela's new moniker should be seen partially in this light, as it did not yet represent a major stylistic change.[89] But if the "afrobeat" tag indicated any clear departure from Fela's earlier music, it was in his attempt to resist the general trend toward exclusively soul repertoires by gradually integrating aspects of both soul and Latin styles into his own music, keeping the foundation rooted in high-life.

The influence and interplay of Afro-Cuban and soul styles is evident in a number of Koola Lobitos compositions. "Oritshe" in particular contains a horn arrangement very reminiscent of salsa in its syncopated, off-beat construction—qualities also apparent in "Abiara."[90] "Wa Dele" and "Àjò" are both examples of the influence of salsa, refracted through the influence of rhythm-and-blues. Both are loping, mid-tempo songs built around the Cuban clave, with salsa-sounding horn ostinatos, syncopated soul bass patterns, blues-derived dominant seventh chord harmonies, and (on "Wa Dele") even occasional hints of a straight rock backbeat. "Alagbara" (Strong Man), "Laise, Lairo" (Innocent), and "Se E Tunde" (You've Come Again), on the other hand, are Koola Lobitos compositions reflecting the influence of soul. "Alagbara" is an up-tempo number that features Fela singing in an urgent, soul-influenced style, backed by a syncopated James Brown–styled bass and rhythm guitar pattern, laid over a highlife percussion groove. Written in honor of his mother, "Alagbara" is in fact one of the few songs of Fela's career that might be considered a praise song:

Won o ni fi iya je mi	They won't punish me in vain
Ti iya mi ba wa won o ni	They won't punish me and get away with it
fi'ya je gbe	As long as my mother is alive
Alagbara ma mero . . .	Strong man who has no thoughts, you won't get away with oppressing me . . .

"Laise, Lairo" presents a short, simple lyric over a bouncing highlife pattern. In this song too, the bass and percussion parts—as well as the percussive horn arrangements—recall many soul numbers of the late 1960s. "Se E Tunde" features declamatory soul-band horn bursts and a bass guitar line seemingly derived directly from Brown's "Licking Stick," again laid over highlife percussion. Fela's vocal is relatively understated until the entry of the tenor saxophone solo, when, in a typical rhythm-and-blues style, he exhorts the tenor player to "Blow!" This is followed by a series of vocal grunts and yells that recall soul singers such as Brown and Wilson Pickett.

Fela responded to the dual challenges of Pino and soul music in several other ways in 1968 and 1969. He took over management of the defunct Kakadu Club in the Idi-Oro area of Lagos, remodeling it, renaming it "Afro-Spot," and establishing it as Koola Lobitos's home base. In an attempt to reach new audiences and make his music more accessible, he introduced daytime concerts at the new club, including the "Friday Break" and "Sunday Jump." Afro-Spot became the site of exciting "battles" between Koola Lobitos and Ghanaian highlife groups such as the Ramblers and Uhuru. But as much as he stubbornly resisted the trend towards soul music, Fela's professional predicament came to a head throughout late 1968 and early 1969. He could either continue in his highlife-jazz style (which would probably mean losing the remainder of his loyal audience to Pino) or capitulate completely and join the ranks of the copyright bands. Effecting a temporary compromise, he began peppering Koola Lobitos's repertoire with James Brown tunes. "The attack was heavy, soul music coming in the country left and right. Man, at one point I was playing James Brown tunes among the innovative things because everybody was demanding it and we had to eat."[91]

Some of Koola Lobitos's songs during this later period, such as "My Baby Don't Love Me" and "Home Cooking," show Fela clearly attempting to compose in the soul style. In contrast to the earlier Koola Lobitos compositions—in which soul-derived guitar patterns and jazz-derived harmonic progressions are grafted onto a highlife/Latin foundation—these later numbers conform to soul conventions rhythmically, harmonically, and even textually.

"Home Cooking" begins, like a number of the earlier tunes, with a horn introduction. Fela then enters with the rest of the ensemble, singing the first verse over a repeating blues-derived horn riff and a soul-derived bass line. The horn riff in particular is noteworthy as a seeming adaptation of the classic blues riff that forms the basis of Muddy Waters's "Mannish Boy" and Bo Diddley's "I'm a Man." The underlying rhythm is vaguely Nigerian highlife, but the text attempts to evoke a completely different mood:

> Let's have a bowl
> it's time for a bowl.
> This home cooking tune
> is a hell of a tune.
> It makes you move,
> it makes me move.
> It makes me jump,
> It must make you too.

As an apparent attempt to evoke the cultural atmosphere of the American south, the "home cooking" metaphor is a major departure from earlier song texts. An even clearer example of Fela's work in a soul-inspired form is "My Baby Don't Love Me," a twelve-bar blues laid over a standard James Brown drum beat with Fela singing a classic blues theme containing his own personal twist:

> My baby don't love me
> Oh, yeah
> My baby don't love me
> She makes me fight all day
> Oh, yeah

My baby don't care—
I'm gonna tell my mama!

Fela's vocal style in "My Baby Don't Love Me" is another significant departure, as he adopts a number of stylizations associated with soul singers such as Wilson Pickett. The two-bar break at the end of each verse—during which Fela sings the punchline—are delivered in a classic "sassy" blues style.

Unsurprisingly, these attempts to battle the soul groups on their own musical terrain were largely dismissed as contrived. To add insult to injury, audiences were increasingly vocal in their demands for authentic soul numbers during Koola Lobitos gigs, despite Fela's measured attempts to integrate soul elements. This was the final straw, as one witness reported:

> That controversial Fela Ransome-Kuti is virtually raving this weekend, and I mean it. Fela is a very angry man and he didn't hide his feelings when he screamed at me "I am through with soul music!" This was sequel to a general clamour at his Friday afternoon "lunch break" at the Ritz Hotel, Lagos, where his fans yelled for soul music. . . . "A lot of the local bands" he went on "are hiding under the cloak of soul music which they copy from foreign artists to establish a name for themselves. . . . I am sticking to my brand of highlife.[92]

While Fela had pursued a very different professional path than his siblings, his stubbornness nonetheless reflected the Ransome-Kuti family ethos. Christian, foreign-educated, and well-traveled, the Kuti parents had been model colonial citizens. However, they were also intensely proud of their native culture, and as worldly as they became, their interests never deviated from their fundamental goal of empowering ordinary Nigerian citizens. Likewise, while Fela had selectively adopted elements from foreign styles in his search for an authentic cultural expression, he considered the multitude of copyright bands embarrassing to African culture and was in the end unwilling to take Koola Lobitos in the same direction. His attempts to compose rhythm-and-blues were contrived and commercially unsuccessful. The "afrobeat" label was an attempt to distinguish his music from both the highlife bands and the copyright bands, but it would take more than a mere name change to accomplish this. Frustrated, at a loss for direction, unable to find more appreciative audiences elsewhere in West Africa, and threatened by Pino's impending return to Lagos, Fela reportedly contemplated giving up music as a career. Shortly after this, however, a remarkable article appeared in the *Daily Times:*

> The stormy Afro-Beat creator, Fela Ransome-Kuti is angry. Angry and dejected. . . . A friend who had just returned from the United States told him that his new beat had caught up fast in the country and some Negro musicians were cashing in on it. The most remarkable thing, Fela said his friend told him, was when he went to a show by the great soul expo-

nent, James Brown, and heard the fiery soulman's band play one of Fela's pieces. "I have been receiving similar reports for a long time. It all became more hurting when all my attempts at getting sponsorship for an American trip failed. Now I am sweating and some others are making the money. It's a most unfair situation" he concluded and stormed off.[93]

Whether these claims were true or an engineered publicity stunt, they paid off shortly afterward when Fela was presented with an offer to take Koola Lobitos on a two-month tour of the United States. The timing could not have been better, as Pino and the Heartbeats were away from Lagos touring the country. A U.S. trip seemed beneficial for two reasons. Given America's preeminence in the international popular music industry, and considering the widespread popularity of soul music throughout sub-Saharan Africa, any African musician who could tour the United States successfully would surely gain prestige on the home front.

Another related reason may have been the recent commercial successes of African musicians in the United States. South Africans Miriam Makeba and Hugh Masekela had both enjoyed popularity—Makeba via her 1967 hit "Pata Pata" (produced by veteran rhythm-and-blues producer Jerry Ragavoy) and Masekela via his 1967 hit "Grazin' in the Grass" and his appearance at the 1967 Monterey International Pop Festival. These musicians, along with other expatriate Africans working in traditional or jazz idioms, including Abdullah Ibrahim (Dollar Brand) and Babatunde Olatunji, comprised the first wave of African musicians to gain widespread acceptance in the United States. By the time of the 1969 Woodstock Music and Arts Festival—a major landmark in America for music, youth culture, and the music industry—the influence of Africa on American popular music was clear; African or neo-African drumming styles were prominent in the festival performances of Richie Havens, Jimi Hendrix, and Carlos Santana. During the same period, artists as dissimilar as Miles Davis and the Rolling Stones were including African percussion in their groups.[94]

Given the cosmopolitan mixture of highlife, salsa, rhythm-and-blues, and jazz in his musical style, Fela calculated that he, too, had the ingredients for success in the American market. Announcing that his tour was to "promote Africa in the United States and help the cause of the Afro-Americans,"[95] Fela and Koola Lobitos departed Nigeria for the United States in June 1969.

America (1969–1970)

Arriving in New York City, Fela and the Lobitos were awed by the grand scale, technological sophistication, and seemingly flawless efficiency of American culture, which must have seemed miraculous compared to the chaotic, unplanned sprawl of modern Lagos. This had an immediate and profound effect upon Fela's worldview; organization and efficiency would become two important criteria by which his native land was measured. At the same time, as in his student years in England, the experience of a foreign culture reinforced a sense of cultural difference that he would address in his songs. "I started thinking; I saw how everything works there, everything functions. I saw how great America is. I realized that to be a great man you have to have a great country behind you. I had no country, just a bunch of Africans running around in suits trying to be Englishmen."[96]

The Lobitos' American tour got off to a heartening start when they were greeted by an enthusiastic contingent of expatriate Nigerian fans at New York's Kennedy International Airport. A chance in-flight meeting with South African singer Miriam Makeba also seemed to bode well for the trip. "I told her I was on my way to America. She, too, was going to the States with her band on a tour. In fact, she was very concerned knowing it was our first visit to the States. I asked her for addresses of promotion agents, which she readily gave to me. But she did not discuss how exploitative the system in America is—probably she did not know much about it then."[97]

Fela sought out Makeba's New York music business connections without success. This was the same year that 400,000 people attended the Woodstock Festival, and the U.S. music industry was reveling in the unprecedented profits generated from the popularity of rock-and-roll artists like the Beatles, the Rolling Stones, and Bob Dylan among baby-boom audiences. African music was an increasing presence in America. Shorn of the psychedelic trappings of late 1960s youth culture, however, Fela's relatively provincial highlife-jazz was not a major commercial priority for American recording companies. Coming from the capital city of a comparatively westernized African nation, neither his music nor its presentation seemed to have the exotic appeal necessary to attract the curiosity of mainstream America. This was in contrast to artists like Masekela and Makeba, who often performed in their native dress and sung in their native tongues. There was certainly a major interest in African music and culture among African-Americans, but while the African-American experience would play a pivotal role in Fela's development during his time in the States, this audience was not the primary target of the mainstream record companies and the African promoters with whom Fela was working.

Complicating matters further, the tour's Nigerian sponsors—African Tours Limited—were nowhere to be found upon the band's arrival. Lacking organized support, the group traveled by car to booked appearances in Washington, D.C., Chicago, and San Francisco before ending up stranded in Los Angeles. Despite their trying circumstances, the band impressed audiences with their jazz-soul-highlife fusion, and prospects seemed to improve following a July showcase performance attended by soul singer Lou Rawls and show business impresario H. B. Barnum. Barnum offered the group a lucrative recording contract and arranged three weeks of concerts at the Disneyland theme park. However, the deal fell through when African Tours materialized and refused to release the band from its exclusive contract.

This became the theme of the Lobitos' American trip. Stranded in Los Angeles without work, ineligible for legal employment, and ensnared in a web of legal complications, they bounced from one thwarted opportunity to the next. When a showcase performance to be attended by show business luminaries like Bill Cosby and Frank Sinatra was arranged for them at an Orange County club, the Lobitos' bassist Felix Jones abruptly disappeared, fearing deportation if he appeared in public. (Jones was of Igbo origin, and the United States was supporting Nigeria's federal government in the Biafran war.) The performance was a disaster, with Fela switching between bass, trumpet, piano, and vocals during the course of each number.[98] Later, the band was presented with an offer to play in the gambling center of Las Vegas, but the city's musicians' union refused to issue work permits, claiming the Nigerians were taking jobs from American musicians.

By the fall, the band's three-month cultural visas had expired and they were without work.[99] Broke and dispirited, some members were forced to take illegal factory jobs to compensate for the lack of income. Although they wanted to return home, Fela was reluctant to leave the States without achieving some measure of success. Having narrowly avoided professional humiliation by Pino when he left Nigeria and announced his visit to "soul country," Fela was especially demoralized by the lack of success in America: "Things were so bad I could not write home. I told them back home that I was going to be a winner when I arrived in America. It got so bad that the people at home thought I was in jail."[100]

The Lobitos seemingly had nowhere to go but up after the series of legal fiascos, and Fela signed a performance contract with a Hollywood club. This move infuriated the group's original promoters, who promptly reported them to U.S. immigration authorities. Although deportation proceedings were initiated soon after, Fela was able to enlist the services of an attorney and the band was granted an extension. With the backing of a Ghanaian record promoter named Duke Lumumba, they turned their attention toward recording their most recent work. In a last-ditch attempt to generate funds, Fela and Lumumba also hatched a plot to exploit the political turmoil in Nigeria by releasing a progovernment record, which they hoped would gain Koola Lobitos the financial sponsorship of the Nigerian government. It was now late 1969 and the Biafran war had escalated into one of the most gruesome military conflicts in modern history. "Viva Nigeria" is a patriotic recitation over a rerecorded instrumental track of the Lobitos' "Wakawaka":

> This is Brother Fela Ransome-Kuti
> This is one time I would like to say a few things . . .
> Brothers and sisters in Africa
> Never should we learn to wage war against each other
> Let Nigeria be a lesson to all
> We have more to learn towards building than destroying
> Our people can't afford any more suffering
> Let's join hands, Africa
> We have nothing to lose,
> but a lot to gain
> War is not the answer
> War has never been the answer
> And it will never be the answer—

Fighting amongst each other
One nation indivisible
Long live Nigeria,
Viva Africa . . .

Fela's simplistic pleas for unity and brotherhood demonstrate—in light of the complex factors surrounding the Biafran war—that his political awareness had not developed much beyond that of his college years in London, and the mercenary "Keep Nigeria One" demonstrated his distance from the political realities of his society. In retrospect, he would profess sympathy with the Biafran struggle and identify the war as a crucial turning point in the spread of officialized tribalism and corruption in Nigeria:

> I was not political at the time we had the Biafran war, but I believed [Biafran leader] Ojukwu was right. . . . Tribalism was used at that time to oppress the Igbos all over Nigeria. I was a witness to that. Igbos were being slaughtered all over Nigeria. Even in Lagos, everywhere. . . . Gowon was saying "To keep Nigeria one, is a task that must be done." What one? To keep Nigeria one, does it mean that innocent Nigerian women, children and other innocent people must die? Do we have one Nigeria today?[101]

Sandra

Events soon took a significant turn for Fela and Koola Lobitos in America. While playing at a social function, Fela met an African-American woman named Sandra Smith, and a relationship quickly developed between them. Smith became the catalyst in Fela's political development and cultural reorientation. A former member of the Black Panther party, she had spent time in jail for assaulting a police officer during the 1967 Los Angeles riots. "Sandra gave me the education I wanted to know. She was the one who opened my eyes. . . . For the first time I heard things I'd never heard before about Africa! Sandra was my adviser. She talked to me about politics, history. She taught me what she knew and what she knew was enough for me to start on."[102]

During the course of their relationship, Smith introduced Fela to a number of political and musical ideas that profoundly reshaped both his worldview and his musical approach. Through her, Fela became familiar with the political ideas and rhetoric of African-American political and cultural figures such as the Black Panthers, Kwame Toure (Stokely Carmichael), Angela Davis, Martin Luther King, Elijah Muhammad, Jesse Jackson, and Malcolm X. It was Malcolm X who made the strongest impact: "This book, I couldn't put it down: *The Autobiography of Malcolm X*. . . . This man was talking about the history of Africa, talking about the white man. . . . I never read a book like that before in my life. . . . I said, 'This is a man!' I wanted to be like Malcolm X. . . . I was so unhappy that this man was killed. Everything about Africa started coming back to me."[103]

Known initially for his espousal of the theories of his mentor Elijah Muhammad (whose Nation of Islam organization Malcolm served as National Minister until 1963), Malcolm X was by the time of his death evolving a more secular philosophy that was equal parts black nationalism, Pan-Africanism, and Marxist-based material/class analysis. One of his major goals during the final phase of his life was the initiation of a political dialogue with leaders of the newly independent African states, in order to internationalize the black struggle while gaining the support of these leaders for the African-American struggle. During 1964 and early 1965, he made two lengthy visits to Africa where he conferred with heads of state and was welcomed as a state guest in a number of countries. These included Ghana, where he was honored by President Nkrumah, and Nigeria, where Yoruba students at the University of Ibadan named him "Omowale"—Yoruba for "the child who has returned." Fela was not politically inclined at the time of Malcolm X's African travels, but the black nationalist leader's influence following Fela's U.S. trip would become strikingly evident in the tone of Fela's new music.

Malcolm X's African sojourn also planted a seed for the growth of the black power consciousness that would flower during in the following decade, and in which Fela would play a major role in the sphere of popular culture. Evidence of this budding movement can be seen in the fact that, concurrently with the Lobitos' U.S. visit, representatives of the Black Panther party were invited to the First Pan-African Cultural Festival in Algiers, listed as one of several anticolonial, anti-imperialist liberation movements, alongside those of Rhodesia, Mozambique, Angola, Namibia, Palestine, and South Africa.

The philosophies of black nationalism and Pan-Africanism held particular relevance for the younger generation of jazz musicians, and through Sandra Smith, Fela also became familiar with more recent developments in jazz. These were mainly the modal jazz of musicians like Miles Davis and John Coltrane, and the free jazz of late-period Coltrane, Albert Ayler, and Archie Shepp. These styles had a dramatic and far-reaching effect on Fela's music, both structurally and functionally.[104] In America of the late 1960s, free jazz in particular had a number of explicit ideological and cultural associations, and the political climate in which Fela encountered these musical styles influenced the way he later applied them upon his return to Nigeria.

Free-jazz musicians presented a radical deconstruction of jazz conventions, and some musicians considered free jazz a deliberate attempt to subvert the dominance of Western-derived musical practices.[105] There were two aspects to this. The first was to fashion a uniquely "black" musical logic that would resist comprehension and financial exploitation by white musicians. The second was to create a style that—through the exploration of existing sonic parallels—implicitly expressed musical and cultural solidarity with other people of color throughout the non-Western world.

Modal jazz—which carried cultural but no such political connotations—evoked comparisons with similar musical approaches in Africa and Asia. Fela acknowledged this connection: "I listened to Miles, Coltrane. After I became ideological, I found the reason why this music got me. Walking through the streets back home, I would hear many tapes of these traditional musicians from the bush. That was when I got the connection—all the sounds that Miles and Coltrane play are very common among people in the bush."[106]

In the context of these developments, the relationship between Fela and Sandra was mutually enriching. For Sandra, her intimate relationship with Fela and her friendships with his band members afforded her a link into the African culture about which she—like so many African-Americans of her generation—was curious. An accomplished vocalist, she would later perform with several popular African bands, including Fela's Afrika 70 and Osibisa, and play a role in the later international explosion of afropop. Ironically, Smith did not perceive the mutual interchange, as she assumed Fela was already aware of the issues they discussed. "At that point in my life I was an extremely passionate person—especially when it came to blackness, Africa, and Malcolm (X), things like that. But the Fela that I met wasn't into Africa as a concept at all. Although I didn't realize it at the time, that was something he was learning from me as we went along. It was like I was turning *him* on to Africa. Later he went to the other extreme, where *everything* about Africa was good, even the bad was good."[107]

If Fela was silent at the time, he was nevertheless aware of the irony. He told John Darnton: "It's crazy; in the States people think the black power movement drew inspiration from Africa. All these Americans come over here looking for awareness. They don't realize they're the ones who've got it over there. Why, we were even ashamed to go around in national dress until we saw pictures of blacks wearing dashikis on 125th Street."[108]

Besides encountering the profusion of African-Americans donning afros and dashikis and adopting African names (usually of Yoruba, Ashanti, and Swahili origin), Fela was exposed to the American counterculture and its mixture of drugs, pop music, cultural awareness, political activism, and sexual freedom. By the late 1960s, black popular groups in a variety of genres, including Sly and the Family Stone, the Jimi Hendrix Experience, the Chambers Brothers, Funkadelic, the Buddy Miles Express, and even Motown groups such as the Temptations and the Jackson 5, clearly reflected the influence of psychedelic rock upon blues, gospel, and soul-based musicians, and their work was, to varying extents, infused with the broader climate of social rebellion. Fela was by now a committed marijuana smoker. and although it is unclear whether he actually experimented with LSD himself, he does refer to the experience in Moore.[109]

Through Sandra, the band—now renamed "Nigeria 70"—was finally able to secure a regular gig at a Hollywood club called Citadel d'Haiti. Although unknown, the Nigeria 70 quickly became popular and built a steady audience. Through their recent trials, they had remained an impressively tight unit showcasing strong talents like Tony Allen, alto saxophonist Isaac Olasugba, Tunde Williams, and female dancer Dele Johnson. Meanwhile, the influence of new ideas from Fela's intense discussions with Sandra—combined with his continued desire for success—forced him to reexamine a number of his own fundamental ideas and ultimately to formulate a new conceptual framework encompassing music, culture, and ideology.

Reading and discussion furnished the ideological and cultural component of the formula; it was during the Citadel d'Haiti engagement that he finally began to discover the musical component:

> One day I sat down at the piano in Sandra's house. I said to Sandra: "Do you know what? I've just been fooling around. I haven't been playing AFRICAN music. So now I want to try to write African music . . . for the first time." . . . I went to play this new number. . . . I didn't know how the crowd would take the sound, you know. I just started. [The club owner] was behind the bar and he almost jumped over it. . . . "Fela, where did you get this fucking tune from? Whaaaat!" The whole club started jumping and everybody started dancing. I knew then I'd found the thing, man. To me, it was the first African tune I'd written 'til then.[110]

The new song, which he titled "My Lady's Frustration," was an homage to Sandra and an acknowledgment of the strain his career troubles placed on their relationship. Aside from citing his conscious integration of African chants and a type of drumming pattern he attributed to Ambrose Campbell, his description of "My Lady's Frustration" as he played it at the Citadel d'Haiti is vague. Still, the song can be analyzed on the basis of its recorded version. A major conceptual breakthrough and artistic epiphany, "My Lady's Frustration" is neither Fela's old highlife-jazz nor pure rhythm-and-blues. Rather it is a hybrid style in which elements from both genres are arranged in a mutually complimentary way. In a rudimentary but very real sense, "My Lady's Frustration" can be called the first true afrobeat song. Built upon a mid-tempo highlife groove, the song begins with a dominant seventh chord vamp in which the soul-styled rhythm guitar is prominent. This is followed by the entrance of a three-part horn theme, over which Fela sings. Like his pseudo-scat singing on the Koola Lobitos material, the "chant" he refers to in Moore seems a kind of nonliteral vocalizing rooted in both African-American and traditional West African vocal practices; there are no lyrics as such. Following Fela's soul-band exhortations to the soloists ("Now blow, man!") there are three horn solos, each supported by a horn background derived from the song's main theme. Following the solos, the main theme returns and the ensemble drops out as Fela offers some a capella vocalizing before the song ends on a sustained dominant chord. Though he would refine his vocal approach further over the next few years, Fela would use this type of song form through 1971–1972, when afrobeat would take, for all purposes, its final form.

It is clear from the rest of the material recorded in Los Angeles that Fela had finally begun to reconcile the jazz, highlife, and rhythm-and-blues elements in his music. He accomplished this reconciliation largely by increasing his use of modal harmony, particularly the minor Dorian and Aeolian modes. Degrees of modalism can be found in the approach to melody within traditional Yoruba genres such as apala and sakara, due to both indigenous practice and the influence of Islamic modalism.[111] Thus, modalism in Fela's work provided a sonic parallel with similar approaches to melody and harmony found in both traditional West African music and African-American modal jazz; this yielded a mood that was deeply "African" in both the traditional and contemporary sense.

Some of the Los Angeles songs, including "Ako," "Ololufe," and the instrumental "Funky Horn," are built exclusively on dominant-based blues forms or juxtapose blues forms with modal vamps, demonstrating that Fela was still working between both styles. However, other songs, such as "Obe," "Witchcraft," "Wayo," and "This Is Sad," show a clear move toward a minor-key modalism. "Obe" in particular is structured very similarly to many of the afrobeat songs Fela would compose during the 1970s, while "This Is Sad" invites comparisons with the 1960s modal work of jazz composers like Joe Henderson, Wayne Shorter, and McCoy Tyner.[112] Other important elements of Fela's 1970s style also emerge here, such as the baritone saxophone ostinato on "Obe" and "Wayo," which he would later use to great effect in songs such as "Shakara" (1972) and "Sense Wiseness" (1975).

The Los Angeles songs are also notable as the first clear examples of Tony Allen's afrobeat drumming style, a unique fusion of highlife, jazz, and rhythm-and-blues drumming. From highlife came the basic rhythmic format, which Allen executes with a propulsion and fluidity characteristic of jazz drumming. Making extensive use of jazz-derived independent coordination, he abstracts and displaces the highlife and rhythm-and-blues patterns around the drum set while interjecting accents in response to the vocals or the horn soloists. Allen's approach to up-tempo numbers like "Obe," mid-tempo numbers like "Frustration," and slow numbers like "Lover" prefigure his later playing on 1970s afrobeat classics such as "Question Jam Answer," "Monkey Banana," and "Trouble Sleep," respectively.

As important as these stylistic breakthroughs were, there were still strong similarities with Fela's earlier Koola Lobitos material. One such similarity lies in their formal development. Although these songs are less harmonically dense through the use of modalism, they generally conform to the same developmental scheme as the earlier works and are built from the familiar sequence of horn themes, sections for improvisation, solo sections, verses, horn interludes, breaks, and ensemble sections. The strongest similarity with the earlier material lies in Fela's lyrics. Although the frequent use of minor keys in afrobeat provides a sympathetic underpinning for the themes Fela would explore in his songs from 1971 on, the lyrics of the songs recorded in Los Angeles are similar to the earlier Koola Lobitos songs. "Obe" declares Fela's preference for spicy dishes:

Mi o le je obe ti o l'ata	I can't eat stew that has no pepper
Mi o le je obe ti o ni iyo	I can't eat stew that has no salt
Mi o le je obe ti o ni epo	I can't eat stew that has no palm oil
Mi o le je obe ti o l'akuko	I can't eat stew that has no chicken
Mi o je	I won't take the stew
Ma fi lo mi o . . .	Don't even offer it to me . . .

Like the earlier "Wa Dele," "Eko" (Lagos) salutes his professional hometown:

Eko layo, e o puro	Lagos is fun, it's the truth
Eko gba ole, a o puro	Lagos harbors vagabonds and thieves, it's the truth
Eko gba ole, o gba ole	Lagos harbors vagabonds and thieves
Eko gba ogbon . . .	It takes wisdom to survive in Lagos . . .

"Ololufe" (Lover) was evidently the last love song recorded by Fela:

Ololufe mi, ti e ni mo fe	Dearly beloved, it's your love I desire
Alayanfe mi, ti e ni mo gba	My chosen one, it's your love I'm crazy about
Ololufe mi, mi o se tiwon mo	Beloved, I'm through with giving my love to others
Wa femi ko mi lenu	Come and consume me with your kiss
Wa fara ro mi l'ara . . .	Come and kiss me all over . . .

Unlike other African bands seeking Western popularity that would languish for years in Europe or America waiting for a break, Fela and Nigeria 70 returned in March 1970 to a petroleum-fueled Nigerian economy rapidly rebounding from civil war, and a restless pop music scene primed for a new development. His dreams of success in America had largely eluded him, but his U.S. trip was a crucial turning point in two ways. While he had given his music the name "afrobeat" as early as 1968, it was during his U.S. sojourn that he was finally able to blend elements from a number of popular styles into his own distinctive style. He had also undergone a crucial political and cultural awakening that finally provided his music with the seriousness of purpose he had long sought, serving to counteract the prevailing image of African musicians as mere providers of good-time entertainment.

According to Lindsay Barrett, had Fela not experienced America he would have gone down in history as a mere "second-string" highlife bandleader.[113] Still, Fela's origins in the struggles of the nationalist era provided his music with a vaguely politicized subtext as he strove to create a sound that would be "a pride to the black race," and this was bolstered by his American experience. The influence of Malcolm X would be clearly evident in Fela's emphasis on black pride, black beauty, and black self-reliance, his revisionist approach to African history, his concert sermonizing, and his ironic, sarcastic humor. The influence of groups like the Black Panthers would be reflected in Fela's belief that political liberation could only be gained by confronting oppressive authority. And Fela's experience of the American counterculture would be fundamental to his own development of an African counterculture in Lagos.

While his American experience was only the most recent catalyst in a process that reached into his childhood, it was also the most potent, bringing him into clear conformity with his family's tradition of artistic talent, protest, and activism, while forging a more active role for his music within contemporary Nigeria. He summed up his American experience:

> In 1969 I was completely almost unintelligent because I had no original African contribution to make. . . . An African meeting an Englishman should have something to offer. He shouldn't be offering an English thing to an Englishman. . . . Africans should be taught to be able to contribute their own mind, their own culture, their own philosophy. Coming back from America in 1970, I then knew that I should not try to impress foreigners. I should impress my own people first. When my people accept me then foreigners will see a need to accept me. They will now appreciate my music."[114]

The psychological consolidation of the cultural, political, creative, and professional sides of Fela's identities released a store of creative energy. After his return to Nigeria, he would continue to refine his musical method, political sensibility, and cultural outlook, resulting in a period of intense productivity and the incendiary style known as "afrobeat." Fela returned to Nigeria a changed man, possessed with the urgency of his new music and new message.

The Ransome-Kuti family, ca. 1940: Rev. Oludotun Ransome-Kuti (left), Dolupo (top), Fela (bottom), Mrs. Funmilayo Ransome-Kuti (center), Beko (held), Olikoye (right). (Photo courtesy of Cheryl Johnson-Odim)

The Ransome-Kuti homestead in Abeokuta, 1988. (Photo courtesy of Cheryl Johnson-Odim)

Rev. and Mrs. Ransome-Kuti with the students of Abeokuta Grammar School, 1947. (Photo courtesy of Glendora Review*)*

Fela (left) and Beko Ransome-Kuti, mid-1940s. (Photo courtesy of Glendora Review*)*

Fela as a student at Trinity College of Music, ca. 1958. (Photo courtesy of Glendora Review*)*

E. T. Mensah and his Tempos dance band. (Photos this page courtesy of John Collins/Bokoor African Popular Music Archives Foundation [BAPMAF], Accra)

Victor Olaiya's Cool Cats.

Bobby Benson and Jam Session Orchestra. (Photo courtesy of John Collins/ Bokoor African Popular Music Archives Foundation [BAPMAF], Accra)

Fela and his first wife, Remi, in London, ca. 1960. (Photo courtesy of Glendora Review)

Geraldo Pino. (Photo courtesy of John Collins/Bokoor African Popular Music Archives Foundation [BAP-MAF], Accra)

Fela and Koola Lobitos at the Citadel d'Haiti, 1969. (Photo courtesy of Sandra Izsadore)

James Brown with Oba Oyekan II of Lagos, 1970. (Photo courtesy of Alan Leeds Archives)

Fela and Afrika 70 at Abbey Road Studios, London, 1971. (Photo copyright EMI Music Archives)

"African Message"
(1970–1974)

It was in America I saw I was making a mistake. . . . I realized that neither me nor my music was going in the right direction. . . . As soon as I got back home I started to preach. . . . And my music did start changing according to how I experienced the life and culture of my people.

FELA quoted in MOORE 1982:89

I went to Africa in 1972 with a group of students. We visited Ghana and Nigeria and two things stand out in my mind from that trip. In Ghana, we went to Nkrumah's funeral and in Nigeria we saw Fela at his Shrine. We really didn't know anything about him or his music then, we just happened to fall into the Shrine one night with some Nigerian people we had met. Fela had a lot of energy and was just up and down and all over the stage and the band played all night. . . . The one thing I remember is that he had these go-go dancers there and that really surprised me. I think we all still had this idea of traditional Africa and it was a trip to see these women up there in their version of hot pants dancing in go-go cages to that funky music!

KATE RUSHIN, interview with author, June 1996

After thirty months of fighting that claimed the lives of an estimated 1 million civilians (mostly through starvation), the secessionist Biafran army surrendered to Nigeria's Federal Military Government in January 1970, ending one of the most gruesome military conflicts in modern history.[1] The Eastern region had been largely reduced to shambles, while General Ojukwu was exiled in Britain. Throughout the rest of the country, the military presence remained strong; Nigeria came out of the war with sub-Saharan Arica's largest standing army, and this would have important implications for the future.

In the war's aftermath, Nigeria was faced with the formidable postwar tasks of physical and economic reconstruction, social reconciliation, and stimulation of a peacetime economy. Although some argued it would also be his eventual undoing, President Yakubu Gowon's conciliatory, nonconfrontational style ultimately inspired Nigerians' capacity to put tragedy behind them in the interest of building a better future, and of serving as a constructive example for the rest of the continent. All Igbo soldiers (as well as others who had fought against the government) were granted amnesty and reintegrated into the Federal army. Igbos also reacquired land, government jobs, and other property that had been seized. Gowon emerged as a national hero. His success at forcibly holding the fragmented Nigerian republic together during the war, and at reconciling the opposing forces after the war, earned him the respect and admiration of Nigeria's neighbors, many of whom were contending with similar problems of subnationalist ethnic tensions and threatened secession. Thus, despite the horrors of the recent past, the decade began with Nigeria resuming the complex process of nation-building.

This project of reconstruction was immeasurably aided by a largely unforeseen development. Oil production in Nigeria had begun as early as 1957 by a consortium of Dutch and British companies who had conducted exploratory drilling in the region for two decades, although without the expectation that the country would become a major petroleum exporter. By 1966, however, production had reached 400,000 barrels daily. While exports were interrupted during the war (the onshore oil fields lay in the secessionist Eastern region), they resumed quickly thereafter, and by late 1970 Nigeria had become the world's tenth-largest oil producer, exporting over a million barrels daily of its highly desirable low-sulphur, low-gravity oil. The country's petroleum industry also benefited from a timely geographical advantage. While the Suez Canal was closed from 1967 to 1975 (complicating oil exports from the Middle East), Nigeria's location on the Atlantic Coast made it easily accessible to freight traffic from Western Europe and the United States, enabling the country to generate massive revenues through contracts with a number of American and European oil companies, including Shell, Gulf, Chevron, Texaco, Mobil, Agip, and Safrap.[2] Virtually overnight, the basis of the country's economy was largely transformed from agriculture to one in which oil exports provided the lion's share of national revenues. Already the most populous and culturally diverse nation in sub-Saharan Africa, with upwards of 70 million people speaking 250 distinct languages, the country's international image and influence increased dramatically as a result of this new economic power.

The early 1970s were thus years of renewed optimism and national solidarity. The changes in the national mood were reflected in the cultural sphere, and a bourgeoning Nigerian literary, visual, and dramatic art scene would ultimately bring international recognition for the country's playwrights, novelists, and visual artists such as Wole Soyinka, Chinua Achebe, Herbert Ogunde, Bruce Onabrakpeya, Jimoh Buraimoh, and Twins Seven-Seven, among many others. The economic upsurge also stimulated intense growth in the Nigerian music industry, which gradually consolidated from its early subnational, regional-ethnic beginnings in the 1920s and 1930s, to a powerful national industry with a budding international presence by the 1970s.[3]

Lagos itself grew into the center of West Africa's music industry, as multinational recording companies such as Decca and EMI embarked on a policy of "Nigerianisation," using the country as industrial and administrative base for their regional activities.[4] Scores of privately owned local companies also sprung up overnight to release records by the growing number and variety of local bands. The prosperity and acclaim that emerging Nigerian pop stars such as Sunny Ade, Ebenezer Obey, Sonny Okosuns, Victor Uwaifo, Prince Nico Mbarga, and Stephen Osita Osadebe would enjoy during this period were the result of the rapid, petroleum-fueled growth of the Nigerian economy, the related availability of time and money to be devoted to leisure activities, and the emergence of a vibrant Nigerian youth culture, particularly in the cities.

Stylistically, however, the country's music industry still mainly offered the older styles such as juju and highlife, in addition to copyright and imported music. During the war, juju had come to dominate the predominately Yoruba capital of Lagos. Rooted in traditional, rural Yoruba values and Christianity, juju musicians like Ebenezer Obey and Sunny Ade accompanied the rise of the Yoruba elite in the postwar period. Highlife, which as a result of the war was now largely confined to the Igbo region of the country, developed into a distinctly guitar-driven variant, generally dispensing with the saxophones and brass of the early 1960s Lagos bands. Advances in recording quality meant that older Yoruba could enjoy the traditional apala and sakara sounds of musicians like Haruna Ishola, Yusuf Olatunji, and Ayinla Omowura in unprecedented fidelity. What the local industry lacked was a contemporary, indigenous popular style that appealed to the young in large numbers. It was an indication of the social mood that older cultural expressions were dismissed by young people as "colo"—that is, as outdated relics of the colonial era.

This is not to suggest that there was no innovation in the popular music sphere. In fact, the changes in popular music that had begun in the mid-1960s had continued during Nigeria 70's absence. As had happened in Ghana, soul music had virtually eclipsed highlife in popularity, while British and American hard rock groups like Cream, Carlos Santana, and the Jimi Hendrix Experience were increasingly emulated by younger African musicians. Groups such as Osibisa, Sonny Okosuns, and Johnny Haastrup's Monomono were in the forefront of an emerging "Afro-rock" movement, combining traditional rhythms with distorted guitar solos and a mixture of traditional African and American psychedelic imagery.[5] Ultimately, these styles held limited currency among Nigerian listeners, who sought a homegrown popular style that was distinctly African in character while thoroughly contemporary, and capable of advancing the country's cultural profile in the international music marketplace. Despite the continued popularity of imported soul, the heady excitement generated by copyright groups began to fade as listeners questioned their wholesale aping of foreign styles and began to demand more original material from local performers.

The personnel changes that took place in a number of major bands toward the end of 1969 reflected the general restlessness within the music scene and the attempt to devise new creative solutions.[6] Victor Dorgu observed that Geraldo Pino "ran out of gimmicks" during a December 1969 Heartbeats appearance in Lagos,[7] while Mac Morgan reported in early 1970:

Recently I watched [Pino and the Heartbeats] perform . . . . After dishing out some old tunes . . . they decided to do the James Brown series. In a nutshell, the "Mother Popcorn" was managed wrongly, the "Mashed Potato Popcorn" wasn't done with any artistic unity, and "The Little Groove Maker Me" was a flop. . . . Fans now ask two questions: first, for how long shall people continue to hear such discordant or fragmentary tunes; and when shall Pino and his copycat group engage themselves in an earnest quest for something more creative and original?[8]

"Blackism"

Fela and Nigeria 70 arrived home from America in a period when Nigeria's popular cultural climate was primed for four developments. One was a homegrown popular music style capable of competing internationally. Second was a cultural-nationalist ideology reflecting the nation's rich cultural composition on one hand, and its growing international status on the other. Third was a voice for the growing underclass, who were increasingly marginalized in the midst of the oil-boom prosperity. Fourth was a style that could express the ideals and aspirations of college-educated students from the emerging middle class. Without a strongly ideological regime and state-supported arts sector as in Ghana, Guinea, or Senegal, it is not surprising that a large part of Nigeria's version of a "cultural revolution" took place within the capital-driven arena of the popular culture industry. The economic prosperity and social transformation of this period fused in a way that permitted commercial forms to be defined as "revolutionary."

Fela was confident of his new music, which he continued to call "afrobeat." While he did not expect overnight success, he was convinced that afrobeat would be recognized at all levels of Nigerian society as a progressive, pro-African expression, and he proclaimed it the "progressive music of the future."[9] He was also confident that the style's ideological component, which he termed "blackism," would resonate with Nigerian audiences.[10] But as much currency as it may have held among Nigeria's educated cultural workers, Fela's new message was not immediately embraced by audiences used to his older, nonpolitical style. Blackism was heavily inflected by African-American culture, and the concept was not widely understood throughout West Africa at that time. Audiences were often confused by his new rhetoric. Greeting Nigeria 70's first post-U.S. audience at Afro-Spot with the clenched-fist black power salute, Fela was met with silence and blank stares—the crowd had little idea what this gesture symbolized.[11] His next challenge was to adapt his African-American vision to his African surroundings.

Nigeria 70 started slowly, performing the recent Los Angeles material while Fela composed a series of songs that would become the first vehicles of his new message. Meanwhile, a number of recent songs were released in Nigeria on an LP entitled *Wayo* (1970). Comprised of material recorded during the group's U.S. sojourn, the release was lauded by critics for its high fidelity but failed to make much of an impression among listeners.[12] *Wayo* occupied a conceptual nether-world between Fela's old highlife-jazz style and his impending political afrobeat, and it confounded audiences. Stylistically, the songs were different from the high-life jazz Koola Lobitos had played prior to their U.S. trip. With his increased use of rhythm-and-blues devices and his newest ideas yet to be presented publicly, many listeners assumed Fela was merely imitating soul music.

As a consequence of his recent politicization, Fela also refused to continue singing the love and romance themes with which many highlife songs—including a number of his own, such as "Ololufe" and "Bonfo"—were concerned. Fela no longer considered such songs truly "African." He has said: "I use politics in my music. That's the only way a wider audience will get acquainted with the issues. It makes sense culturally as well. In Africa, we don't really sing about love. We sing about happenings. That's the tradition. There are no songs like: 'Darling, kiss me.' "[13] Although there were love songs composed in traditional culture,[14] roman-tic love songs in the Western sense did not abound in traditional repertoire, which was largely comprised of praise songs, proverbial songs, and social or philosophi-cal observations, in addition to those accompanying a wide range of sacred and mundane activities.[15] This had substantially changed during the colonial era, as urban highlife bands included Western-styled love songs in their repertoires to suit an audience of elite, westernized Africans and colonial administrators; love songs could also be increasingly found in the repertoires of juju bands for similar reasons. Implicitly dismissing highlife and its song topics as "colonial," Fela was attempting to embed himself and his work within African tradition in a highly self-conscious and selective way—avoiding love songs and praise songs while invoking the traditional spirit of the musician as social observer and critic.

In early 1970, however, he had not yet articulated his new political perspec-tive in song, and excepting the absence of romantic songs, many of his lyrics from this period are closer in style and content to the earlier Koola Lobitos and Nigeria 70 songs than to his later, more politicized work. Like earlier songs such as "Wa Dele" or "Eko," the first post-return songs generally employ an oblique approach vaguely reminiscent of traditional poetry mixed with hip, urban imagery and the latest Lagos slang. The surreal "Egbe Mi O (Carry Me, I Want to Die)" (1970) is an example of this approach. Containing humorous, urbane references to fashion, slang, and crime, it ultimately uses the image of a frantic dance floor to philoso-phize on the importance of maintaining one's composure in the midst of frenzied circumstances:

"Egbe mi o	"Please carry me
Bebe mi ti ja o o	My waistband is loose now
Furo mi ti be o o	My rear end has exploded now
Fila mi ti ja o o . . ."	My cap is deformed . . ."
Ijo lo loo jo ti furo re	It's a dance you claim to be doing, while your whole backside dropped off

Ma gba e o	I'll see to it that you get it together
Ijo lo loo jo to fe yi ku o	You claim to be dancing and you are on the brink of losing your life
Ijo lo loo jo ti bebe re ja o	You claim to be dancing and you snapped your waistband [i.e., by dancing too vigorously]
O wa han ni sale o	It's now hanging loose and showing under your dress
Satide nyo labe Sunday	Saturday is showing under Sunday [i.e., an undergarment is showing inappropriately]
Emi o rii ri	I've never seen this kind of thing before
Emi o mo nipa ti e	I don't know about you
Ijo lo loo jo ti fila re jabo o	It's a dance you claim to be doing, when your cap fell off
Won wa jii lo o	It was then stolen
Orisirisi lo nsele si e to ba njo . . .	All sorts of things happen to you while dancing . . .

As crucial as his U.S. breakthrough was, Fela has admitted that in many respects his work remained in an experimental phase in the first months following his return.[16] A lack of conceptual clarity is evident in the dual approach he took during this period, as he gradually clarified his musical and cultural vision.[17] On one hand, anticipating acceptance of his new message by the country's progressive political elements, he attempted to utilize existing political institutions, businesses, and music industry channels to sponsor his work. Nigeria 70 patriotically represented their country at Ghana's Second International Trade Fair, performing to wide acclaim in Nigeria's pavilion there.[18] The song "Buy Africa," one of Fela's first political songs to be released, was conceived not only as a nationalist theme, but also as an attempt to obtain government patronage for Nigeria 70. Ironically, the band's fan club was sponsored early on by Ambi, a leading manufacturer of skin-lightening cream.[19] And shortly after Nigeria 70's return, Fela's U.S. business partner Duke Lumumba arrived in Lagos to attend the launching by EMI of four of the songs recorded in Los Angeles, including the pro–federal government "Viva Nigeria," which Fela later dismissed with embarrassment.[20] As late as 1972, after his music had achieved widespread acceptance, he would boast on the *Open and Close* LP jacket of having entertained Ghana's President Ignatius Acheampong, and he was supportive of the planned FESTAC well into mid-decade, with his band providing the musical entertainment at one of the festival committee's planning meetings.[21]

On the other hand, he began to refine the vaguely progressive and radicalized image with which he had been associated since the last days of Koola Lobitos, attempting to distinguish himself from musicians whom he felt displayed a "colonial" attitude. He publicly distanced himself from the Afro-rock style, dismissing it as the latest colonial African attempt to ape foreign music.[22] Organizing an "Afro-Festival" to be held at Lagos City Hall in late 1970, Fela deliberately excluded copyright groups, declaring that only groups with "African" approaches to soul music would be invited to perform.[23] This was evidently his way of acknowledging his cross-cultural stylistic debt to soul music while emphasizing the need to indigenize the style.

The same applied to his extramusical borrowings. While distancing himself from Afro-rock, he nevertheless adopted some of the psychedelic styles and symbols he had encountered in America. Advertisements for Nigeria 70's Afro-Spot performances were regularly headed by the word "psychedelic" and contained a cartoon depiction of a man sporting a billowing afro hairstyle (rapidly becoming popular in Africa) and large gypsy earring. Other notices carried the message "everything is cool." Highly unusual for African men, Fela himself briefly sported an earring during performances in 1970, justifying his choice through African jewelry traditions.[24]

Fela also publicly criticized Nigerian bandleaders who adopted British political or military titles such as "Sir" (Victor Uwaifo), "Chief Commander" (Ebenezer Obey), or "King" (Sunny Ade). After expressing his preference for indigenous political titles such as "Onogie" or "Balogun" (both traditional Yoruba military titles), he asked: "Why can't a coloured musician bear his name and be proud instead of looking for prestige which he is not entitled to? The borrowing pride of some of our colleagues in Nigeria has made musicians look cheap to intelligent people."[25]

The issue of "intelligence"—as a signifier for education, elite class status, and privilege—was an important aspect of Fela's budding popularity. Although, in his choice of profession, Fela had rejected the stability and security of his inherited class position, he—more than any of his siblings—was gradually conforming to his family's tradition of protest and activism. His privileged origins were also reflected in the fact that he had been able to avoid a lengthy apprenticeship with an established musician, and to spend an extended period of time perfecting his own musical ideas. College-educated and well-spoken, Fela was ultimately able to use the Ransome-Kuti family's social standing to his advantage. As one observer noted, "In Africa, they really respect family and tradition and all those things. If Fela had just been some person off the street singing those kinds of things, nobody would even listen to him. But since they know he's from a respected family, they figure 'this guy must be saying something.' "[26]

Fela's family legacy provided him a platform to espouse his views that extended beyond the stage, which set him apart from other popular musicians. For example, Fela became vice-chairman of the Nigerian Association of Playwrights, Writers, and Artists, a coalition of educated, progressive artists who sought a more constructive role for their art in society than lionization of the wealthy and powerful. He was also chairman of the Afro-Youth Movement in the early 1970s, the first of a number of collectives of young, left-leaning artists, intellectuals, and activists with which he would be associated during the decade.[27]

The clearest indicator of Fela's break with his musical past was the instrumental sound and structure of his latest music. If his arranging style for Koola Lobitos had demonstrated a clear jazz influence in the band's dense horn charts, the soul influence precipitated a more streamlined approach. Nigeria 70 songs recorded in 1970 and 1971 usually consisted of one-chord vamps; at most, a contrasting introductory overture would be added. Unlike in his earlier work, Fela now sometimes dispensed with horn themes altogether, placing the emphasis on percolating rhythm section patterns, percussive horn riffs, and declamatory vocals. Tony Allen explained: "We decided to simplify things, giving each song two hook lines and a straightforward arrangement so that people wanted to dance."[28]

"Egbe Mi O" is an example of this new arranging style. Opening with a high-powered, ascending rhythm section line punctuated with horn accents, the band modulates to the song's main pattern as Fela enters with the lyrics. There is no horn theme as such—rather, the horns play a repeating three-note staccato figure against the rhythm section and vocals for the duration of the song.

Fela also continued to alter the role of the rhythm guitar in his work. While many of the songs recorded in Los Angeles contain rhythm guitar clearly inspired by rhythm-and-blues, he went one step further after his return and began using an approach to rhythm guitar directly modeled after the guitarists in James Brown's band.[29] This meant using percussively articulated dominant seventh chord voicings that alternated between the fifth, sixth, and seventh degrees of the chord in the upper voice. This style of rhythm guitar playing, known as "chicken scratch," was one of Brown's signature devices, and along with Fela's previous adaptation of the staccato funk bass, it reinforced the growing characterization of Fela as an "African James Brown." Fela adapted the "chicken scratch" style to his modal compositions, often substituting minor-key modal voicings in place of the largely blues-based dominant voicings of Brown's music. This use of the minor modes was adapted to Yoruba vocal tonalities via the modalism and blue note tonalities of modern jazz. Fela's combination of extended instrumental vamping and long-form modal compositions was a conceptual masterstroke, evoking a mood common to rhythm-and-blues, modal jazz, and West African traditional music. The extensive use of minor keys became more important as the decade progressed, providing a moody, often brooding accompaniment that perfectly underscored Fela's lyrics.

Fela was also rethinking his own instrumental role in his music. He abandoned the trumpet entirely (complaining it was too hard on his lips) and began using electric piano and electric organ for accompaniment and solos. Fela's early approach to keyboard improvisation was less complex than his trumpet style had been with Koola Lobitos. He largely eschewed the jazz-derived reliance on chromaticism and harmonic complexity, replacing them with a more diatonic and melodic improvisatory style loosely derived from the Anglican church harmonies of his childhood, more directly from indigenous Yoruba folk melodies, and contemporaneously from the percussive, distorted organ syncopations of late sixties soul musicians such as Sly Stone, Art Neville, Booker T. Jones, and even James Brown.[30]

"J'ehin J'ehin" contains a representative example of Fela's earliest solo work on electric piano, while "Shenshema" contains a fuller realization of his ideas, demonstrating how the organ was transformed in Fela's hands from an instrument of colonial, religious indoctrination to one of incendiary postcolonial cultural and political rebellion. Later, after a bitter dispute resulted in the departure of tenor saxophonist Igo Chico (Okwechime) in 1973, Fela vowed that he would learn the instrument himself and replace Chico within twenty-four hours. He did in fact perform, albeit crudely, on the instrument at the group's next performance, adding a third voice to his arsenal.[31]

By mid-1970, the first of Fela's new "political" music was released in Nigeria. The earliest releases like "Black Man's Cry" and "Buy Africa" feature stark ruminations on blackism over Africanized James Brown grooves. His rhetoric on these songs is heavily influenced by African-American discourse. "Black Man's Cry"—an attempt to redress the psychological damage of colonialism to the African self-image and aesthetic—emphasizes the "black is beautiful" theme, an important component of black power expression at that time:

Nijo wo la maa bo o l'oku eru o?	When will we be free from the shackles of slavery?
Aa bo nijo kan o, l'oku eru . . .	We'll be free one day, from the shackles of slavery . . .
Ta lo so fun mi pe awo dudu ti mo gbe sara mi o da o?	Who is trying to convince me that my black complexion is inferior?
E mu wa kun ri o	Bring that person, let me see him
Ta lo so fun mi pe awo dudu ti e gbe ara yin o da o?	Who is trying to convince you that your black complexion is inferior?
E mu wa ki e ri o	Bring that person so you all can see him
Se e ngbo?	Are you all listening?
Ko si ohun to dara to awo dudu	There is nothing more beautiful than
ti e gbe sara yin . . .	the black complexions you all are endowed with . . .
Ko si ohun to dara to awo dudu ti mo gbe sara yin o e	There is nothing more beautiful than this black complexion I'm endowed with—
E wo mi daada . . .	Look at me closely . . .

"Buy Africa" (1970) emphasizes another important theme inspired by nationalist movements in Africa and abroad—economic empowerment through the patronage of local industry and products:

Se tiwa ni o?	Is it indigenous [i.e., African made]?
Mi o fee!	I don't want it!
Se tiwa ni o?	Is it indigenous?
Mi o ra!	I won't buy!
Se tiwa ni o?	Is it indigenous?
Mi o see!	I won't partake of it!
Se tiwa ni o?	Is it indigenous?
Ko kan mi o!	It's none of my business to be part of it!
Tani maa ba wa jee?	Who will help us eat it [i.e., Who will patronize our own culture]?
Tani maa ba wa see?	Who will do it for us?
Ki la s maa l'owo l'Africa fi taa ba ra tiwa o ee?	How can we get rich in Africa unless we patronize our own products?

Although these funky, politicized afrobeat songs created a major stir in the Lagos music scene, other hurdles remained. Nigeria 70's growing success was heartening, but some listeners resisted the group's new musical and political message. Fela's songs—delivered in an angry, preaching voice derived partly from traditional declamatory styles and partly from rhythm-and-blues—offered uncharacteristically direct political manifestos, and his presentation could sometimes be didactic and heavy-handed, deliberately avoiding the subtle rhetorical techniques and poetic ambiguity of most traditional and neotraditional African styles. And as much as Fela resisted the "Afro-rock" moniker, it was actually an accurate description of the music Nigeria 70 was now offering on tracks such as "Beautiful Dancer," "Don't Gag Me," "Jeun K'oku," and "Eko Ile." His raw Yoruba singing and corrosive, Afro-psychedelic electric organ playing was backed by Tony Allen's aggressive drumming, Igo Chico's tough tenor sax solos, and distorted unison lines between guitar and bass. This combination of sonic and textual led to the perception of Fela and his band as "radicals." A Nigeria 70 concert notice in the *Daily Times* encoded their particular mix of hipness, black pride, and confrontation: "Love, peace, and unity for Africa. Be proud and do your thing. Fight if you have to. But only for Black Africa. This for you to remember."[32]

Fela's insistence on a carefully crafted, politicized, populist message ran counter to cultural expectations that musicians would sing the praises of the rich and powerful. The effects of this significant departure from the established order are apparent in a number of events during this period. Fela was snubbed by a prominent politician he approached in 1970, hoping to gain government sponsorship for his song "Buy Africa."[33] As the political content of his music gradually cut him off from traditional sources of patronage, Fela relied on foreign recording companies in Nigeria for the growth of his career. But even Fela's

British label EMI refused to release Nigeria 70 material it deemed too political, such as "Why Black Man Dey Suffer."[34] And an important early Nigeria 70 performance drew a decidedly lukewarm response from students at the University of Lagos. As one recalled: "We all thought that guy Fela was crazy; the music was funny and he and his boys looked like rascals. We decided never to invite him again."[35]

The perception of Fela as a radical was reinforced by the visit of his African-American mentor Sandra Smith, who arrived in Nigeria in September. For six months she performed regularly with Nigeria 70, despite government harassment, and also granted incendiary interviews to Lagos daily papers, which dwelled upon her connection with the Black Panthers.[36]

That there was an emergent class component to Fela's analysis was clearly demonstrated in his spoken introduction to "Beggar's Lament" (1971), in which he proclaimed: "This song expresses my support for the poor man." Fela's statement functioned on a purely symbolic level—he was not proposing any concrete program of wealth redistribution or economic empowerment—but it was an unusually direct statement that contained an implicit challenge to the culturally sanctioned, boundless accumulation practiced by the upper classes. Further, it is clear that the Ransome-Kuti family still maintained a high political profile, as evidenced by the seizure of Fela's mother's passport upon her return from a women's conference in Budapest in October 1970.[37]

Jeun K'oku

By the end of 1970, the large-scale success Fela and the band desired hung tantalizingly out of reach. Two incidents that occurred at this time proved crucial in the consolidation of his musical and social persona. The first, a physical confrontation with an unruly Muslim patron who refused to pay the entrance fee at Afro-Spot, made Fela notorious around Lagos and was loosely recounted in the songs "Mr. Who-Are-You?" and "Na Fight O." These were the first in a series of narratives in which Fela used his personal experiences as a basis for explorations of topics of wider interest. Such narrative songs later comprised much of Fela's lyrical output, including many of his most famous songs. The lyrics of "Na Fight O" also show Fela extending the religious dimension of the altercation in order to question the cultural orientation of adherents to what he termed the "foreign" religions of Christianity and Islam—another issue he treated frequently throughout his career. Finally, in its mocking, taunting, arrogant tone, it can be heard as a prototype of much of Fela's music throughout the 1970s, allowing him to foreground his growing penchant for abusive humor:

Se o n'waja mi ni o Rasaki o?	Are you spoiling for a fight with me, Rasaki?
Se o n'waja mi ni o, Reverend?	Are you spoiling for a fight with me, Reverend?

Se o n'waja mi ni o, Bishop?	Are you spoiling for a fight with me, Bishop?
Se o n'waja mi ni o, wo mi o daradara	Are you out to fight me, look at me closely
Mo nja gidigbo bi were	I wrestle like a madman
Se o gbo o!	Listen up!
Mo nja karate bii were	I can utilize karate style like a madman,
Se o gbo o!	Listen up!
Mo nja boxer bii were	I am adept at boxing like a madman,
Se o gbo o . . .	Listen up . . .
Se o n'waja mi ni o,	Are you spoiling for a fight with me?
Wo mi o, African ni mi . . .	Then look at me closely, I'm an African . . .
Ma na e pa si Eko yi o bii were . . .	I will beat and kill you here in Lagos like a madman . . .

"Na Fight O" also reflects the social landscape and mindset of young Lagos at the turn of the decade. The lampooning of the *alhaji* (a Muslim who had completed the pilgrimage to Mecca and returned with enhanced social status) is evidence of both Fela's adolescent antagonism toward an authority figure and his growing resentment of the city's affluent classes. "Na Fight O" also demonstrates the gradual transformation of Fela's public personality—from a polite, upper-middle-class highlife musician to a belligerent, outspoken social maverick. He now avowedly embraced both marijuana smoking and the "free-love" philosophy of the American counterculture, and was fast on his way to becoming Nigeria's first major countercultural figure. As Yomi Gbolagunte recalls, "Before Fela left for the States, he was a complete gentleman. He would come in [to a gathering], bow, address everyone very politely and pick up his kids. But after he went to America, people couldn't believe it was the same person, with the women and the smoking and everything—it was like the man had completely lost his mind! I guess he felt that in order to "funkify" his music, he had to "funkify" his life as well."[38]

The second important event was musical in nature. The changes in Fela's music were simultaneous with James Brown's first concert tour of West Africa in December 1970. It was obvious that Brown's music was a major catalyst in the development of afrobeat, so his visit would be a definitive test of Fela's originality. The excitement and anticipation generated by Brown's Nigerian appearances equaled that usually reserved for religious or political leaders. In the three months leading to the performances, the Lagos press ran numerous articles examining the philosophical, cultural, and political dimensions of Brown's music and message and comparing him with cultural icons like Kwame Nkrumah and Martin Luther

King, Jr.[39] When Brown and his entourage arrived in early December, the runway at Ikeja airport in Lagos was mobbed by thousands of fans hoping to get a glimpse of "Soul Brother Number One." After being received by a delegation of the country's leading popular musicians, he was led by military escort to a private meeting with Oba Oyekan, the traditional Yoruba ruler of Lagos, who presented him with a key to the city.[40] This was front-page news the next day, as papers sported photographs of the two accompanied by headlines such as "Meeting of Two Rulers."[41] Fela attended Brown's Lagos performance at Onikan Stadium. After the concert, Brown and his band members sampled the Nigerian music scene. So taken were they with the local sounds that Brown (joined by his troupe vocalist Marva Whitney) recorded a handful of tracks with highlife veteran Victor Olaiya.[42] However, it was Fela and Nigeria 70 who made the biggest impression on Brown and his band, the JB's, when they attended a performance at Afro-Spot.

By this point, the process of cross-cultural influence between West African and African-American musicians had come full circle. The influence of Brown's style on Fela was undeniable, yet the process of creative inspiration clearly was becoming mutual. As for Brown, he was characteristically reluctant to acknowledge any contemporaneous influence on his music. Although he mildly praised Fela's music (calling him an "African James Brown"), he remembered: "It's a funny thing about me and African music. I didn't even know it existed. When I got the consciousness of Africa and decided to see what my roots were, I thought I'd find out where my thing came from. My roots may be imbedded in me and I don't know it, but when I got to Africa I didn't recognize anything that I had gotten from there."[43]

Brown's bass guitarist William "Bootsy" Collins was more enthusiastic in his recollections. "[Fela] had a club in Lagos, and we came to the club, and they were treating us like kings! We were telling them they're the funkiest cats we ever heard in our life and they were replying, 'No, you cats are the ones!' I mean, this is the *James Brown Band,* but we were totally wiped out! That was one trip I wouldn't trade for nothing in this world."[44]

Tony Allen was more explicit about this process of mutual influence. "When James Brown toured Nigeria in 1970, his music arranger—he's a white guy [David Matthews]—he used to come and watch me playing my drums. He watches the movement of my legs and the movement of my hands, and he start writing down. . . . They picked a lot from Fela when they came to Nigeria. . . . It's like both of them sort of influenced each other. Fela got influenced in America, James Brown got the influence in Nigeria."[45]

Fela's innovations on Brown's template were interesting in light of the fact that—despite the musical and cultural assumptions one might draw from the latter's opening of a nightclub called Third World in Augusta, Georgia, after his African trip—Brown himself seemed to be retreating from the polyrhythmic implications of his recent music. Whether this was attributable to the turnover of musicians (Brown lost his bands due to money disputes in March 1970 and again in March 1971) and arrangers (Alfred Ellis had departed in late 1969), or to changes in Brown's own artistic sensibility, is unclear. However, the music Brown and his band created during the 1967–1970 phase, when Ellis was principal arranger, was the most polyrhythmically adventurous of his career, providing a structural link with West African styles that African composers like Fela sought to explore and exploit. Songs like "There Was a Time," "Mother Popcorn," "I Got the Feeling," "Super Bad," and "Brother Rapp" were rich examples of polyrhythmic arrangement, yet in Brown's live performances from 1970 on, these songs had all been simplified into less complex, downbeat-oriented rhythm arrangements.[46] From 1971 on, Fela and Nigeria 70 would continue to mine the rich polyrhythmic vein that Brown's music had opened, despite the growing rhythmic conservatism of Brown's own music.

The song "Jeun K'oku" (Eat and Die, or Glutton to the Point of Death), released shortly after Brown's December visit, was Nigeria 70's breakthrough, summarizing all that had come before—bouncing horn chart, funky, soul-inflected bass and guitars, strident drums—with all that was to come—lampooning, sarcastic humor, and, finally, major commercial success. This graphic, comic portrayal of a glutton—a character much lampooned in traditional folklore—inspired Fela to make full use of his natural talent for parody and lampoon, creating a hilarious song that emphatically established Fela and Nigeria 70's originality:

Jeun K'oku o de . . .	Glutton is here . . .
Mo gbe amala le o tan ta o	I provided yam flour, he ate it all up
Mo gbe eba sile o jee tan o	I provided cassava pudding, he ate it all up
Mo gbe isu sile o jee tan o	I served yam, he ate it all up
Mo gbe obe sile o o laa tan o	I provided stew and he greedily licked it all up
Mo gbe eja sile o jee tan o	I served fish, he ate it all up . . .
Mo gbe emu sile o ba mi muu tan o	I served palmwine, he gulped it all down
Mo gbe obinrin le o ba mi je nbe	I provided women, he had fun with all of them
Ole e ba mi le o!	Thief, help me drive him away!
Onigbese, e ba mi le lo o!	Spendthrift, help me drive him away!

Although "Jeun K'oku" (along with James Brown's "Sex Machine") was banned by the Nigerian Broadcasting Company because of its sexual references, it was a major hit in Nigeria and throughout West Africa, marking the point of departure for Fela's career as a major star.[47] It established Nigeria 70 as a major force in West African popular music and ushered in a period of intensive musical activity that continued through the decade. With this new form of afrobeat, Fela clarified his instrumental conception and invented a distinct sound that successfully transmuted the anger, passion, pride, and self-conscious "Africanness" of the black power impulse into a unique, instantly recognizable style. At the same time, "Jeun K'oku" established him as a popular derisive humorist, fitting into an abusive sub-genre previously hinted at in "J'ehin J'ehin" (a person so greedy he eats his own teeth), "Mr. Who-Are-You," and "Na Fight O." Finally, the song's success drove home to Fela the importance of composing music inspired by, and directed toward, his own cultural environment. He remembered:

> Like [the 1976 song] "Yellow Fever," it was the people at Mushin [a neighborhood in Lagos] who first called traffic wardens Yellow Fever. So I decided to call the [skin] bleaching people "Yellow Fever." It was not my original idea. Even "Shakara," it was from the Mushin people. I don't work in isolation from the society. Shakara was a Mushin word but it was not popular. . . . I made it popular through my record. . . . When I want to write lyrics, I think about my envir-onment, I think about catchy words, words that can easily be identified with society . . . that is why they are very successful.[48]

By early 1971, Nigeria 70 were the storm of the Lagos music scene, and it was clear that they were more than simply the latest musical fad; after nearly a decade of experimentation, frustration, and creative growth, Fela was beginning to be hailed by critics as a musical "revolutionary" whose "scientific" approach had finally managed to "break the abracadabra surrounding soul music."[49] Nigeria 70 also held the distinction of being the only highlife-based band offering a completely original repertoire, devoid of copyright or other currently popular numbers. One long-time observer commented on the band's breakthrough: "The success of afrobeat, that intriguing creation by Fela Ransome-Kuti, stands out as one of the greatest achievements by any Nigerian popular musician this century. Recently, no less than a thousand fans jammed the Afro-Spot club to listen to Fela's band and his message on the African image in "Buy Africa." Sitting back and watching the scene, I could not but recall the several evenings five short years back when the audience strength was constantly FOUR—Fela's brothers, his wife, and I."[50]

A number of changes reflected this growing success. At the beginning of 1971, Fela changed the band's name from Nigeria 70 to Afrika 70, reflecting his new Pan-African frame of reference. The band's growing popularity also dictated a move to S. B. Bakare's Surulere Night Club, a larger venue located in the Lagos neighborhood of the same name. At their new home (again christened "Afro-Spot"), Afrika 70 shared the stage with some of the country's most popular acts, including Geraldo Pino's Heartbreakers, Sunny Ade and his Green Spots, Ebenezer Obey, Segun Bucknor's Assembly, Joni Haastrup's Clusters, the Immortals, the Black Angels, the Hykkers, and Monomono. The summer of 1971 also found Afrika 70 donning new animal skin stage costumes and performing a series of enthusiastically received concerts in London for a mixed audience of Britons and expatriate Africans.[51] Appearing at London venues such as the Cue Club, the Four Aces, and the 100 Club, they quickly became the toast of the town among the city's emerging African music audience.[52]

The band also recorded a series of LPs at EMI's famed Abbey Road studios during this trip, one of which contained a guest appearance by former Cream drummer Ginger Baker. Baker's interest in African music had been well known since he composed a proto-African drum pattern for Cream's influential 1967 hit "The Sunshine of Your Love." By 1971, he had moved to Lagos to help Fela set up Nigeria's first sixteen-track recording studio (financed by EMI), and his presence reflected the growing popularity of African music among the Western pop music cognoscenti. An avid Afro-pop enthusiast, Baker would enter into several ventures with Fela during the early 1970s, including coproduction credits on a handful of Afrika 70 releases.[53] Fela, along with Sandra Iszadore (formerly Smith), also collaborated with Baker during this trip on the latter's *Stratavarious* LP, released in 1972.

On *Stratavarious,* Fela weaves vocals and electric keyboard lines around Baker's improvisational rock sound—replete with guitar and drum solos and rhythm-and-blues singing—while Iszadore layers African melodies and chants on top. The record is a fascinating document of one possible intersection of African music and post-1960s improvisational rock—Baker's drum solos are spiced up with a Yoruba *dundun* talking drum, for example—and also demonstrates the overtones of rock psychedelia that Fela was subtly fusing into his own music. *Stratavarious* also stands as possibly the first high-level collaboration between a Western pop star and his African counterpart, paving the way for later collaborations by such Western pop performers as Paul Simon and Peter Gabriel.

Modern Traditions

The early 1970s collaboration between Fela and Baker also reflected a historical moment in African popular music, when post–World War II advances in the production and dissemination of music (via recording, amplification, and communication technologies) enabled postcolonial African musicians to look simultaneously toward a future of new musical forms and, self-consciously, toward the past and traditional models of inspiration. This dual vision flowered in the 1970s, an era of popular music that was modern and cosmopolitan, yet distinctly African in character. In Ghana, bands like Basa-Basa Sounds and Hedzolleh Soundz fused indigenous styles and instrumentation with jazz and funk elements to create striking neo-African fusions, while in Zimbabwe, Thomas Mapfumo combined electric guitars with traditional *mbira* thumb pianos to create his *chimurenga* style. Somewhat earlier in Nigeria, amplification had enabled indigenous talking drums to become as important an element of local Yoruba juju bands as the previously dominant guitar, facilitating the integration of a wealth of traditional Yoruba musical materials.[54]

More common than the actual use of indigenous instruments was the adaptation of traditional African musical structures to modern Western instruments. Much of the phrasing and interaction between electric guitars in Congolese music is directly traceable to the technique of the indigenous *likembe* thumb piano, for example, while approaches to guitar in Kenya have often been adapted from the local *nyatiti,* a type of traditional lute.[55] Throughout Mali and Senegambia, electric guitarists freely adapted local *kora, balafon,* and *ngoni* traditions in their syntheses of new pop and neotraditional styles, and a remarkable series of recordings of regional dance bands released by the Mali Ministry of Information in 1970 show the different ways this fusion could be achieved. Although these developments reflect the inevitable periodic updatings of tradition, they also represent conscious attempts by postcolonial musicians to revitalize cultural traditions through fusion with contemporary musical materials and technologies.

Both Fela and Tony Allen have cited traditional African music as a conceptually important component in the development of afrobeat. Fela put it this way: "I may listen to [popular music] to see what's happening, but I still prefer to listen to deep sounds from the villages all over Africa. That's where I get a lot of rhythms, spiritualness from."[56] Traditional influences found their way into Afrika 70's music both incidentally and deliberately. In his avoidance of the instruments and social functions of Yoruba neotraditional styles, Fela implicitly eschewed the linguistic component of much Yoruba music, but was still able to evoke a deep traditional mood, sometimes with linguistic undertones. One fan remembered:

> It is through [Fela] that I learned a lot of traditional rhythms. . . . He also has all kinds of slangish ways of tossing in these idioms, and they just flow together. And where, in the case of traditional music, you have a talking drum which people can decode, he has his horns. If one of them goes off into a solo, suddenly some kind of traditional Yoruba adage or proverb or folk song will come out of the horn. There are people in the crowd who will decode it just like a drum, and you will see these people going wild at this point.[57]

While this type of interaction usually occurred in concert settings, which provided the necessary social environment, a superficial example can be found in the solo saxophone interlude in "Gentleman" (1973), in which a male background singer uses Yoruba, pidgin, and nonsense phrases to answer the melodic phrases of Fela's saxophone improvisation.

Other traditional undertones of afrobeat were more deliberate. Fela introduced three important refinements in 1971–1972 that intensified the traditional feeling of Afrika 70 and concretized the structure of the afrobeat style. The first of these was the addition of a third guitar to the ensemble, designated the "tenor" guitar. The tenor guitar played a repeating, single-note staccato figure in the middle register, which functioned as a contrapuntal voice between the bass guitar and the rhythm guitar, and its addition accentuated the tightly hocketed, precomposed rhythmic structures. Despite the three guitars, the sound of Africa 70 was different from African guitar bands in which guitarists took the liberty of loosely interpreting or transforming core melodic material, and in which this type of improvisation was central to overall compositional development. The effect of afrobeat depended on repetition of these precomposed patterns. On top of this, horns or keyboards improvised in specific sections of each song, but this clear separation of solo and supporting parts deviated from most guitar-oriented African styles, demonstrating afrobeat's equally strong roots in traditional percussion, rhythm-and-blues, funk, and big-band jazz. If the guitar bands tended to take their cues from indigenous string and pitched-percussion traditions, Africa 70 produced a sound that most closely replicated the structure of traditional drum ensembles and was powerfully hypnotic when channeled through the band's amplified electric instruments.

Allen's drumming was crucial to this translation. Like Tony Williams's pivotal role in Miles Davis's "second great quintet" of the late 1960s, Allen's role behind the drum set in Afrika 70 often rivaled that of Fela's in influencing the dynamics of a performance. Although limitations in recording quality often make it difficult to hear him clearly, his performances with Afrika 70 marked him undeniably as one of the world's great set drummers of the post–World War II era. On tracks such as "Shenshema" or "Confusion" (as well as all of the band's other work), Allen's playing is distinguished by an almost military stridency resulting from his integration of various snare drum rudiments—flams, drags, ruffs, rolls, and rimshots—into his playing. Like the great jazz drummers, Allen could swing the entire ensemble with his ride cymbal while dropping "bomb" accents with his bass drum. Like the great funk drummers, his syncopated bass drum and hi-hat patterns could simultaneously reign the ensemble in and propel it to the heights of polyrhythmic intensity. Like a traditional West African master drummer, Allen could also interject a crackling snare accent to signal an abrupt change in the dynamic level or to accent the movements of a dancer, or use a mixture of snare rudiments to weave within and around Henry Kofi's rolling conga patterns. His unique approach to the drum set was a major component of the afrobeat sound.

The second important development was the addition of chorus singers, enabling Fela to make extensive use of chorus lines and call-and-response patterns in his songs—a practice universally associated throughout Africa with the most traditional forms of music. The earliest Afrika 70 songs feature the band's male musicians in the responsive role, but by 1972 Fela had integrated a six-member female chorus that provided a stark counterpoint to his smoky tenor. The shrill quality of six women singing in unison was a powerfully effective vehicle for the mocking, sing-song sarcasm of his message. If, in the early Nigeria 70 songs, Fela tended to offer didactic monologues on selected themes, the presence of the chorus offered an opportunity for call-and-response exchange, and this in itself influenced a major change in Fela's lyrical approach, giving his music a more traditionally African sound.

A third element, while not entirely traditional, was crucial in the reorientation of his art. This was Fela's 1972 decision to sing in pidgin English—the lingua franca of Anglophone West Africa—instead of his usual Yoruba. A hybrid of English words and West African syntactic structure, pidgin is primarily spoken in cities and port towns and is strongly associated with merchants, itinerant traders, and urban dwellers—particularly the urban poor. Although pidgin had been used occasionally in highlife, most pop songs were sung in either standard English or local indigenous languages. Fela drew substantial criticism for his decision at the time;

many failed to understand why an elite, English-educated college graduate would choose to sing in the language of West Africa's slums and trading ports. However, the decision made perfect sense in the context of what he was trying to accomplish with his music. Pidgin enabled Fela to dart in and around the rhythm in a strongly jazz-inflected fashion, bending the stresses and accents of standard English to the African syntax and tonal inflections. It also allowed him to integrate nonsense syllables, which had a purely rhythmic value, into his singing.[58]

The most important consequence of this decision was that it made Fela's music accessible to a larger audience. In one deft stroke, he circumvented the customary identification of musical genres with specific ethnic groups and social classes, linking his art with millions of English-speaking Africans across national, religious, class, and ethnic boundaries. In fact, a number of Fela's songs from this period appeal to a youthful, pan-urban, Anglophone West African sensibility. Two examples are "Fogofogo" (Bottle Breaker) and "Shenshema" (Old, Decrepit Automobile)—two slang terms from Accra, Ghana.

Of his decision to sing in pidgin, Fela said: "You cannot use good English to sing in African music. Before, I was using Yoruba but I changed to pidgin English. I had to study it, the accent, I realized it could work so I started to use it. Good English cannot convey the message in African music. Broken [pidgin] English is more acceptable."[59] This was similar to the position taken by Nigerian novelist Chinua Achebe in his consideration of the dilemma faced by the first generation of postcolonial African writers who had been educated in European institutions, but who struggled to find a distinctively African voice in which they could portray their experiences. Some, like Kenya's Ngugi wa Thiong'o, insisted on writing exclusively in local tongues—powerfully affirming indigenous culture while effectively limiting their potential audience. Others, like Achebe, used European languages to portray African experience, raising the question of whether use of the colonial language automatically implicated a text into cultural dependency.[60] Achebe maintained that there could be a distinctively African use of English that was both profoundly African and widely accessible: "The African writer should aim to use English in a way that brings out his message best without altering the language to the extent that its value as a medium of international exchange will be lost. He should aim at fashioning out an English which is at once universal and able to carry his peculiar experience."[61]

Fela's use of pidgin represented such a distinctly African use of English, while it simultaneously functioned as a statement of empathy for and solidarity with the Lagos working class. It was in this vein that his song "Mr. Grammartology-lisationalism Is the Boss" (1975) analyzed the role of language in the reinforcement of class divisions:

FELA: He na the man	*FELA:* He is the man
CHORUS: Which man?	*CHORUS:* Which man?
FELA: He talk oyinbo well well, to rule our land	*FELA:* He speaks European language very well, to rule our land
CHORUS: That man!	*CHORUS:* That man!

FELA: He talk oyinbo pass
English man

FELA: He speaks English better than
the English man

CHORUS: He talk oyinbo pass
American man

CHORUS: He speaks English better
than the American man

FELA: He talk oyinbo pass
German man
First thing early in the morning
na newspaper dem give us to read
The oyinbo wey dey inside
market woman no fit know

FELA: He speaks German better than
the German man
First thing early in the morning
it's a newspaper they give us to read
The English printed inside
the market woman doesn't
understand

The oyinbo wey dey inside
petty trader no fit read
The oyinbo wey dey inside
na riddle for labourer man . . .

The English printed inside
the petty trader cannot read
The English printed inside is a riddle
for the labourer man . . .

The better oyinbo you talk,
the more bread you go get . . .

The better English you talk the
more money you make . . .

The introduction of tenor guitar, chorus singers, and pidgin English all contributed to afrobeat's recognizably African nuance, but as much as Fela drew on traditional African models, his music also departed from these models in certain ways. Harmonically, for instance, afrobeat was strongly rooted in the modalism of jazz and Western classical music, while structurally, the "tight" arrangement of the ensemble sound reflected the clear influence of rhythm-and-blues. Most importantly, Fela maintained a strict conception of the "composition"—specific music accompanied specific lyrics, forms were completely predetermined, and song forms were consistent from performance to performance. In contrast, songs in other genres such as juju or apala often consisted of a set of lyrical themes strung together in a loose "suite" arrangement, over a single musical pattern that could vary substantially from performance to performance. Conversely, the same pattern could be used for different sets of lyrics. In fact, this "modular" approach to song composition is common throughout the world of black music. Even Fela's conceptual template James Brown has recycled rhythm patterns for use in different songs,[62] but all of Afrika 70's songs conformed to predetermined arrangements. This comparatively westernized conception of form probably resulted from both Fela's classical music training and his exposure to dance forms of jazz. It was also somewhat ironic, in light of the fact that many contemporary Western composers have used traditional African and other non-Western models as a way of escaping traditional methods of formal development.

The typical afrobeat song of the early 1970s (such as "Shakara Oloje") was introduced by a simple, chirping staccato line (usually tenor guitar, but sometimes piano) backed by the small percussion (shekere, clips, and lead congas). The rhythm guitar then entered, followed by the simultaneous entrance of bass guitar, rhythm congas, and drum set, completing the rhythm section foundation of the song. Fela, on either saxophone or electric keyboard, then began to improvise over the rhythm section, as a prelude to the horn theme. The horns then entered dramatically with the song's main musical theme or "head," as it is known in jazz. This theme was usually stated twice, with Fela soloing or scat singing throughout. A string of instrumental solos (most often by Fela, Tunde Williams on trumpet, or Igo Chico on tenor saxophone) usually follow the head, accompanied by horn backgrounds derived from the head. Fela's solo was usually last before the entrance of the vocals. After some scat singing or other brief vocalizing, Fela would enter singing the lyric. He would soon be joined by the chorus, and later by the horns in a series of tight, punchy call-and-response structures. These structures became more tightly interwoven and percussive, leading to the climax of the vocal song. A short solo usually followed by Fela on saxophone or keyboards, reintroducing the horn theme and signaling the song's end. The actual song endings varied—the small percussion might fade out, the ensemble might drop out while Fela continued his improvisation until a final, sustained chord by the entire ensemble ended the song. Alternately, the sustained ending chord would come directly at the end of the final horn theme.

At ten to fifteen minutes long, Afrika 70 songs demonstrated the way Fela's conception of form had developed since his return. Unlike the first Nigeria 70 songs (such as those on the *London Scene* LP), which conformed to the three-minute pop song format , an Afrika 70 track now usually occupied the entire side of a twelve-inch record. The twelve-inch record, which heretofore had been primarily used for LPs, became a perfect vehicle for African tastes, in which listeners desired longer songs and more dancing time. It was also the perfect vehicle for Fela's musical manifestos. In concert, Afrika 70's songs could be stretched beyond a half-hour in length with a string of soloists, and Fela usually leading the audience through what he called the "Underground Spiritual Game"—an audience participation chant based on children's songs, nonsense lyrics, names of great African rulers, caricatures of various people, or other random sources—before beginning the actual lyrics. Thus, these songs were eminently danceable and entertaining even as they were vehicles for serious commentary.[63]

These final stylistic refinements completed the foundations of Fela's afrobeat formula. With the structural foundation of his style firmly in place, he could experiment with stylistic ingredients during the 1970s, and a number of songs from this period show the various ways in which the basic formula could be manipulated. "Colonial Mentality" and "Yellow Fever" (both released 1976) show Fela weaving his vocals below the chorus singers in a manner directly traceable to Yoruba traditional singing styles. Two versions of "Monday Morning in Lagos" (1972/1975) wed afrobeat to a traditional 12/8 rhythmic structure. The introduction to "J'enWi T'emi" (1972) utilizes a fuzz-distortion tenor guitar line in unison with the bass. "Who No Know Go Know" (1973) is a textbook study in Fela's method of rhythm section arranging, the bass and guitars following one another in an endless, looping syncopation while drums and percussion chug along underneath. His infrequently used soprano saxophone provides a pseudo–Middle Eastern flavor on "Mr. Follow Follow" (1976), while "Water No Get Enemy" (1974) demonstrates the Afro-

Cuban influence at the root of afrobeat. Finally, songs like "Kalakuta Show" and "Alagbon Close" (both 1975), and "Equalisation of Trouser and Pants" and "Yellow Fever" (both 1976) display afrobeat's seamless blend of highlife and James Brown–styled funk. Fela also occasionally experimented with song form, producing a number of unique arrangements, such as the introductory groove overtures on "Gentleman," "Noise for Vendor Mouth," and "He Miss Road"; the proto-reggae introduction to "Swegbe and Pako"; the spoken-word pauses during "Na Poi" and "African Message"; the free-jazz-styled duet between electric piano and drum set at the start of "Confusion" (1975); the drum solos in the middle of "Open and Close" and "Na Poi" (both 1972); and the solo tenor saxophone interlude in "Gentleman" (1973).

In musical terms, the afrobeat Fela developed between 1969 and 1972 was his major achievement. It clearly drew upon highlife, jazz, and rhythm-and-blues, but Africanized the foreign jazz and soul elements while it deconstructed dance-band highlife, and grafted them all onto a traditional West African rhythmic template. Compared with his previous highlife-jazz, the new style was starker, more aggressive, and rougher-hewn than other styles. This synthesis represented a major innovation in African pop.

The issue of cultural revitalization was an important aspect of Fela's appeal, and a large part of his "progressive" image derived from the fact that he had used his foreign musical sojourns to fashion a uniquely African form:

> [Had I not become politicized], I would still be playing English music, like my counterparts who attended music schools in England. There are many of them who were my contemporaries in England, who still play classical music–they cannot identify themselves with their people yet. It has reached the stage where some of them go and play "African symphony" for the European or American audience. When asked by news men or audiences in Europe why they are not popular at home with the kind of music they play, their answer is that the standard of music they play is far too advanced for their audience way back home in the "jungle" of Africa. Instead of these brainwashed colonial African musicians admitting that they have not related their knowledge of music to their environment, they go about repeating stereotyped propaganda and untruths about African people.[64]

Afrika Shrine

> *The first time I heard Fela was "Shakara." I remember coming out onto the street in Douala [Cameroun] and hearing this incredible rhythm coming out of a record shop–the whole street was literally moving to it! We really had never heard anything like it . . . for a long time after that, all you could hear about was Fela, even in Cameroun.*
>
> JULIUS NDIMBIE, *interview with author, January 1994*

Afrika 70's raw, brash sound took West Africa by storm, bristling with an energy unique in African pop. Releasing a string of national and regional hits sung mostly in pidgin, Fela quickly established himself as a master chronicler of urban life, an outrageous and ironic humorist, and a penetrating, insightful observer of the African postcolonial condition. It was a measure of Afrika 70's success that within less than a year, the band was again moving to a larger venue, one which it would call home for the next five years—the Afrika Shrine. The Shrine, as it came to be known, was actually the courtyard of the Empire Hotel in Idi-Oro near Mushin, owned by Lagos businessman Chief Kanu. In an earlier incarnation as the Ambassador Club it had been one of the main Lagos nightspots during the heyday of highlife, but had declined somewhat since the late 1960s, and by the 1970s it maintained a somewhat seedy profile. However, it was perfectly convenient for Fela, as it was located just across the road from his home on Agege Motor Road.

Like many buildings in Lagos, the Shrine was partially covered with a corrugated tin roof and was surrounded by open sewers. The courtyard, able to accommodate an audience of around a thousand, was ringed with painted flags of all the independent African nations, and a large, neon-lit map of the African continent cast its glow above the stage. Four raised wooden go-go platforms were placed about the interior, and the band performed on a T-shaped stage at one end of the space. With Afrika 70 performing several times a week, the Shrine was doing a brisk business. In addition to weeknight performances, Saturday was the "comprehensive show," which included choreographed dancing, while Sunday was "Yabis Night," in which Fela and audience delighted in derisively poking fun at a variety of targets.

The Shrine audience was unique in its composition, which, unusually for Africa, cut across religious, class, and ethnic lines. Though the bulk of the audience was composed of Lagos youths and students, professionals of all types—university professors, civil servants, government officials, policeman, soldiers, intellectuals, ambassadors, and foreign diplomats—regularly visited the club. A visit to the Shrine was not limited to the enjoyment of Fela's music, as books and pamphlets by a number of African and diasporic authors, including Malcolm X, Marcus Garvey, Cheikh Anta Diop, Walter Rodney, Dr. Ben Jochanan, and Kwame Nkrumah, were offered for sale. Thus, in addition to being a center to hear Nigeria's most innovative music, the Shrine became a vital center for the exchange of ideas, as well as a place to explore progressive visions of a new Africa in which diversity was celebrated over ethnic division, and in which a united Africa—recognized as the birthplace of human culture—interacted with the wider Pan-African world and beyond.

Beyond this, however, the name "Africa Shrine" contained a deeper significance for Fela. More than a mere entertainment club, he considered it an actual shrine to his ideological heroes and the ideology of Pan-Africanism in general—a space in which his political inclinations fused with his musical incantations to assume spiritual dimensions. Many elements of a Shrine performance could be experienced as more than a mere "concert," for both performers and listeners. Several traditional priests even offered libations at the beginning of Afrika 70 performances,[65] but eventually Fela proclaimed himself "Chief Priest of Shrine" and began each performance by pouring a libation at the Shrine's altar, which contained photographs of Malcolm X, Martin Luther King, Kwame Nkrumah, Patrice Lumumba, and others. While he rejected the idea of a Christian "God," the Shrine was a place in which Fela and his audience could pay homage to these political "spirits," each of whom had exerted a profound effect on the history of African people. In this sense, a Shrine performance could be interpreted as an occasion to channel political empowerment to "devotees" by invoking the spirits of important political and historical figures.

In another sense, the Shrine evoked a pseudotraditional mystical atmosphere by communicating "hidden" knowledges such as suppressed or revisionist histories of Africa. The allegorical entrance to other realms of knowledge and experience, as well as the philosophical and psychological significance resulting from black culture's proximity to death and suffering,[66] was clearly represented by the costumed figure of death, which leapt across the stage at the beginning of each performance to the thundering of traditional drums. The marijuana that was freely sold and smoked in the Shrine also helped create a mood conducive to this experience, while intensifying the feeling of community and difference among attendants.[67] Fela explained to the *Independent:* "We smoke in the Shrine all the time. The Shrine is not a club, man. It's a place where we dance, we get high, we play drums to evoke the spirit. The power of the Shrine is very strong—the spiritual power . . . this is why we can smoke dope with impunity."[68]

As is customary in Africa, performances at the Shrine were lengthy, usually lasting until dawn. Interestingly—in light of his promotion of African traditions—Fela appeared on stage clad not in any indigenous dress, but in Western-styled two-piece jumpsuits embroidered with traditional Yoruba symbols and patterns. This sartorial choice led some Western observers to characterize him as an "African Elvis,"[69] although it also reflects his negotiation of the traditional and cosmopolitan.

Fela had also become one of Africa's most visually exciting performers. Far from the studied cool-jazz demeanor of his Koola Lobitos days, he had developed into a masterful dancer, his style a hybrid mixture of traditional steps and rapid footwork recalling James Brown—all projected with a sinuous sensuality. A journalist described his effect on audiences:

> At first glance, Fela seems an unlikely focus for such adulation. . . . He is not prepossessing, certainly not handsome, slight in stature, with a narrow face, high cheekbones and widely set eyes. But when he moves on stage, in restrained, graceful motions like a coiling snake, and when he sings, hunching over the microphone and spitting out the words, the magnetism is unmistakable in any culture: superstar. He struts, turns his backside, arches an eyebrow, twirls the microphone cord like a whip. He pumps a wailing saxophone and pounds an electric organ whose high notes set the tin roof rattling.[70]

While he was unquestionably Afrika 70's leader, composer, and conceptualist, Fela was by no means its sole attraction. Propelled by the jazzy interplay of Tony Allen and lead conga drummer Henry Kofi, the most stable edition of Afrika 70 was rounded out by Okalue Ojeah, Leke Benson, and Oghene Kologbo on rhythm, tenor, and bass guitars, respectively, Nicholas Addo and Shina Abiodun on congas, James Abayomi on sticks, and Isaac Olaleye on shekere. On top of this, tenor saxophonist Igo Chico and trumpeter Tunde Williams offered hard-bop-derived horn improvisations, while Lekan Animashaun, Christopher Uwaifor, and Nwokoma Ukem completed the horn section on baritone saxophone, tenor saxophones, and trumpet, respectively. The chorus section, led by Kevwe Oghomienor, also included Alake Adedipe, Ihase Obotu, Fehintola Kayode, Ronke Edason, Tejumade Adebiyi, Shade Komolafe, Shade Shehindemi, and Felicia Idonije, among many others who passed through the band. By 1972, Afrika 70 had arguably developed into the most formidable rhythm machine in tropical Africa.[71] It was an especially intense phase of activity, with both Allen and Williams releasing LPs under their own names, produced by Fela and accompanied by Afrika 70.

The late 1960s and 1970s witnessed the proliferation of urban African popular music styles on an unprecedented scale, as well as the emergence of the first generation of continental superstars, such as Franco and Tabu Ley Rochereau in Zaire, and South Africans Hugh Masekela and Miriam Makeba. Meanwhile, outside of Africa, the massive worldwide success of Camerounian saxophonist Manu Dibango's "Soul Makossa" in 1973 spurred a new wave of international interest in African pop. Afrika 70's music was released in Europe on a number of labels, including EMI, Decca, and Mercury. As early as 1970, a Nigerian reviewer had voiced the aspirations of this generation of African popular musicians when he noted that "only a band like the Nigeria 70, which has something original to say and knows how to say it musically, can contribute something distinctly African to international popular music."[72]

By late 1972, the Shrine had emerged as the hub of anglophone West Africa's music scene. It had also acquired an international reputation as one of the premier African music haunts, with a number of well-known musicians journeying to Lagos to play with Afrika 70. Besides Ginger Baker, expatriate South African trumpeter Hugh Masekela was a frequent visitor during this period, sitting in regularly with Afrika 70. After an extended exile in the United States in the late sixties, Masekela felt a need to replenish his African roots, a process to which Fela's music proved crucial: "Fela introduced me to his afrobeat, which I found magical. I had to be pulled away from the microphone; I literally could not stop playing with the patterns his wonderful rhythm section wove behind me. From this experience, I found the gateway to West African culture. . . . For this I remain ever grateful to Fela."[73] Masekela and Fela later journeyed to Ghana, where along with Fela's old business associate, Faisal Helwani, they produced an LP by Masekela and the Ghanaian group Hedzolleh Soundz.

Another trumpeter—African-American Lester Bowie of the Art Ensemble of Chicago—would spend a three-month stretch as Fela's featured soloist later in the decade. He recalled:

I went to Nigeria in 1977 on a whim, on a dream, penniless. Fela sort of saved my life. Everyone that I spoke to said: "You're a musician and you're broke, so you should go see Fela." I said: "Where does this guy live?" and they said: "You just get in any cab and tell them to take you to Fela." To me, that sounded really weird. That's like getting in a taxicab in New York City and saying: "Take me to Miles' house." But I got in a cab and he took me right to the hotel where I met Fela. . . . We started playing a little bit and he said, "Stop! Go get this guy's bags, he's moving in with me." So I was Fela's guest of honor for the next three months.[74]

Ex-Beatle Paul McCartney was also a Shrine regular during the 1973 recording of his *Band on the Run* LP at EMI studios in Lagos. On one occasion he was reportedly moved to tears by the power of Fela's afrobeat, to which he had been introduced by fellow countryman Ginger Baker. However, McCartney's first evening at the Shrine ended unpleasantly when Fela privately accused him of coming to Lagos to steal African music. Although McCartney refuted this accusation, he reportedly resisted the impulse thereafter to infuse his music with African elements.[75]

These anecdotes illustrate three important dimensions of Fela's appeal. First and most obviously, they demonstrate the impact his music had on influential musicians far beyond the borders of Nigeria. As far away as the Caribbean, Jamaican session musicians such as Sly Dunbar and Robbie Shakespeare cited Fela's influence and occasionally included subtle shadings of afrobeat in their work.

The McCartney incident also demonstrates the arrogance in Fela's self-appointed role as "guardian" of African music. He was very sensitive to the hegemony of the Western music industry, in which African musicians were frequently relegated to backing status while Western musicians made money performing African songs and styles. He explained his involvement in the Hedzolleh project: "You see if [the foreign producers] came and wanted to record and take the tape away, I wouldn't have helped them. . . . But they wanted to take a band, and that's the kind of thing I like for my people. If you want to take my people on a journey, that's good. . . . I hate artists just coming and just using the [African] artists to record and bring the tapes [abroad]."[76]

Finally, it demonstrates Fela's accessibility. In spite of his growing popularity, he remained approachable in daily life. Yomi Gbolagunte recalls: "In those days, he would walk into the Shrine and greet people individually—friends, neighbors, visitors, black people, white people—very genuinely. People thought he was anti-white but he wasn't anti-white. Although he still lived his life in that radical way, he still had a sense of normalness about him. He genuinely appreciated the support the people were giving him."[77]

African Message

Organized around his innovative music, the Afrika Shrine was the site in which Fela was able to blend the components of his vision of a revitalized African culture most successfully. This vision contained both progressive and reactionary elements. Its inherent contradictions were most immediately apparent in Fela's authoritarian leadership of the Afrika 70 band.

Like James Brown, Fela was extremely strict with his musicians and dancers onstage, maintaining control over every aspect of their presentation. He had already changed his method of rehearsing Afrika 70, feeling that closed rehearsals ran counter to the communal nature of his culture. From the early 1970s, the band's rehearsals were open to the public, becoming virtual performances in themselves. Fela dramatically, and sometimes abusively, taught the parts to each musician, as fascinated crowds gathered to watch the intricate construction of the afrobeat mosaic. It was even widely said that the best time to see Fela was during rehearsals. By mid-decade, he was projecting an even greater air of control on stage. John Collins describes Fela's onstage manner during this period:

> Fela speaks in a mixture of broken English and Yoruba, continuously joking with the audience in between numbers, and they joke back. As soon as Fela is ready, he nods to a young man waiting at the wing of the stage who gracefully leaps up to clip the sax on him. . . . Fela waits patiently, not moving a muscle until the microphone is adjusted and everything is set for him; then one, two, three, they are off. He is strict with his musicians, and if any of them makes a mistake or does not concentrate he may fine him on the spot; consequently they have their eyes fixed on him all the time. As they are playing, four "sexy" dancers perform on shrouded raised platforms or podiums. One is at each corner of the dance floor and the girls are silhouetted onto the lace material by colored lights. Fela is in complete control as he uses four foot pedals to signal anyone of the dancers to stop if she tires; then another clambers up to begin.[78]

Fela's onstage control seemed to increase in direct proportion to the band's popularity. So authoritarian was Fela's stage manner at times that, when he mimicked the orders of a troop commander in his 1976 song "Zombie," the line between parody and the reality of his style of bandleading became blurred.

In creative terms, the relationship between Fela and many of his musicians is encapsulated in the following comment: "I don't find it difficult to find musicians to fit into my concept because I write everything in the band, from the drums to the horns. Everything, I write it myself and I have to teach everybody what to play so it really doesn't matter who plays in my band. . . . I don't write for particular players. I write for myself."[79]

Despite his populist rhetoric, Fela conformed—both creatively and economically—to a pattern of hegemonic bandleaders that scholars such as Christopher Waterman have identified in other styles.[80] Although it would be grossly inaccurate and unjust to minimize the contributions of brilliant Afrika 70 musicians such as Tony Allen, Henry Kofi, Tunde Williams, and Igo Chico, the musicians of Fela's bands—particularly the later ones—were in many cases essentially wage laborers executing the composer's precise instructions, with very limited opportunity for creative input. The younger musicians, especially, tended to have little in the way of formal musical training and thus found it difficult to use a period in the band as a springboard to increased career prospects; in many cases the very instruments they played onstage belonged to Fela. As Fela's star rose and he expanded his entourage and expenditures in line with cultural beliefs that a person's stature is reflected in the size of his retinue, resentment grew among his lower-paid musicians, who could have used the money themselves after years of loyal service.[81]

The economic relationship between Fela and many of his bandsmen is illustrated in the following exchange between music journalist Rob Tannenbaum and one of Fela's band members:

> Victor is twenty-six years old, and lives with his parents in Ghana. He would like to live alone, but can't afford to. The guitar he plays onstage belongs to Fela; Victor has never been able to afford one of his own. He felt lucky to be working, but with Fela earned only thirty naira per week; it costs fifteen naira just to eat three meals a day, thirty-five naira to buy a pair of pants. . . . He asked how much it would cost to fly from London to New York and was clearly disappointed by the answer. "Maybe you could save the money," I suggested hopefully. "Save? Shit, man, how can I save?" he snorted.[82]

The increasing emphasis on African elements in his music and presentation was intimately linked with his continuing exploration of his own African identity away from the stage. Continuing to blur the distinction between art and life, he converted his two-story residence at 14A Agege Motor Road in the Moshalashi area of Lagos into a communal home for family, band members, close associates, and the increasing numbers of Lagos youths who were drawn to him.[83] These youths were given housing and pocket money in exchange for performing tasks in the house or at the club—cleaning, disc-jockeying, or any number of other jobs needed to keep the Afrika 70 organization running.

As on the Shrine stage, an authoritarian organizational style existed in Fela's home. Somewhat in the manner of a traditional African village chief, he presided over his commune—holding daily court sessions, adjudicating disputes, and issuing judgments and punishments that could include fines, cane lashings, or beatings for men, and fines or confinement in a makeshift "prison" for women. Calvin Hernton and Terisa Turner recounted a typical day in the commune:

> The afternoon calm was broken by a child who reported that a resident had slapped him. . . . It was clear that [the grievance] would be brought before Fela in a "court" later that day. . . . The complete household plus visitors attended the court. Fela, fresh from rest, sat in the main concourse. "OK, what happened?" he asked. The child told his story. The man who had slapped him delivered a halting defense based largely on

the argument that a senior had the right to discipline someone younger. "Does anyone want to say more?" After one or two people spoke in the child's support, Fela found the man guilty of shameful behavior. "You, twice the age of this boy, feel you have to be a big man and slap him. You can apologize and curb yourself in the future or leave the commune for good." Deeply shamed, the man apologized to the child before the assembly. . . . In good spirits the commune launched into a birthday celebration before the big Saturday night show.[84]

John Collins, whose recollections of life in Fela's commune chronicle an endless series of disciplinary and spontaneous violence, witnessed a more severe incident:

> My passport was seized by the Lagos inspector general of police. . . . It took almost a month to sort this situation out. The man who took my passport to the [inspector general] was beaten by Fela, as was another young man who sat on and squashed the colonial hat I used in the film. In both cases I tried to prevent the beatings but was told that it was an internal matter and none of my affair.[85]

This authoritarian tendency had probable roots in three sources: (1) the rigid discipline Fela had himself experienced at the hands of his parents; (2) the authoritarian structures of the colonial era of which he was undeniably a product; and (3) characteristically African modes of social organization, with strict emphases on hierarchy, decorum, gestures of respect, and demonstrations of status. Some observers have suggested that these projections of power accounted for some of Fela's immense appeal among disempowered inner-city youth.[86]

"Lady": Gender and Sexuality in Fela's Life and Work

Probably the issue most associated with the inherent complexities in Fela's neo-traditionalist vision is his stance on sexuality and gender relations. His pronouncements on this issue were the source of much controversy and heated debate both within and outside of Africa. In the most generous terms, he has been described as ideologically inconsistent, more frequently as a reactionary traditionalist, and at worst an unrepentant sexist. Certainly, a constellation of factors resulted in a stance on gender relations that strongly contradicted Fela's self-image as a modern African progressive. This stance also seemed strangely reactionary in a world where cultural, economic, and technological issues have forced the fundamental questioning of traditional gender and sexual roles.

As of 1972, Fela remained legally married to his wife Remi (as he would through 1981), but they lived in separate homes. Meanwhile, young women flocked to him in his communal home. Some became his girlfriends; some took jobs in the Afrika 70 organization such as cooks, deejays, dancers, or chorus singers; and others did both. Although he was not formally married to these women, he justified his choice in the context of traditional African polygamy, simultaneously dismissing own his parents' monogamous marriage:

> I did not see the reason why I should follow in their footsteps because one man one wife is not normal in Africa. . . . It was not based on an African concept. My father was a British reverend, an Anglican priest. . . . What I know is that my mind wanted more women. I wanted to be free. By the time I got married in London I was still not an African. I was thinking like a whiteman. I thought that was the safest way, the best way but after that I found out that it was not in my mind.[87]

Fela promoted his new, openly promiscuous lifestyle as more authentically "African," and this outspoken sexual advocacy became an integral part of his public image. He actively promoted an image of himself as a highly sexed man and composed a number of songs about gender relations and sexuality. His girlfriends frequently adorned his album jackets, and he rarely appeared in public without many in tow. All of this resulted in an eroticization of his social profile that became an important component of his overall cultural mission. In grappling with this component of Fela's image, the African press tended towards sensationalism, while the Western press often took a reactive posture that ultimately tended to distort the issues. Matters were further complicated by the uncritical application of Western feminist perspectives to African culture, and by Fela's own delight in making comments calculated to outrage journalists who questioned the depth of his commitment to social change in light of his polygamous lifestyle. The issue clearly requires closer analysis, since Fela made sexuality a significant arena for articulating issues such as power, cultural identity, spirituality, and aesthetics. In fact, Fela's rise to public fame was in some ways strongly predicated upon the role women played in his organization. Even the sound structure and dynamic flow of his musical style have often been metaphorized in sexual terms: "A cynical buddy contends that Fela's been making the same record since 1972, and he's got a point; Fela's pieces do tend to follow a pattern. . . . The beauty of each composition is in the rise and fall, sort of like—I know Fela would approve of this metaphor—a great fuck."[88]

The question of whether or not Fela's sonic structures reflect a particular stance on gender relations or sexuality is probably as ultimately unanswerable as the question of whether the spiked, conical prayer towers adorning mosques throughout West Africa's Islamic regions are phallic architectural manifestations of a male-dominant Islamic culture. But it is clear that there was a highly sexualized aura around his art, which operated inside of a particular expressive framework rooted in the three main components of his social identity: his role as a postcolonial African artist, his role as a derisive singer, and his role as a social maverick.

"Lady" (1972) and "Mattress" (1975) are the songs in which Fela addresses gender issues most directly. He consistently scoffed at the notion of "equality" between the sexes as defined in Western feminist terms, and "Lady" lampoons the "westernized" African women who depart from tradition and claim equality with men:

FELA: If you call am woman,
African woman no go gree
She go say, she go say "I be *lady*-o" . . .
CHORUS: She go say "I be *lady*-o"

FELA: I wan tell you about "lady" . . .

She go say im equal to man
She go say im get power like man
She go say anything man do,
im self fit do
I never tell you finish . . .
She go wan take cigar before
anybody
She go wan make you open
door for am
She go wan make man wash
plate for am for kitchen
She won't salute man, she go
sit down for chair

She wan sit down for table before
anybody

She wan take piece of meat before
anybody
Call am for dance, she go dance
lady dance
African woman na dance, she go

dance the fire dance
She know him man na master
She go cook for am
She go do anything he say
But lady no be so
Lady na master . . .

FELA: If you call her a "woman"
an African woman will not agree
She says "I am a *lady*". . .
CHORUS: She says "I am a *lady*"

FELA: I want to tell you about
"lady" . . .
She says she is equal to man
She says she is as powerful as man
She says she can do anything a
man can do
I haven't finished telling you . . .
She is not ashamed of smoking in
front of anyone
She wants to make you open doors
for her
She wants a man to wash her
dishes in the kitchen
She won't salute man [i.e., by waiting
until he is seated],
she sits down in a chair
She wants to sit down at the table
before anyone else [i.e., in defiance
of established custom]
She wants to take a piece of
meat before anybody
Ask her to dance, she will dance a
ballroom dance
A traditional African woman will
dance
a traditional dance
She knows the man is master
She cooks for him
She will do anything he says
But the "lady" will not
The "lady" is the master . . .

Gender and Postcoloniality

Fela's articulation of the struggle to redefine traditional gender roles in contemporary life can be understood by situating his work within three overlapping analytical spheres. The first of these is the sphere of postcolonial African art. My use of the term *postcolonial* here mainly connotes literature, as it was largely Western-educated African writers who initially assumed the task of articulating the realities of postcolonial Africa to the outside world in a modern art form. There are five dominant themes commonly found in this tradition of literature. The first is the effort to assess the damage of the colonial encounter upon African traditions.[89] The second is a grappling with the question of African identity in the face of such sweeping sociopolitical changes as the nation-state, rapid urbanization, and ethnic displacement.[90] The third is an effort to reinfuse the tarnished icons of traditional culture with a new and vital power, often reinterpreting them in a manner relevant to contemporary African life.[91] The fourth is the encouragement of allegiance to the new nation-state and its institutions. The fifth theme is a class critique that emerges as the communal euphoria of independence gives way to the reality of inequality in the new nation. In Fela's work, "Black Man's Cry" is an example of the first theme, "Gentleman" the second, "African Message (Don't Worry About My Mouth-O)" the third, "Buy Africa" the fourth, and "Ikoyi Mentality versus Mushin Mentality" the fifth. The central role that sexuality plays in Fela's ideology might be considered an example of the third concern of revitalization, as he asserted a more open embrace of sexuality as one way of reclaiming a vital African identity, unfettered by the prudishness associated with the European colonizers. In this sense, his efforts contain implied spiritual as well as cultural overtones.

In the concerted effort to promote allegiance to new political structures while revitalizing the traditional worldview, many postcolonial African artists failed to address inherent contradictions in their idealization of traditional culture. One example is the issue of sexism and the unequal way gender relations were impacted by colonialism. From the standpoint of traditional culture, gender relations in West Africa differ significantly from the West in that traditions that seem male-dominated to the Western observer actually reveal detailed negotiations of power between genders. This is not to suggest that sexism was absent in precolonial Africa. Rather, it has been suggested that women in traditional culture were effective power brokers outside of the political arena (in the spheres of farming, trading, and produce markets, for example), where such influence would normally be sought in Western cultures. On the other hand, colonialism, with its male-dominated political institutions, went a long way toward weighting social balances in favor of men.[92]

When postcolonial African writers idealized the role of women in traditional culture and insisted that women conform to this role in contemporary society, they ignored the fact that while men enjoyed distinct social and political advantages in postcolonial social and political structures, women often suffered under both the patriarchal structures of colonialism and outmoded traditional systems.[93] This was, in fact, the major battle waged by Fela's mother, a battle directed toward traditional as well as colonial institutions of power.

Such male-dominant interpretations of "tradition" have often served in the effort to forge a sense of nationalism and cultural pride, and they offer one interpretative key to Fela's "Lady." To the extent that it attempts to serve these ends, "Lady" works counter to Fela's stated goal of African empowerment. By advocating a proscribed, domestic function for women, it implicitly hinders their advancement in the spheres of employment and education, two clear prerequisites for the social transformation Fela desired. He later said:

> People thought I was trying to say that women had no say, no rights. I was not saying that. I was saying that women had a role, a duty. When they want to have a say in government—though in Africa they are not expected to do that—they are not discouraged. They can do what they want to do. . . . I was not saying that women should take a back seat. If a female wants to do a man's job, no one will stop her from doing it, but women have duties to perform as mothers.[94]

There is an aesthetic component to the postcolonial in Fela's work, reflected in his attempt to reinvigorate an African aesthetic and ideas of beauty. His 1970 song "Black Man's Cry," for example, relies upon African-American sentiments of racial/cultural affirmation such as "black is beautiful" to achieve this goal. The song denigrates practices such as hair-straightening and skin-bleaching for conforming to a Eurocentric standard of beauty, much as they were denigrated in African-American culture during the same period. Thus, in one sense, Fela's placement of bare-breasted, traditionally scarified women sporting traditional braided hairstyles on the jackets of albums such as *Shakara, Expensive Shit,* and *Noise for Vendor Mouth* represent progressive attempts to promote traditionally African standards of beauty. On the other hand, it also seems an objectification of women; although topless women are depicted on the album sleeves, there are no men in similar states of undress. Certainly, when Fela posed semi-nude on his album covers surrounded by dozens of bare-breasted women, he was as equally promoting himself as an African playboy, displaying the women he had accumulated through his wealth and fame. Finally, there is a class component in Fela's exploration of the postcolonial, and in this respect Fela's outlook is similar to his mother's. "Lady" hints at an incompletely articulated class critique, as the "lady" Fela cites—in all likelihood elite, professional, and westernized—is asserting her class status and degree of cultural "refinement" over the crude "market woman" or street trader. In Mercy Oduyoye's interpretation of "Lady," the song contains an implicit criticism of African women who have internalized a Western ideal of woman as weak, frail, and dependent.[95] Both of these points are consistent with a distinction made by Funmilayo Ransome-Kuti, who frequently complained of her difficulties mobilizing elite Nigerian women.[96] She told Sola Odunfa in 1968, "The only class I still can't get at are those so-called educated women; you can never get them to do anything. . . . They cannot identify themselves with the aspirations of the 'ordinary' women because they are the wives of big men. . . . The common women on the other hand know where the shoe pinches. They have been beaten. They have been teargassed. They are those who matter."[97]

Gender and Derisive Humor

The second sphere within which Fela's articulation of gender issues can be interpreted is his role as a derisive humorist. Although both "Lady" and "Mattress" address a concrete social tension resulting from modernization and other factors, they can also be understood as belonging to a genre of playfully derisive songs. Aside from Koola Lobitos's "Iya Me O Se O" (a tribute to Fela's mother), "Who No Know Go Know" (a 1975 song honoring Fela's Pan-African heroes), and "Underground System" (a 1992 tribute to slain Burkina Faso President Thomas Sankara), virtually all of Fela's songs may be heard as fundamentally derisive, abusive, or critical. As a humorous song belonging to a body of such material, "Lady" was not received exclusively as serious social commentary. Rather, it was taken as a jibe at the more extreme departures from traditional gender identities and cultural practices. In one sense, this mocking take on perceived Western feminist notions of "equality" is shared by both sexes in Africa.

Fitting firmly into Fela's role as a provocateur delighting in outraging prudish listeners is his song "Mattress," in which he metaphorizes woman as a "mattress" for man to lay upon. "Mattress" clearly demonstrates the derisive tendency in Fela's music. On a first reading of the lyrics, it is unclear whether he is suggesting that a woman's sexual availability constitutes her sole worth, or whether he is merely celebrating sexual pleasure in general:

FELA: Call am for me, call am for me	*FELA:* Call it for me, call it for me
CHORUS: Mattress, mattress [repeats]	*CHORUS:* Mattress, mattress [repeats]
FELA: He be the plank, wey dey hard for back	*FELA:* It is the plank that is hard underneath
He be the mat, wey he dey cold for ground	It is the mat, when the ground is cold
He be the spring, wey he dey bounce like ball	It is the spring, that bounces like a ball
He be the cushion, wey he dey soft like wool	It is the cushion that is soft like wool
You be plank, you be mat, you be spring, you be cushion	It is a plank, a mat, a spring, and a cushion
When I say woman na mattress, I no lie . . .	When I say woman is a mattress, I am not lying . . .
CHORUS: You no lie, my friend . . .	*CHORUS:* You are not lying, my friend . . .

Although Fela's lyrics represent an extreme formulation of it, the particular fusion of social observation, derisive humor, and male-dominant ideology in songs like "Lady" and "Mattress" has been discussed as a characteristic of dance-band highlife by Nimrod Asante-Darko and Sjaak Van Der Geest (1983). Like most African popular styles, highlife is a male-dominated tradition, and the Afrika 70 band conformed to the social organization of most African popular ensembles in assigning women supportive roles such as dancers or background singers.[98] Unlike female singers who have become leaders in their own rights, such as Miriam Makeba, Christy Essien-Igbokwe, Mbilia Bel, or Oumou Sangare, the female members of Afrika 70 ultimately contributed their talents in a way that reinforced Fela's stance on issues such as gender relations. Indeed, through their singing, they contribute some of the most powerful musical elements in songs like "Lady" and "Mattress."

As much as any other source, Fela's ideas of male supremacy may have been reinforced by his experience of the black power movement, in which a dominant perception of women's potential political contribution was summed up by Kwame Toure in his famous quote about "prone" being the best position for women in the movement. Ironically, Fela's views differ sharply from the later views of his hero Malcolm X, who once observed (following a lengthy trip through Africa and the Middle East) that he could gauge the progressive element of a given society by the extent to which women publicly participated in its political life.[99] By the end of his life, in fact, Malcolm X is said to have remarked that "Africa will not be free until it frees its women."[100]

Gender and Social Deviance

The third sphere within which we can analyze Fela's positions on gender issues concerns his role as a social maverick. His direct takes on sexuality carried the power to shock and provoke in an extremely decorum-conscious African society, something he exploited to the fullest. In one sense, sexuality and eroticism are relatively freely expressed in sub-Saharan Africa, as evidenced by the wide variety of social dances containing highly stylized erotic or suggestive movements, or the exaggerated genitalia in much of the region's figurative sculpture. On the other hand, this ease with sexual matters does not always extend freely into the realm of verbal communication, where it is usually couched in double-entendre, allusion, metaphor, or innuendo.

In such a social climate, Fela's directness was guaranteed substantial shock value, and this was clearly a strong motivation in his foregrounding of gender and sexuality in his work. The cover photo of Afrika 70's 1972 recording *Shakara,* for example, features Fela smiling mischievously, clad in his trademark bikini shorts, outstretched, surrounded by three groups of women holding their breasts in gestures of offering. One group is arranged in the shape of the African continent, the second in the shape of the number seven, and the third in the shape of the number zero—together creating the pictogram "Afrika 70."

It should be noted that Fela's behavior did not differ markedly from other affluent Nigerian men who could afford to sustain several wives, seek additional wives for reasons of increased progeny and sexual variety, and insist that these wives conform to traditional roles. He ultimately differed only in his degree of candor, the extent to which he foregrounded this as an aspect of his public persona, and the extremes to which he often took it, which were directly related to his self-image as a musical superstar. It should also be noted that for all of Fela's posturing, the Afrika Shrine occupied a distinct social space in Lagos's musical nightlife. While virtually all Lagos nightclubs were effectively off-limits to unaccompanied women (who would invariably be harassed as prostitutes), the Afrika Shrine was seen as a space women could attend without such harassment.[101]

In the end, Fela's attitudes seem at odds with the development of his own political awareness, a process to which, by his own admission, women were crucial at each stage. Most ironically, his views differed radically from those of his mother, a pioneering feminist who knew too well the challenges faced by women in postcolonial Africa. Many observers have been unable to reconcile Fela's male supremacy in light of his mother's role in Nigerian society, and some have even explained his own relationships with women as a direct reaction to her harsh discipline of him during his youth.[102] To position Fela's philosophy as the polar opposite of his mother's radical feminism is an oversimplification, however, as their well-documented closeness seems to demonstrate. Many sources report that Mrs. Kuti remained a dominant and solidly supportive influence on her son throughout her life, and that in her absence he lacked his primary source of moral support and encouragement.[103] We must also account for the facts that she lived in her son's communal house during the 1970s, followed suit when he changed his name in 1975 (see chapter 5), and used her influence on several occasions to bail him out of trouble with the authorities. Does it mean she accepted his contradictions in light of his overall contribution to Nigerian culture and his upholding of her legacy of radical activism? Certainly, it would be interesting to hear her analysis of the relationship between her educated, elite, and economically successful son and the steady stream of working-class and/or migrant women drawn to the Afrika 70 commune in search of opportunity, adventure, and acknowledgment. These questions may never be fully answered, and they elude simple conclusions. It is worth noting, however, that all of the Ransome-Kuti siblings agreed that Fela was their mother's favorite, with his elder sister Dolu claiming that Mrs. Kuti would "rather die than see Fela suffer."[104]

Ultimately, the inconsistencies in Fela's traditionalist stance seem rooted in two conflicting goals: one seeks to define a cultural ethos for postcolonial Africa; the other seeks to justify his own habits in the context of tradition. Thus, just as he explained his use of marijuana as an indigenous tradition (refusing to refer to it as "Indian hemp") and his increasingly critical songs as conforming to the African musician's traditional role as social critic, he justified his desire to have many women by reference to the African tradition of polygamy. In the final analysis, Fela relies upon gender to smooth out the inherent complexities in an essentialist conception of culture, in the process providing himself with an aura of unassailable authenticity. As Paul Gilroy has stated: "In a situation where racial identity appears suddenly impossible to know reliably or maintain with ease, the naturalness of gender can supply can supply the modality in which race is lived and symbolized."[105] Consistent with the rest of his work from the period, Fela's musings on gender issues during the early 1970s can be considered relatively light-hearted social observations, but they nevertheless laid the foundations for an incomparably more problematic enactment of these positions at the end of his career.

Colonial Mentality

In addition to the gender question, other Fela songs explore different aspects of the postcolonial African condition. In "Why Black Man Dey Suffer," for example, he explores the division and disruption that are the legacies of colonialism:

Why blackman dey suffer today	Why black people suffer today
Why blackman no get money today	Why black people don't have money today
Why blackman no go for moon today	Why black people haven't traveled to the moon today
THIS is the reason why:	THIS is the reason why:
We dey sit down for our land-e jaiye-jaiye	We were in our homeland, without troubles
We dey mind our business jaiye-jaiyeq	We were minding our own business
Some people come from faraway land	Some people came from a faraway land
Dem fight us and take our land	They fought us and took our land
Dem take our people and spoil our towns	They took our people [as slaves] and destroyed our towns
Na since then trouble start-o	Our troubles started at that time
Our riches dem take away to their land	Our riches, they took away to their land
In return dem give us dem colony	In return they gave us their colony
Dem take our culture away from us	They took our culture away from us
Dem give us dem culture we no understand	They gave us their culture which we don't understand
Black people, we no know ourselves	Black people, we don't know ourselves
We no know our ancestral heritage	We don't know our ancestral heritage
We dey fight each other every day	We fight each other every day
We never together, we never together at all	We are never together at all
THAT is why blackman dey suffer today . . .	THAT is why black people suffer today . . .

Over a moody, mid-tempo groove, "Gentleman" offers a critique of colonial-minded Africans and their imitation of British manners and customs. Perhaps more than any other, this song establishes Fela's essentialist position on the issue of African identity, his goal of dismantling the psychological legacy of colonialism (popularly referred to as "colonial mentality"), and his overall cultural mission during the 1970s. The record's unforgettable cover photograph features a gorilla attired in a European suit and overcoat—sending a clear message to Anglophile Africans—but even this pales in comparison to the scathing lyrics:

I no be gentleman at all, no	I am not a gentleman at all
I Africa man, original . . .	I am an authentic African man . . .
Africa hot, I like am so	Africa is hot, I like it that way
I know what to go wear,	I know what to wear
But my friend don't know	But my friend doesn't know
He put him socks, he put him shoe	He puts on socks, he puts on shoes
He put him pant, he put him singlet	He puts on undershorts, he puts on singlet
He put him trouser, he put him shirt	He puts on pants, he puts on shirts
He put him tie, he put him coat	He puts on tie, he puts on coat
He come cover all wetin hot!	He covers his whole body with hot things!
He be gentleman!	He is a gentleman!
He go sweat—all over	He sweats all over
He go faint—right down	He faints and falls down
He go smell—like shit	He smells like shit
He go piss for body, he no go know—	He unknowingly pisses on himself—
I no be gentleman like that!	I am not a gentleman like that!

The later "Colonial Mentality" (1976) tackles the same theme from a different perspective, ridiculing the African elites and their internalization of Western manners, tastes, technologies, and traditions:

CHORUS: He be say you be colonial man,	*CHORUS:* He is saying that you are a colonial man
you don be slave for before	You were enslaved before
dem don release you now,	Your captors have released you
but you never release yourself . . .	now, But you have never released yourself
FELA: Dem think say dem better pass dem brothers,	*FELA:* They think they are better than their brothers,
No be so?	Isn't it true?
They thing wey black no good, na foreign things dem dey like	Black things are no good, it's foreign things they like,
No be so?	Isn't it true?
Dem go turn air condition, and close dem country away,	They turn on air conditioners, and shut out their country's climate,

No be so?	Isn't it true?
Dem judge go put white wig, and jail him brothers,	Their judges put on white wigs and jail their African brothers,
No be so?	Isn't it true?
Dem go proud of dem name, and put dem slave name for head,	They are proud of their European slave names, and put them at the front of their names,
No be so?	Isn't it true?
CHORUS: It be so!	CHORUS: It is true!

"In This Our Lagos Town"

Many of Fela's songs from this period reflect the atmosphere of urban Lagos. In the wake of the oil boom, millions of Nigerians left their rural village homes and flocked to Lagos, hoping to cash in on the sudden wealth. Almost overnight, Lagos became a civil engineering nightmare, as city planners faced the impossible task of transforming the city's infrastructure to accommodate this mass influx. In less than a decade, Lagos was transformed from a typical West African port city into a sprawling, chaotic, virtually unmanageable metropolis.

This chaos was, ironically, a source of great creative inspiration for the Afrika 70 commune. Living in an area of Surulere adjoining the sprawling ghetto known as Mushin, they experienced the lively streets and market places of Mushin as well as the poverty and challenges facing its inhabitants. This proximity was important in the development of Fela's art, as he was able to tap into the immense reservoir of adaptive creativity required to survive in such a setting. This was expressed most immediately in the endless circulation of street slang, which seemed to evolve by the week, and much of which found its way into Fela's art. Some of Fela's songs also served a social function established by the earliest urban African musicians—to interpret the absurdities of inner-city life and comfort and reassure a displaced rural population during a period of intense social transformation.[106] "Go Slow," "You No Go Die Unless You Wan Die," and "Trouble Sleep, Yanga Wake Am" examine the complexities of modern urban life from both public and private perspectives.

"Go Slow" is the Lagos slang for traffic jams. During the 1970s, it was not uncommon for motorists to spend an entire day ensnarled in traffic, and the city's infrastructural problems became legendary around the world. With a humor characteristic of the typical Nigerian's method of dealing with seemingly insurmountable social problems—a mixture of resignation, exasperation, outrage, and irony—Fela bemoans the daily frustration and chaos faced by Lagos motorists:

FELA: Go slow, go slow	FELA: Go slow, go slow
CHORUS: Go slow, go slow . . .	CHORUS: Go slow, go slow . . .

FELA: You dey make your business every day
Then you buy your motor car
Or you join your public transport
Then you start to go for work
Then suddenly, suddenly, suddenly—
Lorry dey for your front
Tipa dey for your back
Motorcycle dey for your left
Taxi-moto dey for your right
Helicopter dey fly, fly for your top-o
You self don dey for cell
Go slow catch you!

FELA: You take care of your daily business
Then you buy yourself a car
Or you take public transportation
And start to leave for work
Then suddenly, suddenly, suddenly—
A pushcart is in front of you
A dumptruck is behind you
A motorcycle is on your left
A taxicab is on your right
A helicopter flies above
You are imprisoned
The traffic jam has caught you!

In "You No Go Die Unless You Wan Die," Fela metaphorically warns of the dangers of life in the "concrete jungle" of transformed Lagos:

You no go die unless you wan
die, but if you wan die sa o
you go die . . .

You won't die unless you want to
die, but if you desire to die,
you will surely die . . .

To ba r'iku o ko maa sare

If you see danger or death, you'd better run

Ko ma sare, ko maa sare

Please, run for your life

To ba r'ejo koo maa sare

If you see a snake, please run

To ba ri danfo ko maa sare!

If you see a passenger van, please run!

To ba ri molue ko maa sare!

If you see a public bus, please run!

Omo elere lo ri ye n o, ko ma sare . . .

That's the speedster for you, keep running . . .

The lyrics of these songs can be thought of in one sense as reflecting the confluence of pedestrian and symbolic streams of thought concerning roads. In traditional lore the image of the road is a rich metaphor for destiny—an idea found especially frequently in the crossroads iconography of the Yoruba deity Eshu-Elegba. On the other hand, road fatalities in Nigeria escalated dramatically during the 1970s, allowing a very concrete interpretation of the road as a site of destiny, with its machine-mediated carnage also functioning as metaphor for the modern tragedy of the colonial encounter. A similar parallel was drawn by Wole Soyinka in his play *The Road,* which draws on traditional Yoruba mythopoetic strategies to use the highway as metaphor for the tragedy of the postcolonial Nigerian nation-state.[107] (It is a reflection of the country's dismal road safety record that Soyinka actually served on the Nigerian Road Safety Commission, encouraging the nation's drivers to follow traffic regulations.) Years later, Tony Allen would explore a similar set of themes in his 1979 song "Road Safety."

Over a slow, lilting neo-highlife arrangement and plaintive horn and choral line that perfectly underscore the melancholy lyrical portraits, Fela's "Trouble Sleep" (popularly known as "Palaver") describes the struggle to survive and maintain dignity in spite of the absurdities and contradictions of urban life. The song—uncharacteristically poignant and one of Fela's most enduring—remains very popular in Nigeria today, having lost none of its relevance:

FELA: When trouble sleep, yanga go wake am— Wetin he de find?	*FELA:* When trouble sleeps, someone must wake him What will he find?
CHORUS: Palaver, he dey find . . .	*CHORUS:* Palaver [trouble] is what he will find . . .
FELA: My friend just come from prison Him dey look for work Waka, waka day and night Policeman come stop am for road He say "Mister, I charge you for wandering" Wetin he dey find?	*FELA:* My friend was just released from prison He looks for work Walking day and night A policeman stops him on the road He says "Mister, I charge you for wandering" What thing will he find?
CHORUS: Palaver . . .	*CHORUS:* Palaver . . .

"Trouble Sleep" implies a sympathy for the prisoner that would never be expressed in a juju song; Fela implicitly empathizes with the struggle for survival even if it includes strategies that sometimes operate on the far side of the law. Living in Mushin was a stark reminder of the relationship between class and culture, and Fela's appreciation of the excitement and dynamism of urban African life clearly grew in direct proportion to his awareness of the increasing disparities of wealth and power. "Ikoyi Mentality versus Mushin Mentality" explores the lifestyle contrasts between the affluent (Ikoyi) and working-class (Mushin) areas of Lagos in order to dramatize class differences in contemporary Nigeria:

Make we hear how people different, for this our Lagos town . . .	Let us hear how people differ in our Lagos town . . .
Some people dey Ikoyi, some people dey Mushin-o . . .	Some people live in Ikoyi, some live in Mushin . . .
Ikoyi man dey travel	The man from Ikoyi travels
Him travel all over the world	He travels all over the world
Him bring "civilization" for us,	He brings "civilization" to us
Civilization we no understand	Civilization we don't understand

Mushin man dey for home	The man from Mushin is at home
Him never travel anywhere at all	He never travels anywhere at all
Him understand him people language	He understands the language of his people
The language of Africa	The language of Africa
Make we hear how people different, for this our Lagos town . . .	Let us hear how people differ in our Lagos town . . .

Not all of Fela's songs concerned pressing social issues. "He Miss Road" is a comical rumination on the misfortune wrought by confused or mistaken plans, "Shakara Oloje" lampoons braggarts and haughty women, and "Monday Morning in Lagos" describes the difficult transition from the carefree mood of the weekend to the austerity of the work week. "Gbagada Gbogodo" ["Pluckety-Splackety Sound"] is a lighthearted child's folktale recounting a war from the mythical Yoruba past:

Ogun Adubi s'oju re ja?	Was the Adubi War fought while you were present?
Ogun Adubi le l'opo l'opo	The Adubi War was most fierce
Iwo nikan soso da pa soja mefa	You singlehandedly killed six soldiers
Oro o wo mo o pada s'ehin	When the battle became too fierce, you made a hasty retreat
O pada s'ehin, o wa fi ewe bora	You beat a hasty retreat and took refuge under a heap of leaves
Iya re nke lo bi ewure	Your mother started bleating like a goat
Baba re nke lo bi aparo	Your father was screeching like a sparrow
Iwo na nbe lo bi igala	You also took off and started galloping like an antelope
Omi ireke le nbu sebe	You all started using sugar cane extracts to do your cooking [indicating rough times and scarcity of food]
Le nbu sebe, le tun fi ya omo	You not only used sugar cane liquid for stew, you also fed the extracts to newborn babies
O ya o, eni omo wu o ya ka lo o	Yeah, it's time—anybody who wants and cherishes a child, let's go!

"My Country, Why Not . . . ? "

The period between 1970 and 1974 was a time of productivity, financial reward, and good times for Fela and the Afrika 70 organization. He continued to refine his instrumental conception while forging a more organic relationship between his art and his society, clarifying his subject matter and channeling his sense of humor into pointed social observations. It could be argued that as a result of his enormous popularity, he almost singlehandedly brought the black power revolution to Nigeria, at least in the sphere of popular culture, in his own way helping to fill the ideological and cultural vacuum that had existed since the end of the colonial era. The success of the Shrine and his communal living environment were clearly huge boosts for Fela's creativity. His work had not yet become the political "weapon" he would later designate it, in response to a number of external factors. Free from these concerns, he composed much of his most enduring material between 1972 and 1974, celebrating the black aesthetic and the new African nation state. The mood and goals of Fela's music through 1974 are nicely encapsulated in his song "Confusion," in which, following a string of observations chronicling the chaos of Lagos, he laconically remarks "For me, I like am like that—na my country, why not?" (i.e., "It's my country, why shouldn't I like it?").

Throughout the seventies, Nigeria would struggle to live up to its new image as the "giant" of sub-Saharan Africa. At the same time, the country wrestled with the problems of grossly unequal distribution of wealth, military intervention, and ethnic tension, among many others. As Fela's analysis of these problems sharpened, and as his confidence increased in proportion to his popularity, he would become an increasingly vocal critic of Nigeria's elite class and political leadership. This would have serious consequences, and by the end of the decade, he would be—in addition to Africa's best-known musician—one of its foremost political dissidents.

"The Black President"
(1974–1979)

It is being educated in the English way that makes you a big man [in Nigeria]. *That is what I disagree with. My message was: "Think African. Make students read African history." The people listened, but the government did not. That was when my confrontation with the government started.*

FELA *quoted in* BOEHM 1989:21

If you could see Fela in the seventies—the man turned Nigeria completely upside down! He had the whole country in his hand, it was like he owned Nigeria! To tell the truth, Fela at that time was a law unto himself and did whatever he pleased in Nigeria, until he met an equally lawless group—the army.

UNIDENTIFIED NIGERIAN FAN, *Lagos, March 1992*

National Problems, Official Sensitivities

By 1974, with its new *naira* currency growing stronger than the British pound, Nigeria was riding the crest of its oil-fueled prosperity and influence. It had become one of the world's largest petroleum producers, and was benefiting from the world petroleum shortage of 1973–1974, as well as the simultaneous embargo of Arab oil to the United States. With the largest standing army, most prosperous economy, and most diverse population, Nigeria could claim the military, economic, and cultural leadership of black Africa. The country's leaders spent the better part of the decade doing just this; presidents Yakubu Gowon, Murtala Mohammed, and Olusegun Obasanjo presided over the most prosperous and idealistic period in Nigeria's postindependence history. It was also a turbulent time.

The boomtown oil economy had transformed Nigeria in ways unimaginable just a decade earlier, multiplying its exports ten times, and eventually providing 80 percent of the its revenue.[1]

The social implications of this transformation were enormous. The social optimism and economic prosperity of the oil boom period were accompanied by an equal degree of civil chaos, as expectations were continuously outstripped by a grossly inadequate civil and organizational infrastructure. At the end of the war in 1970, the Gowon government proclaimed its commitment to improving the quality of Nigerian life in its four-year Second National Development Plan, in which huge amounts of public funds were allocated to large-scale civil projects such as revamping the educational system, providing more housing in the cities, conducting a new national census, and upgrading the infrastructure through improvements in such areas as transportation and communications.[2] But development was hampered by a chronic shortage of trained professionals qualified to undertake these tasks, as well as the pervasive corruption that often prevented the qualified from advancing. These problems decreased productivity and increased frustration; even as government public spending reached epic proportions, civil projects became mired in webs of inefficiency, corruption, and bureaucratic red tape.

The most graphic illustration of Nigeria's crippling inefficiency occurred during 1975, when—as a result of inadequate staff and berthing facilities, and dilapidated offloading equipment—congestion in Nigeria's port system was so high that the estimated time between arrival and berth was as much as three months. More than four hundred ships congested the Apapa ports in Lagos, and untold thousands of pounds of goods perished before they could be unloaded.[3] Much of the backlog consisted of cement ordered by the government for various public works projects, and much of this was ultimately dumped into Lagos harbor, with the government accruing millions of naira in demurrage fines on the remaining floating tons.[4] The situation was much the same at the Ikeja International Airport in Lagos, which, incredibly, was not under the supervision of any centralized airport authority. Facilities at Ikeja were completely inadequate to the increasing traffic of goods and passengers, and customs authorities gained an international reputation for disorganization and corruption. A simple passage into the country might take hours as the passenger negotiated the abyss of lost, stolen, or mishandled baggage and uncooperative customs officials demanding bribes.[5]

Corruption not only undermined productivity and complicated international commerce immeasurably, it also symbolized the nation's difficulty in adhering to a coherent vision. Corruption had been a problem prior to the war, but by the mid-1970s it reached unprecedented levels, becoming a pressing national concern. At all levels of society—from the military to the civil service to the street peddler—virtually no business could be transacted without the requisite bribe or "dash," as it was known. In a perversely ironic way, the widespread corruption—as much as it undermined efficiency and accountability—may have reflected traditionally egalitarian attitudes regarding the importance of sharing and recirculating one's accumulated wealth.[6]

It was becoming clear, however, that the primary beneficiaries of the nation's new wealth would not be those who needed it most. Although revolutionary rhetoric flowed freely in pre-independence Nigeria, the country had pursued a less radical course following independence, largely maintaining the political and administrative apparatus established by the departed British colonialists. At independence, control was simply transferred to the various native ethnic elites, with a good share eventually usurped by the military through the succession of coups. This may be due in part to the fact that Nigeria's experience of colonialism was less severe than it had been in other places that subsequently developed strongly ideological regimes. The country also lacked a charismatic leader like Nkrumah, Senghor, or Toure who could galvanize the diverse population around a specific ideology or social agenda. The absence of these factors ensured that the beneficiaries of the postwar economic prosperity would mainly be the military and the elite, who grew wealthy functioning as Nigerian middlemen, providing foreign firms access to the country's abundant natural resources—cocoa, peanuts, palm oil, cotton, timber, rubber, and especially petroleum.

Outside of the cities, where people maintained faith in ethnically rooted "trickle-down" networks of patronage and wealth redistribution, the effects of the new economic order were not as readily apparent.[7] In Lagos, however, the disparity of wealth and privilege was glaringly obvious. On the one hand, the downtown business center on Lagos Island sprouted scores of modern, Western-styled office buildings, and its streets were full of Western luxury vehicles. The nouveau-riche national elite rubbed heads at night-long celebrations where opulence was the rule and vast amounts of currency were lavished upon the musicians who sang their praises, while the urban poor danced on the periphery until dawn, waiting for leftover food.[8] In upper-class areas such as Ikoyi and Victoria Island, the country's wealthiest businessmen erected palatial mansions complete with ornate flower gardens, private mosques and chapels, and personal security forces.

On the other hand, large tracts of the Lagos mainland consisted of areas in which basic human dignity was often tested to its furthest limits. In the fishing village of Maroko, corrugated-iron shacks were perched above open sewers, and residents could be seen fishing in waters brimming with human waste. These areas swelled far beyond containable limits as country dwellers flooded the city, hoping to capitalize on the soaring economic climate even though annual income for the average Nigerian remained barely $400 U.S. throughout the decade.[9] Lagos's infrastructure was no match for urban drift of this magnitude. Disruptions in electric power were frequent, and housing was in chronically short supply, with thousands sleeping nightly on public roads, bridges, and intersections. These conditions also created serious health hazards. Only one in six Nigerians had access to running water, and no Nigerian city could boast of a central sewerage system—streets were lined with unsanitary open sewers festering in the tropical heat. In a country that had only one physician per every eight or ten thousand citizens, access to health care was also a major problem.

Possibly the worst consequence of this rapid and massive urbanization was the increasing neglect of the country's once-profitable agricultural sector. Before the oil boom years, Nigeria had exported a variety of foodstuffs, but by the early 1980s it was having trouble meeting its own food requirements and importing indigenous staple crops such as rice and palm-oil.[10]

Although there were middle-class areas such as Surulere and Ikeja, Lagos as a whole had been irrevocably transformed into a city of hustlers, with begging and poverty rampant, and seemingly everyone trying to make a fast buck. The rise of a new, ruthless breed of armed robbers demonstrated that some of the less-privileged were determined to share in the national bounty, on their own terms. Public gatherings such as Yoruba *ariyas* (lavish parties or celebrations),[11] weddings, and even services at elite churches were the most frequent targets of such robberies. By 1976, President Olusegun Obasanjo was urging his countrymen to adopt a low profile and shun excessive and ostentatious displays of wealth. But violence was also endemic in poorer areas such as the "jungle city" of Ajegunle or the rougher parts of Mushin, with armed robbery soaring despite increasingly harsh government measures including public executions. Pitched gun battles between police and bands of robbers became a regular occurrence in the industrial areas of Lagos. In the residential sections, it was not uncommon for armed gangs to descend on a block, cordon off the entire area, and systematically loot and pillage each home while police and soldiers remained conveniently unavailable. Police or army collusion in these raids was not uncommon; the surge in violent crime was often linked to the prevalence of weapons following the civil war.[12] And foreigners visiting Lagos were advised to keep their arms inside vehicle windows while stuck in go-slows, lest their limbs be macheted off by street criminals on the prowl for rings, bracelets, and watches.[13] Nigeria had the world's worst road safety record, and its roads functioned as a metaphor for the entire nation and its difficulty in adhering to a vision of national unity, as drivers regularly and flagrantly disregarded basic traffic regulations such as one-way streets and stop signs.[14]

The continuing presence of the military became another highly contentious public issue at the turn of the decade. While President Gowon had emerged as a postwar hero, and while it was generally accepted that the military's presence had been critical in holding the nation together during the war, continued military rule was viewed with suspicion. Gowon argued that the country required the continuity of government in order to guarantee stability in the postwar oil-boom era, but this argument was counterbalanced by the public's vision of military men stuffing their pockets with the country's oil receipts. This image certainly fueled some of the more cynical, laissez-faire attitudes toward corruption among the general public. In any case, Gowon promised the nation that his regime would hand power over to a democratically elected civilian administration in 1976.

Despite these problems, Nigeria was at the peak of its power by the mid-1970s, and President Gowon scored several major symbolic victories for the nation. Besides chairing the Organization of African Unity in 1974, he was the primary catalyst behind the 1975 formation of the Economic Community of West African States (ECOWAS)—a supranational economic alliance of sixteen nations, largely established at Nigeria's initiative, and realizing to some degree Kwame Nkrumah's vision of Pan-African cooperation.[15] Around the same time, Nigeria was selected to host the second World Black and African Festival of Arts and Culture—known as FESTAC—a huge international festival scheduled for November 1975, devoted to the celebration of African and diasporic creative and intellectual arts. The first FESTAC had taken place in Senegal in 1966, and the decision to appoint Nigeria as the 1975 host was a clear indication of the country's status. If Nkrumah's charismatic leadership and progressive ideology, as well as his country's early independence, had made Ghana the political leader of sub-Saharan Africa during the 1960s, and if Senegal—as the continental torch-bearer of "Negritude" under Senghor—had been its cultural leader, Nigeria's enormous human resources, rich cultural heritage, and oil-derived economic power enabled it to usurp both roles during the 1970s.

In sync with the nation at large, Fela and Afrika 70 were riding the crest of their own success. This period was the group's commercial high point, as afrobeat had become overwhelmingly popular as the youth music of Nigeria. Fela maintained a fleet of cars and buses emblazoned with the Afrika 70 logo; the Shrine was packed to capacity nightly, and the band embarked on several nationwide stadium tours performing to tens of thousands of listeners at a time; and Afrika 70 was releasing six to ten top-selling LPs a year. The group's popularity also extended far beyond Nigeria's borders, throughout West Africa and beyond. In cities as far away as Accra, Douala, and Dakar, Fela's afrobeat was a rallying point for fellow musicians, urban dwellers, social rebels, and progressive students. Its popularity reflected the potent social resonance of his music and its broad impact among African youth. For those in urban Africa, afrobeat was a contemporary, cosmopolitan style that offered both enjoyment and symbolic protest against the residual strictures of colonial culture. For students and intellectuals, it offered a form of progressive, pro-black dissent from the prevailing climate of staid conformity and materialist acquisition, embracing a vision that was neither the materialism of the elite nor the spent cliches of the nationalist era. Political radicals related to Fela's rhetoric, with its overtones of Marxism and black power, while social rebels could relate to Fela's flouting of convention. And most everyone could relate to the fusion of highlife, funk, jazz, and traditional music at the root of the afrobeat style. With his fiery rhetoric and ready clenched-fist salute, Fela became a focal point for introducing the ideology, rhetoric, and symbols of African-American black power not only into Nigeria, but into West African popular culture in general. Nigeria's tolerance of Fela's music and image, though it would be severely tested and ultimately shattered, demonstrates that the country—then at the peak of its affluence and influence—was confident enough as a society to entertain the utterances of a socially critical musician without undue crisis.

Fela's music was not yet explicitly political in early 1974, but his impact on Nigerian society should nevertheless be understood in the context of the social, cultural, political, and economic upheavals of the period. He was one of the country's highest profile voices—from the Shrine stage, in the streets, and even through his own classified advertisement in the *Daily Times* entitled "Chief Priest Say," in which he offered acerbic, running commentary on a variety of public issues. During the floating cement debacle, for example, Fela quipped that as a result of the port backlog, it would be quicker to reach England by jumping from ship to ship than by flying[16]—a comment subsequently cited by both Lagos papers and international magazines in their profiles of Nigeria and its problems of modernization. Incidents such as this increased government sensitivity during a season in which Nigeria, despite its successes, had become the laughingstock of the world business community.

Moreover, the very sound of afrobeat, while championed by Nigeria's underclasses and progressives, offended the sensibility of its elite and sent an unsettling message to the country's military rulership. Blaring from record shops throughout Lagos, its stabbing horn lines, aggressive jazz solos, and irresistible rhythm—all united under Fela's coarse, hemp-smoked voice—came to be heard as the sound of rebellion itself. Even the sound of Africa 70 changed as the decade wore on, as the rough-edged "Afro-Rock" ramble of the early 1970s was gradually replaced by a deviously funky, slinkier sound suffused with attitude and marijuana. The Afrika Shrine was frequently host to the children of Nigeria's elite, to foreign diplomats and dignitaries, and to left-leaning political aspirants, dissident intellectuals, and radical students, which made the "Fela question" even more loaded. The authorities resented his lionization during a period when student unrest was rampant, there was general alarm about the rising use of marijuana, and faith in the country's leaders was waning.[17] John Collins reported: "Everywhere he goes, people stop what they are doing, shout his name, and give the black power salute. Once, at the Surulere football stadium in Lagos, he received an overwhelming ovation, greater than even the Head of State had received. Fela had a larger retinue, with scores of musicians, chorus girls, dancers, bodyguards, and wives accompanying him."[18]

Fela's regal comportment and the seriousness with which he (and his followers) embraced his deviant vision also irritated the authorities. Carlos Moore and Sylviane Kamara describe a typical "morning" at Fela's home:

> 3 P.M.: Fela Kuti, also known as the "King of afro-beat," the "Black President" wakes up. In white briefs, he leaves his poster and bill-plastered room and enters [the living room], a room with broken armchairs, dirty mattresses and jumbled sheets. One of his followers, whose only function is to serve Fela beverages, hands him a drink. Another man brings him a dish of rice, that being his only function. Fela has not even finished his first spoonful when a third man presents himself and opens a black box. Fela takes a joint out of the box; the joint is as thick as one's thumb and as long as one's hand. He makes himself comfortable, takes a drag, and man, now he's ready. Ready to start the day, a day which will only end at 6:00 A.M. the next day."[19]

Throughout the country, his popularity had reached unprecedented levels for a popular musician, with Fela also arguably more popular than any foreign musician. During a much-anticipated 1974 concert by Jamaican reggae singer Jimmy Cliff at the National Stadium in Lagos, for example, Fela was spotted entering the arena, and the concert ended prematurely as members of the crowd hoisted him on their shoulders and paraded him around the stadium.[20]

"Don't Worry about My Mouth-O": Social Criticism and Derisive Singing

Despite Fela's distance from social and musical norms, his forays into socially critical singing following his return from America in 1970 increasingly embodied a musical tradition nearly universal throughout sub-Sarahan Africa. To fully understand this, his work must be seen in light of the traditional West African musician's common roles as praise-singer, social critic, and oral historian. From his childhood, Fela had ample opportunity to experience these modes of music-making in Yorubaland and throughout Nigeria in general.

The famed *jalis* or *griots* of the Senegambia and Western Sahel (i.e., the countries of Senegal, Gambia, Mali, and Guinea) are the best-known exponents of a type of musical activity that is virtually universal throughout West Africa. A class of endogamous, court-based musicians usually in the employ of traditional rulers, jalis are often responsible for the preservation and transmission of oral histories, usually recited in musical form.[21] The jali may recount the historical saga of his people in the form of an epic song-poem, or he may recount the exploits of a particular family lineage or individual patron. In a more itinerant version of this social role, there are wandering musicians who travel the countryside, relating current events to villagers and offering verses of praise to individuals.[22] Throughout West Africa, these overlapping musical traditions continue today in both urban and rural settings. Like their traditional forebears, typified by the jalis, many contemporary musicians continue to sing the praises of the most powerful members of society—which, in addition to traditional rulers, now include politicians, religious leaders, soldiers, businessmen, and other people of prominence. Similarly, the wandering praise singer has persisted in contemporary life through the street musicians in modern urban centers like Dakar and Lagos, singing or drumming verses of praise for passersby. The marked emphasis throughout sub-Saharan Africa on social grace and decorum is embodied in the activity of the praise singer, whose virtuosity at improvised flattery enables him to turn any situation to his financial advantage.

The Yoruba, whose traditional rulers trace their ancestry to an apotheosized ancestor/cultural progenitor, have an especially strong history of arts patronage.[23] Much of this art served to glorify rulers or commemorate their images, and resulted in stunning artistic achievements such as the Ife and Owo bronzes, as well as a huge corpus of praise and divination poetry.[24] In music, praise singing is fundamental to neotraditional genres such as apala, sakara, and fuji, often accounting for the lion's share of the singing in both live and recorded performances. This particularly close historical relationship between artists and political rulers continues in contemporary life. In the nationalist period of the 1940s and 1950s, for example, popular juju musicians accompanied the gradual rise of the Yoruba elite in the march toward national independence.[25] During the 1960s, as the Biafran war decimated the multiethnic highlife scene in Lagos, juju gradually emerged as the dominant sound of the nation's most powerful city. Throughout Yorubaland in the 1970s, money flowed profusely at all-night ariyas, as the Yoruba elite, like other ethnic elites, celebrated and consolidated gains made since independence and intensified by the oil boom. No such occasion would be complete without a juju band offering verses of praise to the prestigious, affluent, and powerful in attendance, in exchange for currency "sprayed" (pasted) onto the perspiring forehead of the praise-singing musician. At juju nightclubs such as Ebenezer Obey's Miliki Spot or Sunny Ade's Ariya, or at the appearances of fuji musicians like Sikiru Ayinde Barrister or Wasiu Ayinde Barrister, the evening's inevitable highlight is the line of patrons dancing their way to the stage, awaiting their turn to shower currency upon the lead singer in appreciation of his improvised verses in praise of them.

In such a climate of pervasive patronage, explicit criticism of powerful figures is rare. Musicians seldom address political issues in their songs, and when they do, salient points tend to be expressed elliptically, refracted through the multiple possibilities of interpretation found in traditional oral poetry. Gary Stewart, writing about Ghanaian highlife singer Nana Ampadu, describes a characteristic approach. Ampadu's explanation could apply equally to Yoruba singers:

> Many of Ampadu's compositions . . . tell a story through the skillful use of metaphor. . . . "Okwaduo," [which] tells the story of a wild ox who tricks a hunter into releasing him, thus ensuring more severe treatment for the next to be caught, was widely believed to be about the members of the Nkrumah government, which had recently been overthrown. "Few of them were political," Ampadu slyly explains. "I just wouldn't say directly political, but the listeners would just refer to an incident that happened in the country and say: 'Look, you think this musician sang this song about this case?' But maybe that is not the real motive behind the composition."[26]

Praise singing sets up an inescapable duality in the social appraisal of musicians. On the one hand, they are lionized and venerated, since music is integral to a wide range of activities. On the other hand, they are derided as sycophantic beggars singing the praises of anyone willing to pay them. Among the Yoruba, most performing artists were habitually regarded as "vagabonds and beggars," at best necessary evils, regardless of their centrality to traditional culture.[27] In Senegal, the social marginality accorded griots meant they lived in enforced physical isolation from other social classes, and custom often forbade them to be buried in communal grounds after death. Rather, their bodies were left to decay in the open savannah.[28]

Roots of Abuse Singing

As fundamental as praising continues to be to much African music, there are occasions in which the general reluctance to criticize is suspended. As Kofi Agovi notes, the close integration of artistic and political activities not only served ruling interests, but also stimulated a large body of personally, socially, and politically critical art.[29] Thus, the musician's power to praise is accompanied by an ambivalently tolerated and rarely exercised social responsibility to offer critical social commentary. In extreme instances, the musician may also directly lampoon, insult, or otherwise verbally abuse a target. No one—including political leaders or other powerful persons—is exempt from this type of criticism. In the social dynamic of communal African societies, in which the awareness of one's social standing is acute and ever present, ridicule is relied upon heavily as a character-molding device, as well as a corrective remedy in the maintenance of social equilibrium.[30]

In addition to departure from social ideals, Isidore Okpewho identifies a number of other common motivations for criticism in music, including recreation, personal grievance, and professional competition.[31] On occasions such as the Avudwene festivals held among the Nzema of southwestern Ghana, for example, cooperatives of young male musicians operate as "instruments of public policy,"[32] explicitly articulating the grievances of the governed to those who govern and subjecting the ruling paramount chiefs to direct attack and insult in the form of satirical songs. The communally sanctioned boldness of these young musicians results from the belief that they are vehicles of ancestral sentiment mitigating against the abuse of power by ruling elders.[33] Among the Urhobo of southwestern Nigeria, by contrast, songs of explicit abuse and insult are composed for pure enjoyment among competing villages in the periodic Udje festival. Unlike the Nzema, criticisms in Udje poetry need not be rooted in fact; the goal, according to Okpewho, is "to use the resources of words, coupled with music, dance, and spectacle, in the most poetically effective way to do the utmost harm to the object of the attack." As the author notes, the viciousness of such attacks has recently been compromised by the threat of libel suits.[34]

Charles Keil, in his study of singing traditions among the Tiv of central Nigeria—a group noted for their skill at oral composition—broadly concludes that "the raising and lowering of status, including one's own, is every composer's stock in trade,"[35] an observation consistent with other studies of praise singers.[36] Keil's survey of Tiv composers provides insight into the varying individual motivations for abuse singing, as well as the changing institutions, patronage relationships, and economic conditions that support this tradition.[37] The career of Tiv composer Aneke Tire, for example, reflected shifting allegiances that themselves reflected shifting patronage relationships. During the nationalist period in Nigeria, Tire alternately praised and abused rival political parties during times of increased political activity, depending on the source of his income. On other occasions, he was hired by individual patrons to compose songs insulting personal enemies and rivals. Keil also chronicles a number of highly personal catalysts for careers in abuse singing. The composer Auta Anwuna gained fame throughout Tivland for his abusive songs directed at a politician who had earlier seduced his wife. According to Keil's informants, the politician's eventual death was widely attributed to the heartache and indignity caused him by Anwuna's songs. At the time of Keil's study, the composer Kuji Iyum had made a thirteen-year career of abuse songs directed at a former girlfriend and her subsequent lovers before being restrained by a court order. Similarly, the composer Jato Nyamikongo spent twenty years abusing a runaway wife in his songs.[38] The fact that all of these singers achieved wide-reaching notoriety despite highly personalized subject matter demonstrates the cherished place that abuse, insult, and derision often occupy in African oral arts.

These same qualities are plentiful in Fela's native Yoruba culture. Joel Adedeji's study of traditional Yoruba dramatic forms surveys the institutionalization of satire, derision, and burlesque and their centrality to even the most culturally profound rituals, in which they are used to "expose social evil and deviant behaviour."[39] The role of satire and burlesque is central to the performance of the Gelede, a masquerade danced to placate female elders of the community, and integral to a host of other festive occasions. Another example is the festival commemorating the divinity Orisa-Nla, in which Adedeji reports that "people flock around to listen to tales which reveal, in the open, certain obscure conducts of highly-placed citizens which call for reproach. Such people are ridiculed and abused, but their names are not mentioned."[40] In the Egungun masquerade rituals commemorating deceased ancestors, the dancer engages in a type of caricature including "a deliberate distortion of the mannerisms of certain individuals he uses as a target. . . . [The public] find out from him the latest bits of the locality, especially about deviant behaviour. . . . His form of entertainment brings a sense of relief to the mind of his listeners."[41] In the Orisa-Oke festival, satire takes the form of "obscene displays and utterances,"[42] while in the Okebadan festival, "Bands of people roam the town and are notorious for their licentious songs and sex display. . . . Many of the shouts and songs are stock phrases of ridicule and abuse. . . . Prominent people hardly escape their sarcasm or ridicule."[43] In Ibadan, the second-largest Yoruba city, the Baruwa troupe operate as professional satirists, hired to express personal grievances through slanderous song.[44]

Abuse singing is a common feature of contemporary popular music as well. Both Keil and Christopher Waterman cite abuse songs as a competitive strategy for aspiring musicians. This is also true of the most successful and established performers, and of the most commercial forms of popular music. As noted by Waterman, series of abusive songs have often been traded on successive recordings between Yoruba megastars; in the case of fuji stars Salawa Abeni and Ayinla Kollington, these represented actual, personal feuds as well as profitable publicity stunts that encouraged fans to purchase an entire series of recordings.[45] In Zaire, rival bandleaders Franco and Tabu Ley Rochereau were known to have a long-running feud despite their public civility toward each other; this only heightened the significance (and commercial impact) when they publicly declared a "peace pact" and recorded two best-selling albums together in 1983.[46] Clearly, the complex relationships among praise singing, abuse singing, and critical singing continue to inform the content of African popular arts on many levels.

Fela had already made a clear statement on the issue of praise singing on stage at the Shrine, where he physically avoided (sometimes to comical effect) audience members who attempted to climb onstage and paste currency onto his forehead. Obviously, a musician fashioning himself as an activist and champion of the poor could not participate in such ostentation. This in itself set Fela far apart from most other Yoruba popular musicians, a social distance that was graphically dramatized in early 1976 when armed robbers descended on a party at the University of Lagos at which both Afrika 70 and Sunny Ade's African Beats were performing; the robbers invaded Ade's ballroom while the Afrika 70 concert continued uninterrupted.[47] Fela would later characterize his position between the Nigerian haves and have-nots to a French journalist:

> I was driving and there was a wheel right in the middle of the road. I saw it but it was too late and I drove on it. The car broke down. It was about two a.m. Suddenly we were surrounded by about fifteen thieves. My friends shouted: "It's Fela, it's Fela!" After that, they stopped and I started the car. To tell the truth, I was not afraid. I don't think that any thief would hurt me in Nigeria. . . . Burglars would strip the other houses without coming to mine. I could see them carrying the plunder. That would happen nearly every night.[48]

Fela's contemporary articulation of the abuse-singer model could also be compared with the work of Yoruba playwright Hubert Ogunde (1916–1990), a founder of the modern Nigerian theater. Ogunde's satirical plays drew on the local Apidan and Alarinjo theatrical traditions, and his work often generated friction with the authorities. Ogunde was detained in 1945 by the colonial administration for his anti-British plays *Worse Than Crime* and *Strike and Hunger,* and again in 1950 for his play *Bread and Butter,* which dramatized the massacre of striking miners in the town of Enugu by colonial soldiers. In 1964, his most famous play, *Yoruba Ronu,* which satirized the machinations of Yoruba politicians following independence, was banned "for life" from being performed in the Western Region by Western Premier Samuel Akintola.[49] There was a clear continuity between the work of the two men; in fact, according to Frank Fairfax, it was Ogunde's young son who often danced as the shrouded "figure of death" on stage at Fela's Shrine.[50]

Despite Fela's populist orientation, some incidents nevertheless suggest deeper similarities between his motivations and those of other popular and traditional musicians. When he returned to Nigeria in 1970 after the group's American trip, for example, one of his first moves as his popularity rose was to publicly criticize the "colonial" orientation of Lagos juju and copyright musicians and their habit of adopting Western military and political titles as stage monikers (see Chapter 4). Another telling example is Fela's comments regarding former Ghanaian head of state Ignatius Acheampong. In 1972, he dedicated the *Open and Close* LP to "his Excellency Col. I. K. Acheampong, Ghana Head-of-State, the first head-of-state I ever entertained. It was beautiful." Fela's career was on the rise, and it was a mark of great status to count a head of state among one's audience, especially for a musician fashioning himself as a champion of the people. Later, however, after the Afrika 70 troupe had been deported from Ghana an action Fela attributed to Acheampong), Fela recalled the military coup that ousted the leader: "That

Acheampong motherfucker, who's dead now, got his ass kicked good by [subsequent head of state] Jerry Rawlings!"[51] It is unclear whether Fela's indirect praise of Rawlings was also motivated by the fact that the latter had in 1982 overturned Acheampong's 1977 order banning Fela from Ghana.[52] This is one instance of what Waterman calls "the Janus-faced relationship of praise and abuse."[53]

These varieties of cultural rhetoric fused with the political convictions Fela inherited from his family, his social milieu, and his foreign travel experiences. It was not surprising that a modern abuse singer should emerge from the politically radical Ransome-Kuti family, and Fela's mother stated emphatically on many occasions that she felt her son was continuing her radical legacy.[54] It was equally unsurprising that such a musician would emerge from the turbulent cultural matrix of Abeokuta. In another sense, however, Fela's public role belonged to a Lagos political tradition of urban populism and youthful irreverence for authority that had its roots in the political machinations of the nationalist era. He also clearly embraced Kwame Nkrumah's Marxist-derived tradition of targeting and mobilizing "youth" as a distinct segment of the urban proletariat.[55] A constant subtext in Fela's work is a belief in students and young people in general as the progressive vanguard of the nation; this would become especially clear with the formation of his own "youth action" group a few years later.

"Kalakuta Republic": The Rise of an African Subculture

I saw these African people coming off the plane in the Milan airport. They were mostly speaking an African language and they were wearing all the traditional jewelry, but they had jeans with holes in them, they all reeked of pot, and they had a city edge to them. They were cursing and causing a big ruckus in the airport. It was like a bunch of African hippies, unlike any African people I had ever seen. Then when I saw the instruments coming out, I realized—these were Fela's *people! Then it all made sense!*

JAY HOGGARD, *interview with author, July 1997*

The idea of "youth action," given a somewhat different spin, is particularly relevant to the subculture that coalesced around Fela's music, and is perhaps the most provocative element of his work in the mid-1970s. As much as traditional African life was the template upon which Fela fashioned his community, his version departed radically from the traditional models in a number of ways. Although he unquestionably ruled over his commune with an iron hand, an atmosphere of mischief and irreverence prevailed. The young people living at the communal house—often high school truants, artists, runaways, or just plain free spirits—freely smoked marijuana and used loud profanity in public areas, generally reveling in the increasing public scandal caused by their anti-establishment lifestyle.

By 1974, the lifestyle of Fela and his troupe became *the* popular scandal of Nigerian society. Tabloids abounded with sensationalized accounts of rampant drug use and promiscuity, and Fela's every move was the subject of intense scrutiny by the press. As Fela's popularity skyrocketed, his sense of the outrageous was increasingly reflected in his music, and he began to express his less conventional views in song with a frankness some listeners found shocking. The unrecorded "N.N.G." (for "Nigerian Natural Grass"—a play on the acronym used by the Nigerian Petroleum Corporation to advertise its product, "Nigerian Natural Gas") opposed the classification of marijuana as a "drug," advocating its use as a natural, beneficial product of African soil, and an effective means of dismantling the colonial mindset. Marijuana was clearly crucial to Fela's musical and social vision in a number of ways. Sonically, it was reflected in the loping, insistent patterns, whose hypnotic effect was similar to the Jamaican reggae of the same period (in the creation of which marijuana also played a integral role). At the Shrine, it fostered a sense of community, alternative reality, and intensified experience among attendants. In the larger social scheme, it was one practice through which Fela's subcultural community could enact its rebellious social vision.

These meanings were by no means shared by the larger society, in which marijuana smoking was not only generally looked down upon as a degenerate habit (synonymous with hard drug addiction and inevitably leading to moral depravity and mental insanity), but was also highly illegal—the penalty for possession of a single marijuana cigarette at the time was ten years imprisonment, and the penalty for cultivation was execution. In early 1975, the papers were filled with the stories of otherwise "respectable" citizens—a physician, a hotel stewardess, a community counselor, and a fifty-year-old traditional drummer, among others—all dealt ten-year prison sentences despite being found with as little as one half-smoked joint in their possession.[56] Although the draconian law was modified in late 1975, public opinion remained overwhelmingly negative on the issue, especially concerning the purported increase in hemp smoking among university and secondary school students.[57]

Fela's foregrounding of his own sexuality was also a mark of difference and dissent in decorum-conscious Nigerian society. The sexualization of his public persona was in some senses an inevitable result of his community's general vilification by the mainstream society, and also the degree to which he consciously highlighted the issue of sexuality But as common as it is for outlaw communities to be suspected of all sorts of deviance by the conformist public, Fela took deliberate steps to provoke the public. On stage, his undulating dancing style projected far more explicit eroticism than was the rule among popular singers in any style, and the Afrika 70 dancers, including Aduni Idowu, Funmilayo Onilere, Omolara Shosanya, and Najite Mokoro, presented highly eroticized solo dances.[58] A typical maneuver might involve a dancer bouncing around the stage on her haunches, thrusting her pelvis forward while gesturing outward with her hands as if she were ceremonially bestowing sex upon the audience. A dancer might feign intercourse by thrusting her hips against the floor while skittering about the stage on all fours, or might lift one leg high in the air while rotating her hips against an invisible partner. Another became legendary for the way in which she would allow her buttocks to vibrate rhythmically to the music while the rest of her body remained perfectly still. Fela sometimes carried this explicit sexuality to his songwriting. In "Going In and Out," he uses a crude metaphor of sexual intercourse to invert a biblical proverb on the nature of change:

FELA: Anywhere you enter you must come out again it's the law of god, you no fit change am . . .	*FELA:* Anywhere you enter, you must come out again it's the law of god, it cannot be changed . . .
To ba wonu yara lo wa tun jade ni	When you enter a room, you must come out again
To ba wo'nu ewon lo wa tun jade ni	When you enter prison, you must come out again
To ba wonu obinrin lo wa tun jade ni	When you enter a woman, you must come out again
To ba wo ibi kan lo to ba ri e mo	If you go into a place and you are not seen again,
Na so you go so	That means you're gone for real
CHORUS: O di gbere ni yen!	*CHORUS:* It's farewell for you!
FELA: Na die you die so	*FELA:* That means you've really died
CHORUS: O di gbere ni yen!	*CHORUS:* It's farewell for you!
FELA: You go rest in peace	*FELA:* You will rest in peace
CHORUS: O di gbere ni yen!	*CHORUS:* It's farewell for you!
FELA: O di oju ala o . . .	*FELA:* We'll only see you in our dreams . . .

"Na Poi" (1972/1975) demonstrates his willingness to sing about sex in the most graphic terms:

When man see woman, and him hold im hand	When a man sees a woman, and he holds her hand
and he carry am go him house,	and carries her inside of the house,
and he carry am inside room,	and carries her inside the room,
and he lock door	and locks the door
the thing wey dem dey do	the thing they do
behind the door wey dem lock—	behind the locked door—
Na Poi!	It's sex!
Fi sii	Put it in, please
Ibe ko lo fi si yen	That's not the right spot,
Sun mo waju die die	it's the wrong place
Move am forward, small-small	Move it forward—gently, gently

O di poi!	It's sex!
Fi ha!	Do it!
Shock am	Guide it in
Ma je o yo	Don't let it slide out
Ma ran mo . . .	Rub it in, please . . .

A newspaper review of "Na Poi" reflected the ambivalent public opinion of Fela, his music, and his image in Nigerian society:

> One has to admit, irrespective of one's opinion about Fela and his faults—there are many of them—that he is a very hard-working musician. It surely takes a dedicated artist to be turning out records at the rate Fela does. There are divided opinions over his ability at composing songs. . . . "Na Poi" will surely sound [like] a lot of meaningless and vulgar lyrics to some people. But to many others it is all about the lighter side of life reflecting [on] the relationship between man and woman.[59]

At the compound, crowds regularly thronged the gates, waiting for the moment late in the day when Fela would finally emerge, usually clad only in bikini briefs and surrounded by any number of his girlfriends—his tenor sax slung around his torso and a cigar-sized stick of Indian hemp in one hand. Seeming a simultaneous reaction to the residual rigidity of colonial culture and a deliberate deconstruction of his own strict upbringing, this sense of the outrageous extended into most areas of Fela's life, in which he adopted a "punk" approach—thumbing his nose at decorum and subverting the African popular musician's common role as arbiter of elegance, fashion, and social grace.[60] John Collins recalled Fela's reception of guests:

> Fela would often talk to his entourage while sitting on a toilet that adjoined the cushioned "session room" where he held court and entertained visitors. This alcove had no door, and . . . no curtain either. . . . When I went there the second time, he had put a thin curtain between the toilet and the session room so that you could only see his legs and knees; as a result of his growing international popularity, he was advised that some sort of partition was necessary because of the increasing number of foreign visitors who might be shocked.[61]

Like most countercultural movements, the Afrika 70 commune was vilified in mainstream society, characterized as an immoral den of drug-induced filth, depravity, criminality, and disrespect. One reader complained to the *Daily Times* that Fela

> has no regard for God and humanity. . . . I once watched Fela declare "My father died a foolish man. He was telling people to go to church." . . . The

late Rev. Ransome-Kuti is now resting with our Lord. How can a person defend a man who has neither respect for God nor his late father? The problem here is that this country has never been blessed with leaders who have moral conscience and who are interested in the morals of her citizens. In some civilized countries, a person like Fela will find himself in an asylum where qualified psychiatrists will look after him.[62]

In reality, life in the Afrika 70 compound only vaguely resembled what the authorities or tabloids presumed. Many observers have characterized the communal life there as highly organized and disciplined. Justin Labinjoh observed during his visits that "drug taking [marijuana smoking] was not as rampant as the general public perceived and sexual promiscuity [apart from Fela's own lifestyle] was non-existent."[63] Nevertheless, as creator of this homegrown counterculture, Fela displayed a highly provocative sense of the outrageous, guaranteed to test the boundaries of social and official tolerance in his conservative, decorum-conscious African society.

Even these controversial and unconventional elements of Fela's lifestyle and image were not entirely without precedent. As noted earlier, a sense of the burlesque often went hand-in-hand with a mission of social critique, dramatizing the trespass of social boundaries implied by the liberty of direct criticism. Marijuana smoking had also been a symbolic presence in an earlier phase of popular music—the highlife subgenre known as toye, which fused highlife and juju and took its name from local slang for marijuana.[64] The major toye exponent was Orlando Owoh, who began performing with his own band in the late 1960s using the moniker "Dr. Ganja." In a sense, Fela's work can be placed in a tradition of educated Lagos Yoruba musicians like Owoh, Julius Araba, and Ambrose Campbell who, by virtue of their education, could self-consciously combine the stereotypically carefree attitude of the palmwine musician with the studied discipline of the trained musician.[65] In Fela's radicalization of the highlife tradition, the stereotypical proclivities of the palmwine musician—musicmaking, womanizing, and palmwine drinking—were partially "modernized" with elements adopted from the American counterculture: marijuana smoking, funky music, and modern jazz, among other infusions.

These factors were instrumental in Fela's emergence as one of Africa's first bona fide countercultural heroes. Over time, a distinct, full-fledged subculture coalesced around him whose physical location was the communal house and whose ritual space was the Afrika Shrine. Its primary creative expression was afrobeat music and *yabis* (abusive joking), while its most prominent ritual practice was marijuana smoking. Its mode of communication was the pidgin English of the streets, infused with African-American slang, and its stated ideology was a mixture of Pan-Africanism and black power. In this mixture of progressive political sentiment and social rebellion, Fela offered a distinct social countervision in which, as Labinjoh notes, individuality and freedom of expression were valued as necessary prerequisites for innovation and development.[66]

This process had consequences beyond the confines of Fela's house. The Afrika 70 organization came to dominate the area between the communal house and the

Afrika Shrine, with Fela acting as a kind of paramount urban chief. Eyewitnesses recount that traffic on Agege Motor Road would be stopped nightly so that the entire Afrika 70 entourage, with Fela leading on a donkey, could cross en route to the Shrine while hundreds of passersby chanted his name.[67] Marijuana was smoked openly and publicly (Fela himself often smoked on stage at the Shrine), and as a general rule the police preferred to leave the commune members to themselves rather than risking a confrontation with "Fela's boys," as his street-tough bodyguards were known. The Afrika 70 commune also spawned a red-light district in which all sorts of activities flourished, including prostitution and marijuana peddling. This in itself was not notably different from other Lagos nightclubs, which were in particular havens for prostitution. As much as Fela attempted to banish prostitution from the confines of the Shrine (so that unaccompanied women could attend free of harassment), it remained an integral part of virtually all Lagos nightclubs. Fela was, in fact, a champion of area prostitutes and beggars, to whom he distributed hundreds of thousands of naira on a weekly basis.[68]

The excitement generated by the "Chief Priest" likely resulted not only from his music, but also the thrill of being on the edge of social mores and, sometimes, the law itself. This, along with his semi-nude public appearance, his expressed indulgence in habits considered degenerate, his embrace of street language and profanity, and even the alleged conditions of his home, positioned him as purveyor of a subversive social direction. One fan remembers: "Tell our parents we were going to the Shrine? No way! Everyone said it was a place where people on run from the law hung out, just criminals, hemp smokers, prostitutes, school dropouts, and people like that. . . . We went anyway because there were a lot of progressive things happening there, a lot of progressive people."[69]

In a broader sense, this aura of conflict surrounding the afrobeat subculture also reflects the role that a sense of risk, mischief, and even danger plays in fostering an atmosphere of excitement around a performance in traditional West African expressive culture. Just as the divinities commemorated in traditional ceremonies regularly engage in various forms of mischief and outright chicanery, the energy and excitement generated by these public events is often expressed in ritualized communal conflict.[70] Despite their deep cultural significance, for example, Yoruba masquerade performances such as Egungun or Gelede resist being simplistically interpreted as well-organized public performance events. Rather, the masquerade is the focal point of a fairly chaotic event in which the dancer careens impulsively and unpredictably across public spaces, sometimes placing spectators and even fellow performers at risk. As far away as Freetown, Sierra Leone, descendants of repatriated Yoruba slaves maintain traditional masking societies that play a unique role in the country's cultural landscape.[71] These societies are part of a distinct, mostly male subculture in which masquerading, traditional drumming, reggae music, and marijuana smoking comprise the main activities. As depicted by John Nunley in his 1987 study *Moving with the Face of the Devil,* the masking societies represent both the creative vanguard of urban Freetown and a threat to the civil authorities. Injury and violence often accompany processions, as masqueraders dart impulsively about crowded streets in costumes that include sharp quills (often dipped in poisons and other toxins) or jagged objects. Heated preperformance disputes between the societies and their patrons, as well as physical confrontations with the Freetown police, are considered essential to a successful performance. While the public has generally frowned upon government harassment of the societies and seizure of masquerade costumes (since the masquerade is considered a manifestation of an ancestral spirit), the authorities have viewed them as both a threat to civil order and a potential breeding ground for political radicalism. One society, for example, named itself "Civilian Rule"—a direct challenge to Sierra Leone's military government. The chaotic artistry of the Freetown societies permeates the artistic, spiritual, physical, and political spheres, leading to inevitable conflict with civil authorities. As Nunley notes, "Mistrust prevails on both sides. During the masked performances, societies support their patron, yet the affective experience they obtain extends beyond the political realm and into the religious and the sacred. Such ambiguity is not well-tolerated by governing institutions that rule by establishing clearly-defined roles, governing departments, and the black-and-white letter of the law."[72]

Fela's afrobeat subculture moved through Nigerian society of the 1970s with the same reckless trajectory as the Freetown masquerades. What it ultimately shared with the masking societies was the endeavor to revitalize traditionally rooted worldviews in the face of contemporary, conformist postcolonial culture and authoritarian political governance. Long after its demise, Fela would continue to refer wistfully to his commune as an "authentic" remnant of "Africa." Obviously, many of the freedoms enjoyed therein were impossible in traditional culture, characterized as it was by all sorts of strict social controls. Fela's comments reflect his idealization of the precolonial African past during a period of rapid transformation. His nonconformity and irreverent populism were organic responses to the dominant social climate in which, as Labinjoh theorizes, "the tension of acquisitiveness, generated by the capitalist ideology of development, had almost completely denied individuals a sense of identity and the possibility of self-fulfillment."[73]

"Everything Scatter"

Fela's presence in Nigeria was much more of a loaded issue than that of the masqueraders in Freetown. The critical factor that distinguished Fela from traditional socially critical musicians was the fact that as a popular artist working via mass media such as radio, television, and sound recording, he could impact society on a much broader level than his traditional forebears, whose impact was necessarily limited to their immediate surroundings. Ben Okri remembered of Fela in the 1970s that "so strong was his voice, his biting jibes and pokes, that a whole language of abuse came into existence."[74] Thus, the "Fela question" became increasingly loaded as the decade progressed. Regardless of their progressive appeal, the Afrika 70 community began to be targeted by the authorities for involvement in drug dealing, prostitution, and other forms of criminality. In addition to his outspokenness, Fela's real crime was the openness with which he flouted convention. His popularity and influence, his flagrant use of Indian hemp, and his open consorting with underage women made him an obvious target for official harassment.

There had been friction as early as 1971, when the Nigerian Broadcasting Corporation banned "Jeun K'Oku" because of its overt sexual references. In 1972, EMI refused to release "Why Black Man Dey Suffer," objecting to its anticolonialist content. (Later in the decade, Decca would similarly refuse to issue a rerecording of the song.) In the same year, Fela was involved in a dispute with S. B. Bakare, owner of Surulere Night Club, which ultimately involved the Lagos police; it is suspected that Bakare objected to the messages in Fela's songs.[75] In fact, it was rumored that a number of Fela's earliest abusive songs such as "Na Fight O," "Jeun K'oku," and "J'ehin J'ehin" were partially aimed at Bakare.

The friction with Bakare was a motivation for Afrika 70's 1972 relocation to the Empire Hotel. Shortly after the group's arrival, however, shows at the new venue were violently disrupted by hired thugs initially thought to be religious fanatics objecting to Fela's message and lifestyle. Mabinuori Kayode Idowu reports that on a number of occasions, these thugs would wreak havoc by spraying the Shrine dance floor with glass bottle fragments: "On several occasions, the Shrine would be swinging at night, when suddenly from nowhere, you just see broken bottles flying into the dance floor, causing the audience to run in pandemonium."[76]

These attacks began a protracted neighborhood siege between Fela's organization and the allegedly offended parties. Ultimately, according to Fela, it was not a moral difference but rather an extortion attempt that lay at the root of the conflict:

> Whenever we were attacked, we made sure we attacked them back. This time carrying the fight into their individual houses and homes. Bottles, stones, sticks, etc., were among the weapons used in this war of survival. It got to a point where I realized that these gangs were doing the attacks, with the hope that I would come and pay them protection money. But for that, them lie. I promised never to pay anybody protection money to play my music. If they want to fight it out, I am ready. In the end after almost a year and a half, we succeeded in subduing them.[77]

Regardless of the actual motivation for these attacks, the Shrine acquired a criminalized aura as a dangerous locale, and a precedent was set for using Fela's deviant behavior and outspoken opinions as a pretext for harassment. But if the gang violence accompanying the opening of the Afrika Shrine set a precedent for state-sponsored harassment of Fela, it also set a precedent for his own response. The street-tough bodyguards he surrounded himself with eventually dominated the neighborhood to such an extent that policemen were wary of persecuting them. Some have claimed that Fela's personal security force was such a formidable institution that it became a spawning ground for later organized crime gangs.

"Expensive Shit"

LAGOS, May 2–Quantities of Indian hemp were found in Afrobeat king Fela Ransome-Kuti's sitting room when his house was searched by the police on Tuesday. Fela and his colleagues will appear in court to

*answer charges of hemp peddling. Fela will also answer whatever
charges arise from the current probe into the circumstances in which 24
underage girls came to his premises.*

Daily Times, *May 2, 1974*

By mid-decade, besides routine surveillance of Fela's commune, Afrika 70 could count on agents from the Police Central Intelligence Division being represented in any audience, anywhere in the country. The first serious brush with the authorities came on April 30, 1974, when the Afrika 70 commune was raided by fifty heavily armed riot policemen, accompanied by tracking dogs, who claimed they were investigating reports of "hemp peddling, drug addiction, and underage girls on the premises."[78] Fela was arrested on suspicion of possessing Indian hemp and, along with the roughly sixty occupants of the house, was jailed at Alagbon Close prison in Lagos. Although most of those imprisoned were released the following morning (the group was about to leave for a tour of Cameroun), the police returned the following evening on a second surprise raid. This second raid set the precedent for a pattern of interrupting Fela's attempts to spread his music beyond Nigeria, which would continue throughout the rest of his career. The house was clean but the police—determined to lock Fela away for a long time—brought a stick of hemp themselves to plant. Fela was able to grab and swallow the stick, causing the police to detain him in a prison cell until he passed the incriminating evidence. With the help of his cellmates (and his mother, who smuggled him fresh vegetables to help cleanse his bowels), he was secretly able to use the communal toilet at night while the prison guards slept. When, on the third day, he finally agreed to provide a "specimen" for his captors, his stool was clean:

> Ooh, see the commotion in the police station, man! "Fela wants to shit!" Helter-skelter! Everybody looking for chamber pot—policeman, orderly, constable, everyone! They all want Fela's shit! They took me to the backyard, put the chamber pot under my yansch [behind]. I shit. When I look at my shit, man, it was clean like a baby's shit. Clean! That's how I got myself out of that shit that time, man. The motherfuckers couldn't charge me for any fucking thing. No evidence!"[79]

Upon his release, Fela composed two songs, both directly inspired by his prison experience. In "Expensive Shit," Fela gets the last laugh on his captors in this humiliating account of their desire to obtain his stool:

FELA: Obo na monkey, for Yorubaland (repeat)	*FELA:* "Obo" means monkey in Yorubaland (repeat)
Him go bend him yansch, he go shit	He bends his behind and shits
He go comot away from the shit	He goes away from the shit
The shit be the last thing wey he go like to see—	The shit is the last thing he would like to see—

Because why-o?	Why?
CHORUS: Because the shit de smell!	*CHORUS:* Because the shit smells!
FELA: Me I be Fela, I be black power man (repeat)	*FELA:* Me I'm Fela, I believe in Black Power (repeat)
I go bend my yansch, I go shit	I bend my behind and shit
I go comot away from the shit	I come away from the shit
The shit be the last thing wey I go like to see—	The shit is the last thing I would like to see—
No be so for some fools wey I know!	But it's not the same for some fools that I know!
No be so for some stupid people I know!	It's not the same for some stupid people I know!

Fela's first encounter with Nigeria's criminal justice system was brief in comparison to others, such as Malcolm X, who experienced prison as a catalyst for politicization. Nevertheless, it was a conversion experience of sorts, bolstering his embrace of revolutionary rhetoric and reawakening latent anti-authoritarian tendencies:

> That first time [in jail], it's a funny feeling. . . . You know how people are brought up thinking that jail is just for criminals, man. For people who've "gone against society." . . . But after they put me in that cell with the people they call "criminals," I started thinking: "who the fuck is Society? Who jails Society when it does horrors to people? . . . I used to think prisoners were criminals until that day. Inside there I found guys who were also looking for a better life.[80]

The charges were later dropped due to inconsistencies in the police account,[81] but the experience influenced a substantive change in Fela's music. Broadening his subject matter beyond his usual sociocultural critiques, he began to directly question the Nigerian political establishment and its agents of "law and order." "Alagbon Close," also composed in response to the police attack, directly addresses brutality, corruption, and civil rights abuses by policemen and soldiers, while challenging the basis of their authority:

For Alagbon,	In Alagbon
Dem go point dem gun for your face	They point their guns in your face
the gun wey dem take your money to buy	The guns which they have taken your taxes to buy
Dem go torture you and take your statement from you	They torture you and take your statement from you
Dem dey call am investigation	They call it an "investigation"

If you know dem for Alagbon	If you know them at Alagbon,
Make you tell them, make them hear	Tell them so they can hear
Uniform na cloth, na tailor dey sew am	A uniform is cloth, sewn by a tailor
Tailor dey sew am like my dress	A tailor sewed it, like my clothing
Tailor dey sew am like your dress	A tailor sewed it, like your clothing
Nothing special about uniform . . .	Nothing is special about a uniform . . .

It was thus during 1974 that Fela began to assume the confrontational posture in his music for which he has since become renowned. On stage, as Randall Grass observed, "his lips pouted petulantly, his jaw was thrust out defiantly . . . his every gesture proclaimed a defiance and assertion of self that would not be appropriate in traditional African music."[82] Even on a purely instrumental level, "Expensive Shit" and "Alagbon Close" convey—through their fleet up-tempo patterns and whiplash call-and-response structures—Fela's outrage in no uncertain terms, dispensing with the remaining highlife stylizations, and replacing them with a tougher, tighter ensemble sound.

This approach extended to the artwork that adorned Afrika 70's releases, which alternately flaunted Fela's rebellious lifestyle or condemned the authorities through damning photographs by Afrika 70 photographer Femi Bankole Osunla and garish cartoon caricatures by Ghariokwu Lemi, Kenny Adamson, Maxo-Max-Amoh, Okanlawan Banjoko, Ajao Bello, Frances Kuboye, Boniface Okafor, Remi Olowookere, and Tunde Orimogunje. These young artists' work carried as much punch as the music itself. Osunla's photos depicted government violence against innocent civilians, while the cartoonists brutally deconstructed the Europhile affectations of the country's rulers, replacing them with barbaric, animalistic depictions and gross caricatures. The front cover of the *Expensive Shit* LP featured Fela and twenty women standing bare-chested on the compound grounds, their fists raised defiantly in the black power salute, while the back cover contained hazy photographs of a semi-nude Fela lazily reclined on a giant bed, exhaling clouds of marijuana smoke. In addition to photographs showing Fela relaxing behind the compound's newly installed barbed-wire fence, the cover of *Alagbon Close* featured Lemi's grossly distorted caricatures of barbaric policeman brutalizing pregnant women and briefcase-carrying professionals. Other covers featured evil-eyed religious figures clutching bags of currency; corrupt judges accepting bribes from businessmen; or obese, wealthy businessmen driving their limousines over the backs of gasping, emaciated masses.[83]

The growing tension between Fela and the authorities, and the dangers he was courting by this point in his career, were reflected in two significant lifestyle changes he enacted during 1975. He dropped the English "Ransome" from his name, dismissing it as a slave name, and replaced it with "Anikulapo"—Yoruba for "he who carries death in his pouch." The choice of name reflected Fela's budding interest in traditional mysticism as a means of physical protection from the authorities, an interest that would grow in later years.[84] In a quite unusual departure from tradition, Fela's mother followed suit, adopting "Anikulapo" in place of her late husband's name—a clear statement of solidarity demonstrating that Fela had come a long way from when he was regarded as the black sheep of the Ransome-Kuti family. But it also conformed to Mrs. Kuti's own longstanding sentiments, since she had dropped her own English names decades previously and insisted that her pupils in Abeokuta use their African rather than European names.[85]

Fela also renamed his communal compound "Kalakuta Republic," proclaiming it an autonomous zone free from the laws and jurisdiction of Nigeria and open to people of African descent worldwide—especially to all persecuted Africans. To drive the point home, he erected a barbed-wire fence around the compound.

He explained the significance of the new name to John Collins:

> It was when I was in a police cell at the C.I.D. [Central Intelligence Division] headquarters in Lagos; the cell I was in was named "The Kalakuta Republic" by the prisoners. I found out when I went to East Africa that "Kalakuta" is a Swahili word that means "rascal." So, if rascality is going to get us what we want, we will use it; because we are dealing with corrupt people, we have to be "rascally" with them.[86]

The newly fortified Kalakuta Republic was fairly self-sufficient, with farm animals, a free health clinic, and facilities for rehearsing and recording. Fela's declaration of Kalakuta's independence was a symbolic act calculated to express his dissent from the prevailing climate; in no realistic sense could his Kalakuta be seriously considered an independent "republic." Nevertheless, as a popular symbol, it was an affront to the country's rulers. The secessionist Biafran war was still fresh in the national memory, and the authorities were uncomfortable with the way Fela's interpretation of Pan-Africanism was linked to a vocal disregard for the nation-state idea at a time when national sensitivity to the question of ethnicity and national unity still ran high. Further, Fela wielded a huge amount of influence among Nigeria's youth, and the Shrine was increasingly a rallying point for disaffected intellectuals, student activists, and left-leaning political aspirants. After a major police raid on the Afrika 70 retinue following a concert in the town of Ilorin, for example, five hundred students from Kwara State College of Technology were expelled for their violent protests against the treatment of Fela and his organization at the hands of the police.[87] The authorities responded with further harassment, on one occasion even trailing the Afrika 70 entourage into neighboring Cameroun and arresting them in Douala, where they had traveled for a concert.[88]

"Kalakuta Show"

LAGOS, November 25—Afrobeat king, Fela Ransome-Kuti, has been admitted into Lagos University Teaching Hospital for injuries he received when anti-riot policemen were called into his home at 14A

*Agege Motor Road on Saturday morning. Fela was reported to have
refused entry into his barbed-wire fenced home to plainclothes
policemen who had come for a "routine search." Saturday's search was
the third to be conducted at Fela's house by the police during the last
six months.*

Daily Times, *November 25, 1974*

Back in Lagos, the next major police raid on Fela's house took place on November 23, 1974. On that occasion, anti-riot police raided the commune on the pretext that an underage girl living in the compound had been kidnaped by Fela. Although the girl refused to cooperate, the police—armed with tear gas and axes—cut down the fence, stormed the house, and brutalized the occupants, including Fela, who was hospitalized for seventeen days as a result of his injuries.[89] John Collins was visiting Fela at the time, along with the members of the Ghanaian groups Basa Basa and Bunzu Sounds, and reported:

The very first morning we were there, Fela's place, which is opposite the Shrine, was attacked by about sixty riot police with tear gas. They were looking for a girl they claimed had been abducted (being so near, we too were gassed). . . . When he did return, it was in style. . . . He was accompanied by about ten-thousand people from the court in Lagos to the Shrine, played there that very night, and helped us with our recordings the next day.[90]

The brutality of this attack drew outcries and demands of a probe from, among others, the University of Ife Student Union, the National Union of Nigerian Musicians, and even the government-owned *Daily Times*.[91] Fela himself chose to channel his rage and personal turmoil directly into his art. Relating the experience in 1975's best-selling *Kalakuta Show* LP, he continued to use his personal experiences as basis for his social critiques. This time the record jacket also featured photographs of the police raid and the head wounds Fela sustained. Again, he was able to depict himself as victimized hero, and the authorities as repressive thugs. Musically, *Kalakuta Show* finds Fela and Afrika 70 at the height of their Afro-funk powers, with Fela's tenor sax mocking and squealing over a rhythm guitar figure that slashes through a tightly woven fabric of Allen's stuttering trap drums and Kofi's rolling traditional congas. The song "Kalakuta Show"—like "Expensive Shit," "Gentleman," "Upside Down," "Yellow Fever," "Equalisation of Trouser and Pant," and "Alagbon Close"—is one of Fela's most successful fusions of James Brown–styled funk and West African highlife. By 1977, Larry Birnbaum would remark in the American *Down Beat* jazz magazine that "Fela has risen from jazz-loving student to musical idol and now political martyr. His sound, once considered too sophisticated to sell at home, has evolved from heavy-handed imitation to powerful originality, an amalgam of African and Western styles that rocks with a vigor unsurpassed in American or Caribbean idioms."[92]

Ramatism

In his October 1974 Independence Day address, Gowon postponed his government's promised transition to civilian rule by 1976. By mid-1975, both public dissatisfaction with the Gowon regime and the demand for civilian rule had reached a fever pitch. As always, the nation's campuses were a bellwether for the national psyche; all across the country, campuses were rocked by riots as students demanded a return to civilian rule by 1976 and the immediate formation of a civilian constitution drafting committee.[93] The national press was also vigorous in its criticism of continued military rule, corruption, skyrocketing inflation, mismanagement, and the lack of adequate preparations for FESTAC, scheduled to take place in November 1975. Thus, despite Gowon's ECOWAS and FESTAC triumphs, a sense of relief and renewed possibility was felt throughout the country when General Murtala Mohammed assumed power in a bloodless coup in July 1975, while Gowon was away attending a meeting of the Organization of African Unity (OAU) in Kampala, Uganda.

During the first months of his presidency, Mohammed seemed to make headway against the country's problems, seizing the moment and endearing himself to the Nigerian public despite his continuation of the military rule. Building his cabinet around a coterie of prominent civil war veterans including Olusegun Obasanjo, Mohammedu Buhari, and Ibrahim Babangida (all of whom would succeed him, in turn, as military heads of state), Mohammed promised to sweep away corrupt officials and straighten out the bureaucratic tangle that was strangling the country, He also promised to hand power over to a civilian government in 1979. He canceled the results of the much-disputed 1973 census and postponed FESTAC until 1977, declaring that preparations were inadequate and that the nation had higher priorities at the moment. He reorganized the Ports Authority, treating the port congestion as a military exercise and clearing it in a matter of months. He not only retired corrupt military governors and civil servants, but fired corrupt officials (or "deadwoods," as they were known) by the thousands throughout the country. More ominously, Mohammed also considered executing corrupt officials and took tentative steps toward deactivating sections of Nigeria's huge postwar military.[94]

Almost immediately upon assuming office, Mohammed declared that his administration was essentially a corrective one with no specific ideology—partly honest admission but also a calculated move intended to downplay the country's close economic ties to the capitalist West and emphasize its nonaligned status. His focus on self-determination and implicit anti-Americanism endeared him to the Nigerian public, although the ideological vacuum (which was reiterated by the subsequent regime) ultimately created the conditions for what John Darnton observed as "capitalism in its rawest form."[95] During and even after Mohammed's reign, this vacuum was filled by a philosophy that came to be known as "Ramatism," which—taking its cues from Marxism and Maoism—aspired to the pantheon of personality-generated (and personality-glorifying) African political philosophies such as "Nkrumahism" (Kwame Nkrumah), "Awolowoism" (Obafemi Awolowo), and "Zikism" (Nnamidi Azikiwe). Ultimately, Ramatism was a simple celebration of the fact that Mohammed (whose middle name was Ramat) was able to inspire cooperation and efficiency among the nation's diverse citizens.[96]

Under the General's leadership, Nigeria adopted a much more aggressive profile in Africa and toward the Western powers. This was reflected, for instance, in the harsh press criticism directed toward the United States and President Gerald Ford on the issue of Angola, which had recently become the focus of another Cold War standoff between the Americans and the Soviet Union. It was also reflected in the government's aggressive stance toward the apartheid regime in South Africa, which, it loudly proclaimed, was strongly supported by American interests despite international anti-apartheid sentiment and United Nations resolutions. In fact, the eventual establishment in 1976 of the Nigerian Atomic Energy Commission was motivated in part by the desire to challenge South Africa, which was also developing nuclear capability, with what became popularly known as the "Black Bomb." Nigeria was also embroiled in an ongoing dispute with the British government to recover a number of prized antiquities, including a carved mask which had been designated the symbol of FESTAC, but which had been seized by the British during a "punitive" raid against the Benin Kingdom in 1897 and subsequently housed in the British Museum.[97]

This national mood of military, racial, economic, and cultural pride continued even after Mohammed's presidency, reaching a peak in mid-1976 when Israeli commandos conducted a raid on Uganda's Entebbe Airport to free Israeli citizens on a plane hijacked by Palestinian terrorists and forced to land in the Ugandan capitol of Kampala. In the eyes of many Africans, this was a flagrant violation of African soil and sovereignty, and for months tension mounted between Uganda (then under the stridently anti-Western rule of President Idi Amin, who had also recently expelled all Asians from his country) and neighboring Kenya, which had allegedly allowed the Israeli planes to refuel on its soil.[98] These tensions reached a critical point when it was revealed that Kenya was receiving arms from both the United States and Britain to forestall a potential Ugandan military reprisal. Nigeria was the most vocal African nation in the face of these events, ultimately leading a protest withdrawal of African and Arab countries from the 1976 Olympic Games in Montreal.[99] When the Nigerian government—following an OAU emergency meeting on the Angolan situation—publicly advised U.S. Secretary of State Henry Kissinger that he should cancel the Lagos leg of his scheduled African visit, it was clear that the country had designated itself the African nation most willing to stand up to the Western powers. One editorial noted that

> with regard to African-American relations, it would require more than frequent shuttling by a U.S. Secretary of State, before mutually satisfactory relations are established. . . . All through the period of nationalist struggle against Portuguese colonialism, the U.S., for reasons best known to her, made common cause with Portugal which was generously supplied with military weapons. . . . The U.S. has always found

devious means to support the white minority regimes in Zimbabwe and in apartheid South Africa. Dr. Kissinger does not have to jet from Washington to selected African capitols, merely to reiterate America's double-faced policy of giving support to white minority regimes, while at the same time pretending to sympathise with Africa's yearning for freedom.[100]

Given the precarious state of Nigeria's own internal affairs, it is difficult to distinguish which of these actions represented substantive advances, and which were more or less pure rhetoric. But it is clear that the country was flying high on the tide of its affluence and influence. Even the ever-critical Fela had thrown his support behind Mohammed, through his public comments and in his "Chief Priest Say" classified ads.[101] He told John Collins: "I'm very cool with this government. We feel that we are going to progress now because this government sees the sense of having a change. So we are with them."[102]

This era of Nigerian optimism and idealism was abruptly shattered by Mohammed's assassination in an abortive coup on February 13, 1976. The General had taken pride in his austere lifestyle, which often included driving himself to work in his own car, without personal security; ironically, his assassination took place while his car was stuck in a Lagos go-slow.[103] The coup directive was eventually traced to the deposed General Gowon (exiled in Britain) and was carried out by Lieutenant Colonel B. S. Dimka, a senior military officer related to the former head of state by both marriage and ethnicity.[104] Dimka's stated goals were to return Gowon to power, as well as to reinstate the military governors dismissed by Mohammed. Within hours of the assassination, students had stormed the British and American embassies in Lagos, violently protesting those countries' alleged involvement in the attempt to restore Gowon to power.[105] Uncharacteristically in sync with official sentiments, Fela issued a statement bemoaning Mohammed's death, and he even performed a day of "mournful music" at the National Stadium on the last day of the official mourning period.[106] Mohammed's successor, General Olusegun Obasanjo, pledged to continue the progress of his predecessor, but he immediately moved to establish closer ties with the West, enjoying a cordial relationship with U.S. president Jimmy Carter.

Obasanjo pledged to continue a program of officially encouraged cultural awareness and revitalization. This process, which had been delayed since independence by the Civil War, resurfaced with a new urgency in the months leading to FESTAC, as Nigeria consolidated its leadership role in black Africa. The media during this time was a lively forum for public discussion and debate of various cultural issues. Was skin bleaching an acceptable practice? How could gender relations be adjusted to contemporary life? What were the true merits of indigenous medicine? Was nudity in traditional life "cultural," "primitive," or pornographic? Were native chewing sticks preferable to Western toothbrushes? Was scarification cosmetic enhancement or disfiguration? The government also formed the National Policy Development Center, the first national think tank devoted to the discussion of pressing political and economic issues.[107] Outside of the official sphere, however, it was Fela's music that engaged these issues in the most direct and visceral way. The period between Mohammed's coup and FESTAC, with its strong public emphasis on issues of culture, was the perfect setting for Fela's message of African cultural pride and revitalization.

A temporary respite from official harassment allowed Fela and Afrika 70 to concentrate on their art to an unprecedented degree. Fela also benefited from the connections of his mother, who still wielded enough influence in political circles to help him avoid criminal convictions. Another guardian angel appeared in the person of M. D. Yusufu, who had been appointed Inspector-General of Police by General Mohammed. Like his boss, Yusufu brought a decidedly humanist bent to his job, at times not even bothering to wear a uniform while on duty.[108] Forcefully advancing the position that Fela was an artist and not a criminal, Yusufu restrained the police from harassing Kalakuta. Free of these disruptions, Fela and Afrika 70 entered their most intense and productive stretch of music-making. They signed on with Decca (despite the company's initial misgivings about Fela's reputation as a trouble-maker)[109]—the major recording company in the region—and began releasing records through their Afrodosia imprint. Afrika 70 headlined a huge, all-night festival concert at the Lagos State Sports Stadium in late 1975 that also featured Afro-Cult Express (from England), War Head Constriction, Perry Ernest's Afro Vibrations, and films of the Jackson 5, Marvin Gaye, Eddie Kendricks, and Stevie Wonder. Plans were made for a major film biography and soundtrack of Fela's life called *The Black President,* to be coproduced by Fela's old Ghanaian business associate Faisal Helwani and Ghanaian filmmaker Alex Oduro.

The music recorded by Fela and Afrika 70 between 1975 and 1977 is their most focused, cohesive, and incisive work, and Fela's continued explorations of social and political themes are decidedly more pointed in this period. The issues raised in these songs encapsulate the postcolonial African dilemma: the hegemony of Western attitudes, products, and cultural practices over indigenous ones; infrastructural disorganization; local and global power relations; and the cultural allegiance of an increasingly remote and economically insular elite class. His talent lay in his ability to articulate these complex issues using the language and humor of the streets.

"Confusion," "Upside Down," and "No Buredi" use the infrastructural disorder of West Africa as a point of departure for explorations of global power imbalances. "Confusion" uses the traffic problems of Lagos and the variety of national currencies throughout West Africa as metaphors for larger problems of African cultural unity and economic division, legacies of the colonial era:

Dem be three men wey sell for roadside-o	There are three men selling at the roadside
Dem three speak different language-o	The three speak different languages
Dem speak Lagos, Accra, and Conakry	They speak Lagos, Accra [Ghana], and Conakry [Guinea] dialects

One white man come pay them money-o	One white man comes and pays them money
He pay them for pounds, dollars and French money	Paying them in pounds, dollars and francs
For the thing wey he go buy from them	For the thing which he bought from them
He remain for them to share am-o	He remains while they try to make sense of the various currencies
Me I say, na confusion be that . . .	Me, I say that's confusion . . .

"Upside Down"—composed by Fela but sung by his African-American mentor Sandra (Smith) Iszadore, who visited Nigeria in 1976—compares Nigeria's civil chaos with the order experienced in Western countries:

For overseas, where I see	Overseas, I see
Communication organise	Communications are organized
Agriculture organize	Agriculture is organized
Education organize	Education is organized
Electric organize . . .	Electric is organized . . .
For Africa my house I don see,	In Africa my home, I see
Communication disorganize	Communications disorganized
Agriculture disorganize	Agriculture disorganized
Education disorganize	Education disorganized
Electric disorganize . . .	Electricity disorganized . . .

"No Buredi (Bread)" discusses the rampant poverty of African life, despite the continent's wealth of natural resources:

Land boku from north to south	Land is plentiful from north to south
Food boku from top to down	Food is plentiful from top to bottom
Gold dey underground like water	The gold in the ground is plentiful as water
Diamond dey underground like sand	The diamonds are as plentiful as sand
Oil dey flow underground like river	Oil flows underground like rivers
Everything for overseas, na from here him dey come	Everything abroad comes from here

Na for here man still dey carry shit for head	But here men still carry shit on their heads
Na for here we know the thing dem dey call	Here we know the thing called
"No Buredi . . ."	"No bread (money) . . ."[110]

A number of songs vilify the ostentation and unbridled material accumulation of the Nigerian elite and ruling classes. "Noise for Vendor Mouth" describes the street-level gang violence resulting from elite political rivalries, while both "Don't Make Ganran Ganran" (Don't Brag Like a Big Man to Me) and "Before I Jump Like Monkey, Give Me Banana" condemn the ostentatious, obnoxious behavior of the Lagos nouveau-riche elite. Other songs are more proverbial in tone, offering social and political critiques from a more traditionally oblique, poetic stance. "Unnecessary Begging" is a fable with a clearly revolutionary message promising retribution for injustice:

Everyday, everyday, I dey hungry	Everyday I am hungry
Everyday, everyday, no house to stay	Everyday, I have no place to live
Monkey dey work, baboon dey chop	The monkey works, the baboon eats
Baboon dey hold the key of store	The baboon holds the key of the store
Monkey dey cry, baboon dey laugh	The monkey cries, the baboon laughs
The day monkey eye come open now—	The day the monkey's eyes open—
Baboon dey vex	The baboon worries
Monkey refuse to work	Monkey refuses to work
Baboon dey vex and craze	Baboon worries and becomes agitated
Then he start to beg and beg—	Then he starts to beg and beg—
Unnecessary begging, as we dey call am for area . . .	That is unnecessary begging, as we call it in this area . . .

One of Fela's most popular tracks, "Water No Get Enemy" uses the flowing motion of water as a metaphor for the natural "flow" of society, emphasizing the importance of harmonious interaction:

> *FELA:* T'o be fe lo we omi l'o ma'lo
> If you want to wash, na water you go use
> T'o ba fe s'ebe omi l'o ma'lo
> If you want cook soup, na water you go use
> T'o ri ba n'gbona o omi l'ero re
> If your head dey hot, na water go cool am

T'omo ba n'dagba omi l'o ma'lo
If your child de grow, na water he go use
T'omi ba p'omo e o omi na lo ma lo
If water kill your child, na water you go use
Omi o l'ota o (nothing without water)

CHORUS: Water, him no get enemy

FELA: If you fight am unless you go wan die . . .
You don't fight him unless you want to die . . .

Even such oblique imagery carried political undertones. As Yomi Gbolagunte notes, "What he was saying in that song was that the society has a natural flow to it, and the government must go with that flow. If they refuse, the results can be disastrous. He was saying the government and the people must work together."[111]

Second World Black and African Festival of Arts and Culture

FESTAC . . . A rip-off! Corruption left and right! . . . FESTAC was just one big hustle, so a whole lot of military men and useless politicians could fill their pockets. . . . I didn't go to that thing-o! I stayed at the Shrine and made my "counter-FESTAC" there! All the big musicians and artists FESTAC brought in wanted to see me, man. For one whole month man, every night, Shrine was packed with blacks from all over the world. And since they wanted to know what was happening in Nigeria, I told them. I used the stage at Shrine to denounce all of the shit and corruption of that government which had invited them. That one they never forgave-o. . . . I didn't know my resigning would cause so much shit.

FELA quoted in MOORE 1982:137

Murtala Mohammed's assassination had plunged Nigeria into a fit of self-doubt, and the outside world wondered if the "giant" of sub-Saharan Africa would be able to withstand the economic and political instability plaguing the rest of the continent. However, FESTAC provided another important chance for the country to consolidate its economic and cultural leadership of black Africa. The largest Afrocentric cultural exhibition ever staged, FESTAC brought together thousands of scholars and performing artists from fifty-five countries throughout Africa and the African diaspora for one full month of concerts, dance exhibitions, poetry readings, colloquia, and dramatic presentations. The importance the Nigerian government attached to the event was reflected in the amount of money spent—the festival ultimately cost over 140 million naira (the naira was roughly on a par with the U.S. dollar at the time),[112] with 45 million alone spent on the showpiece National Theatre, which the government touted as "a symbol of our cultural awareness."[113] The political significance the government attached to the event was reflected in its open invitation to all African liberation movements.[114]

The Nigerian government clearly wanted to showcase Fela, the country's most popular musician. Not only was he invited to perform, the Mohammed government panel in charge of planning the event solicited his input. However, relations between Fela and the panel soured under the Obasanjo administration. The organizing committee rejected his list of recommendations for the festival, and he ultimately withdrew after a string of highly publicized accusations and counter-accusations in the national press. Fela publicly questioned the choice of a military general to organize a cultural event and claimed the government refused to allow him to perform with his own band. The army general in charge of planning claimed that Fela withdrew after the government refused his demand that they purchase new equipment for his band.[115] What was clear was that Fela was just one of a number of prominent Nigerian artists and intellectuals (including Herbert Ogunde and Wole Soyinka) who complained of the rampant corruption, poor organization, and lack of opportunities for participation by the Nigerian public. One reviewer noted: "What was unfortunate in the context of the historical importance of FESTAC, was that so many radical Nigerians pulled out. . . . With entrance tickets to almost all FESTAC events at first costing three naira . . . an unacceptably elitist debarment, most Lagosians felt excluded from their own festival, and became increasingly resentful as the millions of their tax money seemed to be frittered away on bare breasts and war dances."[116]

In its planning stages, FESTAC had already been dogged by an ongoing public debate about its feasibility and relevance. Critiques of the festival ranged from pragmatic protests that it was merely a multimillion-naira government "ego-trip" and that the money would be better spent on pressing concerns such as health and education, to the "colonial" critiques which held that the festival—with its bare breasts, chants, and traditional drummers—would merely present a "primitive" view of African culture confirming the negative stereotypes of the wider world.[117] At various times, the governments of both Guinea and Senegal threatened to withdraw their countries' participation due to disputes with Nigeria about the planning of the festival.[118] Chief Anthony Enahoro, former president of the festival committee under President Gowon, was under arrest for corruption and "abuse of office."[119] Now, with the country's leading musician publicly critical, the Fela flap was yet another embarrassment to a government obsessed with the festival's international prestige value. These tensions seemed to have simmered for quite some time before erupting into open conflict. When British music professor Ian Hall attended a FESTAC planning reception at the National Museum in 1973 (at which Afrika 70 was providing the musical entertainment), he witnessed an incident that probably says much about the strained relationship between Fela and the festival's administrators:

> Much to my delight, music was being played by Fela's renowned band. Then, a curious thing happened! While the music was being played, waiters began to serve refreshments. Fela stopped his band, demanding that no eating should take place during his musical performance. This was a most audacious deed, especially since many of Nigeria's most important politicians were present at the function, among them Major-General Haruna, Maitama Sule, and Chief Enahoro. The gathering was

compliant. But I saw how such an act could be seen as pure impudence and it doubtless caused resentment in high places.[120]

At the end of 1976 the FESTAC opening ceremonies were fast approaching and the government began taking a draconian approach to the traffic problems in Lagos in anticipation of the influx of foreign tourists. "Operation Ease the Traffic" stationed Nigerian army soldiers with horsewhips at major Lagos intersections, instructing them to deliver on-the-spot whippings for traffic offenses. The public outcry against this was immediate, and Fela, planning what he called a "counter-FESTAC," railed against this and other government policies from the Shrine.[121] While juju singers such as Ebenezer Obey put their most patriotic faces forward in support of the festival and government programs such as the "Operation Feed the Nation" agriculture campaign, Fela railed against what he termed "Operation Beat the Nation."

The government officially discouraged delegates from visiting the Shrine, but Fela's international reputation guaranteed that he was the unofficial star of the festival among the visiting delegates and artists. After arriving in the country, superstar Stevie Wonder made his first public appearance at the Shrine,[122] while Archie Shepp, members of Sun Ra's Arkestra, and the Art Ensemble of Chicago jammed with Afrika 70; the American delegation even staged a "mini-FESTAC" at the Shrine. This evidently provided the visiting delegates a welcome change of pace. One correspondent wondered:

> Why was the modern Nigerian music at FESTAC such a travesty of what the country has to offer, just a group of tired old hustlers on the bandwagon? . . . We went to the Africa Shrine, where Fela Anikulapo-Kuti had invited some far-out American musicians to share the stage in an African-American solidarity night. It became an alternative FESTAC, with Fela preaching against corruption, openly smoking weed on stage, his go-go girls writhing away in their wooden cages, the place totally packed with hip Lagos youth, the big-time prostitutes, Fela's respectable family and of course hundreds of FESTAC visitors eager to see where Nigerian music was really at.[123]

The FESTAC debacle was the most obvious evidence yet that Fela was becoming the thorn in the boot of the Nigerian military, inheriting his mother's disgust of the machinations of high-level politicians and exposing the underside of the Nigerian oil dream. Although many Nigerians felt that Fela should have played patriot and supported his country in the festival,[124] he had won the battle of forcing his presence into the festival despite his official absence, as evidenced by the Shrine's capacity crowds, the growing talk of launching him onto the international music scene,[125] and his ongoing suit against the government stemming from the November 1974 attack, which was front-page news during this time. During the same period, he publicly ridiculed a private offer made to him by a group of prominent "big men" in Ikoyi who wanted to hear him in person but did not want to come to the Shrine; they asked him to entertain them privately at an exclusive elite club for a fee nearly ten times the amount he was earning nightly at the Shrine.[126]

Fela's impact during this time reached beyond the festival, the press, and his shows at the Shrine. As the tension between he and the Nigerian authorities grew more and more palpable, he began confiding to intimates his interest in holding public office, hoping to parlay his popularity as a musician into viability as a politician, and his ideas into concrete policy. Now popularly hailed around Lagos as the "Black President," he formed a vaguely socialist youth action group called Young African Pioneers, which distributed thousands of stridently antigovernment pamphlets condemning the organizers of FESTAC and "Operation Ease the Traffic" throughout Lagos—causing further embarrassment to the Obasanjo administration at a time when over 50,000 people had flooded the country for the festival.[127]

By the end of 1976, he had publicly proclaimed his intention of running for the nation's presidency in the civilian elections of 1979, declaring that "after 1979 music will be my profession and politics my calling."[128] As early as the 1975 police raid in Ilorin, Fela had vowed to his captors that he would become president expressly to fight such abuses of power.[129] With his popularity at an all-time high and Kalakuta's barbed-wire fence newly electrified, Fela began damning the government from the Shrine stage. John Darnton noted: "On Sunday afternoons, when he laced his show with rambling, pot-inspired diatribes against Christianity and the rich people on Ikoyi island . . . he began saying things that no Nigerian newspaper would dare publish. 'You think dey go give up power,' he scoffed at the military's promise to hand the government back over to the civilians in 1979. Then lapsing into Oxford English, 'Tell me, what African man in a uniform with shiny brass buttons has ever done that?' "[130]

To top it all off, he recorded "Zombie"—his most popular and biggest-selling song to date—which mocked soldiers as robotic idiots mindlessly following orders:

Zombie no go go, unless you tell am to go	Zombie won't go unless you tell him to go
Zombie no go stop, unless you tell am to stop	Zombie won't stop unless you tell him to stop
Zombie no go turn, unless you tell am to turn	Zombie won't turn, unless you tell him to turn
Zombie no go think, unless you tell am to think . . .	Zombie won't think, unless you tell him to think . . .
Tell am to go straight—joro-jara-jo	Tell him to go straight—left, right, left
No brains, no job, no sense—joro-jara-jo	No brains, no job, no sense—left, right, left
Tell am to go kill—joro-jara-jo	Tell him to go kill—left, right, left
No brains, no job, no sense—joro-jara-jo	No brains, no job, no sense—left, right, left

Tell am to go quench—joro-jara-jo	Tell him to go die—left, right, left
No brains, no job, no sense—joro, jara-jo . . .	No brains, no job, no sense—left, right, left . . .

"Unknown Soldier"

LAGOS, March 7—An inquiry has been ordered into the cause of the disturbances at the home of Fela Anikulapo-Kuti at Agege Motor Road, Lagos. As a result of the disturbances, the musician and 80 members of his organization were arrested. It is also reported that his mother, Mrs. Funmilayo Ransome-Kuti, was hurt during the fight with soldiers and police, as was his doctor brother, who was admitted to hospital. A fire subsequently destroyed the house.

West Africa, *March 7, 1977*

"Zombie" demonstrates that Fela's yabis was increasingly directed toward official targets, and at the same time the song began to be sung and danced by youths who, to taunt the soldiers in the streets of Lagos, marched robotically and used sticks as mock rifles.[131] Fela's people also grew increasingly cocky toward the soldiers from the nearby Abalti barracks. A week after the festival ended they allegedly burned an army motorcycle during a dispute with soldiers over a traffic violation, and the military retaliated with a vengeance. On the afternoon of February 18—ironically, eighty years to the day after the British invaded the Benin Kingdom in the "punitive expedition" (in which the mask symbolizing FESTAC was seized)—over a thousand armed soldiers surrounded Kalakuta. After barricading the building and parading with signs imploring area residents to run for their lives,[132] soldiers set fire to the generator that electrified the fence, stormed the compound, and severely brutalized the occupants. Fela later alleged that he was dragged by his genitals from the house, severely beaten, and sexually mutilated by the soldiers, only escaping death following the intervention of a commanding officer.[133] His mother—then seventy-eight years old—suffered a broken hip when she was thrown through a window, and his brother Beko was so severely beaten that he spent several months in a wheelchair. A number of the men reportedly had their testicles smashed by the soldiers, and the women were beaten, forced to strip, and carried naked through the streets on flatbed trucks to the army barracks, where they were reportedly raped and tortured. Some had their nipples smashed with stones, while others had broken bottles inserted into their vaginas. One female commune member reportedly died in the attack after suffering a fractured skull.[134] Finally, the soldiers set fire to the entire compound, attacked firefighters who arrived to extinguish the blaze, and severely beat several press photographers who attempted to cover the melee. The Kalakuta Republic, including its recording studio, musical instruments, master tapes, and Beko's free health clinic, was completely gutted. Also destroyed in the fire was the multimillion naira soundtrack to Fela's film autobiography-in-progress, *The Black President*. Following the army's siege, all sixty occupants of the house were either in jail or in the hospital, where they remained for the better part of a month. There were widespread reports that rampaging soldiers, not content to destroy Fela's commune, engaged in thefts, looting, violence, and other abuses directed at civilians in the area.

Regardless of Fela's relentless goading of the powers-that-be and his deviant social image, most Nigerians were troubled by the viciousness of what Fela termed the "Kalakuta Massacre," and the public outcry was immediate. With over 250,000 soldiers, Nigeria had Africa's largest standing army, and many civilians were already cynical and uneasy about the prospects for peaceful transition to civilian rule as 1979 approached. In fact, the Kalakuta episode was only the most brutal of a number of violent confrontations between soldiers and civilians in the mid-1970s. Unruly soldiers had ransacked the town of Epe in 1975 and had clashed with civilians in the Orile Agege area of Lagos and in the town of Shendan in Plateau State in 1976. In Kwara State, a reporter was beaten nearly to death by a gang of soldiers who claimed he had looked at one of their wives.[135] In the months following the Kalakuta attack, soldiers rioted in Lagos after one of their own was struck by a civilian auto—setting fire to the civilian vehicle, destroying five others, and vandalizing buildings in the area. In September, soldiers reportedly killed one civilian and seriously injured twenty others in Lagos after a motorcyclist allegedly sideswiped a soldier's wife. In the ensuing riot, the soldiers smashed the windshields of all automobiles along a stretch of road they had barricaded. Civilians retaliated in Cross River State, lynching two soldiers who had reportedly castrated a young boy.[136] And in Lagos, an irate mob beat one soldier to death, set fire to another, and destroyed an army motorcycle following a dispute between a soldier and a civilian.[137]

The Kalakuta incident was thus one of a number of military-civilian clashes reflecting indiscipline among the army's lower ranks on the one hand, and a rising tide of public hostility toward the soldiers on the other. In this climate, Fela became Nigeria's foremost popular dissident and a conduit for public enmity toward the military. Amnesty International began investigating his case, and the Ransome-Kuti family brought a 5 million naira suit against the army and senior military officers, which was later increased to 25 million.

The Lagos state government inquiry set up to investigate the incident took evidence from 183 witnesses over several weeks in the new National Theatre. Despite the testimony of several witnesses who claimed they could personally identify by name all of the soldiers who set the blaze, the report in late April 1977 concluded that Kalakuta was unintentionally destroyed by "an exasperated and unknown soldier."[138] Having exonerated the soldiers of virtually all responsibility, the report castigated Fela for proclaiming his commune an independent republic, forbade Afrika 70 from performing in public, and recommended that the political activities of Young African Pioneers be probed. The report also berated the police for "the levity with which they treated allegations of crimes against Mr. Fela Anikulapo-Kuti," and for failing to enforce the law in the area surrounding Kalakuta and the Shrine.[139] The government permanently closed the Afrika Shrine, revoked the Empire Hotel's liquor and entertainment licenses, and purchased the remains of

Kalakuta Republic and its environs, forcibly evicting several thousand area residents in the process. In the ensuing public outcry against the ruling, even the government-controlled *Daily Times* was deluged with enraged letters. One wondered: "For how long shall we be at the mercy of these unknown, deranged, or even invisible persons who are easily cleared after committing atrocious acts? One feels that a situation whereby culprits are allowed to go scot-free on such apparently flimsy grounds is a potentially explosive one."[140]

Probably the most articulate statement of public sentiment came from a *Daily Express* editorial:

> It is rather sad that at this stage of our social development, some people can still believe that Nigerians are not discerning enough to make sound and correct judgement over issues of public interest. For how else can one explain the incredible finding in the report that it was some "Unknown Soldier" in sympathy with his colleagues after being exasperated . . . that set fire on "some rubbish" under the vehicles? If this is the best Anya's panel could produce, then it is the view of the *Daily Express* that either the panel lacked the diligence and industry necessary to determine and identify the cause of the fire and to apportion blame, of the whole exercise was a theatrical mockery, staged in the National Theatre.
>
> For if at the end of it all, we are to believe that some "unknown soldier," as distinct from the troops admittedly sent to surround Fela's residence, came and set "some rubbish" on fire, and without authority, right before the eyes of our vigilant and alert troops, we say it loud and clear that it says very little of the Army's traditional and statutory duty of protecting lives and properties.[141]

The Kalakuta attack and its aftermath dealt a severe blow to Fela and his organization, destroying virtually all of his material assets, profoundly shaking him psychologically, ending the triumphant work of his classic period, and leaving the entire Afrika 70 organization homeless. Although his potency as a political and cultural icon would grow even broader in many ways following the attack, he would never again enjoy the same financial affluence, physical health, or freedom to create.

"Stalemate"

Penniless, dispirited, and still healing, Afrika 70 attempted to get back to work. In theory, the closure of the Shrine should not in itself have presented a major obstacle to performing, since Afrika 70 had always done selected gigs outside of the Shrine at venues such as Popson Hotel, Mobolaji Sports Centre, and various university campuses nationwide. By the spring of 1977, the court order prohibiting their public performances was overturned and concerts were attempted at Lagos City Hall, Yaba College of Technology, and the Plaza Cinema in order to generate desperately-needed cash flow. However, with cordons of armed police and soldiers assembled at each venue to physically prevent Fela's entry, intimidated hotel and club owners were reluctant to book Afrika 70—suffocating them financially and effectively silencing Fela in the months following the attack.

With no prospects for work inside Nigeria and concerned for his safety, Fela went into self-imposed exile with his entourage in Ghana in the fall of 1977. There he met Kwesi Yopee, the harassed editor of Ghana's dissident *Catholic Times,* who became his liaison to radical students in Ghana, as well his chief spokesman for the next year.[142] While in Ghana, Fela attempted to have the soundtrack of *Black President* redubbed at the Ghana Film studios, but this proved too difficult and the project had to be abandoned, with the film remaining uncompleted to date.[143]

Fela became immediately popular in Ghana, as well as controversial. His song "Zombie" was a favorite of the students, who scheduled meetings with him in which they complained about the brutality of their own military government, headed by General Ignatius Acheampong. After securing a gig at Accra's Apollo Theatre, Fela began speaking out onstage against Acheampong's regime, and created another stir when he became involved in an Accra dispute between street vendors and Lebanese merchants. Several of his bandmembers were also arrested for marijuana possession after a police raid on his room at the Hotel President.

One fan remembered Fela's time in Ghana:

> Fela was extremely popular in Ghana. In 1977 he would go to all these villages around the countryside, almost like he was campaigning or something. . . . The people would come out offering them sacks of Indian hemp, saying "ours is better than the one you are smoking." Or they would pick him up and carry him around the village like a hero. In some of the places he might have a meeting with the village chief, or in others, the chief would refuse to see Fela, and would tell the people to chase him away. It all depended on how colonial the place was.[144]

During the next few months, the group returned to Nigeria several times in connection with the pending court case, and it was on one of these visits in February 1978 that Fela married twenty-seven female members of his troupe in a communal wedding at the Parisonna Hotel in Lagos, on the anniversary of the Kalakuta attack. In a ceremony presided over by Ifa priest Yusufu Olaleye, Fela simultaneously wed Funmilayo Onile, Alake Adedipe, Kevwe Oghomienor, Tejumade Adebiyi, Ngozi Olisa, Najite Mukoro, Adejunwon Williams, Adeola Williams, Fehintola Kayode, Ihase Obotu, Emaruagheru Osawe, Bose James, Kikelomo Oseni, Aduni Idowu, Olaide Babalaiye, Tokunbo Sholeye, Ibe Agwu, Orode Olowu, Iyabo Chibueze, Omowunmi Adesumi, Omolara Shosanya, Oluremi Akinola, Dupe Oloye, Folake Orosun, Omowunmi Oyedele, Chinyere Ibe, and Idiat Kasumu.

Although the ceremony was private and attended only by family and close friends, the event was sensationalized in the press as a "historic mass wedding."[145] While John Collins claims the move was a ploy to allow Fela's entourage into Ghana (the women could enter as Fela's wives, but not as his girlfriends),[146] Fela explained that he was providing the women the social status they were denied as his mere girlfriends (they were frequently dismissed as street women and prostitutes), as well as showing his appreciation for their continued support through his many personal and public crises.[147] He also justified his controversial move by defining it within the traditional custom of polygamous marriage.

Fela's actions conformed in some ways to traditional motivations for such a polygamous arrangement, one of which is increased sexual variety and access. As early as "Shenshema" (1971), he had advanced the idea of hypersexuality as fundamental to African manhood when he sang "You be man, you get 33 women—you say you no fit get 99 . . . you be Shenshema [i.e., outdated, colonial]!" There were other factors. Throughout Africa, polygamy is almost exclusively practiced by prominent "big men" who can afford to sustain a household of such size, with the number of wives in many cases being an important criteria in appraising a man's social standing. Accordingly, one 1937 survey of the most powerful traditional rulers in Yorubaland found each man's wives numbering well into the hundreds without exception.[148] To take a contemporary example, the wives of the late Yoruba businessman and philanthropist Moshood K. O. Abiola were said to number in the dozens. Another motivation is the importance of women as laborers. In traditional culture this mainly concerned farming and market work; in Fela's case, all of his new brides performed some function within the Afrika 70 organization.[149] Fela's decision might also be seen as his strategy for shoring up his self-esteem and celebrity status following the indignity of the Kalakuta incident, as well as a reflection of the enhanced status derived from his political ambitions.

As with most matters concerning Fela, the public response was sharply divided. While some supported his move as an authentic embrace of tradition, others dismissed the wedding as a mere publicity stunt. Among those who questioned the authenticity and sincerity of the ceremony, many did so either because of Fela's failure to fulfill the traditional expectations for such a wedding, or because of the wide class disparity between Fela and the brides. Most of his brides had failed to finish secondary school, had been socially marginalized for their association with him, and had been long-alienated from their natal families at the time of the wedding. Fela was thus relieved of two crucial factors formalizing the fusion of two family lineages in Yorubaland[150]—the traditionally expected economic and symbolic exchanges between a groom and his in-laws,[151] and the issue of mutual family consent. Those who felt the wedding contained overtones of show business gimmickry could point to the fact that unlike Fela, most polygamists married their wives sequentially as they gained in wealth and prominence, not all at once. They could also criticize the marriage setting; although the ceremony was conducted by an Ifa priest, it took place not in a traditional shrine or compound but at a Lagos hotel (although this had been Afrika 70's de facto residence since the Kalakuta incident).

The anti-Fela position was expressed in an irate letter to the *Daily Times*:

That so-called wedding is a gimmick and no marriage by any standard. Fela has openly defied the tradition that he purports to uphold. And the fact that he has got away with it shows how grossly lacking we are in discipline. Never mind his own admission that the bunch of delinquents he now possesses under his spell are deviants and rejects from their homes. Fela has merely used the cloak of tradition to grab cheap apples to munch, washing his hands of the customary demands that would have been too costly for his insatiable tastes. . . . If anything intrigues me, it is the statement of Fela's mother "God bless Fela and his brides." Mrs. Funmilayo Ransome-Kuti is well aware that her son's legal marriage still subsists and she has five grandchildren by it. Just what could have changed the proud ideals of a great lady who has done so much to inspire Nigerian womanhood?[152]

Fela's wife Remi had lived in her own house, with the couple's children, since Fela's return from America in 1970, when he had converted his mother's Agege Motor Road property into a communal residence for his ever-increasing cadre of musicians, dancers, girlfriends, and others. Prior to the communal wedding, Fela implied that he had Remi's blessing when he proclaimed that they had been "living in the unrealistic English system of marriage" but that now they wanted "to live in the reality of African marriage."[153]

From Remi's perspective, the 1978 communal marriage—more than any of his other actions—may have represented the most symbolic act in Fela's process of cultural reorientation—or what is more derisively known as "going bush." This process, a theme often explored in the works of postcolonial African writers such as Chinua Achebe, Kole Omotoso, and Ayi Kwei Arnah, was particularly pronounced in the generation of politically conscious "been to's"—students of the late nationalist era who married abroad and then moved with their expatriate wives back to Africa to assist in the heady process of nation-building. These men from elite backgrounds received colonial educations abroad and then returned to African societies in the midst of postcolonial identity crises. As a social class, they embodied the cathartic and often contradictory attempts to decolonize the cultural mind while modernizing and revitalizing traditional culture, a process with unforeseen consequences for their wives.[154] At the time of the wedding, in fact, Fela claimed that the ceremony was only the first in a series of periodic expansions of his household, pledging to marry additional "deserving new female members" of his organization every two years henceforth.[155]

Afrika 70 had planned to return to Ghana following the wedding ceremony, but they were met by officials at Accra's Kotoka Airport and informed that Fela had been deported due to the dispute with the Lebanese merchants and the size of his entourage.[156] In reality, the Acheampong government did not look kindly upon his meetings with dissident students. The troupe returned to Lagos, where Fela continued to stir controversy and make headlines. In a humiliating conclusion to the Kalakuta affair, and despite a government panel's recommendation that the Kuti family be compensated for their losses in the Kalakuta attack, a Lagos High Court judge dismissed their 25 million naira suit against senior army officials in February 1978, on the dubious grounds that the nation's constitution "did not provide for award of damages when a citizen's fundamental human rights had been infringed."[157] Nigerians had diverse opinions about Fela as a public presence, but a more general fear had been confirmed—the nation's constitution did not hold the military culpable for any atrocities it might commit. The ruling held ominous implications for the nation's future, most of which would be lived under a succession of progressively brutal military kleptocracies.

Events took another tragic turn when Fela's mother died in April, having never fully recovered from the injuries she sustained in the Kalakuta attack. It was reported that she had fallen ill upon hearing of the court's ruling in the family's suit; she reportedly gasped and collapsed, never to regain her health.[158] Funmilayo Anikulapo-Kuti was eulogized in the press and by prominent Nigerians— including President Obasanjo, who called her a "freedom fighter."[159]

Obasanjo would retire from office in 1979 with the singular honor of having been the only Nigerian head of state to relinquish power voluntarily, but Fela would never forgive the president, whom he held directly responsible for the soldiers' role in his mother's decline. Long before the Kalakuta attack, Funmilayo had been forced to move into Kalakuta after the government took over Abeokuta Grammar School without providing her with what the family considered adequate compensation.[160] For the rest of his career, Fela's determination to avenge the circumstances of his mother's death would be one of the primary fires of his creative muse.

A clue to one of the ways in which Fela intended to honor his mother's tradition of radical activism, as was revealed in October when he became embroiled in yet another controversy. A bitter dispute emerged between Afrika 70 and the Decca recording company and its chairman, Chief M. K. O. Abiola, over unreleased recordings and unpaid royalties. Afrika 70 had mustered a string of recordings in the wake of the Kalakuta crisis such as "Shuffering and Shmiling," "Stalemate," "I Go Shout Plenty," "Fear Not for Man," and "Cross-Examination of the Colonial African Soldier." That at least some of these tracks were hastily composed attempts to comply with the terms of the Decca contract is evident from their sketchy, minimal sound and development.[161] Despite their formal simplicity, the new songs found Fela addressing more political concerns, defiantly declaring his intent to continue his criticisms in spite of government harassment. In light of recent events, Decca balked at releasing some of the material it deemed "seditious," such as "Sorrow, Tears, and Blood" and "Observation No Crime." Ultimately, the affair degenerated rancorously, with Decca refusing to release Fela's material, the government confiscating Afrika 70 master tapes, and royalties on existing releases slowing to a trickle despite substantial sales. For the homeless and penniless members of the Afrika 70 organization, the company's refusal to release the contracted albums during the specified period constituted a breach of contract (an interpretation verified by a police lawyer). Fela saw it as an instance of neocolonial exploitation, as well as an attempt to force him out of the music business. He had lost faith in the legal process following the Kalakuta rulings; rather than pursuing the matter in a court of law, he resorted to other means to achieve his ends in the Decca case. Recalling his mother's occupation of the Alake's palace in Abeokuta thirty years earlier, Fela and the entire Afrika 70 entourage took over the Decca offices on Ajike Faramobi Street in the Anthony Village section of Lagos, effectively shutting the company down for seven weeks. The matter was only resolved through the intervention of Fela's police friend M. D. Yusufu, but still without any financial settlement for Fela.[162]

As a result of the dispute, Decca chairman Abiola became one of Fela's chief nemeses during the next ten years. An Abeokuta native of humble origins, Abiola had earned a degree in accounting from Glasgow University and joined International Telephone and Telegraph in as a staff accountant in 1969. By the mid-1970s, he had become the company's vice president for Africa and the Middle East (due in part to his relationship with former head of state Murtala Mohammed), and had also assumed the chairmanship of Decca Records Nigeria.[163] By the late 1970s, Abiola had become one of Nigeria's most powerful businessmen, securing millions of dollars in government contracts and gradually maneuvering himself into the political arena. Despite his professional success, reputation for philanthropy, and advocacy of Pan-Africanism, Abiola's professional path led his critics to deride him as the prototypically corrupt comprador and elite businessman.[164] Fela became chief among these antagonists when documents found by Afrika 70 in Decca's files indicated that Abiola had acted on instructions from the company's London headquarters to prevent the release of Afrika 70 material, and had even traveled as far as London to discuss the matter. Fela frequently quoted from books on multinational corporations in Africa to denounce Abiola as a puppet of Western imperialists, a line of attack that would culminate in his song "I.T.T. (International Thief Thief)" a few years later.

He was eventually able to win a court order forcing the return his master tapes, and he subsequently issued "Sorrow, Tears, and Blood" as the first release on his own Kalakuta Records. Perhaps reflective of his recent experiences, the exuberant hubris of his pre-inferno music was replaced by a moodier, more subdued, more reflective sound. The lyrics, however, continue in the mode of explicitly critical songs such as "Alagbon Close." "Sorrow, Tears, and Blood" offers a poignant but direct recounting of the Kalakuta attack over a subdued mid-tempo rhythm pattern. The middle portion of the lyric—alternating between a critique of political apathy and the depiction of a woman's attempt to resist seduction—perfectly demonstrates Fela's subversive use of social deviance as an metaphor for political action:

FELA: My people sef, dey fear too much . . .	*FELA:* My people, we fear too much . . .
We fear to fight for freedom	We fear fighting for freedom
We fear to fight for justice	We fear fighting for justice
We fear to fight for liberty	We fear fighting for liberty
We fear to fight for happiness	We fear fighting for happiness
We always get reason to fear:	We always find a reason to fear:
"I no wan die	"I don't want to die
I no wan wound	I don't want to be wounded
I get one child	I have a child
Mama dey for house	My mother is in the house

Papa dey for house	My father is in the house
I won't enjoy . . ."	I won't enjoy . . ."
So policeman go slap your face, you no go talk	So a policeman slaps your face, you remain silent
Army man go whip your yansch you go dey look like donkey	A soldier whips your behind, you look like a donkey
Rhodesia dem do dem own, our leaders yab for nothing	Rhodesia and South Africa violate human rights,
South Africa dem do dem own . . .	our own (corrupt) leaders hypocritically criticize them
Dem bring sorrow, tears, and blood . . .	They bring sorrow, tears, and blood . . .
CHORUS: Dem regular trademark . . .	*CHORUS:* Their regular trademark . . .

He reserved his harshest sentiments for "Shuffering and Shmiling," an attack on Christian and Muslim complicity in foreign cultural imperialism and local political oppression. The song can be more specifically read as Fela's response to the growing incidence of violent confrontations between Nigerian Christians and Muslim fundamentalists, which he interpreted as a proxy war fought between Europe and the Muslim world, on African soil. It can also be read as an attack on the Christian Obasanjo and the Muslim Abiola. In his classified ad, Fela expressed his feelings regarding Christianity and Islam in Nigeria in no uncertain terms:

Chief Priest Say: If expenses of 80,000 pilgrims who go to Mecca is at least 600 naira each, then Nigeria spends 48 million in Saudi Arabia this year for religious pilgrimage. What do we get in return: sick pilgrims and brainwashed Africans. For me it's not worth it.

. . . For pope country, 30,000 die every year because of alcoholism, kidnappers dem boku, armed robbers, thieves, rapists and orishirishi criminals like sand-sand, police like animals, so wetin pope wan tell us for our own country? Make him repair him own country first!![165]

Now, in his most audacious song to date, he introduced a clear class dimension into the equation, placing the struggles of the working class in direct opposition to the privileges enjoyed by leading clergy and prominent adherents:

I want you all to please	I want you all to please
Put your minds into any goddamn church	Put your minds into any goddamn church
or any goddamn mosque:	or any goddamn mosque:
Suffer, suffer for world	Suffer in this world
Enjoy for heaven	Find enjoyment in heaven
Christians go dey yab:	Christians talk nonsense:

"In spiritum heavinus"	"In spiritum heavinus"
Muslims go dey call:	Muslims call
"Allahu Akubar"	"Allahu Akbar"
Open your eyes everywhere	Open your eyes everywhere
Archbishop na miliki	The archbishop has much pleasure
Pope na enjoyment	The pope has much enjoyment
Imam na gbaladun . . .	Imam has good times
Archbishop dey for London	Archbishop is from London
Pope dey for Rome	Pope is from Rome
Imam dey for Mecca	Imam is from Mecca
My people dem go follow bishop, follow Pope, follow Imam	My people follow the bishop, the Pope, the Imam
Dem go carry all the money . . .	And carry our money to these places . . .

Responses were sharply divided about Fela's most explicitly critical song to date. One listener felt that the song

> could be of great lesson [to the country's rulers]. Many people are suffering on our roads, people have no good water to drink, no proper medical care, etc., and yet our lawmakers want heaven on earth for themselves. I doff my hat to Fela Anikulapo-Kuti—a man with the message of truth. It is true that the truth is bitter. . . . I therefore implore him to keep it up.[166]

Others found the track highly insulting:

> It is unethical, at least in Africa, for a youth to spite or deride an elder. It is blasphemous the world over for anybody young or old to speak with disrespect about God or the worship of Him. But with the jet age flying fastest here, this order is fast [disappearing]. This is the lesson of Fela Anikulapo-Kuti's album "Shuffering and Shmiling" in which he castigates and mocks Christians and Moslems alike for no offense other than their religious beliefs.[167]

Although many Nigerians felt Fela had disgraced their country by openly abusing its leaders in front of a European audience, he and Afrika 70 gained much international prestige when they were invited to headline the Berlin Jazz Festival in September, a concert televised in several European countries. The concert's highlight was "Vagabonds in Power" ("V.I.P."), another new song that explored class divisions in Nigeria. While Fela and Afrika 70 were away premiering "V.I.P." and other new songs in Berlin, the Lagos state government used the opportunity to demolish the gutted remains of the Kalakuta Republic, dashing not only the most visible symbol of Fela's reign, but also his hopes of ever returning to the property. *Punch* reported that on the morning of October 29,

> as early as 8:00 A.M., bulldozers had arrived in two heavy-duty trailers. The drivers went into action, starting with 14A Agege Motor Road, building of the late Chief Funmilayo Anikulapo-Kuti. In less than thirty minutes, the two story building in which a mock coffin and the Afrika 70 Organization flag were displayed had been pulled down. Despite the heavy downpour, hundreds of people stood by and as the "Kalakuta Republic" gave way, they all shouted in unison "KA-LA-KU-TA, Going! Going! Gone!!"[168]

The Berlin performance also turned out to be the great Afrika 70's swan song. Citing low pay and insufficient credit, and balking at Fela's forays into politics, the band broke up acrimoniously following the trip. The musicians of Afrika 70 felt underpaid and exploited. As Frank Fairfax noted, most had never been able to achieve a comfortable standard of living despite belonging to one of the most popular bands in the country.[169] Fela's intention to use the bulk of the profits from the Berlin trip to finance his own political aspirations (a practice he repeated on later European tours) was the final straw for many of them. Tony Allen explained his own reasons for leaving:

> I discovered that this guy is a real slave driver. He never paid what he was supposed to pay his musicians. . . . I told Fela when we were in Berlin that I was going to resign when we got back to Nigeria. Fela went into politics. He was telling me that the money we make in Berlin, he was using on politics and he wants to be elected as the president of Nigeria. . . . I told him I am not a politician, I'm a musician. So I left.[170]

Most of the band left with Allen, ending a decade of creative growth. This would have major consequences for the subsequent development of Fela's music. Despite the afrobeat classics to come and the outstanding musicians who would pass through his later groups, Fela was not subsequently able to maintain as stable or talented a group of musicians as Allen, Henry Kofi, and the original Afrika 70.

The turbulent and tragic events of 1977 and 1978—the death of Fela's mother, the army sacking of Kalakuta, the takeover of Decca, and the break-up of Afrika 70—were each major turning points in Fela's career, ending a period of his greatest productivity, commercial success, moral support, and public presence. Just as the American counterculture of the 1960s collapsed under the weight of various hard realities at the turn of the new decade, Fela's countercultural experiment collapsed in the wake of the Kalakuta debacle into a new reality at the dawn of the 1980s. If he had led the high-flying lifestyle of a celebrated pop star during the 1970s, the 1980s would find him living something more akin to the harried life of a political dissident. As early as 1979—barely a year after the communal wedding—some of his wives had left, tiring of the constant harassment. As Lindsay Barrett noted, Fela's post-Kalakuta life and music assumed "a brilliance that was, however, shadowed by a doom-laden sense of inevitable confrontation."[171]

The years of afrobeat's birth and peak popularity in the late 1960s and 1970s reflected an African musical moment in which styles such as rhumba, soukous, mbalax, highlife, and juju took their places alongside the modern urban popular musics of the world—sonic assertions of Africa's postindependence euphoria and revitalization of its traditional culture in the service of the nation and the city. Among these styles, Fela's afrobeat was the most vigorous and explicit interrogation of the postcolonial African condition, a stance that would intensify in the next phase of his career. From the 1980s, as Africa entered a neocolonial era marked by the increased influx of multinational capital and economic aid, the resulting "world music" phenomenon would have a transformative effect on the careers of these musicians in terms of audiences, mediums, and markets.

Both FESTAC and the sacking of Kalakuta in 1977 represented crucial turning points in the lives of Fela and the Nigerian nation. If Fela's critical music and the celebratory festival symbolized two opposing poles of Nigeria's ambivalent postcolonial ascendance, they also beckoned toward a more austere and difficult era. As early as 1978, Nigeria had begun heavy borrowing of various European currencies to keep its various development programs afloat.[172] After the festival, Nigeria would coast along on its petroleum wealth for a few more years before the bottom fell out of the oil market and, like most of the continent, the country entered an era characterized by successive military coups, protracted dictatorships, mounting foreign debt, renewed ethnic tension, collapsing infrastructure, and health pandemics. In this climate, the intensified political and cultural convictions of Fela's post-1977 music held major consequences for both his life and musical career. Yomi Gbolagunte recalled that for some of Fela's detractors in Lagos, Funmilayo's death made the man seem more vulnerable.

> Back in the sixties with Koola Lobitos, Fela was singing this song ["Alagbara"] which said something to the effect of "As long as my mother is alive, nobody can do anything to harm me." After his mother died in '78, people in Lagos were taunting him by saying: "Fela what will you do now? Now that your mother has gone, the government will just toy with you at will."[173]

"A Serious
Cultural Episode"
(1979–1992)

The first time I heard Fela, I thought "That's the guy that's going to put Africa on the world map." But he blew the whole thing . . . he went too political . . . and the further he goes, the more he loses the African elements.
A FORMER PRODUCER OF FELA, *quoted in* BERGMAN 1985

Seeing my mother die has made death very unimportant to me now. . . . I swore on the day I first saw her dying that I would put my struggles into top gear. . . . My mother's death has made me see death in a clearer perspective. Before she died, I might have been restrained from protesting to Dodan Barracks [seat of the Military Government]. *But after the death, Dodan Barracks became just like Race Course* [the Lagos dog racing track].
FELA *quoted in* Sunday Punch, *June 25, 1978*

To many Nigerians, the 1979 civilian elections were an opportunity for a new era of civilian politics following years of military rule, and the lifting of the military ban on political activity in late 1978 was accompanied by a groundswell of new contenders, including many younger politicians. Unfortunately, their hopes gradually soured as older politicians emerged to dominate the show, competing for the presidency as what Chinua Achebe called a "compensation prize" for their thirty years of dubious "service" to the nation.[1] Ultimately, out of approximately forty parties that formed after the lifting of the ban only five were allowed to register, and most of these were headed by veterans of Nigeria's "First Republic" civilian government (1960–1966) such as Obafemi Awolowo (Unity Party of Nigeria), Nnamidi Azikiwe (Nigerian People's Party), Shehu Shagari (National Party of Nigeria), and Aminu Kano (People's Redemption Party).[2] The hopes of younger progressives for substantive political realignment were thus dashed for the 1979 elections.

In the end, Shagari emerged as the victor of a hotly contested election. The unprecedented corruption of his administration, as well as the 1982 oil glut that turned the country, virtually overnight, into Africa's largest debtor nation, resulted in a pervasive national cynicism and disillusionment that grew progressively stronger throughout the 1980s.

In this twilight of the Nigerian oil dream, though Fela continued to compose explicitly political, confrontational music, reflecting his commitment to his mother's legacy of radical activism, he offered this music in a Nigeria that was less able to absorb such criticism. The world at large, however, was growing more receptive to his music and message. Fela's mediation of these two roles—resident dissident and international pop star—would govern the trajectory of his music and career during the 1980s.

While Afrika 70 had given only a handful of performances since the army siege of Kalakuta, Fela had nonetheless remained in the public eye through the scandals and misfortunes of the intervening months. The Kalakuta trial, the suit against the government, and the Decca affair had been front-page news throughout 1977, as had his communal wedding, his expulsion from Ghana, and the death of his mother in 1978. The last Afrika 70 releases—*Vagabonds in Power* and *Shuffering and Shmiling*—became major hits despite being banned by government-controlled radio stations. Fela was also in demand on the university lecture circuit, usually addressing students on subjects such as Pan-Africanism and the importance of embracing African history and culture. It was a measure of his popularity among students and his engagement of the critical issues confronting society that he delivered some sixty university lectures related to cultural themes during this period, usually in panel discussions or colloquia placing him alongside more conservative academics.[3] In a 1981 symposium called "The Essence of Culture in Development," for example, Fela arrived at the University of Ife with a pile of books such as G. M. James's *Stolen Legacy,* Yosef Ben-Jochanan's *Black Man of the Nile,* and Walter Rodney's *How Europe Underdeveloped Africa.* These invoked tropes familiar to Afrocentrists, revisionist Egyptologists, and black nationalists: black Egypt as cradle of world civilization, Greek civilization as the stolen cultural legacy of black Egypt, the Moorish influence on medieval Spain, and linguistic similarities as proof of Africa's underlying cultural unity and genesis in ancient Egypt.[4]

At other times, Fela would completely flout the conventions of academia, with an approach to the lecture stage as unorthodox as his approach to the concert stage. In a 1981 lecture at Ogun Polytechnic entitled "The Role of Music in Communication," for example, he arrived with a soccer ball and retinue of traditional drummers, maneuvering the ball to the sound of drums to demonstrate his point that African footballers would fare much better in the World Cup if they patterned their movements after indigenous African war dances instead of relying solely upon European training techniques.[5]

As a result of the Kalakuta episode and his increasing extramusical activities, Fela's political visibility was in some ways higher than it had been prior to the attack. In fact, so newsworthy was he at this time, that the *Punch* newspaper rose from relative obscurity to become one of the major Lagos dailies, based largely on its coverage of his endless travails.[6] However, this enhanced visibility also meant the stakes were raised in his ongoing battle with the Nigerian authorities. He continued to set his sights on the country's presidency, working with Young African Pioneers and distributing more antigovernment leaflets of the type that had helped incur the wrath of the Obasanjo regime. The Kalakuta affair had bolstered his status as a lightning-rod for public discontent, making him more of a nuisance to the establishment as the elections neared. With the lifting of the military ban on political activity in late 1978, Fela finally formed his own political party, Movement of the People (M.O.P), and pulled off a huge concert/political rally at Tafewa Balewa square in November. The party was disqualified in late 1978 by the Federal Electoral Commission (FEDECO), along with most of the others, allegedly because of its failure to meet organizational guidelines.[7]

Fela's Movement of the People party claimed offices in fourteen of the nineteen state capitals around the country, but the extent to which his organization was a bona fide political party, rather than a glorified fan club, was unclear. The party's symbolic lineage was more obvious. Fela cited "Nkrumahism" as the party's ideology, and in its manifesto, the M.O.P. relied heavily upon the recommendations of a FESTAC colloquium report that advocated African socialism, Pan-Africanism, and cultural revitalization as fundamental to the fulfillment of Nkrumah's vision of an empowered Africa.[8] The M.O.P. logo—a clenched fist imposed on a background of red, black, and green—was an obvious nod to the African-American black power movement that had provided Fela with his political and cultural epiphany. However, despite the manifesto's four-year development plan for the "economic, cultural, social, political, technological, and ideological reconstruction of Nigeria in particular and Africa in general," its concrete policy applications remained vague. Fela spoke in broad strokes, declaring that the party's main objectives were to establish cultural pride among people of African descent, fight against corruption, remove all forms of oppression, establish a democratic civilian government, and encourage research into traditional culture (especially traditional medicine).[9]

On some issues, the party assumed highly unconventional and sometimes contradictory positions. Fela claimed that—in line with his mother's struggle—women would play an active role in the affairs of the nation. But he went on to designate motherhood as the ideal "active role," suggesting that women form "Women Associations," which he called the most "viable medium for the transmission of African culture."[10] Discussing the issue of education in the presidential campaign (this had been a major theme for all candidates since the Obasanjo government launched a program of universal primary education in September 1976), Fela declared education "a fundamental right of every Nigerian child."[11] However, following his meeting with a senior M.O.P. official, a reporter from the *Punch* informed readers that "the first act of their party in power would be to abolish free education. The Movement of the People sees free education as the evil canker [*sic*] destroying the Nigerian society. It enabled parents to send their children to school instead of farms. Schools would be banned, therefore, and children sent to farms to learn all about nature, farming and herbs. The art of reading was unnecessary in their scheme of things."[12]

Following FEDECO's disqualification of his party, Fela defiantly vowed that there would be no election without his movement's participation.[13] But the reality was that as much press as he had garnered from his recent extramusical activities, his primary source of income remained music, and he could not expect to remain either relevant or solvent on the basis of mere scandal. Despite his notoriety, he did not have enough money coming in to support his commune, band, political party, or other projects such as *YAP News.* Having finally settled into a new communal house on Atinubu Olabinjo Street in the outlying Ikeja section of the city (the house had formerly belonged to his old friend, J. K. Braimah), with his political aspirations temporarily dashed as a result of the FEDECO restrictions, and with the performing ban against him lifted, he turned his attention to the full-scale revival of his performing career.

The first order of business was to assemble a new band to replace the departed Afrika 70, and this was complete by the spring of 1979. The new edition was largely comprised of younger recruits such as set drummers Nicholas Avom and Masefswe Anam, conga player Essiet Udoh, bass guitarists Idowu Adewale and Kalanky Clement, guitarists Mardo Martino and Tunde Brown, rhythm pianist Durotimi Ikujenyo, trumpeters Oye Shobowale and Olu Ifayehun, and saxophonists Oyinade Adeniran, Kola Oni, and Mukoro Owieh. Also joining the horn section was Fela's eighteen-year-old son, Femi, on alto saxophone. These new musicians took their places alongside Afrika 70 veterans like Nwokoma Ukem, Okalue Ojeah, and Lekan Animashaun (the new bandleader following Tony Allen's departure). Unlike the former group, where Fela had gradually developed his sound in conjunction with his colleagues, he was clearly the patrician in this band, instructing a younger group of players in the art of afrobeat.

Certainly, enemies in high and low places dreaded his return. On the eve of his reemergence, a letter to *Punch* from the Federal Ministry of Education criticized Fela's influence on the nation's youth and lamented: "It will be recalled that society enjoyed a lease of unpolluted, dignified, and unvulgarised music those peaceful months of Fela's holiday."[14] Others doubted whether the "Chief Priest" would be able to command the stage with the same confidence, vigor, and humor he had before his personal crises. Thus, speculation, anticipation, and trepidation were all high when Fela and the new Afrika 70 gave their first major comeback concert at the University of Ife in July 1979.

By all accounts, the concert—featuring all newly composed material—was a triumphant return, with the new band sounding tight and confident, Fela's creative powers seemingly undiminished, and the political content more direct than ever before. In his review of the show, Fola Arogundade wrote:

> After watching Fela perform, I have no doubt that [he] has lost nothing musically. Money, cars, and some "queens" he has lost, yes. But he is still in touch with music and, if anything, he has had time to reflect and improve on his composition, arrangement, and even his dancing. . . . If

and when he does come back to playing live music regularly, he'll be found to be the old vibrant, dedicated and good musician that he was before the series of deprivations that landed him low all these years.[15]

The high point of the Ife concert was the new song "Unknown Soldier," an epic composition recounting the 1977 Kalakuta attack and written in memory of Fela's mother. Through six mid-tempo verses of his most elaborate vocal arrangements to date, he detailed the horrors of the incident and its aftermath, using a range of traditional choral styles to create a mood of somber reflection. "Unknown Soldier" was released in the fall of 1979 to general acclaim, and Fela said in interviews that he considered his latest song not only a tribute, but "the proper burial of my mama."[16] As with most of the music to follow, "Unknown Soldier" is a lengthy song—over thirty minutes long in its recorded version, which comprised two sides of an LP; the first side contains an instrumental version, while the second side continues with the vocal.[17]

The rest of the new material presented at Ife offered Fela's new vision and new priorities for his music at the dawn of the new decade. He was quoted as saying his new music would be "more definite, less satirical," and in it he clearly sought to address corruption at all levels of government and society, to discuss the nation's predicament in no uncertain terms, and to keep the memory alive of the injustice that had been committed toward the Ransome-Kuti family.[18] He was also foregrounding the political content in anticipation of the next civilian elections, scheduled for 1983. From 1979 on, his songs became virtual manifestos, as he began to focus—and personalize—his analysis of Africa's problems. Where earlier songs tend toward humorous observations of society, Fela's post-Kalakuta work tends toward sardonic indictment of specific segments of society. These songs attack issues of government corruption, bureaucratic mismanagement, and religious complicity in political and economic oppression with a new intensity. While some, songs such as "Perambulator" and the plaintive "Power Show," offer the type of humorous observations he had perfected with Afrika 70, most of Fela's new texts were devoted to harsh and explicit criticisms of Nigerian government policies, specific government officials, events from Nigerian history, and detailed analyses of the colonial encounter. In songs like "International Thief Thief," which contains jibes at former president Obasanjo and ITT/Decca chief M. K. O. Abiola, he took abuse singing to new dimensions, focusing on some of the most powerful personages of the society. "Authority Stealing" compares street criminals to their white-collar counterparts, while the unrecorded "Football Government" uses the analogy of a football game to describe the way Nigeria's natural resources are "kicked" about in a "game" between local elites and foreign interests. "Cross-Examination of the Colonial African Soldier" is an indictment of military leaders, whose actions in Fela's view reflected their colonial-era training, and whom he blamed for the progressive demoralization of the continent. Singing in standard English to simulate the language of the courtroom, he was also clearly reacting to his own his bitter experiences under the military:

FELA: Calling you African people—
This is an African court

Those who want to hear this court
Come in and sit down . . .

My brother you are accused for this case . . .
You now have to tell me, colonial African soldier:
Where were you trained?

CHORUS: I can't remember

FELA: I put it to you, you were trained overseas, the uniform is foreign

CHORUS: I don't know!

FELA: Some time ago, our people fought for independence
It was forties and fifties—
did you fight along with the people?

CHORUS: I don't know!

FELA: You did not struggle with the people!

CHORUS: I don't know!

FELA: The colonial master used you!

CHORUS: I don't know!

FELA: They killed our prisoners and tortured our people!

CHORUS: I don't know!

FELA: How come you are rulers?

CHORUS: I don't know!

FELA: You took power by force!

CHORUS: I don't know!

FELA: How come you are rulers?

CHORUS: I don't know!

FELA: You took power to steal!

CHORUS: I don't know!

FELA: I will now pronounce the judgement, the people will now
comment—You are guilty!

As much as these outcries reflect Fela's disgust with the military's domination of Nigerian politics, they may also have deeper roots. Like Fela, President
Olusegun Obasanjo was a native of Abeokuta, but the similarities between the two
men end there. In contrast to the highly educated Ransome-Kuti family, Obasanjo
came from humbler origins and had risen to prominence through the military. The
antagonism between these two social positions was expressed by Fela's brother
Beko:

I think the military government was a disaster for this country. . . . General Obasanjo was a year below me in school at Abeokuta. People who
joined the army at that time were either people who could not read or

were so poor that they could not get on on their own. With that group of people ruling the country, they tended to develop a complex and they really didn't understand what they were doing, and they made a mess of things as a whole.[19]

"Classical African Music"

*I want to play music that is meaningful, that stands the test of time. . . .
It's no longer commercial, it's deep African music, so I no longer want to
give it that cheap name* [afrobeat].

FELA *quoted in* BROWN 1986:29

The historical and political perspectives of Fela's new music were matched by an evolution in both his method of composition and the mood of the music. He began to refer to his compositions as "classical African music" in order to emphasize this new breadth of vision and seriousness of purpose. The quest for depth and meaningfulness was reflected in a number of ways. The new Afrika 70 gradually expanded during the decade, until at upwards of thirty members it could be considered a small orchestra, carrying for Fela many of the familiar Western connotations of the orchestra as a symbol of "high" artistry and cultural depth. There were stylistic changes as well. While the fundamental afrobeat structure remained, the new personnel stimulated both a new sound and a new approach to composing. For example, in the absence of Tony Allen, the drum set now played a more circumscribed role, laying down repeating, precomposed patterns as opposed to Allen's looser, jazz-inflected style.[20] On top of this, Fela wove a dense, moody texture of guitars (bass, rhythm, and tenor) and a newly added rhythm pianist played a counterharmony line to the rhythm guitar. This last element, an extension of Fela's own rhythmic patterns on keyboard, strengthened the music's modal feeling and showed a clear debt to jazz pianist McCoy Tyner's modal "comping" style. Fela also began to compose extended passages of traditionally styled chorus singing, and to integrate choral lines into the horn arrangements. Harmonically, his music began to sound increasingly polytonal, with horn lines, rhythm patterns, and choral singing often based around different tonal centers. His compositions, which had rarely lasted less than ten minutes, now often approached an hour in length, and album releases were increasingly taken up by single tracks as he lengthened his music and message in line with audience tastes and his new vision. He told Fola Arogundade: "I can't stand all that short music. We dance long distance here, so no three-minute music for me."[21] Still, Fela's vision extended far beyond the dance floor, and he began to downplay his music's function as dance music in interviews, emphasizing its reflective, didactic qualities.

Taken together, these changes resulted in a music that was orchestral in its complexity and more serious in its mood. Where the original Afrika 70 was brash and youthfully arrogant, the new band was moodier, restrained, and more reflective, functioning simultaneously as a vehicle for cultural and political commentary, mystical reflection, and social dancing. Based on the evolution of Fela's music from the early days of Afrika 70 through the band's later music and on to this latest stylistic phase, one could also argue that as the marijuana influence grew stronger, Fela's composing became smoother, spacier, and less edgy. The new band could still turn the fire on, however, and new arrangements like "International Thief Thief" and "Original Sufferhead" featured a barrage of horns over the types of driving, up-tempo grooves that made Afrika 70 so exciting.

New Afrika Shrine

Shortly after the Ife concert, the Afrika 70 organization countered all reasonable expectations when they opened a new Afrika Shrine on Pepple Street in the outlying area of Lagos called Ikeja, two-and-a-half years after their forced exile from Surulere and the Empire Hotel. Located thirty minutes from downtown Lagos, Ikeja was known for its street traders, nightlife, drug trade, and prostitution. Although the new site was not as immediately accessible as the old Shrine, its creation was nevertheless a major triumph surmounting considerable political and economic opposition. A newspaper advertisement presented Fela's new vision for his music and his assertion of its place in society. In Fela's vision, the new Shrine offered a religious, cultural, and political—as well as the expected musical—experience: "After a long battle with the authority, we are staging a big comeback at the new Afrika Shrine. . . . We want the authority, the news media, the public and everybody concerned to know that *Afrika Shrine* is not a NIGHT CLUB—it is a place where we can worship the gods of our ancestors."[22]

With characteristic humor, the flyer continued the religious theme, drawing contrasts with the Christian church in order to emphasize the Shrine's stated cultural mission:

a) THE CHURCH is an ideological centre for the spreading of European and American cultural and political awareness.

THE SHRINE is an ideological centre for the spreading of Afrikan cultural and political awareness.

b) THE CHURCH is a place where songs are rendered for worship.

THE SHRINE is a place where songs are rendered for worship.

c) THE CHURCH is a place where they collect money.

THE SHRINE is a place where we collect money.

d) THE CHURCH is a place where they drink while worshipping ("holy communion").

THE SHRINE is a place where we drink while worshipping.

e) THE CHURCH is a place where they smoke during worship (burning of incense).

THE SHRINE is a place where we smoke during worship.

f) THE CHURCH is a place where they dress the way they like for worship.

THE SHRINE is a place where we dress the way we like for worship.

g) THE CHURCH is a place where they practice foreign religion.

THE SHRINE is a place where we practice Afrikan religion.[23]

Black Power

The religious imagery was partly tongue-in-cheek, and partly calculated to minimize potential opposition to the Shrine as a center for renewed political activism. However, it also reflected Fela's growing interest in spiritual matters, as well as a new set of goals for his music. The early 1980s were a period of soul-searching and reassessment as he grappled with his recent tragedies while attempting to rejuvenate his creative muse. Crucial to this process was his developing relationship with Professor Kwaku Addaie (usually known as Professor Hindu), a Ghanaian magician of some renown. Hindu reportedly came to Lagos at Fela's invitation in the spring of 1981, and shortly thereafter Fela began referring to him as his "spiritual advisor." He said: "I'd almost given up hope of helping to change my society; everything seemed to be going against me—*everything*. . . . For me, I just couldn't compromise my ideas and philosophy. Then I met him. And since I've met him I've seen so much spiritual light."[24]

Under the influence of the Professor (and of his own readings), Fela's work began to reflect a conception of African history that reached far beyond the boundaries of his native Yoruba culture. He began to articulate a view of African culture stretching from classical Egyptian civilization, through the establishment of the Yoruba spiritual/cultural center of Ile-Ife, and on to the contemporary Pan-African world. In the spring of 1981, Fela had a spiritual epiphany, which he often recounted later, and after which he changed the name of his band from Afrika 70 to Egypt 80 "to make people, Africans, recognize that Egyptian civilization was African."[25]

Using the historical achievements of classical Egyptian and Yoruba civilization as a cultural backdrop, Fela began to interpret both historical and contemporary sociopolitical phenomena in terms of his evolving mystical beliefs. According to his new perspective, the impetus for Western technology was provided by a sacred Yoruba "power pot" stolen by explorer Mungo Park from Ife in 1633 and taken back to Queen Victoria in England.[26] In the same vein, he espoused a literal interpretation of the legend that holds that the Ashanti Kingdom was founded when a golden throne descended from the sky.[27] He also began to vilify the African leadership responsible for the continent's current condition in supernatural terms, seeing them as reincarnated malevolent spirits: "You see, here's what happened. In the fifteenth century, at the beginning of the slave trade it was the African gods and the European gods that conspired together to make the slave trade successful. So those leaders in Africa today are those ancient gods that have come back to replay those parts that they played in those times to make Africa what it is today."[28]

As much as Fela embraced a Pan-African cultural vision, he tended to draw on the icons of his own Yoruba culture for inspiration. In songs such as "Just Like That" and "Give Me Shit, I Give You Shit" he chanted the names of mythical Yoruba figures like Oranyan, Orompoto, and Oranmiyan.[29] In his own twist on Yoruba orisha worship, he installed a photograph of his mother on the new Shrine's altar, giving her the name *Afa Ojo* (She Who Commands Rain) and pouring libations to her along with the other Pan-African heroes making up his pantheon. Fela's occasional lack of distinction between the local, national, and continental elements reflects the essentialist tendency in his postcolonial effort to forge a Pan-African identity. The elevation of his mother to orisha status reflects a systematic personalization and hybridization common in postcolonial African religion; he took this liberty although he was not a traditional priest or adherent in any sense of the term.[30]

Another major theme to emerge in Fela's work during the early 1980s was his espousal of traditional forms of knowledge. In his view, one of the major crimes of African leadership was its reluctance to explore this area, remaining instead dependent on imposed Western forms of expression, thought, and technology. Fela did not explore this them much in his songs, but it was central to the university lectures he gave between 1979 and 1981, in which, in addition to preaching Pan-Africanism, he extolled the values of naturalism, herbalism, and "African science." Essentially, he was advocating a form of science that operated in harmony with nature and drew on indigenous traditions to create a distinctly African technology. In Fela's view, Western culture was too dependent on a technology that degraded the environment and thus was unsustainable. An African variant could offer a more natural alternative. On the university lecture circuit or on stage in yabis sessions, Fela regularly criticized the government's suppression of research into herbal medicine and other aspects of traditional culture.

In line with his new vision of nature, culture, and spirit, Fela by 1981 was clearly trying to use his music to create a "sacred space" in which musical and textual symbols would interact to add a more profound cultural resonance to the music. The spacier, more languorous mood of his new songs complemented his reflective, sardonic lyrics, broadened cultural vision, and increasingly mystical inclinations. Waterman noted a similar development in juju music of the nationalist period, where the slowing of tempos "represents a convergence with Yoruba secular dance drumming . . . much of which is markedly slower than early juju music. Informants describe it as a move 'downward,' toward 'cooler,' more 'solemn' feelings. The slowing of tempos in the postwar period . . . made juju more deeply and self-consciously Yoruba in form, feeling, and content."[31]

1981's "Movement of the People" is built upon a hypnotic, neofunk pattern highlighting the interplay between the rhythm piano and traditional hand drums, with the song's instrumental introduction—a series of atonal organ trills over percussion—recalling the eccentric sound of a traditional incantation. The mid-tempo "Army Arrangement," from the same year, juxtaposes the straight eighth-note march of the bass guitar against the complex, swirling motion of the rest of the ensemble, resulting in a belligerent, entrancing rhythm pattern. Both of these songs also contain multimovement horn and chorus themes over sauntering modal grooves, occasionally recalling the formal complexity of Fela's horn writing for Koola Lobitos. Fela also introduced a new compositional device. Although they are still fundamentally modal vamps, both songs contain harmonic modulations to contrasting sections, heightening the tension and release in the music's development. In distinction to his Afrika 70 work, in which he often performed on electric piano, the early 1980s often found Fela relying heavily on his electric organ playing. Clearly, he was clearly presenting music of a different order than "Lady," "Jeun K'oku," or even "Zombie."

He said in an interview around this time: "Africans are the only people who have not been able to use their knowledge for human benefit because of oppression. I think the African concept is the concept of the future. . . . Africa will be able to create a new knowledge of naturalism, spiritualism, being able to create through higher forces, being able to treat ailments of the body by natural means and not through chemicals . . . being able to have a new science. . . . This is my message. That is what I want to achieve in my music."[32]

Besides reinforcing Fela's ideas about African culture, African history, and a higher purpose for his music, Professor Hindu had another, more remarkable influence on Fela, who began to stretch beyond conceptions of history into the realm of the supernatural. During the Professor's initial Lagos visit in May 1981, he gave a number of public demonstrations of his reputed powers. In two appearances at the Shrine, he reportedly hacked open one man's throat and fatally shot another. In both cases, the bodies were buried outside of the Shrine for several days before being revived by the Professor.[33] Fela announced to the public in a full-page newspaper advertisement:

> On Wednesday 6th of May 1981 (at) 10 P.M., Professor Addaie shot and killed a man at the Shrine. The body is buried right in the Shrine, you can go there and see; the body is still in the tomb. At 7 P.M. today Friday the 8th of May, 1981, the body will be resurrected by Professor Addaie himself. We hereby invite all press, doctors, Police, C.I.D. [Central Intelligence Division], N.S.O. [National Security Organization], Presidential Guards, etc. to come and see true Afrikan powers with their own two eyes. With this, there is no Jesus—THERE IS AFRIKA.[34]

In some senses, Fela could draw upon a cultural tradition of musicians as guardians of esoteric knowledge to justify his forays into mysticism. Many musicians had been trained in the Christian church, for example, resulting in a substantial influence of Christianity in popular music through the inclusion of hymns, proverbs, and biblical verses. Juju star Ebenezer Obey pursued a parallel career as a Christian minister (using his born surname, Fabiyi), and juju pioneer I. K. Dairo even founded his own Christian Yoruba church known as Aladura, of which he was the pastor. A similar influence can be found in Muslim popular styles like fuji, sakara, and apala, which abound with Koranic verses, praise lyrics for Allah, and Yoruba proverbs. A more concrete interpretation of Fela's actions would hold that the Nigerian music business is frequently treacherous, and musicians need whatever protection they can manage; reliance on magic had occasionally been used as a strategy among competing Yoruba musicians. In one remarkable incident, for example, early juju innovator Tunde King is said to have spent fifteen years in exile after a malevolent magical object was nailed to the Lagos pier from which he departed.[35] This pattern held true throughout sub-Saharan Africa. In Zaire, witchcraft was assumed to be an important factor in the success of popular musicians.[36] The entourage of legendary Zairean bandleader Franco was alleged to routinely include a team of sorcerers, for example. Far from denying these rumors, Franco, when asked about his alleged involvement in sorcery, replied: "Why do you ask me that? Even the Cameroun football team took twelve doctors to the World Cup. Don't you think there were some sorcerers among them?"[37]

In the eyes of some Nigerians, Fela's championing of what many derisively termed a "witch-doctor" reflected a retreat into mysticism betrayed a true political mission and confirmed his lack of critical political insight.[38] Others felt he was reasonably attempting to find a means of psychic empowerment that would also repel government violence directed at him and his followers. Frank Fairfax speculated that Fela's indulgence in mysticism tended to increase in direct proportion to the amount of stress on his household,[39] and indeed, in "Unknown Soldier" he had cited the soldiers' use of witchcraft against him during the Kalakuta attack.[40] Perhaps this was his motivation for so openly inviting his armed establishment enemies—soldiers, policeman, and security officers—to the Professor's demonstration. But to most, including some of his family members, Fela's embrace of mysticism confirmed a growing suspicion that his suffering had affected his sanity; this was confirmed to some when he claimed that he was now able to communicate with the spirit of his deceased mother, as well as to identify his own previous bodily incarnations in dynastic Egypt.[41] It was also evidently draining his resources. Fela's son Femi claims his father was "a victim of his belief."

> Fela changed when Hindu came into his life. Everyone now got worried because Fela wouldn't listen to anyone except for Hindu. My mother said I should come out of it because it was getting too diabolical and deceitful. But I told her "If I leave him now, it is possible he will get killed and we will lose him forever." I felt this because Hindu once told Fela that if he wore a special African bulletproof vest, they could shoot him and he wouldn't die. To prove it, Hindu got a gun and put the jacket on a goat and fired six shots to show it really worked. Later, we found out he had used blanks. But my father thought this was wonderful and he wanted to put the jacket on himself. Luckily, his elder brother said "Let's try it on another goat, just in case." So they took this double-barrelled gun—and the goat died. And Fela cried and cried. Obviously, they were cheating him.[42]

"International Thief Thief"

It was not surprising that Fela sought supernatural protection, as his recent vitriolic attacks on some of the country's most powerful political and business were unprecedented. "Gimme Shit, I Give You Shit" included a direct attack on Decca chief M. K. O. Abiola, whom Fela continued to blame for nonpayment of hundreds of thousands of naira in back royalties, dating to the 1977–1978 dispute. In 1981's "International Thief Thief" (the title is a derisive play on the multinational company's acronym), Fela depicts both Abiola and former president Obasanjo as "thieves," "rats running over and under," and "men of low mentality." An uptempo indictment in the tradition of "Zombie," "Alagbon Close," and "Expensive Shit," "International Thief Thief," like "Alagbon Close" and "No Buredi" before it, uses the image of the *agbepo* (human waste carter) to great effect:

FELA: Long time ago, Africa man, we no dey carry shit We dey shit inside big-big hole For Yorubaland na "shalanga" For Iboland na "onunu-insi" For Hausaland na "salga" For Ashantiland na "tifi" . . . And during the time dem come colonize us Dem come teach us to carry shit . . .	*FELA:* A long time ago, African people didn't carry shit We shat inside a very big hole called "shalanga" in Yorubaland "Onunu-insi" in Iboland "Salga" in Hausaland "Tifi" in Ashantiland . . . During the time Europeans colonized us They taught us to carry shit . . .
Many foreign companies dey Africa Carry all our money go Dem get one style wey dem dey use Dem go pick one African man A man with low mentality Dem go give am million-naira bread To become one useless chief Like rat dey do Pass under under Pass out out Pass in in Pass up up Like Obasanjo and Abiola—	Many foreign companies in Africa Take our money and run They use a similar style— They pick an African man A man with low mentality They give him a million naira To become a useless chief Like rats, they run under, out, in, and up Like Obasanjo and Abiola—
CHORUS: International Thief Thief!	*CHORUS:* International Thief Thief!
FELA: We don tire to carry anymore dem shit . . .	*FELA:* We are tired of carrying their shit . . .

These provocations increasingly extended beyond his songs. The occupation of Decca in 1978 marked the beginning of a campaign of sporadic public mischief that would continue for the next few years as Fela attempted to antagonize the authorities by all means at his disposal. On the eve of Independence Day, October 1, 1979, as the military regime of Obasanjo prepared to transfer power to the civilian regime of Shehu Shagari, Fela and fifty-seven members of his organization mounted a ghoulish protest at Obasanjo's residence at Dodan Barracks in the Obalende section of Lagos Island. After bursting through a military roadblock while armed soldiers fired machine guns at their speeding van, they placed a symbolic mock coffin on the steps of the barracks, a silent protest against Fela's mother's death at the hands of the military. While Fela later claimed that the successful protest proved the power of the human spirit over the power of the gun, the entire Afrika 70 organization was later beaten and arrested when they refused to remove the coffin;[43] the soldiers assumed there was sorcery involved and found the coffin "spiritually threatening."[44]

Months later, police were summoned to the headquarters of the *Punch* newspaper after Fela physically threatened Chief Abiola when the two encountered each other in the paper's offices.

> Policemen were called in on Thursday night to escort Chief Moshood Abiola of ITT from *Punch* premises at Ikeja because of threat of assault by musician Fela Anikulapo-Kuti. Both Chief Abiola and Fela were on official visits to the *Punch* when they met. Fela accused Chief Abiola of not allowing Decca Recording company to pay him some money and he threatened to "deal" with him . . . a contingent of policeman were called in to ensure Chief Abiola's safe journey home.[45]

Soon after, it was reported that ten buckets of human feces had been dumped at the gate of Abiola's Lagos mansion and smeared on its walls.[46] These were accompanied by anonymous signs imploring "Abiola and Decca" to "give us our money." It appeared that Fela and his entourage had literally given Abiola shit, as he had promised in his song. In another incident, he took a Mercedes-Benz automobile from EMI following a payment dispute with the company, and—in desecration of its prestige value—used it to haul crude firewood from the countryside (the company later repossessed the car with the assistance of the police).[47] This continued goading of Nigeria's most powerful public figures worked counter to his attempts to cultivate an image as a credible politician, confirming many Nigerians' perceptions of him as a troublemaker. As one letter to a Lagos daily paper complained:

> Every time I hear Fela Anikulapo-Kuti say "I am going to rule Nigeria," I get ulcers in my stomach. Just how is he going to do that? How is Fela, who balks the rule of law at every opportunity and with so much impunity, going to rule the nation, since the practice of democracy calls for a lot of self-restraint? Can we possibly entrust the economy of this nation to someone who couldn't manage his own resources which, I'm sure, is why he is broke now? . . . One can't but acknowledge Fela as a great talent in African music but he is wasting away this talent.[48]

Fela's actions also had more serious consequences. In one 1979 incident, he was arrested and charged with armed robbery after one of Abiola's wives charged that he had robbed her at gunpoint. The charges were later dismissed after it was established that Afrika 70 was performing in another part of the country on the date in question. The band's planned 1980 tour of Italy, sponsored by the Italian Communist Party, was an opportunity for a major political statement. Upon arrival in Naples, however, 45 kilograms of marijuana were found stitched into the lining of the band's luggage. The American woman who eventually confessed to planting the marijuana was later rumored to be an associate of both the Nigerian government and of Abiola. Even though he was eventually cleared of all charges, the bust was a substantial setback for Fela's political aspirations, as the Communist Party distanced itself from him to avoid further embarrassment.[49]

Fela and the Rise of "World Music"

I cannot tell you it's gonna take this, gonna take that, before African music breaks into America, into the world. . . . It will break into the world, but it will take its time, very gradually but very systematic and consistent, because that is the best way for the music to break. The gods do not want the music to break into the international scene as a fashion. [They want] it to break in as a serious cultural episode.

FELA *quoted in* STEWART 1992:122

If Fela's attempt to rebuild his domestic career proved complicated in light of personal tribulations and the post–oil boom economic climate, other prospects loomed. The growing "world music" market held great promise for Fela, who returned to the Nigerian music scene in a period when the halcyon days of the oil-boom 1970s were gradually fading into memory and the country was slowly descending into economic recession. This weakened the country's music industry, leaving the market more vulnerable to imported disco and funk music, the latest American styles and artists to "invade" the region. Live music also declined as discotheques began to replace live bands in many major nightclubs, including Afrika 70's former haunt, the Surulere Night Club.[50]

During the mid-1970s, at the height of his popularity, Fela never performed outside of Africa, declaring that his music was inspired by the African experience and was meant for Africans first and foremost. This refusal to perform abroad was also his way of protesting the "colonial" attitude displayed by many musicians smitten by the prestige and glamour associated with performing in the West. Since the destruction of Kalakuta, however, Fela's financial state, as well as the general economic climate, spurred his interest in building an international audience for his music, and the international music industry became an important factor in the revival of his career. In fact, there had been talk of promoting Fela abroad since the FESTAC period, when he made a lasting impression among the visiting delegates and had several major profiles written on him in the Western press.[51]

Apart from his prepolitical days with Koola Lobitos in the United States, Fela's face-to-face interaction with Western audiences began with the original Afrika 70's performance at the 1978 Berlin Jazz Festival, the group's first major performance outside of Africa. Fela and Afrika 70 were invited as part of a program celebrating the African roots of jazz, and Fela's reputation as the continent's most popular and notorious musician preceded him to Berlin. Certainly, he must have remembered the favorable impression gained during his 1958 visit to East Berlin, and he no doubt expected that the audience would be receptive to his political music.

The event encapsulates many of the issues that would surround Fela's reception in the West. By consensus the most provocative and controversial performer on the program, Fela drew a decidedly mixed response from the audience in Berlin's Philharmonic Hall. Although Afrika 70 gave an excellent performance (the recording of "Vagabonds in Power" was taken from the show), Fela was misunderstood as a musician, booed as a performer, and dismissed by critics, who considered a neotraditional percussion ensemble led by his old British associate Ginger Baker the evening's only "authentic" African music. One review reported that Fela "presented a long, drawn-out and rather uninteresting show related to the old soul music which becomes embarrassing when he puts aside his saxophone for electric organ," while another characterized Afrika 70's music as "unfortunately very Western, namely a variation of the most primitive disco music with faint African undertones . . . received by the Berlin audience with boos and cries of 'No disco' and 'No Travolta.' "[52] The Berlin audience's problem with Fela rested on three main counts: he was dismissed as a progressive political figure because of his despotic stage demeanor and his harem of wives; he was misunderstood as an instrumentalist by jazz fans who expected technical virtuosity in the jazz sense; and he was derided as a performer by African music purists who resented the pop stylings of his music and presentation.

This implicitly political misunderstanding was fundamentally a clash of two conflicting notions of what constituted the "legitimate" concerns of African music. In Fela's view, his art remained faithful to a fundamental African spirit in its rejection of the strictures of colonial European culture, its overt embrace of Pan-African musical and cultural elements, its communal social function, and its aura of grassroots politicization. The Berlin audience, on the other hand, was expecting a traditional, nonconfrontational musician whom it could appreciate on purely aesthetic grounds, independently of cross-cultural power dynamics or aesthetically "impure" cross-influences. Instead, it got a politically engaged contemporary musician whose art was directly rooted in global politics, diasporic African musical styles, and the power relationship between Africa and the West—in short, one reflecting the complexities and contradictions of the African postcolonial experience. The dynamics of the Berlin Festival would continue to characterize Fela's negotiation of the international music audience in the coming years.

Number 25 Olavsgate, Oslo is a sprawling building of ancient Norwegian architecture. Its main entrance leads to several floors of entertainment. The crowd is full of anticipation as the joint peaks—an hour before midnight—

*and if you happen to have come from Nigeria, you can't help being
surprised as Mr. Deejay erupts with Fela Anikulapo-Kuti's "Lady" which
instantly engulfs the entire audience in bouts of euphoria. There are shouts
for more Fela, and they get it. You have gold in your hands if you happen
to own a Fela album in Scandinavia. Our "black president" has suddenly
become an international superstar and his music is steadily winning
Nigeria more friends than our new dynamic foreign policy.*

TONY AMADI (1976)

Much had changed by 1981. International interest in African popular music, initially spurred in the late 1960s by expatriate South African musicians such as
Hugh Masekela and Miriam Makeba, followed an upward trajectory throughout
the 1970s, intensified by the huge international success of Manu Dibango's 1974
dance hit "Soul Makossa." Such was the growing international influence of musicians like Fela and Zaire's Franco that by the beginning of the 1980s, a feeling
existed in certain quarters of the music industry that with the proper promotional
and marketing strategies, African pop might well represent the next major trend
in international popular music.

In large part, the way for Afropop had been paved by the growing popularity
of Jamaican reggae music in Europe and the United States since the late 1970s. The
work of musicians such as Bob Marley offered a popular style that was at once
accessible, exotic, and politicized. The sound of Jamaican patois and the neo-
African rhythms of "roots" reggae had also primed the Western public's ear for
African sounds. While many reggae performers maintained strong Western followings, the style's initial international explosion was largely due to the output of
a single group of three charismatic singer-songwriters—the Wailers (Bob Marley,
Peter Tosh, and Bunny Wailer)—and the international music industry machine that
propelled them to worldwide stardom. Within Jamaica, as Peter Manuel has noted,
reggae's aura of authenticity and conviction strongly reflected a period of sociopolitical ferment that culminated in the election of Michael Manley's socialist People's National Party in 1972.[53] This era effectively ended with Marley's death from
cancer in May 1981, as well as Manley's ouster from office in 1980. Although a
number of reggae groups continued to tour and release recordings internationally,
reggae lost its most visible, charismatic, and articulate spokesman, and the post-
Marley Jamaican music industry largely returned to its studio and dancehall—as
opposed to live performance—orientation.

Another reason for Afropop's rising international star was its influence on the
more experimental forms of Western rock music and its practitioners like David
Byrne and Brian Eno. The pervasive influence of Yoruba culture in particular was
demonstrated in the title of Byrne and Eno's 1981 collaboration *My Life in the Bush
of Ghosts,* the title of which was taken from a well-known magical-realist work by
Yoruba novelist Amos Tutuola. Byrne titled a juju-influenced track from his 1982
Catherine Wheel score "Ade" in homage to the Nigerian juju star, while Eno produced Edikanfo, a Ghanaian highlife band. In fact, Eno had originally wanted to
produce Fela, but the project never materialized. Even in the realm of mainstream

popular music, emerging megastar Michael Jackson had borrowed from Manu Dibango's "Soul Makossa" in his 1983 hit song "Wanna Be Startin' Something."

The specific attraction of Western audiences to Fela's music was rooted in several elements. Musically, it was simultaneously familiar, cosmopolitan, and exotic to Western ears. The funky beats and jazzy horn lines were familiar enough to Western ears attuned to James Brown, salsa, and jazz, while still containing a strongly African nuance. The same was true for afrobeat vocals, which, like Jamaican patois, were at once familiar in their use of the English language and exotic in their Africanized nuance. Fela's message of naturalism, antimilitarism, and social rebellion struck a chord with the concerns and sensibilities of late Cold-War European youth, which were similarly rooted in a mixture of postwar, antinuclear, postcolonial, and ecological sentiment, and similarly infused by the spirit of America's social struggles of the 1960s.[54] Fela's image was also fueled by *Music Is the Weapon,* a widely shown European television documentary on his life and work, which inspired the subsequent visits of hordes of left-wing European journalists to his home in Lagos. Their reports, as Lindsay Barrett notes, presented the image of "this pop singer with a message that seemed to engender more wrath in government than anyone in their own tradition seemed to be able to do. They left with the impression of an unbelievably virile, uncompromising hedonistic lifestyle that was somehow both totally free and highly-disciplined. . . . They succeeded in building up the image of a national martyr whose ideas, although totally unconventional in terms of European mores, were even more unacceptable to his own society."[55]

Island Records president Chris Blackwell, searching for a charismatic third world musical superstar to succeed the recently deceased Marley, expressed interest in bringing African pop to an international audience in 1981, and the company had already released a series of Afropop compilations.[56] With the expressed interest of a major international record company experienced in promoting third world artists, it appeared that the equally charismatic and legendary Fela was poised to duplicate Marley's international superstardom. He joined forces with Martin Messonier, a French producer active on the Nigerian music scene and connected with Island. Despite his client's prior problems with multinational companies, Messonier arranged a record deal for the distribution of Fela's music in Europe, as well as a limited European tour. Arista Records released *Black President,* a compilation containing three edited Afrika 70 songs, followed by *Original Sufferhead,* Fela's current Nigerian release, issued in unedited form.

The reception Fela and Egypt 80 received during their spring 1981 mini-tour of Europe seemed to confirm him as the inheritor of Marley's mantle of politicized, Afrocentric pop. Not only were the concerts in Paris, Brussels, and Strasbourg huge successes, but Fela's political message was given equal time to the music. A translator stood onstage at concerts and interpreted Fela's between-song "yabis" for the French-speaking audiences, and preshow press conferences were arranged in all tour cities, allowing him to elaborate his political views. One observer noted:

> Hardly anyone from Nigeria in that [Paris] audience had realized the extent to which Fela has become a folk hero of European youth. The

roar that greeted not even his own appearance but the appearance of the band onstage at the Nouvel Hippodrome in Porte de Pantin could be heard nearly a mile away on that Sunday night. This, it turned out, was only the beginning. Throughout the show security men were carting away fainted enthusiasts and several times the stage was almost stormed. . . . The crowd was totally his for the entire duration of the concert which ran more than two hours over schedule.[57]

This scenario was repeated at each of three remaining stops on the tour. However, conflicts arose away from the stage. Fela's European performances were sometimes listless, a development that some attributed to his heavy use of a blend of liquified THC extract and native Nigerian *ogogoro* gin which he called "Felagoro."[58] Further, he was not receptive to his promoters' main suggestions: first, that he decrease the size of his entourage in order to maximize profits (on one European tour he traveled with an entourage of seventy, only twenty or so of whom were actual performers[59]); second, that he lessen—at least temporarily—the political emphasis in his recordings and performances, in order that they might be more palatable to Western audiences; third, that he temporarily relocate to Europe to avoid further government harassment and to create a Western base from which his career might be more effectively managed; and fourth, that he relax his long-standing policy of presenting only new, unrecorded material in concert, and that he perform familiar, less political classics from his 1970s repertoire.

There was widespread speculation on the question of whether Fela—said to be virtually penniless at the time—would compromise his confrontational message and lengthy anti-entertainment presentation in order to gain the mass audience and wealth that were presumed possible, along with acknowledgment as the major innovator in contemporary African music. Ian Watts noted: "The direction of Fela's music will be watched very closely to see if he can sustain his original fire and spirit, as there is speculation as to whether he may compromise his political message, even if briefly, to attract much needed funds—a story similar to the artistic problems encountered by the late Bob Marley."[60] Marley's 1978 LP, *Kaya*—largely a collection of love songs and paeans to marijuana—was perceived by many as a retreat from the political themes dominating his previous release, *Exodus* (1977), in the wake of intense political violence in Jamaica that included an attempt on the singer's life. It was also considered by some to be a direct attempt to court nonpoliticized American and European audiences.

The 1981 Paris performance indicated that Fela was not willing to compromise his music on any terms—the unrecorded compositions he presented on this occasion were among his most political to date. "Army Arrangement" discusses the Nigerian presidential elections of 1979, widely dismissed as fraudulent. "Movement of the People (Political Statement #1)" traces the process by which the British colonized Nigeria and instituted a trained, modern military that progressively evolved into a tool of the indigenous ruling classes, to be used against the poor masses in the face of hardening class divisions in modern Nigeria:

FELA: Now let us ask ourselves, wetin be government?
Government na father of the people, father must like him son
Son must like him father too
But the things wey dey happen for Africa, I will make an explanation:
The government whey we get, na overseas sense dem go get
Dem no be father, we no love dem as son
Dem be the masters, we be the servants
Food na plenty money, not enough houses to stay

They houses wey e de, dem dey cost plenty money
You go for any town, no water for the town
The government wey we get, dem be blackman for di face
The government wey we get, dem be whiteman for di yansch . . .

That is why you go see-o:
Judge dey go—

CHORUS: One police go follow am

FELA: Assemblyman dey go—

CHORUS: Two police go follow am

FELA: Senator dey go—
CHORUS: Three police go follow am

FELA: Speaker dey go—
CHORUS: Four police go follow am

FELA: President dey go—

CHORUS: Hundred police go follow am

FELA: Now let us ask ourselves, what is government?
Government is the father of the people, the father must like his son
The son must like his father too
But I will explain the things which happen in Africa:
The government we have has a western orientation
They are not our fathers, we don't love them as sons
They are the masters, we are the servants
Plenty food and money exist, but there are not enough houses to live in
They houses they live in cost plenty money
But any town you visit lacks water
They government is black to the appearance
But white underneath . . .

That is why you see:
A judge appears in public—

CHORUS: One policeman accompanies him

FELA: An assemblyman appears in public—

CHORUS: Two policemen accompany him

FELA: A senator appears in public—
CHORUS: Three policemen accompany him

FELA: A speaker appears in public—
CHORUS: Four policemen accompany him

FELA: The president appears in public—

CHORUS: One hundred policemen accompany him

FELA: Thousand police go follow am-o	*FELA:* One thousand policemen accompany him
CHORUS: (repeats)	*CHORUS:* (repeats)
FELA: Riot soldiers go line up-o	*FELA:* Riot soldiers line up
CHORUS: (repeats)	*CHORUS:* (repeats)
FELA: N.S.O. go dey hang around you	*FELA:* The National Security Organization[61] hangs around
CHORUS: (repeats)	*CHORUS:* (repeats)
FELA: C.I.A. go dey hide somewhere	*FELA:* The C.I.A. is hiding somewhere
CHORUS: (repeats)	*CHORUS:* (repeats)
FELA: Dem dey take chance-o . . .	*FELA:* They take chances . . . [i.e., by appearing in public]

Despite the sophistication of Fela's new music, audiences often wanted to hear older Afrika 70 classics. Fela explained his refusal to perform a "greatest hits" show, a decision at least partially rooted in his long-standing policy of not performing material that had already been commercially released: "I don't believe in falling on old tunes to play to the audience. I want my audience to feel me where I'm at, not where I was. To feel me where I'm at gives me progress, makes me feel I am communicating. So to fall back and start to play old tunes, for me it's retrogressive. It doesn't give me the challenge and the impetus to write new songs. . . . With that kind of decision, I'm forced to keep writing."[62]

The management grew frustrated at Fela's intractability in the face of both prospects for international stardom and his own precarious financial situation. In addition to the obvious market considerations, there was also the serious problem of conducting business with a high-profile political dissident living under a military government. This was evidently a factor when the London-based Arista failed to help organize a London show despite the obvious success of the other European shows.[63] An attempt at a second European tour ended in financial disaster when a three-day rainstorm ruined a series of planned concerts in Holland and the tour promoter absconded with the money.[64] Shortly thereafter, Messonier and Fela parted company bitterly, and the Frenchman began to work with Fela's countryman, juju star Sunny Ade. Greg Tate, in a 1983 profile on Ade, reported:

> Both [Ade's road manager] Sammy and Martin [Messonier] came to work with Sunny after leaving Fela. Sammy says he left Fela because the man is getting old, smokes too much, mixes music and politics, and was responsible for Sammy getting arrested. . . . Fela, Sammy says, is an honest man but a hardhearted man who believes he's always right and that kind of man you cannot communicate too well with about business.[65]

Even local businessmen often found it difficult to conduct business with the Chief Priest. Nigerian concert promoter Aib Igiehon encountered him as not a man who cared much about making money. . . . He was very weird, superstitious and most of the time in the mood of a man who had gone out of it and into the spirit world. You could not discuss with him successfully on business matters. If you said anything that he did not like, that was the end of the business talk. When you praised him so much, he could get annoyed and if you did not praise him, he could get annoyed too.[66]

"Synchro System"

Sunny Ade and his band, the African Beats, subsequently enjoyed a short but substantial period of international success and critical acclaim, generating ecstatic press notices and providing European and American audiences with some of the most exciting concerts of African music ever given in the West. Ade was an obvious candidate for several reasons. The Island Records organization characterized him as receptive to new ideas and easy to work with, and he had already established a reputation for innovation in juju music, having variously experimented with the pedal steel guitar, electric keyboard, vibraphone, and synthesizer in his juju lineup.

Another factor was also significant. Since the late 1970s, Ade's juju style had gradually come to reflect the influence of Fela's afrobeat. Ade himself characterized this as a simple decision to compose in minor keys in addition to the major keys favored by most juju composers. He also distinguished the styles on the basis of instrumentation: "Everybody is based in African rhythms, and what you put on top makes you define it. Like afrobeat, they're using horns, and they normally play on minor . . . but we always play on major-minor, and our rhythms are fully loaded with percussion. But afrobeat only has a conga, shekere and clefs. It doesn't have the others, except it has all horns."[67]

Ade's 1976 release "Synchro System" partially supports his comments. Although the arrangement already reflects the subtle influence of afrobeat in its use of a tenor guitar and funky, syncopated electric bass line, the harmony has an ambiguous modal quality, which, it could be argued, characterizes much West African guitar music. In addition, the drum set is mixed almost inaudibly low, with the percussion section dominated by a variety of small instruments, while the rhythm guitar plays a gentle, finger-picked figure characteristic of palmwine or guitar-band highlife music.

However, by the time of Ade's heavily backed international tours of the early 1980s (including support from the Nigerian government, which payed for the band's plane tickets), his recordings and concerts contained melodic and structural passages borrowed directly from Fela's compositions and arranged for the African Beats. Two examples of this are Ade's 1977 song "Oba Adeyemi," which contains an excerpt of "Sorrow, Tears, and Blood," and the mid-1980s release *O Ti To (The Truth)*, which contains a reworked arrangement of Fela's "Excuse-O" as an instrumental interlude. Less directly, Ade's older juju staples such as "Ma Jaiye Oni" were reworked for live performance so that the lilting major-key sections were dramatically interspersed with minor-key afrobeat interludes, driven by the assertive, afrobeat-influenced style of the band's set drummer, Akanbi Moses, and the psychedelic pedal-steel guitar of Ademola Adepoju. The updated version of "Synchro System" released for the international market in 1982 abandoned the traditional modalism and palmwine-styled guitar work of the earlier version in favor of minor-key Dorian mode harmony, a James Brown–styled rhythm guitar line, and a typical Tony Allen drum set pattern—all explicit elements of afrobeat. Many of Ade's more recent tracks such as "Ja Funmi" or "Penkele" were, at least instrumentally, composed completely within an afrobeat style (minus the horns, of course), and both 1982's *Synchro System* LP and 1984's *Aura* LP are filled with many instrumental passages of pure afrobeat; *Aura's* opening track, "Ase," sounds particularly close to Fela's "Alagbon Close." Tony Allen (who made a guest appearance on the track "Oremi") explained the similarity: "Bob [Ohiri, former guitarist with Afrika 70 and subsequently a member of Ade's African Beats] arranges the guitar works of the tunes—he got the ideas from Fela. Because, since Sunny started going to afrobeat—you know he's a juju musician but has infused it with afrobeat—Ohiri had that knowledge of afrobeat so he just started helping."[68]

Whether these borrowings reflect a deliberate strategy or a more organic process of stylistic influence, Ade and other musicians often earned Fela's ire, and he derided them as "thieves" for their occasional lifting of his music. Borrowing among musicians and styles is commonplace, and Fela's stance in one sense reflected his comparatively strict notion of "composition" and "originality." At the same time, he seemed less judgmental of musicians who drew stylistically on afrobeat while remaining relatively true to its social meaning. It seems took the most exception to those who placed his musical innovations at the service of what he considered trite or "colonial" social sentiments.

The clear stylistic distinctions I have drawn between the juju and afrobeat styles are not necessarily distinctions made by Nigerian listeners, since music in this context often derives its ultimate social meaning not only from its sonic character, but also from the social context in which it is performed. Thus, while juju music resonates with images of traditional Yoruba values, traditional philosophy, Christianity, refinement, prestige, rural settings, and connections to power, afrobeat resonates with images of disrespect toward and antagonism of authority, hemp smoking, promiscuity, urban life, and general social deviance. These associations will, in all likelihood, remain hard and fast even as the stylistic characteristics sometimes overlap.

The inclusion of afrobeat structures was a major component of Ade's international success. The Western press consistently noted the uncanny similarity between juju music and African-American funk, but generally attributed this to a universalist, Pan-Africanist musical impulse, as opposed to a specific process of stylistic adaptation and hybridization facilitated by a specific individual. *Down Beat* writer Bill Milkowski mused that Ade's band "held down a funky staccato root that sounded as gritty and nasty as James Brown's 'Get On the Good Foot.' "[69] Greg Tate made the musical connection clearer, drawing comparisons with African-American dance music to describe a performance of Ade's juju:

The energy and enthusiasm is so infectious and so on-the-One that everywhere you look, people is getting happy feet, giving it up to the funk, getting down, getting off, moving, grooving, working up a sweat and being swayed, soothed, and cooled out in a single motion. . . . Would the same folk whose life-force is responsible for Trouble Funk, Grandmaster Flash, Slave, Cameo, and even Michael Jackson check the righteous connection between juju music and the funk and go with it?[70]

Along with the prior successes of musicians like Hugh Masekela, Miriam Makeba, and Manu Dibango, Ade's success can be credited with laying the foundation for Afropop's widespread acceptance in the West, and this had both local and continental implications. In the wake of his success, Nigerian bands led by Ebenezer Obey, Sonny Okosuns, Dele Abiodun, and Segun Adewale lined up for international recording contracts, as did older, established continental stars such as Masekela, Franco, Tabu Ley Rochereau, and Manu Dibango, as well as newer acts like Senegal's Toure Kunda and Gambia's Foday Musa Suso. On the home front in Nigeria, top juju stars Ade and Obey competed to consolidate their growing status as important social personalities and prominent Christians. Obey publicly proclaimed a renewed commitment to his Christian faith,[71] while Ade was ordained an apostle in the indigenous Aladura Christian church. In an interview, Ade suggested his musical mission was divinely sanctioned, while reassuring his fans that the spiritual commitment would not compromise his music: "This is because I can't see myself deviating from my life ambition which is to modernise our Black music to world standard, at least now that God has shown me that he is with me."[72]

In the budding Afropop market, the buzz was that due to Fela's stubbornness and lack of business acumen, his popular rival Sunny Ade had "stolen" his fire and gained the international acclaim rightfully due Fela as an Afropop innovator. Ian Pye thus proclaimed in the British *Melody Maker:* "Kuti's whole approach is outrageously spaced out; his near 20-strong band holding the same churning rhythm endlessly while their leader deliver[s] Third World sermons. . . . Ultimately I can't help but think it will be Sunny Ade who is destined to make the biggest impact on Western music, simply because what he has to offer has a freshness and originality that Kuti sorely lacks."[73]

"Confusion Break Bone"

While Ade and other African musicians were taking the West by storm, Fela remained marooned in Lagos, broke, without a manager or record contract to speak of. He was able to release a few titles through local companies such as Lagos International and Skylark, while a handful of others were released through his own independent Kalakuta Records. However, a general economic downturn—attributable to the cumulative effects of long-term corruption and mismanagement, as well as a 1982 oil glut—was having a serious effect on Nigeria's music industry. As austerity measures were gradually implemented through the 1980s, independent record companies folded and many petroleum products—including polyvinyl chloride, the primary substance used in the manufacture of vinyl records—were in short supply. Recording studios were also on the decline due to the difficulty of purchasing and maintaining equipment. Exacerbating the situation was the growing trend toward bootlegging; it was becoming increasingly difficult for artists to collect royalties from their legitimate recordings.

A number of prominent juju and fuji musicians were able to rely on their accumulated assets or the support of wealthy patrons during this rough period. For Fela, who had made a career of attacking the Nigerian elite, this was not an option. Having acrimoniously severed his relationships with Decca and EMI while losing millions in the Kalakuta raid, he lacked the money to release many records independently, and few Nigerian companies would release his records either out of fear of government reprisal or in light of Fela's past conflicts with record companies. He attempted to beat the bootleggers in 1981 by importing cassettes of his latest music pressed during Egypt 80's most recent tour of Europe, but the material was confiscated by Nigerian customs officials upon arrival in Lagos.[74] In 1982, his former company Decca won a 120,000 naira judgment against him for his illegal occupation of its offices in 1978.[75] In combination, these factors virtually silenced Fela inside Nigeria. Whereas in 1976 alone he was able to release six new albums containing fifteen new compositions, he managed a total of only five albums containing nine new compositions between 1980 and 1984.

Other factors contributed to Fela's difficulties. Nigeria's deteriorating economic climate during the early 1980s had serious consequences for the country's morale, as scandal after scandal shook the faith of the nation in its institutions and elected officials. In 1980, fifty prisoners suffocated to death inside an overcrowded transport vehicle, raising long-overdue questions about police brutality and misconduct. Later in the year, soldiers in northern Sokoto state massacred an estimated 1,500 tenant farmers involved in a land dispute with the government, and months later they opened fire on demonstrators at the University of Ife, killing several students.[76] It was also reported in 1981 that the military officers in charge of the 1977 FESTAC had collectively embezzled over 55 million naira (more than a third of the total money spent on the festival),[77] followed by the disclosure that the health ministry was broke.[78] In a move that exacerbated tensions between Nigeria and its neighbors, the Shagari government expelled 2.2 million alien immigrants from the country in early 1983 as one of a number of measures attempting to adjust to the drastic change in the country's economic condition.[79] By far the most shocking news of the period, however, was the revelation that 2.8 billion naira was missing from the Nigerian National Petroleum Corporation treasury. When it was claimed that the money had been paid into the private account of a single individual, an official investigation was launched that even probed former president Obasanjo, but the culprits were never identified and the probe was widely dismissed as another ineffectual investigation of corruption by corrupt politicians.[80]

Inevitably, dissident voices began to feel the pressure as government paranoia mounted in response to the growing tide of public discontent. In 1982,

FEDECO outlawed the registration of any new political parties, crushing not only the hopes for substantive political realignment, but also Fela's hopes of candidacy in the 1983 elections.[81] Journalists critical of the Shagari regime such as Ray Ekpu and Dele Giwa were arrested on fabricated murder charges, and Fela's brother Beko—who was emerging as one of the country's loudest dissident voices—was subjected to harassment when he led a doctors' strike in early 1981 protesting government health policies. Fela himself was particularly targeted since, despite his financial troubles, he showed no signs of compromising the political messages or the personal attacks in his music for either economic gain or personal safety.

> **Chief Priest Say:**
> if you get enemy for town, follow am go for street, point finger to am, shout ole! [thief!] dem go put tire for him neck and dem go help you burn am alive. Nigeria don spoil o. If you no fit lynch General Obasanjo, you no fit lynch poor man.

Fela had already provoked the wrath of officials with the release of "Authority Stealing"—a response to both the increasing public outcry over market theft and a series of widely publicized cases of official embezzlement—in which he compares street criminals to their white-collar counterparts flourishing at the highest levels of government and business. "Authority Stealing" was composed during a period when the high level of public frustration was reflected by the increasing trend toward vigilante mob executions of market thieves, who were usually "necklaced" or "re-tyred" in the South African manner with gasoline-soaked automobile tires and set aflame. In an attempt to stem the rising tide of violent crime, the Shagari administration reinstituted public executions of convicted armed robbers. In this climate, Fela's song—vilifying the country's rulers as the "real" criminals—suggested that Nigeria's corrupt politicians were deserving of a fate worse than that reserved for the armed robbers. During the fall of 1980, in fact, he claimed repeatedly—onstage and in the press—that he had hard evidence linking the missing petroleum funds to Obasanjo. An issue of *Y.A.P. News* with a cover story on this subject was included with the *Authority Stealing* LP.[82] Rejected as too inflammatory by Nigerian record companies, *Authority Stealing* was later recorded in Nigeria, manufactured in Ghana, and subsequently smuggled back into Nigeria and released on Fela's own Kalakuta Records.[83] The lyrics offer an excellent example of his traditional use of irony and analogy:

FELA: Authority People, dem go dey steal
Public contribute plenty money

Na him authority him go dey steal
Authority man no dey pickpocket
Na petty cash him go dey pick
Armed robber, him need gun
Authority man, him need pen
Authority man in charge of money
Him no need gun, him need pen

FELA: Authority figures steal

The public contributes plenty money (in taxes)
The politician's authority is stolen
He doesn't pick pockets
He picks from petty cash
The armed robber needs a gun
The politician needs a pen
The politician in charge of money
Doesn't need a gun, but a pen

Pen get power gun no get	The pen is stronger than the gun
If gun go steal eighty thousand naira	If a gun can steal eighty thousand naira
Pen go steal two billion naira	A pen can steal two-million naira
You no go hear them shout:	You don't hear the people shout
CHORUS: Thief, thief thief!	*CHORUS:* Thief, thief, thief! [i.e. as they do in the case of petty market thefts]
FELA: Different way be them way	*FELA:* They have a different method of stealing,
Na similar style be them style . . .	But a similar style—
Authority stealing, pass armed robbery!	Stealing by the authorities is worse than armed robbery!

During Egypt 80's celebrated 1981 European tour, Fela had openly denounced corrupt Nigerian leaders from the stage. Eluding security officers who waited at the airport to arrest him upon his return to Nigeria, he soon released "Coffin for Head of State," which celebrated the 1979 protest march to Dodan Barracks (the song also pokes fun at Obasanjo's "big, fat stomach," and describes Lieutenant-Colonel Shehu Yar'adua as having "a neck like ostrich"). He also revived his weekly classified ad "Chief Priest Say" in the *Punch* newspaper, although the paper later canceled the series—due ostensibly to a payment dispute, but more probably because they no longer felt safe serving as a forum for Fela's ire. Between 1981 and 1984, it seemed the ruling powers were determined to silence Fela, as policemen and soldiers repeatedly raided the Shrine and arrested all attendants. More ominously, they began paying regular visits to Fela's Ikeja commune, spoiling for another Kalakuta-styled debacle.

> *LAGOS, December 4—Afrobeat music king Fela Anikulapo-Kuti was arrested by the police yesterday. Fela was held at his home on Atinuke Olabinjo street, Ikeja, after a "fierce battle" with the police. Fela was eventually overpowered and his home searched. Assistant Commissioner of Police Lucas Thomas, who led policemen there, said Fela was arrested because he helped the escape, on Wednesday night, of a suspected leader of criminals staying at the "Shrine"—headquarters of Fela's organization. Mr. Thomas said the police discovered a garden of weeds suspected to be Indian hemp in the compound, and also found a large quantity of dry weeds, also thought to be Indian hemp. The police commissioner said his detachment later went into the "Shrine," where 31 persons were arrested.*
> Daily Times, *December 4, 1981*

In December 1981, Fela—like a number of outspoken journalists—was charged with armed robbery. Police alleged that he had harbored criminals and had, along with two accomplices, used a semi-automatic weapon to rob a soft drink bottling plant in Ikeja. The charges were eventually dismissed, but Fela was severely beaten by the arresting soldiers. He recalled: "They beat me so much that for the first time, I left my body. . . . They used gun-butts on my head. By the eighth blow I stopped feeling pain, I just heard the noise on my head. . . . Something slapped me back into my body and I found myself lying in the gutter where they had kicked me when they thought I had died."[84]

Miraculously, he survived this assault (attributing his survival to Professor Hindu's power), but he suffered numerous fractures, including particularly severe damage to his left hand that prevented him from holding his tenor saxophone. He was thus forced to use the smaller, lighter soprano saxophone during this period, and his injuries ended a period in which his saxophone playing was gaining a new fluency.

With a new band, new music, new Shrine, new spiritual vision, new repertoire of public pranks, and numerous lecture engagements, Fela had kept a high and lively profile since his return to performing in 1979, but this 1981 beating seriously compromised his post-Kalakuta resurgence. Femi Kuti later referred to this incident as the worst beating his father ever received—one that profoundly affected him both physically and psychologically. The incident marked the beginning of an inward focus as Fela cut back on performing, recording, and lecturing, spending most of his time at home and out of the public eye. He was said to be indulging heavily in both Professor Hindu's mysticism and a variety of concentrated THC products, and some of his closest associates began to question his sanity and mission. Tiring of the constant harassment and lean lifestyle, his wives continued to leave; by mid-decade, less than half of the original twenty-seven remained. Usman Abudah of *Punch* visited Fela in early 1982:

> Inside a wide-angled sitting room was a fragile and pale-looking Fela, coiled up in a sitting-chair. On his left side was a package of assorted cigarettes. . . . About four females, whom I gathered were the remaining loyal ones out of his twenty-seven wives, were all making up their faces. Fela said "My house was burnt and I was later charged for armed robbery. A lot of evil things have happened to me but I will not die. I will rule Nigeria, but I don't know when. You see, they are now laughing at Fela but for how long can they laugh with an empty stomach?"[85]

Attendance at the Shrine slowed considerably as the government mounted pressure, publicly declaring it a "danger zone." The reluctance of Lagosians to attend was compounded by a dramatic increase in night crime. Along with his inability to release new material, and the alien law that resulted in the expulsion of many of his non-Nigerian musicians, this led to fewer performances and, occasionally, an under-rehearsed Egypt 80. On this matter, Fela commented that "when the Shrine is very dry like this, you don't feel like blowing so much. . . . I don't work the band so much now."[86]

The hardcore devotees who continued to attend the Shrine despite these circumstances danced to an afrobeat that was both increasingly mystical and more mordantly political than ever. The Shrine became a Bakhtinian "carnival" site in which traditional African magic fused with Fela's interest in classical Egyptian civilization; his derisive, scatological humor; his self-styled counterculture; and his political activism. Stalking the stage in recently added white face paint (which he felt facilitated easier communication with spirits), Fela attempted to construct a musical dimension simultaneously sacred, sexual, and politically charged.

The lyrics of mid-1980s songs such as "Confusion Break Bone," "Government Chicken Boy," and "Just Like That" cover the same grim textual terrain as literary works like Chinua Achebe's *Anthills of the Savannah* in their graphic depictions of class conflict, economic decline, corruption, and ethnically inflected backroom political infighting. These subjects became highly combustible in combination with the sex, smoking, and abusive humor infusing the aura around afrobeat. Onstage at the Shrine, Fela profanely denounced the government in yabis sessions interspersed with raw scatological humor. "Army Arrangement," one of his most explicitly political songs, was regularly prefaced with a monologue comparing the sizes of women's buttocks, and on the back cover of *Original Sufferhead*, Fela posed in his briefs shortly after the 1981 police attack, baring his bruised and battered body for the public to see. In the *Music Is the Weapon* television documentary of the same year, he slipped his underwear down for the camera in order to expose government-inflicted wounds on his buttocks. Clearly, he was perfectly willing to deconstruct even his own celebrity aura to buttress his credibility as a dissident and reveal the underside—pun intended—of modern Nigeria. If the various aspects of Fela's lifestyle—womanizing, hemp smoking, music, yabis—were merely the expected by-products of his celebrity status during the 1970s, they solidified into hard ideological strategies in the 1980s, symbolic weapons in his ongoing confrontation with the authorities and elites.

Ladi Ayodeji discussed the complexities of afrobeat's commercial impact in a 1984 review, while confirming the style's ascension beyond the sphere of "pure" popular music:

> Afrobeat does not make the global breakthrough reggae made because its originator refuses to commercialize it at the expense of his belief. This is where Fela stands head and shoulders above every artist. His music could make him a Michael Jackson ten times over if he sings "I wanna love you . . ." The saxophonist would rather "yab" government and provoke hate from the people against the authority. . . . Either way, the point is made that afrobeat has taken its place among the popular musical forms which graduate into the ranks of classical music—the tonic of the mind.[87]

European Tour, 1983–1984

I'm lying a bit low myself. I'm just as political but I don't want to keep repeating myself. If I had the money, I would have stood for election and it would be a mass movement towards my party. I thought that since I don't have any money now, I can't operate, so let me wait, keep my mouth shut and just see what they're going to come up with. They are trying to make me redundant, so I thought I must get myself together, make some money and start over again. I've written a lot of new material, everything we play on this European tour will be new. When I went to America in 1969 I knew Africa had the music to go around the world but I thought it was going to be quicker. I have been waiting for this a long time.

FELA *quoted in* KILBY 1983

Despite his domestic problems, European interest in Fela remained strong. Pascal Imbert and François Kertekian, two Frenchmen who had been captivated by Fela's 1981 Paris show, drove across the Sahara Desert to Nigeria and proposed a management deal that Fela, having no representation at the time, accepted.[88] Plans were made for a major European tour, and a record deal was finalized with Fela's old label EMI.

With new management, a record deal, and dates set, Fela and his new management planned his second major attempt to crack the Western market. He kept a low profile during most of 1983, performing at the Shrine, rehearsing the band into shape, and working up new material for the upcoming tour and recording sessions. He claimed his political ambitions remained, and he planned to use profits from the tour to finance future presidential campaigns. The combination of his reputation, memory of his celebrated 1981 concerts, and the growing success of African pop music in Europe guaranteed that, despite his recent difficulties, the European tour of late 1983 and 1984 was highly anticipated. Build-ups like the following were typical: "It's been a long wait, but you can bet it's going to have been worth it. . . . Stories don't come much more exciting than Fela's—who, despite at least two state-inspired attempts on his life—continues to extend the boundaries of permitted artistic commentary on political and social affairs. And what's more, you can *always* dance to it!"[89]

Fela returned to Europe commanding an Egypt 80 ensemble that had grown to thirty members, including a nine-piece horn section, six chorus singers, and six dancers, offering a series of unrecorded, densely political, and virtuosic big-band arrangements familiar only to regular attendants of the Shrine. This latest edition featured a number of soloists, including afrobeat heir apparent Femi Kuti on alto saxophone, Dele Sosinmi on rhythm piano, Yinusa "Y.S." Akinibosun (formerly of Sonny Okosuns's and Bongoes Ikwue's bands) on tenor saxophone, Lekan Animashaun on baritone saxophone, and Nwokoma Stephen Nkem on flugelhorn. The music presented on this tour was substantially longer and more ambitious than any he had previously presented. The double LP *Live in Amsterdam,* taken from this tour, contained a total of three songs: the album-length "Movement of the People #1" (in two parts), with "Gimme Shit, I Give You Shit" and "Custom Check Point" occupying a side each. *Fela Live*—an hour-long videotape of a 1984 festival performance in Glastonbury, England—contains two songs that run thirty minutes apiece even after extensive editing: "Teacher Don't Teach Me Nonsense" and "Confusion Break Bone." "Just Like That" and "Army Arrangement" were also performed on this and other occasions. Musically, these were Fela's most complex compositions to date. Unlike the Afrika 70 material, in which two brief, jazz-styled "heads" bracketed the vocal section of his songs, the Egypt 80 songs contained lengthy, polytonal, multimovement themes encompassing intricate horn charts and choral singing.

These works also continued the trend of overtly confrontational, political lyrics. Discussing the political chaos resulting from the presence of imposed, colonial political institutions in Africa, "Teacher Don't Teach Me Nonsense" examines the relationship of culture and tradition to politics, as well as the contentious 1983 elections, before indicting the former colonial powers for what Fela views as a deliberately flawed transfer of European political institutions to independent Africa. The song's stubborn, halting rhythm pattern is graced by a gentle, finger-picked rhythm guitar line reminiscent of palmwine or juju styles, and extended passages of chorus singing styled after schoolyard chants:

FELA: If good-u teacher teach something And the student make mistake Teacher must talk so But oyinbo no talk so	*FELA:* If a good teacher teaches something and the student makes a mistake The teacher must tell the student But the European hasn't told the student
Na support dem dey support	Instead, they support [corrupt African regimes]
That mean to say dem teaching get meaning Different, different kind of meaning	So their teaching has a different meaning That is why I sing, that is the reason of my song
That is why I sing, that is the reason of my song I sing, I beg everyone to join my song:	I sing, I beg everyone to join my song:
CHORUS: Teacher, teacher o tabi na lecturer be your name Teacher, teacher o tabi and lecturer be di same Make you no teach me again-o Na student teach finish yesterday don die today-o Me and you no dey for the same-o category	*CHORUS:* Teacher, teacher—lecturer is your name Teacher, teacher and lecturer are the same Please don't teach me again The student you taught yesterday has died today You and I are not in the same category [i.e., European political institutions will not work in Africa]

"Confusion Break Bone" (a partial reworking of 1975's "Confusion") is one of Fela's most complex arrangements—polytonal, lavishly choral, and densely architectural. Rhythmically, the song is constructed upon a solemn 12/8 traditional rhythm pattern; harmonically, it is based in the melodic minor mode, with the modal harmony complementing the traditional tonal inflections of the chorus. Lyrically, "C.B.B." presents the morbid image of an abandoned, decomposing body being picked apart by thieves as a metaphor for state corruption and the decay of the Nigerian body politic. When the song was eventually released later in the decade, the cover painting depicted all of the country's heads of state since independence, with a caption underneath asking, "Which Head Never Steal?"

The first one na leg-e robbery	The first crime is a stolen leg
Where man go go pick pocket	When a man picks a pocket
He go take leg and run	He takes the leg and runs
The second one na arm-u robbery	The second crime is armed robbery
Where man go go steal big thing	When a man steals a big thing
He go take gun, defend himself	He takes a gun to defend himself
The third one na head-e robbery	The third crime is a stolen head
Where oga patatpata go steal	When the boss steals excessively
He go take position, steal for free	He uses his position to freely steal
Free stealing na him policy	Free stealing is his policy
Which head we get e no dey steal?	Which of our heads of state has never stolen?
Which president we get e never steal?	Which of our presidents has never stolen?

Discussing the troubled Kainji Dam electrification project,[90] the Biafran war, the endlessly multiplying number of regional states, and Fela's relationship with Professor Hindu, "Just Like That"—like the earlier "Unknown Soldier"—uses the metaphor of magic, this time to describe the haphazard nature of Nigeria's postindependence development. Fela concludes that all the apparent chaos is in fact planned by the country's rulers, a "magical" smokescreen functioning to divert the attention of the masses from the steady siphoning of public resources. The song's horn arrangement is one of his most distinctive, a complex sequence of call-and-response structures rotated throughout the ensemble and building to a violent, clashing, chorus.

One of Fela's most unique arrangements, "Custom Check Point" features a traditional 12/8 rhythm taken at breakneck pace and a frantic horn theme recalling a traditional choral chant. The song is a protest against borders between African nation-states on three fronts: as administrative vestiges of colonialism; as Western-imposed disruptions to the cultural unity of West Africa; and as sites of considerable bureaucratic red tape, inefficiency, corruption, and inconvenience.

Other songs performed during this period include "Look and Laugh"—a somber litany of Fela's confrontations with the Nigerian authorities, and "Government Chicken Boy"—detailing government interference in private industry.

Reviews of the tour were mixed. Some felt Fela had presented weak and boring material confirming the loss of his musical powers, while others felt the material was his strongest and most ambitious yet. The contention that Fela's latest music had been compromised by his political ambitions and personal troubles was contradicted by the scale and complexity of the music he presented in Europe, which demonstrated clearly that both his political commitment and his composing had taken a quantum leap from the days of "Lady" and "Zombie." This was, in fact, one recurrent criticism of his latest work: as much as songs such as "Just Like That" represented strong musical advances, their lyrics tended toward catalogues of suffering and corruption, almost completely lacking the humor of his earlier work. Many times during the tour, in fact, it seemed Fela was more interested in politics and the flawless presentation of his intricate compositions than in providing a party atmosphere for the audience. Always a perfectionist, he was in a particularly stern mood during many of these concerts. In addition to prefacing his songs with long political diatribes, Fela frequently berated his musicians onstage; conducted the band with stomps, scowls, and angry hand gestures; and sometimes even halted the music altogether to harangue the band or the sound technicians when he was displeased with the music or sound mix. While regular attendants of the Shrine in Lagos were used to Fela's rambling monologues and his authoritarian stage demeanor, European audiences often perceived him as a musical dictator or provocateur who was ruining the good-time mood they expected of African performers. Greg Stephens observed in *The Beat:*

> Fela has the aura of one who incites, almost wants the type of violence he seems to attract. . . . There was little of the joyful group interplay that one has come to expect from African bands. The whole orchestra carried themselves solemnly. One doesn't know whether this was because they were under Fela's thumb or whether this was a reflection of them sharing his sense of mission. Since that mission seems to be an unending documentation of suffering and corruption, their gravity was understandable.[91]

Clearly, the mood and performance of these new compositions was thickly political and directly confrontational, in contrast to the colorful, festive mood that characterized the European performances of Sunny Ade and other African or Caribbean musicians. Visually, Egypt 80 presented a very different image than the juju bands. The members of Sunny Ade's African Beats, dressed in traditional attire, projected the genial, contented bearing of Christian family men equally at home entertaining European audiences, esteemed traditional rulers, or wealthy politicians. By comparison, Fela's presentation was decidedly more rough-edged, featuring a mixture of older, veteran horn players, sexy female chorus singers; and a core crew of young, streetwise Lagos musicians whipped into musical shape by their rebel leader.

Although, in the wake of Bob Marley, political content and an enjoyable night of music and dancing were no longer mutually exclusive, Fela's brash afrobeat was marked by a very different tone than that of Marley's reggae. Rob Tannenbaum described the opening moments of "Just Like That" at the Glastonbury concert:

> The band trumpeted his arrival with a thundering, atonal clamor as Fela saluted the crowd with two clenched fists high above his head. . . . The music built from several simple riffs into complex counter-rhythms which clashed together forcefully. The band responded to Fela like a well-rehearsed orchestra. He glared at [guitarist] Victor [Tieku], who picked his staccato riff a bit lighter, urged on the drummer with beating fists, and waved the nine horns into a unison chart. Then Fela walked to center stage and embarked on a keening organ solo which wove between the horns and percussion like Booker T. [Jones] trying to topple the walls of Jericho. . . . Afrobeat is not pretty like so much African music. Its shrillness can be threatening, especially when augmented by Fela's coarse voice.[92]

Complicating the band's reception was the fact that some reviewers, having read about the jazz influence in Fela's music and expecting a saxophone or keyboard virtuoso in the jazz sense, derided his instrumental abilities and the musicianship of Egypt 80 in general: "On stage, one of his greatest errors is to assume an annoying bogus jazz status for himself and his fellow saxmen. Now Fela on soprano is no Coltrane, and neither are his baritone players potential Mulligans. At best their contributions are perfunctory, at worst a losing battle to spark explosions with damp gunpowder."[93]

It is true that by the standards of modern jazz, the Egypt 80 soloists would be considered rudimentary improvisers. As opposed to a long-term, methodical study of the instrument, Fela himself had taken up the tenor saxophone in 1973 in a fit of professional competition (see Chapter 4), and the roughness of his playing had been a point of contention for Western jazz critics ever since the first Afrika 70 performances at the Berlin Jazz Festival in 1978. Now that he had switched to the higher-pitched, more piercing soprano sax (a more technically challenging instrument requiring a tighter embouchure and extreme attention to intonation) in the wake of his hand injuries, their cries became louder. The other Egypt 80 soloists made varying impressions on the critics. Y. S. Akinibosun was the most formidable, offering a tough, rhythm-and-blues style rooted in players like Junior Walker, but with hard-bop overtones, and an overall approach that was quite similar to his Afrika 70 predecessor, Igo Chico. The improvising style of Lekan Animashaun was percussive and textural in conception, comprised of short bursts of melodic shapes juxtaposed with staccato repetitions, and shorn of the melodic and harmonic intricacies of modern jazz. The moody flugelhorn style of Nwokoma Ukem reflected the influence of Lester Bowie as well as his Afrika 70 predecessor, Tunde Williams, with a language of slurs, squeals, and other valve tricks. Altoist Femi Kuti was at this stage still a relative newcomer to his instrument.[94]

Besides the fact that, like many composers, Fela's primary "instrument" was his orchestra, critics often failed to realize that neither he nor the other musicians of Egypt 80 were aspiring to virtuosity in the Western sense of the term—and, despite the fact that Fela has often been thought of as a "jazz" musician in Nigeria, their local audiences did not expect this of them. Ultimately, such virtuosity was peripheral to the overall significance of Fela's music. The term "jazz," when applied to Fela, did not refer to solely to his music, but also encompassed a lifestyle of nocturnal hedonism and a more philosophical freedom of creative expression.

Still, as much as his music had advanced in conception, it was clear that the constant personnel changes had compromised the energy of the music; it was reported in the Nigerian press that Egypt 80 likely had the highest membership turnover rate of any leading Nigerian band.[95] It was also clear that the constant hassles with the authorities had taken their toll. Besides the alternating flashes of lethargy and impatience in Fela's onstage demeanor, as well as the occasional lethargy of the band, often it was the force of the compositions—as opposed to Fela's own enthusiasm—that supported the music. Perhaps this was what one reviewer sensed when he called the *Live in Amsterdam* version of "Movement of the People" "forty minutes of dishwater."[96]

The tour's organizers made an effort to recruit Tony Allen to provide a spark for the music, but although the drummer agreed, Fela vetoed the move.[97] Allen, meanwhile, had begun to capitalize on the Afropop explosion himself. Besides his collaboration with Sunny Ade, he had released a well-received EP on the Sterns/Earthworks label entitled *N.E.P.A.* (Never Expect Power Always). With the derisive acronym title (referring to the unreliability of the Nigerian Electrical Power Authority) and classic afrobeat retread (the song "When One Road Close, Another One Go Open" was a reworking of his 1976 Afrika 70 track "Hustler"), Allen was clearly working within the stylistic and rhetorical models he established with Afrika 70.

As tightly focused as Fela was on the presentation of his work, the critical response to these shows often centered on the extramusical aspects of the performances, such as his clothing and sex life. He had worked hard to present his most ambitious material, and this must surely have contributed to his sour mood as the tour progressed. But on at least two counts, Fela must share part of the responsibility for the sensationalized media coverage of these performances. Already dismissed by many as an authoritarian and sexist, Fela often offered comments in the British press that made him seem a complete reactionary. In one fashionable pop-culture magazine, for example, he claimed that homosexuality did not exist in Africa and that known homosexuals met death by stoning. He was also loathe to retract any of his statements on gender relations, leading to protests by British feminists outside of his London concerts.[98] Despite the notoriously capricious nature of the British pop music press, such comments did not help to endear him to British audiences steeped in a tradition of irreverence and questioning of authority.

The second factor for which Fela must take responsibility was the format of the concerts on this tour, which routinely began with stage presentations by Professor Hindu. As he had done in Lagos, the Professor mutilated human bodies onstage in order to demonstrate his restorative powers, to the horror of audiences across Europe.[99] The Professor often accompanied Fela onto the stage in concert, was present at interviews, and is even pictured on the inside cover of the *Live in Amsterdam* LP. Fela also sponsored the Professor's solo demonstrations in Europe. But while Fela credited the Professor's powers with saving his life during the savage 1981 beating, most journalists took a less-than-sympathetic view; these performances inevitably inspired the type of coverage that reinforced the most sensationalized European stereotypes of Africa. Some observers felt this was an intentional distraction from the music; one even speculated that "the infamous Professor Hindu was putting his stamp on the proceedings, to disguise quite how untogether the Egypt 80 were."[100]

"Just Like That"

Although it had not passed without controversy, the tour was an overall success, largely free of the mishaps that had frustrated previous European tour attempts, and Fela's management began organizing a long-anticipated tour of the United States. This trip was to include a massive third-world "festival" concert in Los Angeles, with Trinidadian calypso giant Mighty Sparrow and Jamaican reggae legend Peter Tosh also slated to appear. The work of both singers had often contained pointed social observations, and Tosh in particular was no stranger to politically tinged pop controversy or its consequences, having been unrelenting in his criticisms of the Jamaican political system (or "shitstem," as he called it) and its politicians. The singer was savagely beaten by Jamaican policemen on several occasions, most notably in April 1978 following his vitriolic concert-stage tirade against current and former prime ministers Michael Manley and Edward Seaga, who were both in the audience.[101] Thus, the Los Angeles concert would bring together three black music giants and would contain strong political undertones. The timing was perfect, as American interest in African music in general, and Fela in particular, was at its peak. Imbert and Kertekian hustled a deal with Capitol Records, which promptly reissued *Black President, Original Sufferhead,* and the new *Live in Amsterdam* to appreciative audiences in the United States. They also arranged a deal with the independent company Celluloid, which began a reissue campaign of Afrika 70 classics such as *Zombie, Shuffering and Shmiling, No Agreement,* and *Mr. Follow Follow.*

Meanwhile in Nigeria, the military government of General Mohammedu Buhari had seized power from Shehu Shagari in a bloodless coup on New Year's Day 1984, ending a short-lived, chaotic period of civilian rule. Appropriating the no-nonsense image of Murtala Mohammed's "corrective" military regime, Buhari's administration was initially welcomed after the flagrant abuses and excesses of the Shagari years. However, the mood in the country quickly turned to cynicism and pessimism as the administration dispensed with the few democratic vestiges of the overthrown civilian regime and embarked upon what was widely viewed as a repressive program. When the new administration waged a much-touted "War

Against Indiscipline" aimed at eradicating the disorganization of Nigerian society, journalists noted the continuing corruption of soldiers and government officials, suggesting that they should first set a proper example before condemning the society for its faults.[102] As public sentiment turned against the administration, a series of draconian decrees were issued—including Decree #4, which threatened journalists with imprisonment for public criticism of any government official or program. The harshness of the new regime may have been a factor in Fela's extended stay in Europe during 1984, in addition to his extensive schedule of recording and performing. By the time of his August arrival in Lagos to prepare for the upcoming U.S. tour, several prominent journalists and social critics such as Tai Solarin, Haroun Adamu, and Rufai Ibrahim were already behind bars, and Buhari had issued an ominous warning to musicians, urging them to "avoid inciting anything that might promote violence, aggression, and above all, indiscipline in our people."[103]

In what seemed a blatant capitulation to the forces of the state to some observers, Fela accepted a position on an Ikeja police-community relations board in 1984, perhaps hoping this would take the official heat off of him.[104] As much as two years earlier (shortly after the 1981 police attack), he had publicly declared to the press that he was no longer in a mood for confrontation. In the same vein, he played in a send-off concert for the Los Angeles–bound Nigerian Olympic team at the National Stadium. However, these were small gestures in the scheme of things. The Buhari government had a strong interest in preventing Fela, who was riding a renewed wave of international popularity, from spreading his antigovernment message abroad, especially at a time of considerable public disenchantment. Besides the fact that Fela was perhaps the symbolic personification of the "indiscipline" the government was attempting to eradicate, the administration also had a close petroleum-based relationship with the U.S. government to protect. Just months before, as Shagari officials routed the national treasury and brutally silenced dissident voices, President Ronald Reagan had praised the "miracle of Nigerian democracy."[105]

> *LAGOS, November 9—Afrobeat generalissimo Fela Anikulapo-Kuti took a ten-year jail sentence yesterday. The Port Harcourt Zone of the Currency Anti-Sabotage Tribunal convicted him for five years for each of two-count charges of currency trafficking. The sentences run concurrently. Both offences were said to have been committed on September 4, 1984 at the Murtala Mohammed Airport, as Fela was bound for the United States with his group. A hush fell on the courtroom as the judge pronounced the sentence. If Fela was ruffled, he did not show it. Even as his queens broke down in tears on seeing the "king" being led into the Black Maria, Fela smiled it off and gave a "Black Power" salute.*
>
> Punch, *November 9, 1984*

On September 4, as he was about to board a plane bound for New York to begin the tour, Fela was arrested on an alleged currency violation. The rest of the entourage traveled to New York as planned, expecting him to follow shortly after the resolution of the matter. Instead, he was detained and charged with two counts of illegal currency exportation. Egypt 80 played a handful of dispirited U.S. gigs before returning home, losing an estimated $3 million in the process.[106] Ironically, the band returned to Lagos on the same flight as Sunny Ade and his band, who had just completed a triumphant world tour with reggae supergroup Black Uhuru. Although Fela claimed he had declared the 1,600 British pounds that were found on him, his currency declaration form was mysteriously lost, the customs officials who offered to testify on his behalf were arrested, and he was sentenced by a military tribunal to two concurrent five-year prison terms on November 8, 1984. Once again, his chance to claim his place as a major innovator in contemporary African music had been thwarted.

The response of the international music community was immediate and vocal. Numerous petitions were circulated protesting Fela's imprisonment, and important profiles of him were written in the Western press. Tribute concerts were organized in major American and European cities, and a "Free Fela" movement began, organized by a coalition of left-wing political organizations, musicians, and human rights organizations. Fela was adopted as a prisoner of conscience by Amnesty International in October 1985. Initially confined at Kiri-Kiri Prison in Lagos, he was later moved to a distant northern location in Maiduguiri after granting a secret interview to a French reporter from the magazine *Liberation.*

In Lagos, Egypt 80 maintained its regular performance schedule at the Shrine, led by Fela's son Femi and financed by his brother, Beko. The political climate in Nigeria was such that Beko was also imprisoned for his leadership role in organizing a strike of the Nigerian Medical Association in protest of government health policies. The authorities also clearly sought to thwart his efforts on behalf of his brother; Beko kept the Shrine operating in Fela's absence and was Fela's main contact with the outside world. Fela's manager Pascal Imbert was also briefly jailed in Lagos when he was arrested with copies of the recently released *Army Arrangement* LP in his possession.

Although he had signed with Capitol Records shortly before his arrest, both that company and EMI abruptly canceled Fela's contracts following his imprisonment. His work remained in the public ear through the New York–based company Celluloid, which, besides reissuing some of his classic 1970s work, also released the recently recorded *Army Arrangement,* along with a remixed version (on an EP also containing edited and remixed versions of "Government Chicken Boy" and "Cross-Examination") produced by Bill Laswell. Laswell had recently scored successes with projects for Rolling Stones vocalist Mick Jagger and jazz keyboardist Herbie Hancock, and his production style was distinctly modern and electronic, making full use of the latest computer sequencing technology. Following his success with Hancock's computer-driven "Rockit," he experimented with a similar approach to projects with Camerounian saxophonist Manu Dibango, Senegalese group Toure Kunda, and Jamaican toaster Yellowman. Seeking to modernize Fela's sound, Laswell erased the original solos and some of the rhythm tracks, overdubbing a number of musicians including Parliament/Funkadelic keyboardist Bernie Worrell, reggae session drummer Sly Dunbar, and multipercussionist Aiyb Dieng.

The songs on the remixed *Army Arrangement* feature heavy, electro-percussion backbeats, altered tempos, processed studio textures, and overdubbed solos. Although the project later sparked a press feud between Fela and Laswell, it helped keep Fela's name in the public eye during his imprisonment, as did a 1985 tribute version of "Lady," recorded by Hugh Masekela.

Yet another (bloodless) military coup took place in Nigeria in August 1985, overthrowing Buhari and bringing General Ibrahim Babangida to power, and raising hopes that Fela might be freed. The new government released many political prisoners of the Buhari administration and promised to review all remaining cases. The most dramatic breakthrough in Fela's case occurred during the fall of 1985, when it was leaked to the press that he had been visited by the judge heading the military tribunal that had sentenced him, Justice Gregory Okoro-Idogu. During this visit, the judge allegedly apologized to Fela, admitting that although there had not been sufficient evidence for a conviction, he had been pressured from the highest levels of the Buhari government to hand down a harsh prison sentence. The meeting ended with the judge promising to write a personal letter to President Babangida requesting the commutation of Fela's sentence.[107] This revelation, and the public controversy that followed, began the countdown to his release. Fela was transferred to a location in southern Benin City where he was again allowed visitors, and finally regained his freedom on April 24, 1986, having served a total of eighteen months in prison.

After his release, Fela held a celebratory press conference at the Afrika Shrine, as well as interviews with foreign journalists. Effectively answering the question of whether or not his eighteen-month imprisonment had finally broken his spirit, he promised to revive his political party and reiterated his plan to run for the presidency. Disregarding the political establishment, he vowed that he would eventually be elected by popular acclaim. This is a theme he voiced repeatedly during 1986: "My popularity is so great now that I could even be made President by acclamation. I don't think anyone will have the guts to stand against me."[108]

He also explained the low atmosphere which existed prior to his arrest: "I devoted myself to a long introspection that helped me realize that if the authorities had succeeded in putting me in jail, it was because I was low-spirited. I had to rebuild myself and get into shape. Half of my body was constantly in pain. I could not play saxophone anymore. . . . This eighteen-month incarceration has enabled me to identify the forces acting against me and to analyse my own energies."[109]

He criticized the Babangida government's transition program, demanding that it reschedule the projected 1990 civilian elections to an earlier date. Finally, he ended the press conference by proclaiming himself "Double Fela" and promising that his new music would surpass his old. Feeling renewed, recharged, still stubborn, yet uncharacteristically gracious, he thanked his international fans for their support: "I won't thank government for releasing me, but I thank all Nigerians, Africans, Asians, and Americans who have in one way or the other called for my release. To all of you I thank from something more deep than the bottom of my heart."[110]

"Double Fela"

A number of Fela's longtime observers wondered whether he would take the opportunity of a fresh post-prison start to sort out what was by many accounts a chaotic domestic situation, which had gradually alienated him from his friends, family, and other close associates. The degeneration of Fela's commune was evidently one point of contention between him and his son Femi, who moved out of his father's house, left the Egypt 80 band, and began work on an LP with his own Positive Force Band, which also featured ex–Egypt 80 pianist Dele Sosimi. Fela was reluctant to discuss his son's departure publicly, but the *African Guardian* suggested Femi was dissatisfied with both his own musical progress and the domestic environment that he felt had long hindered his father's creativity:

> Femi says he left the band for two reasons. The first is that his father is surrounded by people who would never allow his political ideals which he (Femi) fully accepts, to blossom. And the second reason is that: "My father never sent me to a music school. He never encouraged me and I felt I had gotten to a stage where I needed to cut my own teeth. . . . Most of us who love him are no longer around him as we should be because we cannot stand some of the things which happen around him. . . . If I go to him now and tell him I want to stop people selling drugs around the Shrine, I will make a lot of enemies and he too will not listen to me."[111]

In fact, Femi's education had been the subject of a long-standing dispute between Fela and his first wife, Remi; she felt their son should be educated in England, while Fela insisted he should study in Ghana.[112] In the end Femi, who left secondary school early to join his father's band, never continued his education, and his departure from Egypt 80 ended a period during which he was being groomed as heir to the afrobeat throne. Several years would reportedly elapse before father and son spoke again.[113] However, the public and private relationship between them seemed repaired by the early 1990s, when Fela publicly praised his son's brand of afrobeat, and Femi began keeping regular Sunday night gigs at the Afrika Shrine with his own band, while releasing his music domestically on his father's Kalakuta label.

Fela did make some changes in his domestic situation following his release, the most significant being his decision to divorce those of his remaining wives who wished to leave (eight or so ultimately remained with him), while publicly declaring his disdain for the institution of marriage in general. There seemed to be several reasons for this. One was an acknowledgment of the strain that constant economic hardship and harassment had placed on his day-to-day domestic life. Another was his despair over the fact that only two of the wives had borne children since the 1978 wedding. Fela also seemed to be reacting to stories circulating in the Nigerian press of his wives' alleged infidelities during his incarceration, some of which even maintained that certain wives had babies fathered by Egypt 80 bandmembers. Fela commented on this in an interview with Azuka Molokwu:

FELA: A lot of prisoners heard stories about their wives fucking outside their marital homes. You cannot blame the woman for fucking outside. Not when you are in prison. You can also not blame the man whose wife is fucking another man. But he's blaming himself for going into marriage in the first place.

Q: You heard such stories as regards your marriage and queens?

FELA: Many, not just one story.

He concluded in another interview:

> Marriage is an institution. No matter how you protect a woman, if she wants to have an affair, she will have it. I condemn the institution of marriage. Marriage brings jealousy and selfishness. . . . I just don't agree to possess a woman. I just don't want to say: "This woman is mine, so she shouldn't go out with other men."[114]

The third apparent reason was a renewed desire for freedom. He elaborated in a later interview:

> After I got married [in 1960] and we separated, I thought I was free from marriage, and I was enjoying myself. I went to marry twenty-seven women again. . . . For me to have called it marriage at that time was very wrong. . . . When I married them, they became possessive. They never wanted me to meet any other women. . . . In prison I decided not to marry again. I will have an association with women but not marriage.[115]

Without knowledge of their precise whereabouts, it is difficult to say how life in Kalakuta payed off for Fela's ex-wives in the long run. In Carlos Moore's book, Fela frequently depicts his sex life in the most explicit terms, and a few of the wives match his tone in their own accounts. But however much ambivalent public notoriety they derived from their highly publicized exploits, it is highly doubtful that ex-wives derived an equal amount of postmarriage benefit from their association with him. That some had allegedly turned to prostitution within two years of the "divorce" was, in the public's eyes, a confirmation of his failings as a husband, the shallowness of his embrace of polygamy, and the ultimate reality of their objectification. On this theme, Nick Fadugba of the *Daily Times* had visited Kalakuta back in 1979 and noted:

> Near the door leading outside is a boldly handwritten notice, 'Go NOW, Why Wait?' "Some people have misunderstood the notice" says Fela. "Now and again a few of my wives tell me they are leaving so I decided to put it there. It's all yabis" he explains. He is anxious to point out that the notice is "fun really" and not an indication of disloyalty. "There was even another notice which said: 'Take your choice, in or out?' But it was removed by some of my wives," he says.[116]

Now, having divorced his wives, Fela discussed the issue with Molokwu, relying on linguistic tactics to deflect charges of irresponsibility:

> Q: It is being alleged that some of the queens who have left you have gone into prostitution because you have failed their aspirations of having a dedicated husband. To what extent would you hold yourself responsible for their misfortune?
>
> FELA: How can you call prostitution a misfortune? There's nothing like "prostitution" in African language. What is prostitution? In Yoruba . . . you say *asewo*. Asewo itself does not mean "prostitution." It means "money-changer." In Ibo language you say *akunakuna* which means "somebody who walks about." It does not mean "prostitution." . . . Do you know you cannot have a wife in Africa without paying? You call it dowry. In white man's society, you don't pay the dowry; that was where they got prostitution from. To smell the yansch [private parts] of a woman in Africa, you pay, whether you are going to marry her or it is a one night stand. . . . That is their problem if I disappointed them as a husband. . . . But I still see nothing wrong in their new job. Marriage is contract. Prostitution is not a bad thing.[117]

Whether or not Fela was conscious of the similarities between his view and the broader Marxist interpretation that marriage is, in the end, a form of institutionalized prostitution, his words and actions reflected such an interpretation. On the other hand, if we follow Vivien Goldman's alternate interpretation that Fela's treatment of women sprang partly from a desire to avenge himself on his mother, the above quote implies that he took a perverse pleasure in providing a cultural justification for the ultimate social devaluation of his former wives.

This latest pronouncement was greeted with some derision by the Nigerian public, another indication that despite his trials and age, Fela would continue to live resolutely outside of social boundaries. However—regardless of the public's opinion of his personal life—his imprisonment, like the Kalakuta attack nearly a decade earlier, had boosted his notoriety; he was probably second only to Nelson Mandela among African political dissidents. In July, he traveled without his band to the United States to take part in a benefit concert staged by Amnesty International at Giants Stadium in New Jersey. Out of his element in front of the huge rock crowd and unusually subdued, Fela appeared on the festival stage only briefly, jamming with the Neville Brothers on congas, joined by Ruben Blades, Yoko Ono, and Sean Ono Lennon. He also took the opportunity of his U.S. visit to lambast Bill Laswell's remix of "Army Arrangement," criticizing the project in the most vehement terms (attributing it to a CIA attempt to sabotage his music) and sparking a press war of words. He told Spencer Rumsey:

> I did not like it. It's not my music, simple as that. I have a reason for everything I write in my music. I'm not writing for commercialism as

such. I'm writing African music not only for myself but for the future generations so that they can understand African music. What Bill Laswell has done is not African music the way I hear it.[118]

Laswell responded:

Those tapes were badly done, badly played, and all of Fela's horn solos were abysmal. I have no respect for bad musicianship and I have no interest in politics. Fela's solos were erased. We mixed the LP in five minutes, as a favor. . . . I would never have produced a record like that, and I would never work with musicians at that low a level. . . . You can talk about Africa and fucking politics for days, but the fact is that [the overdubbed musicians] are high-grade musicians and Fela's in jail.[119]

British producer Dennis Bovell, who recorded the initial sessions, provided a mediating perspective on the dispute:

It was an idea I had to get Fela to play with new sounds, but not to change his composition. I just wanted him to play what he played, but with new equipment. [Fela's management], they didn't understand. I told them "you wait till I finish with Linton Kwesi Johnson, and I'll finish the album." They were like "we gotta go now, man. The iron's hot, we gotta strike!" They changed the whole shit to what they thought was new. And they fucked it up.[120]

With the *Army Arrangement* LP released internationally and a number of his 1970s classics reissued, Fela maintained a high profile on the African music scene, riding a new wave of celebrity and credibility. At home, he showed up often to jam at his niece Frances Kuboye's Jazz 38 nightclub on Victoria Island, sporting a new tenor saxophone—an instrument he had not been able to play since the 1981 beating. Still, his fans wondered whether he would be able to maintain the same level in his art after his stint in some of Nigeria's harshest prisons. Fela started slowly—rehearsing Egypt 80, hinting at changes in his band, and working on a new composition, "Beasts of No Nation." He told Chuzzy Udenwa: "When I say 'beasts,' I'm not abusing [i.e., for fun] . . . and those people who have spiritual knowledge will know I'm not abusing. . . . Really, there are animals who walk the street in human clothing. If you have the third eye, you will know; you can even see the type of animals they are—antelopes, and others."[121]

By September, he and Egypt 80 were ready to take the stage again. A "comeback" concert was planned for the National Stadium in Lagos, with tours of Europe and the United States to follow. Although an ongoing financial dispute between Fela and the show's promoters resulted in high ticket prices and a lower turnout than expected, the Lagos concert was a triumph. Playing three numbers he had performed prior to his imprisonment—"Just Like That," "Confusion Break Bone," and "Teacher Don't Teach Me Nonsense"—he also introduced the new "Beasts of

No Nation," which was enthusiastically received at the September concert in Lagos:

> A masterpiece composed by Fela in prison, "B.O.N.N." could mark the beginning of a new Fela afrobeat. Lyrically, it was a pleasant reminder of Fela in the 70s, at the peak of the afrobeat journey. His lead vocal blended smoothly and melodiously with the chorus. He used two bass guitarists, first to complement each other and then for emphasis. The effect was terrific. He also brought in the long, guttural-sounding native drums to further increase the baritone undertone of the music. The horns again poured out unrestricted, closing up the loose ends and asserting, more than ever before, Fela's seat among the masters.[122]

International in focus and sardonic in tone, "B.O.N.N." condemns the brutality of oppressive regimes worldwide, with Fela using the injustice of his own imprisonment as a point of departure to explore human rights abuses by Nigerian soldiers (including the violent suppression of student uprisings at Zaria and Ife), as well as the support given to the apartheid South African regime of P. W. Botha by the British and American governments of Margaret Thatcher and Ronald Reagan:

FELA: Dem go hold meeting, dem go start yab human beings	*FELA:* [World leaders] hold meetings in which they abuse human beings
Animal talk don start again	Animal talk has started again—
Dash dem human rights	"Bribe them with human rights"
Animals wan dash us human rights	Animals want to bribe us with human rights
Animals can't dash me human rights	An animal cannot bribe me with human rights
I beg you, make you hear me well well—	Please, listen to me very closely—
Human rights na my property	Human rights are my property
You can't dash me my property	You cannot bribe me with my own property
CHORUS: Many leaders as you see them	*CHORUS:* Many leaders, as you see them
Na different disguise dem dey-o	Are wearing different disguises
Animal in human skin	Animals in human skin
Animal put tie-o	Animals wearing ties
Animal wear agbada [African garment]	Animals wearing agbada [African
Animal put suit-u . . .	Animals wearing suits . . .

"Beasts" introduces several new elements into Fela's composing style. Built on a natural minor vamp that lopes along at mid-tempo, the song modulates for a choral refrain at the end of each verse. The guitars and keyboards blend into an almost bluesy, melancholy ambience that becomes more propulsive with the addition of the new instruments Fela hinted at during his spring press conference. A second electric bass plays a counterline to the first bass during emphatic passages, while an eight-foot-long traditional *gbedu* drum is used for additional emphasis under the horn and vocal arrangements.[123]

In Europe, reviews heralding Fela's return noted the sophistication of his new music and the tightness of Egypt 80. The French magazine *Liberation* reported on the band's Paris concerts:

> Fela conducts the band with a shrug of the shoulder or with a motion of his hand. . . . The brass sound magnificent. . . . As soon as the band plays the first chorus, it sounds like the golden days. . . . The four chorus singers begin singing and their voices swing between the reeds. The whole sounds perfect. . . . This attitude he shows suggests he has finally reached his musical maturity. . . . He is the one who will put African music back on track.[124]

Like the European tours earlier in the decade, anticipation for the long-awaited American concerts was particularly high among "world beat" enthusiasts who sought a successor to Bob Marley. Greg Stephens observed that "Fela's first American appearance in 17 years . . . created a fervor unequalled since Marley's final tour. . . . The Fela legend . . . has been given context by the continuous flow of African orchestras who have made their way through, beginning with King Sunny Ade three and a half years ago, then building with a string of prophets whose real purpose, it sometimes seemed, was to widen the path enough for Fela to enter."[125]

Critical response to the American concerts was polarized but mostly very positive. While the new music was universally praised (though some thought it lacked the fire of his older work), some were turned off by Fela's stage manner and others had trouble accepting him as a credible political candidate as a result of either his ideological contradictions or his stage manner. Stephens felt the music contained "a heavy marijuana vibe" and described Fela's stage manner as "very stoned indeed—a man whose thoughts seemed very important to him, but who had trouble remembering the words to describe them."[126]

The 1986 tour was Fela's shining moment on the international stage, a moment when he was taken most seriously musically and politically. Despite Egypt 80's ejection from an airplane in Denver, Colorado, for allegedly smoking marijuana and throwing food in flight, Fela was received as a hero on the U.S. leg of the tour, performing to sold-out audiences and receiving civic honors such as the keys to the cities of Detroit, Michigan, and Austin, Texas. In Washington, D.C., he was presented with a plaque by the mayor, and the mayor of Berkeley, California, proclaimed November 14 "Fela Day." The international triumph also gave his domestic career a shot in the arm; despite his consistent railing against the "colonial mentality" of African musicians who sought Western recognition, Fela was lauded in the Nigerian press for his Western breakthrough. One article even suggested that by getting himself thrown off an airplane, he had mastered the "American" marketing tactic of boosting ticket sales by committing highly publicized illegal acts.[127]

In the years that followed, both Nigeria and its musicians would turn inward as the economy dovetailed, the country's international image plummeted, and tastes changed in the international demand for African pop. Even Sunny Ade, on whom so many hopes were pinned, was abruptly dropped by Island Records in 1985 when his albums failed to generate sales in the numbers the company had anticipated.

One of the most immediate effects of Nigeria's increasingly troubled economy on the music industry was the decline in local recording studios, and a tragedy of Fela's later career is that the small amount of music he bothered to record (only a fraction of what he was actually performing) was often poorly captured on tape. Unlike the relative ease with which the medium-sized Afrika 70 band could be recorded, the Egypt 80 orchestra represented a greater challenge for the recording process. The increased complexity of his music in the 1980s and 1990s unfortunately also coincided with both a marked decline in the quality of Nigerian recording facilities and the prohibitive cost of recording abroad. Under optimal conditions in the Shrine, Fela's music could be experienced according to his ideal sense of ensemble balance, but in translation to record, this complex balance has often been lost, with recordings sounding flat, muddy, and narrow in dynamic range. This problem—compounded by the low-register additions of the second bass guitar, second baritone sax, and gbedu drum—is evident on a number of later recordings, including the original version of *Army Arrangement, Beasts of No Nation,* and *Overtake Don Overtake Overtake.*

Part of the problem was Fela's own ambivalent relationship to the issue of fidelity and recording technology. While working in a popular medium, he maintained a purist stance rooted in the aesthetics of dance-band highlife and rhythm-and-blues of the late 1960s. This manifested itself as an open hostility to any signal-processing devices besides those that served the basic functions of amplification or recording: "I use electric guitars to amplify, but not for effect. . . . Anything that changes the natural sound of my instruments, I don't use. . . . I will not do music with computers and electronic gadgets because African music is natural sound. I am a pan-Africanist."[128]

Fela's linking of musical aesthetics with culture and ideology was understandable in the context of cultural definitions of sound "quality." As much as it is sometimes admired as a symbol of westernization and/or modernization, overuse of electronic devices such as drum machines, effects pedals, and synthesizers is considered an overt concession to the Western pop aesthetic. Such was the criticism of Sunny Ade's heavily electronic LP *Aura,* aimed at Western audiences but universally dismissed by his core juju fans in Nigeria. Still, distinctions can be made between the more dramatic signal processors and those that enable an ensemble's sound to be accurately and artfully captured on tape. In an age of computerized mixing and other postproduction practices, Fela's music stubbornly remained primarily a real-time performance art, with records essentially serving as the most basic documents of actual performances. Along with his music's strong political content, this contributed to a decline in his popularity in Nigeria, as other artists strove to "modernize" their sounds according to largely Western criteria.

Song length is another issue that compromised Fela's ability to prosper in the world music market, a consequence of the somewhat misguided notion held by some Western recording companies that African artists could achieve massive market success if they deconstructed their music into shorter, radio-friendly songs. On several occasions, Fela's music was edited after having been leased to foreign companies. Although this strategy has been arguably successful with some other African artists, it did a disservice to Fela's compositions, which last fifteen to forty minutes, and which develop a single musical and textual idea. As John Miller Chernoff observed, "The potential impact of Fela's conception of musical arrangement . . . has been negated by the record producers who distribute Fela's music in Europe and America. They cut the bulk of the early improvisations in order to place the vocal sections nearer the beginning."[129]

Fela challenged culturally and commercially conditioned expectations regarding the scope of his work, and he drew analogies with Western art music in order to convey his sense of the music's seriousness of purpose: "You cannot class my music like [popular] American music, because . . . my music is in different movements . . . so you cannot say Fela is writing one song. No! Fela is writing a song with five movements. . . . It's like a symphony but in the African sense."[130]

Changing international tastes also played a role in the popularity of various African artists and their accessibility to the international audience. While the initial phase of international interest was dominated by musicians like Fela, Sunny Ade, Ebenezer Obey, Franco, and Tabu Ley Rochereau, subsequent trends originated from other parts of the continent, and these musicians increasingly had to share their role as the spearheads of African "world beat" with a younger generation of musicians from around the continent as the market for African pop continued to diversify and audiences became more selective in their tastes. South African musicians such as Mahlathini and the Mahotella Queens and Ladysmith Black Mambazo garnered attention during the late 1980s, in part due to the dramatic changes in South Africa's political landscape, as well as Paul Simon's hugely successful *Graceland* LP and world tour, which featured a number of black South African musical styles and crack studio musicians. *Graceland*'s popularity also fueled a resurgence in the careers of South Africa's first wave of internationally known musicians such as Hugh Masekela and Miriam Makeba, even spilling over to noncommercial jazz artists like Abdullah Ibrahim (Dollar Brand), Johnny Dyani, and Dudu Pukwana.

Since the late 1980s, much attention has been focused on performers from Francophone West Africa, including Youssou N'Dour (who toured and collaborated with former Genesis vocalist Peter Gabriel), Salif Keita, Baaba Maal, Ali Farka Toure, and Alpha Blondy. These performers have often achieved unique blends of traditional instrumentation with modern recording technology, resulting in a distinctly Pan-Francophone–West African aesthetic that differs from the rougher sensibility of their Anglophone neighbors. Projects by Oumou Sangare and other Malian artists are especially interesting in this regard. And a new generation of Congolese musicians such as Kanda Bongo Man have also continued to forge a strong international musical presence from Paris.

Within Nigeria, other factors eroded the massive popularity Fela had previously enjoyed. Most important was the changing mood of the country. During the halcyon days of the 1970s, the country, relatively confident in its role as economic and cultural leader of black Africa, could self-consciously critique its own shortcomings. In Nigeria of the 1980s and 1990s, however, audiences out for a good time preferred not to be reminded of the country's political and economic predicament. One listener's comments encapsulated the criticisms of Fela's later music:

> One can't but acknowledge Fela as a great talent in African music but he himself is wasting away this talent. He says his music is not for pleasure but [no] one wants a political or ideological lecture for the price of a long-playing record. . . . I hope next time he comes out with a record, it will not be about his quarrel with the government, the press, his business associates, or whoever he is presently disagreeing with. Confrontation is no music.[131]

After his prison stay, he also had other popular styles to contend with. Since the 1980s, Yoruba popular music had been dominated by the ascendance of fuji music, a neotraditional style spearheaded by musicians such as Sikiru Ayinde Barrister, Wasiu Ayinde Barrister, and Ayinla Kollington. Stylistically, fuji was a youthful, popular reaction to the increasing westernization of juju bands that were performing for European and American audiences. These new performers took their inspiration from the older generation of neotraditional musicians such as Haruna Ishola and Ayinla Omowura. While continuing the tradition of praise singing, fuji bands eliminated Western instruments altogether, replacing them with more traditional percussion, and foregrounding the talking drums. Initially associated with Muslim musicians, fuji grew to become the overwhelmingly popular Yoruba youth and street music of Nigeria. Comprised of large batteries of percussion playing relatively simple parts hocketed into densely complex patterns, fuji demands much less technical facility on Western instruments than either afrobeat or juju, two styles which it suddenly cast into a comparatively westernized light.

Fela was operating at a different point on the stylistic continuum. Having established his politicization and cultural consciousness beyond doubt, he seemed since the early 1980s to be assertively reclaiming a semi-westernized aura of the "composer," as in his Koola Lobitos period. By 1990, he would even depict himself in the manner of a classical Western composer, on an album cover painting showing him in front of a grand piano with a European-styled, naturalistic bust of his mother arising from a lily pond.[132]

Along with complaints that Fela's art had become static, the notion that it had become too complex and demanding in the facility it required on Western instruments seemed to be the implicit criticism of one Nigerian review from 1990:

> Since the debut of his hit track "Jeun K'oku," afrobeat has remained the sole preserve of Fela. . . . No one seemed to have found the formula, the keynotes to afrobeat. And, for lack of variety, the Fela pattern [has become] a bit boring. Now and again, Fela attempts a few innovations, particularly in his singing pattern which lately has become longer, more message-oriented, more confrontational and political. Rhythmically, his horn arrangements particularly, have become more complicated and out of the reach of upstart musicians.[133]

Unlike other Yoruba styles in which innovation has occurred as a by-product of competition between two or more leading musicians, the lack of competition within the afrobeat genre probably meant that Fela felt less need to revamp his style dramatically over time. Despite his continuous development as a composer, his later work tended to conform to a single formal model. This is in contrast to his work of the 1970s, when he experimented with form in songs such as "Swegbe and Pako," "Open and Close," and "Na Poi."

"Cross-Examination"

Apart from an abortive tour of Canada in 1987, a swing through Europe in 1988, the African Sunsplash tour of the same year (staged in Monrovia, Kinshasa, and Lagos), and various Nigerian tours, Fela and Egypt 80 kept largely to their Shrine base following the 1986 tour, and it was another three years before they returned to the United States. When Fela did return to perform his latest manifestos there in the late 1980s—largely without the messianic hype that had accompanied his earlier tours—it provided an opportunity to scrutinize the way his Pan-Africanist message played out in different settings.

Pan-Africanism has often been dismissed as romantic, outdated, idealistic, and impractical,[134] but, as Paul Gilroy has stated, if the concept has any immediately demonstrable viability, it would most certainly be in music, where musical styles have flown freely as vehicles of identity throughout the "Black Atlantic."[135] While limiting his performances to Africa during the 1970s, Fela's music powered his image throughout Africa and the world, and his embrace of this ideology went relatively untested in the wider sense. When he began performing internationally, however, the complexities involved in actually applying the Pan-African vision cross-culturally emerged. As easy as it is for most people of African descent to relate to the sound of Fela's music, the messages it contained have been received and interpreted in dramatically different ways, demonstrating the different ways "blackness" is conceived and articulated in different settings. This was made abundantly clear by the interaction between Fela and his audiences at a series of concerts given over a two-year period around the New York metropolitan area.

In July 1989, the band arrived at the city's famed Apollo Theatre in Harlem to perform two benefit concerts for singer James Brown, who had been imprisoned the previous year on charges of evading arrest. The event was highly charged with political, cultural, and musical significance, with the audience an even mixture of Afrocentric African-Americans and expatriate Nigerians (many of whom seemed to be Shrine regulars from back home). Also in attendance backstage were a handful of musicians who had been members of Brown's band when they toured Nigeria and visited Fela's Afro-Spot in 1970. Although opposed in theory to benefits, Fela had agreed to perform because of Brown's predicament, his stature as a cultural icon, and Fela's own obvious musical debt to him. Fela and the band took the stage to a supportive audience and rapidly converted them to their afrobeat message with their powerful big-band sound, provocative dancing, and political singing. The evening's compositions—"Underground System," "Overtake Don Overtake Overtake," and "Akunakuna, Senior Brother of Perambulator"—were among Fela's most political works, and some of his between-song rap sessions (on the subject of the Nigerian government's Structural Adjustment Program and his latest theme of "second slavery") ran as long as forty minutes. However, all were well received by the culturally and politically minded audience. The "second slavery" theme was particularly resonant, given that Nigeria's leaders were submitting to socially and economically humiliating structural adjustment programs with the International Monetary Fund, while in America unprecedented numbers of African-American males under the age of thirty-five were in prison, punishment was among the fastest growing industries in the country, and the movement toward privatization of prisons was gaining momentum. The Apollo, a symbol of black cultural pride and artistic achievement, was an ideal venue for Fela and his message, which successfully struck a Pan-African chord that evening with the Nigerian students as well as African-Americans facing many similar problems and concerns.

The following night's concert at a hotel ballroom in Newark, New Jersey, was an entirely different affair. The Newark area contains a sizable West African community, and the audience at this concert was overwhelmingly comprised of Nigerians. While most would probably be considered working-class by American standards, many are budding entrepreneurs, and the very fact that they were living in the United States placed them in a drastically different economic and cultural position than Fela's regular attendants of the Shrine, many of whom will probably never travel outside of Nigeria. The traditional attire and formal, reserved demeanors were markedly different than the jovial, casually dressed Nigerian students at the previous night's concert, who had received Fela like a favored uncle and sung along with every line. Attending Fela's show much as they would one by any Nigerian musician touring the United States, the Newark audience seemed to come primarily for a night of musical entertainment and cultural community. Although at the beginning of the concert some audience members urged Fela to "yab dem" (abuse the government), few of them actually shared his political sensibility, and this urging was more along the lines of the type of interaction they had come to expect from him. The confrontational tension in the room was palpable as Fela embarked on an intense, thirty-minute political monologue detailing how he had "paid with his blood" to sing and speak his antigovernment opinions, to an audience of upwardly mobile Nigerians who were striving hard for the American dream while back home the Babangida government pummeled the masses through stringent economic reforms. The mood was lightened during "Overtake . . . ," in which the Egypt 80 dancers took the stage while Fela sang a brief medley of his old themes, to the nostalgic delight of the audience. By the last song of the evening, the tension was superficially relieved; most of the audience seemed to ignore Fela's political lyrics (about government harassment of street traders) while dancing in couples to the neo-highlife flow of "Akunakuna . . ." much as they might have danced to the music of Bobby Benson or Victor Olaiya decades earlier. Afterwards, however, one Nigerian man held forth angrily in front of a circle of people in the lobby, offended because Fela had insulted his countrymen in attendance by suggesting they had abandoned the struggles of their homeland, working menial jobs in pursuit of American affluence.[136] Had this been a Shrine audience, his comments might have been interpreted differently, but Fela was forcing the audience to confront—on his own socially transgressive terms—the raw underside of Nigeria just as they were trying hard to put their "best front" forward in pursuit of American-styled success.

A year later, Fela and band returned to New York City to perform at the International African Festival, a huge cultural fair held annually on the field of Boys and Girls' High School in Brooklyn. Comprised equally of Africans, African-Americans, and Afro-Caribbeans, the audience was probably the most Afrocentric one the band faced on the tour, and the atmosphere, in the heart of all-black Bedford-Stuyvesant, was probably closest to that of the Shrine. Taking the stage well after midnight, Fela obviously felt relaxed and at home, taking much time for his between-songs yabis sessions and mixing his political commentary with a steady stream of profane humor. While portions of the audience seemed to appreciate some of this (particularly the Jamaican contingent, used to the explicit "slackness" lyrics of modern dancehall), it also offended many. Most of those at the Brooklyn festival attended the concert primarily as a cultural event, many coming with their entire families despite the late hour. A large contingent of the festival audience also consisted of African-American women stylishly adorned in traditional African attire—wraps, headpieces, prints, and batiks, as well as elaborate braids and dreadlocks—for whom African culture was embraced for its dignity, grace, and tradition, as opposed to the harshly political, streetwise African sensibility Fela offered. Fela evidently assumed that the type of street humor he indulged in was a universally valued mode of black communication, but on this occasion it was an affront to those African-Americans in the audience who identified with Africa as a symbol of cultural affirmation and dignity.

Fela also made a series of strong remarks during his song "M.A.S.S.," criticizing the role of Islam in contemporary Nigerian affairs. In the song's introduction, for example, he told the audience: "I'm disappointed. Americans don't know what is happening, man—African-Americans especially. The Muslim religion is not for Africans at all." As the song faded, he continued his tirade, imitating the call to prayer: " 'Allaaaaahu Akbar!' What the fuck is that, man? I'm African, man, I don't understand that shit! Our ancestors can throw Allah away with one little finger."

Some in the audience—already offended by Fela's vulgarity—left as a result of these comments. Jazz pianist Randy Weston (who had jammed with Koola Lobitos during his mid-1960s visits to Nigeria) was scheduled to make a guest appearance with Egypt 80. But Weston was apparently among those who took offense at Fela's remarks and departed early. Fela had alienated a large portion of the audience for whom the Muslim religion was an important source of cultural affirmation, if not actual religious faith. Despite the fact that even familiar Afrocentric exponent Molefi Kete Asante had recently voiced a similar hostility to Islam in his book *Afrocentricity,* many seemed unwilling to entertain the notion that Islam, despite Elijah Muhammad's assertion that it was "the true religion of the blackman," has functioned as a force of division in the black world as often as it has functioned a force of unity.[137]

To say that Fela failed to account for the degree to which Islam was closely tied to dissent and cultural awareness in African-American culture is probably inaccurate. Having been influenced by *The Autobiography of Malcolm X,* and enjoying a close relationship with the cultural segment of the African-American community, he was certainly aware of this. It would be more accurate to assume that besides his antagonism toward Islam (and Christianity) in Africa, and the fact that his own activism was infused with the aura of traditional African cults, his identity as a derisive singer took precedence over any considerations of nuanced analysis or cross-cultural tact. A year later, during a July 1991 return visit to the Apollo, he continued this theme in another preface to "M.A.S.S.," this time vilifying Nation of Islam leader Louis Farrakhan for his alleged snubbing of the "common" people during a recent visit to Lagos.[138] A longtime Nigerian Fela fan who witnessed both events remarked: "You think he cared? He doesn't care who he offends. Back home he does the same thing. He just likes abusing people—that's his main thing! And he will abuse anybody! After he gets that Indian hemp inside of him, he probably doesn't even care what he is saying."[139]

With three radically different audiences and receptions within the same metropolitan area, these encounters demonstrate the difficulty of assuming Pan-African political, cultural, or philosophical unity, and the importance of factoring the politics of location into the cultural equation. Even in Nigeria, while many native Lagosians would never have been caught in the hemp- and crime-filled devil's den they believed the Afrika Shrine to be, many of the Western tourists and dignitaries seen by day in the city's upscale areas such as Ikoyi or Victoria Island could inevitably be counted among the Shrine audience by night.

The misunderstandings that marked Fela's international tours can be attributed, in many cases, to the disparity between Fela himself and the ways he had been "framed" by the Western concert promoters and recording companies, as well as the complexity of his style and presentation. Those concertgoers who expected a raging African political firebrand (as suggested by the cover painting of *Live in Amsterdam,* which depicts a bare-chested, spear-wielding Fela dressed in a traditional loincloth and beads) experienced instead a man dressed in Western stage clothes. Those who expected a performance of traditional music experienced an electric, Western-influenced popular style. Those who expected a virtuosic African jazz experienced instead a social, communal dance music in which virtuosity in the Western sense was not a prime consideration. Those who expected a progressive, leftist ideologue experienced instead an authoritarian, neotraditional polygamist presenting a stage show often bordering on the burlesque. Those who expected a greatest hits show got completely unfamiliar material, substantially different in conception than Fela's older music. And finally, those who simply wanted to have a "good time" listening and dancing to African party music experienced instead a heavily politicized music and lengthy political sermons.

The shift in international tastes for African music was by no means a professional defeat for Nigerian musicians like Fela and Sunny Ade. With the continent's largest music market as their audience, they still commanded huge domestic followings—and even at the height of their fame, there was never the sense that they wanted to become international stars on the order of Youssou N'Dour or Bob Marley, at least not at the risk of sacrificing their loyal fans at home. In retrospect, the consideration of Fela for international stardom by Western companies was clearly based on the power of his instrumental sound, his rebellious legend, and his personal charisma, as opposed to the ideas expressed in his music. In no realistic sense could his 1980s music be expected to command an international audience without a revolution in the very notion of what constituted "popular music." While Bob Marley's political songs such as "Africa Unite," "Zimbabwe," and "Top Rankin'" were ultimately broad enough in their articulations to appeal to nonpoliticized audiences unfamiliar with respectively, Pan-Africanism, African nationalism, and political violence in Jamaica, it is difficult to imagine Western audiences joining a chorus of "Army Arrangement" or "Movement of the People." Further, while Rastafari-infused reggae contained a strongly pastoral, back-to-nature streak that resonated with the exoticist, environmental, and utopian strains of America's counterculture, Fela's Afro–black power sensibility was thoroughly urban and only utopian in a Marxist sense (i.e., utopia as ultimate revolutionary triumph). The fact that this material generally found a more welcoming response in Europe was likely due to a relative familiarity with the issues expressed in Fela's songs, rooted in the history of colonial interactions between Africans and Europeans. In the United States, where the historical context was not colonialism but a racial antagonism rooted in the history of slavery, Fela's music and presentation, with its undertones of African-American black power, was more difficult for mainstream European-American audiences to accept. Simultaneously, the complexities of his African vision contradicted the romanticized images of African-American listeners. Virulently hostile to African elites, Fela rejected their culture of symbols—clothing, titles, language, and bearing—which many African-Americans uncritically accepted as symbols of "nobility," not of hegemony.

John Akpederi once noted that "Stripped down to the basics, Fela's whole yabis session [says] one thing: 'Let me be me. . . . ' " Fela's involvement in the world market can be characterized by this same ethos; it is ultimately marked by the same stubbornness and reluctance to compromise as the rest of his career has been marked.[140]

Despite his domination of the Nigerian music scene during the 1970s, Fela by this stage in his career was clearly not the type of musician who cared to cultivate, pursue, or exploit his own commercial "moment"—that mythic period in the career of an artist when all the facets of his work and personality seem to fuse magically with the dominant cultural mood and the commercial trends of the music marketplace. In truth, he was too complex a personality to accomplish this, and had in any case become completely disillusioned with the music industry.

Fela doesn't seem to have held any regrets about this. By this latter stage of his career, he had completely withdrawn from recording and international touring, playing his backlog of unrecorded music exclusively for his devoted Shrine audience and, occasionally, elsewhere in Nigeria. As late as 1994, he reportedly turned down a multimillion-dollar offer for his back catalogue from the Motown recording company "on advice from the spirits."[141] As he explained to Gary Stewart in 1990: "To play African music, you cannot economize. . . . The culture of Africa is not based on economy, it is based on naturalness, being natural. And if you try to put money first before the culture, then you will destroy the beauty of what you wanted to represent. . . . I don't have any intention to destroy the beauty of African music for money. I will never do that. So I'm the poorest musician in town right now."[142]

Fela returning to the Afrika Shrine following a court case, 1974. (Photo courtesy of John Collins)

Fela with some of his wives and band members after the communal wedding, 1978. (Photo courtesy of Glendora Review)

Tony Allen, 1983. (Photo courtesy of C. C. Smith)

Bob Marley, the reggae superstar who prefigured Fela's rise as an Afropop star. (Photo courtesy of Leni Sinclair)

Sunny Ade, Fela's Nigerian "world beat" competitor. (Photo credit: Daniel Ray, courtesy of Andrew Frankel/Graviton)

Fela's son Femi Anikulapo-Kuti onstage in Naples, 1984. (Photo courtesy of Juliet Highet)

Lekan Animashaun in Naples, 1984. (Photo courtesy of Juliet Highet)

Ghariokwu Lemi, who drew and designed many of Fela's album covers. (Photo courtesy of Glendora Review*)*

Egypt 80 horn section onstage in Europe, 1983. (Photos this page courtesy of Juliet Highet)

Egypt 80 onstage in Europe, 1983.

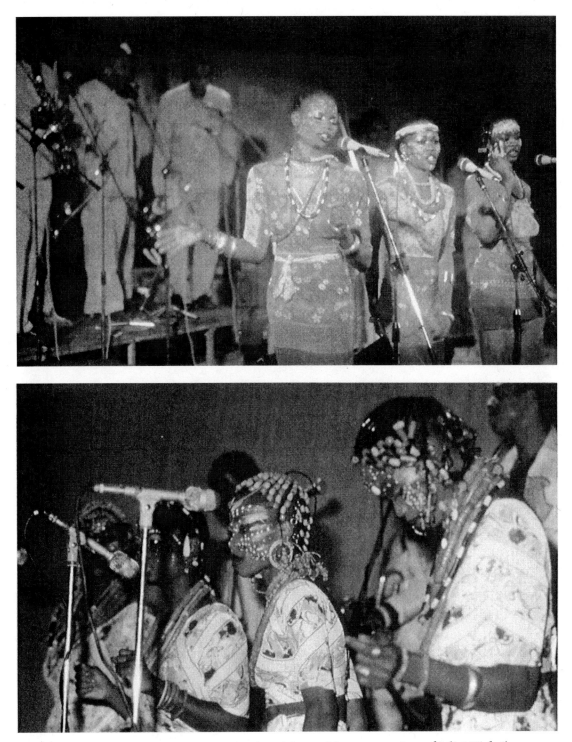

Fela's wives singing onstage in Europe, 1984. (Photos this page courtesy of Juliet Highet)

Fela's wives dancing onstage, Paris 1984. (Photo courtesy of Juliet Highet)

"Yabis time" in Naples, 1984. (Photo courtesy of Juliet Highet)

Fela playing soprano saxophone onstage in Naples, 1983. (Photo courtesy of Juliet Highet)

Fela, Sandra Izsadore, and Ginger Baker, 1986. (Photo courtesy of Sandra Izsadore)

The last Kalakuta commune, Ikeja, 1994. (Photo courtesy of Miki Kagami)

Lighting up at the Shrine, 1994. (Photo courtesy of Miki Kagami)

Fela, 1994. (Photo courtesy of Miki Kagami)

Fela's daughter Yeni Anikulapo-Kuti, 1999. (Photo by Michael Veal)

Femi Anikulapo-Kuti, 1999. (Photo courtesy of Drew Fitzgerald/FACET)

"Fear Not for Man"
(1985–1997)

*The African governments have been willing to compromise with what
they think is only a little evil. Even today, with all the recent history of
vicious little tyrants, these nations fail to realize that when they
compromise about restoring democracy, they become unwitting
accomplices in the greater evil.*

WOLE SOYINKA *quoted in* GATES *1995:14*

*When I went to Nigeria in 1970, I was ready to give up on America
completely—I was ready to become an African. Nigeria was such a
beautiful country, and people were so hopeful and optimistic there, you
KNEW that country was gonna achieve great things. But the way things
became by the 1980s, [I was] not interested in going back.*

SANDRA ISZADORE, *interview with author, February 1999*

*I don't have to enter the mainstream of politics. I can have a program,
which is much more productive than entering the system, which would
mean that I agree with that system. We can never win, so I will educate
instead.*

FELA *quoted in* HIGHET *1989:42*

Sweeping away the unpopular regime of Mohammedu Buhari and proclaiming a
new era of economic reform, infrastructural revitalization, and human rights, the
administration of President Ibrahim Babangida stole its way into office in August
1985 on a wave of ambivalent public hope. A veteran of the Civil War and Murtala Mohammed's regime, and one of the longest serving rulers in Nigeria's postindependence history, Babangida had an affable manner and apparent willingness
to consider his critics that initially masked what nevertheless became, by most
accounts, the worst administration in the nation's history to date. Its ultimate dis-

grace would be the astronomical greed and arrogance of Babangida and his cohorts, the grossly unequal shouldering of the burden of harsh economic reform, and the president's reluctance to leave office and turn power over to a civilian administration. Ultimately, Babangida would bequeath to his nation a legacy of unprecedented poverty, brutal repression, kleptocracy, political chaos and—if the most pessimistic forecasts are to be believed—the possible collapse of the Nigerian nation-state as constituted since independence.[1] By the end of his eight-year tenure, many Nigerians would openly wonder whether the country was in fact a better place to live during the years of colonialism.[2]

Babangida's first years in office were comparatively rosy, as the administration released political prisoners (including Fela) and paid lip service to human rights. The previous administration's refusal to implement structural adjustment policies dictated by the International Monetary Fund (IMF) may have been a crucial factor in its overthrow in what has been termed a "palace coup" (Babangida had been Buhari's military chief of staff). Julius Ihonvbere thus suggests that Babangida assumed power with a clear but covert agreement with his foreign backers that the country would adopt the stringent economic measures without question.[3] The Structural Adjustment Program (SAP), a set of conditions attached to a loan from the IMF, was implemented between October 1985 and July 1986— even though the country, following an intense public debate, never actually accepted the loan. These conditions, designed to save money and promote government earnings, included massive layoffs, pay cuts for government workers, banning of basic food imports, a wage freeze, removal of subsidies for petroleum and other industries, and currency devaluation. It also required Nigeria to embrace an American-style free market system through controversial measures designed to provide incentives to foreign investment, including revoking indigenization decrees passed in the 1970s and introducing a debt-equity swap program.[4] It was misguided to expect that local industry, already highly underdeveloped in the global economy, would be able to compete with multinational capital once the floodgates of foreign investment were opened. Foreign companies merely increased their local holdings and profits, while indigenous elites consolidated their economic power exponentially both as local entrepreneurs and as middlemen for the foreign multinationals.

Babangida insisted that for SAP to be successful, Nigerians of all walks of life had to shoulder the burden through sacrifice, harder work, and a more austere lifestyle. But in reality the burden fell squarely on the shoulders of common citizens—the middle, working, and urban underclasses—who had to contend with reduced salaries, longer work hours, weakened currency, massive inflation (food prices alone increased by an average of 500 percent), and scarcity of basic resources. The Babangida era was one in which Nigerians saw their quality of life decline rapidly, while the military and elites made unprecedented gains in both consolidating and displaying their wealth. The culture of corruption, already central to Nigerian life, became completely entrenched, and working in the service of the state offered the fastest route for accumulating personal wealth.[5] Even discredited politicians of former regimes, many of them dismissed by Murtala

Mohammed for corruption in 1976, were reinstated and placed on government allowances. Billions of additional naira were squandered on leisure activities and projects designed to project the prestige of the government, including sports tournaments, extravagant building projects, and importation of expensive luxury items. In one highly publicized episode, the Babangida administration purchased over fifty six-door Mercedes-Benz limousines for a conference of the Organization of African Unity held in Abuja. This event took place in the same year in which the government gave 300,000 inhabitants of the Maroko slum area in Lagos seven days to relocate, with no alternative housing arrangements, before the entire property was bulldozed to make way for the designer houses of government officials, reportedly among the most expensive and breathtaking in the world. As Ihonvbere notes, many of the residents of Maroko had already been made jobless as a result of SAP and took to various criminal means as the only hope of survival.[6]

The inevitable result of this culture of official arrogance and mass suffering was an increase in crime and civil unrest. Anti-SAP riots took place in major cities in 1986, 1989, 1990, and 1992. In most instances, students were the catalysts, but they were joined spontaneously by frustrated citizens from all walks of life. In response, the proclaimed "human rights" facade of the Babangida administration began to crack; in the end, it became the most brutal regime to yet rule Nigeria, arresting more dissidents and executing more Nigerians than any previous regime.[7] Babangida crushed political opposition (especially among student associations) and was not above fostering primordial ethnic and religious animosities as a divisive tactic; by the end of his tenure, the country would witness a dramatic resurgence in ethnic and religious violence.

Fela remained a highly charged political symbol during the Babangida years. Although he sporadically reiterated his claim that he would one day rule Nigeria, whatever political aspirations he still held were frustrated under Babangida's rule—and in any case, he increasingly tended to delegate the country's overwhelming problems to otherworldly forces. He told Gary Stewart in 1990: "I know I will rule my country. . . . Whether I want to do it through politics or through spiritual means is what I have to decide myself. You see, I'm still trying to balance and decipher exactly what should happen in my country."[8] By 1993, he had concluded: "This country has many leaders: 'My own different, my own different' [i.e., everyone proclaims allegiance to a different leader]. . . . Our ancestors have taken over the running of the country."[9] By the early 1990s, in fact, he was more likely to tell inquirers that he was spending his time internally—engaging in spiritual contemplation or communing with the spirits of African ancestors—than in any worldly pursuits.

His retreat from the political frontlines did not affect his potency as a political symbol, which only increased with the events of the late 1980s and early 1990s. The tenth anniversary of the Kalakuta attack in February 1987 was marked by a week-long series of events including films, jazz concerts at the Jazz 38 nightclub, and a symposium entitled "Kalakuta Inferno and Human Rights in Nigeria" chaired by novelist Festus Ijayi. In May 1988 Fela was invited to London by the Global Cooperation for a Better World as "Africa's Ambassador of Cooperation and Goodwill." A play entitled *Water No Get Enemy* (after Fela's 1975 track) was staged in early 1989 by Tunde Fatunde, a radical lecturer at the University of Benin. And the Shrine remained a rallying point for political dissidents, as evidenced by a major concert/rally celebrating the release of the "Kuje 5" political detainees, Beko Ransome-Kuti, Olusegun Mayegun, Baba Omojola, Femi Falana, and Gani Fawehinmi, in July 1992.[10]

In contrast to the post-Kalakuta dog days of the early 1980s, when Fela was intent on advancing his political profile, he seemed simply happy to be back on the scene making music following his release from prison in 1986. While his postprison work continued to grow more political, it was also reinfused with some of the humor that had been lacking since the late 1970s. He seemed to experience a period of creative rejuvenation, reflected in a string of remarkable compositions devoted almost exclusively to political themes. These include "Overtake Don Overtake Overtake" (lamenting military dictatorships around the continent); "Chop and Clean Mouth Like Nothing Happened, Na New Name for Stealing" (vilifying the country's postindependence leaders for their looting of the national treasury); "Country of Pain"(examining the hardship of Nigerian life in the late 1980s); "Government of Crooks" (detailing the embezzlement of Nigeria's oil wealth by corrupt politicians); "Music Against Second Slavery" (examining the impact of Islam on contemporary Nigerian politics and power dynamics); "Akunakuna, Senior Brother of Perambulator" (criticizing the government's "wandering" law and harassment of petty street traders); "Underground System" (a tribute to slain Burkina Faso president Thomas Sankara); and "Big Blind Country" (similar to the earlier "Yellow Fever" in its lampooning of foreign cultural practices). In characteristic form, Fela explained the inspiration for this last number, implicitly commenting on the notorious "toothy grin" with which Babangida kept his critics at bay:

> The tune I'm thinking of now is about African women who palm [straighten] their hair. It's becoming disgraceful that every African woman's hair is shining like white man's hair. It's a chemical from America, big business. I will ask these women one question: Why the hair on the head is shining, but not the hair down there? . . . This chemical makes their hair soft and it destroys it. . . . In the same way that woman is treating her hair to make it look artificially nice, how many of our leaders are looking artificially nice?[11]

Despite the recurring criticism that his music had become too political, Fela seemed only strengthened in his resolve to highlight the underlying causes of Nigeria's political turmoil. In a period when Nigerian reggae musicians such as Sonny Okosuns, Majek Fashek, and Ras Kimono were jockeying to criticize the crumbling apartheid regime in South Africa, Fela's work alone continued to explore the complexities of military leadership and corruption throughout Africa, and particularly on the Nigerian home front, in the most graphic terms. During this era of unprecedented economic polarity, the roster of Yoruba megastars was almost entirely dominated by praise-singing musicians; even as the economy was nosediving, President Babangida donated 10 million naira to the Nigerian Musician's Union (PMAN) in 1992.[12] In this context, Fela's music remained relevant, vital, and entirely distinct from other styles.

"Overtake Don Overtake Overtake" is probably most representative of his later work. In it, he criticizes unmandated military governments and decries the common suffering induced by the austerity programs. The song's choral refrain juxtaposes images of this suffering against images of police and soldiers extorting money from innocent civilians.

FELA: When we want to call Nigerian government, we give am name "Federal Military Government" For Libya dem give am name "Liberation Council" For Liberia dem give am name "Redemption Council" For Zaire dem give am name "Revolutionary Council" Dem get different different names for different different governments	*FELA:* When we refer to the Nigerian government, we use the name "Federal Military Government" In Libya they use the name "Liberation Council" In Liberia they use the name "Redemption Council" In Zaire they use the name "Revolutionary Council" There are many different names For many different [military] governments
But the correct name na "soja come, soja go . . ."	But the correct name is "soldiers come, soldiers go" [i.e., an endless succession of military governments]
CHORUS: Soja go, soja come, soja come, soja go (repeat)	*CHORUS:* Soldier go, soldier come, soldier come, soldier go (repeat)
FELA: Na so Africa man life dey bi, suffer don dabaru him sense	*FELA:* This is the life of an African man, suffering has compromised his common sense
When you wear police uniform, na to collect money for road Police station don turn to bank	When you wear a police uniform, and extort money from drivers The police station has turned into a bank
D.P.O. na bank manager	the Divisional Police Officer is the bank manager
Police station don turn to bank	The police station has turned into a bank
I.G. na managing director	The Inspector General of Police is the managing director
Na big-e wahala for man to waka for walk on road at anytime . . .	It is a big problem for a man to the street at anytime . . .

Familiar only to regular attendants of the Afrika Shrine, the unreleased "O.D.O.O." became notorious in Lagos for its frank depictions of police and military corruption. By the time the 1988 Reggae Sunsplash Festival arrived at the National

Stadium in Surulere, the tour promoters, fearing government reprisal, asked Fela (who was headlining) to omit the tune from his set. Reports indicate that he agreed, then bounded on to the stage to huge fanfare and announced "O.D.O.O." as his first tune, to the shock and delight of the thousands in attendance.[13] There are unsubstantiated rumors that a highly placed official in the Babangida administration sent Fela a message following the concert warning him that there would be serious consequences if "O.D.O.O." were released. Nevertheless, the song was recorded during the group's 1989 world tour, appearing later in the year on Fela's Kalakuta label and leading John Nwaobi, in his review of the album, to speculate that Fela had a not-so-latent death wish.[14] The release party at the Shrine was attended by leading social critics, demonstrating Fela's continued status as a political symbol and elder dissident of sorts. Nwaobi reported:

> Two weekends ago, "O.D.O.O." was formally launched at Fela's Afrika Shrine in Ikeja, Lagos. If Fela ever thought he was alone in his crusade for improved social conditions in Nigeria, such kindred guests as Gani Fawehinmi and Alao Aka-Bashorun—two radical lawyers—were among many other guests whose presence gave credibility to Fela's social criticisms. . . . [Nothing] could damn the flow of bitter condemnations of government's policies and seeming apathy to the privations of Nigerians.[15]

Fela also continued to use his music to comment on events around the African continent. "Underground System" was his tribute to the late President Thomas Sankara of Burkina Faso. A Marxist ideologue, recreational musician, and longtime fan of Fela's music, Sankara met Fela after the latter's release from prison. Fela was impressed by Sankara's revolutionary rhetoric, his mass appeal among Burkina Faso's youth, and his love of music. In fact, Sankara often "trained" his country's pop groups ideologically, and he occasionally accompanied himself on guitar in state speeches. It was thus natural that the two men would share a musical and ideological bond. So impressed was Fela by Sankara that he began composing a song in praise of the young leader. However, following Sankara's assassination in a coup on October 15, 1987 (in which the Nigerian government was accused of complicity),[16] Fela changed the song to a posthumous tribute, decrying the "underground system" by which the continent's most progressive leaders seem to perish:

When one good man rise for Africa today,	When one good man rises in Africa today,
Bad leaders dem go wan finish am-o	Bad leaders want to eliminate him
When one good man rise for Africa today	When one good man rises in Africa today,
useless leaders dem go wan finish am-o	useless leaders want to eliminate him
Dem go plan against am, lie against am	They plan against him, lie against him

Lie against am, talk against am	Lie against him, talk against him
You no see Nkrumah dem finish am-o	Don't you see Nkrumah, they have eliminated him
You no see Sekou Toure dem finish am-o	Don't you see Sekou Toure, they have eliminated him
You know see Lumumba dem finish am-o	Don't you see Lumumba, they have eliminated him
You no see Idi Amin dem finish am-o	Don't you see Idi Amin, they have eliminated him
You no see Mandela dem wan kill am-o	Don't you see Mandela, they want to kill him

Although many reviewers took issue with Fela's inclusion of Ugandan dictator Idi Amin on a list of "progressive" African leaders,[17] "Underground System" was released internationally in 1992 to enthusiastic reviews, sparking a gradual reappraisal of Fela's work after a period in which he seemed to have fallen out of the international limelight.

Fela's relationship with the Nigerian rulership into the 1990s was marked by a tenuous peace interspersed with preemptive measures. Realizing that it was dealing with an internationally known dissident, the government largely refrained from its previous drastic measures. Whenever there was civil unrest, however, he was sure to be rounded up or harassed, along with other outspoken critics such as his brother Beko, Wole Soyinka, Alao Bashorun, Femi Falana, and Gani Fawehinmi.

During 1988 student uprisings in response to rumors of the excessive wealth amassed by President Babangida (who would reportedly leave office with 30 billion francs in foreign accounts, surpassing even Zaire's legendarily corrupt Mobutu Sese Seko),[18] along with government clampdowns on several national student organizations, police shot and killed a man in front of the Afrika Shrine, sending a clear message to those who viewed the club as a site of popular mobilization. When the nation erupted again in anti-SAP riots in April of the following year (the severity of which were only dwarfed in intensity and international news coverage by the concurrent protests of Chinese students in Beijing's Tiananmen Square), Fela's planned hometown concert in Abeokuta was canceled by soldiers who, arriving in trucks and armored tanks, surrounded Asero Stadium and threatened to shoot on sight any civilians attempting to enter.

In January 1993, Fela was arrested and charged with ordering the fatal beating of a former employee; he denied any involvement in the beating. Like previous incidents, his arrest was apparently politically motivated, this time part of a larger sweep of dissidents associated with the Campaign for Democracy (CD). Chaired by Beko Ransome-Kuti before his imprisonment, the CD is a coalition of trade unions and civil rights organizations that emerged as the leading opposition to Nigeria's military government. In a page 2 article on Fela's arrest, the *New York Times* suggested that "as many Nigerians see it, the [murder] case is being used by the authorities as a way of getting back at Fela, his brother Beko, and other dissidents who have formed the core of an increasingly effective opposition movement."[19] This suspicion seemed confirmed when—following Babangida's annulment of civilian elections reportedly won by Fela's old nemesis M. K. O. Abiola in June 1993, and the installation of the departing president's handpicked interim government—all concerned were released and the charges against them dropped.

Babangida's annulment of Abiola's victory, which seems to have been a remarkable popular mandate across regional, religious, and ethnic lines, marked the beginning of an era of unprecedented political chaos and public frustration in Nigeria. The president's installation of Chief Ernest Shonekan as head of an "interim" civilian government was widely interpreted as a veiled invitation for former military chief of staff Sani Abacha to usurp power and claim his share of the national spoils—and this is exactly what took place in November 1993. After less than six months' respite, military rule continued in Nigeria under the brutal rein of a new dictator.

It is unclear just what soured the formerly close relationship between Babangida and Abiola. The latter had benefited tremendously from his close relationship with the government, winning millions of naira in government contracts while gradually maneuvering himself into the political arena. By 1992, however, with the nation clamoring for a return to civilian rule and Abiola himself eyeing the presidency, the businessman was using his Concord group of publications to call for Babangida's departure. It has also been alleged that Babangida was pressured, by northern military officials fearful of southern economic domination, to annul Abiola's victory. After traveling abroad to canvass for support for his election mandate, Abiola was imprisoned by General Abacha for treason when he returned to Nigeria and defiantly proclaimed himself president. In the two years that followed, prominent prodemocracy activists—among them many prominent Yorubas from Abeokuta—were rounded up and imprisoned for their opposition to Abacha's government. Fela's brother Beko was given a fifteen-year sentence and former president Obasanjo sentenced to death for their roles in planning an alleged coup, a charge widely dismissed as a pretext for the silencing of dissident voices. Obasanjo's sentence was commuted to twenty-five years imprisonment following an international outcry; former U.S. president Jimmy Carter even traveled to Nigeria to appeal on Obasanjo's behalf.

Such international pressure was unfortunately not enough to save the life of Ken Saro-Wiwa, a novelist best known for *Basi and Company,* a highly popular television series of veiled but pointed social and political criticism. During the course of his public career, Saro-Wiwa had taken varying positions toward the government and its activities, at one point serving on the government of his native Rivers State. Despite his varying relationship to the state, however, he was a consistent and staunch advocate for the rights of his native Ogoni people and their plight as an ethnic minority. During the late 1980s, Saro-Wiwa's commitment intensified in response to the environmental despoliation of Ogoni homelands by the drilling operations of Shell Oil Company in the Niger River Delta region. Forming the Movement for the Salvation of the Ogoni People (MOSOP), Saro-Wiwa and his colleagues demanded reparations for environmental damage that had rendered large portions of their homeland uninhabitable, a larger share of oil revenues, and greater control over the conduct of oil companies in their region. By 1992, taking his cue from developments in the Soviet Union and Eastern Europe, he was actively calling for the dissolution of Nigeria into a federation of separate ethnic states, by peaceful or even nonpeaceful means.[20] He proclaimed in 1992:

> Nigeria is a multi-ethnic state. And there's no need pretending that it's anything else. You cannot be a Muslim from Sokoto and a traditionalist from Ogoni and you say they're going to make one country. What sort of confusion is that? Allow everybody to go his own way. . . . The Hausa-Fulani people cannot take everything away and the others have nothing and you think that the country will stay together. . . . They should stop using trickery and violence, preaching one Nigeria in public and then in private, they're running the place on an ethnic basis. . . . The whole notion of the state called Nigeria doesn't exist in fact in the minds of the people. It only exists because there's oil money to be stolen from the Delta.[21]

Saro-Wiwa had been hostile to Biafran nationalism during the Biafran war, but his stand echoed that conflict insofar as both were at least partially concerned with the issue of who controlled and profited from natural resources (i.e., petroleum) crucial to the economic survival of the nation. MOSOP's campaign of militant activism and civil disobedience, which had caused Shell to withdraw its drilling operations from Ogoniland in 1993, brought Saro-Wiwa into direct conflict with the Abacha regime, 90 percent of whose revenues derived from oil exports, and whose officials relied upon embezzlement of these profits as their chief source of personal enrichment. One-half of the government's oil receipts came from Shell's operations and, as David Rieff noted, these revenues "were all that stood between the regime and economic collapse."[22] In May 1994, Saro-Wiwa and eight other MOSOP members were arrested and charged with the murder of four Ogoni tribal chiefs who had opposed their efforts. Tried by a secret military tribunal, they were all sentenced to death and, despite considerable international attention to their case, executed in November 1995.

Saro-Wiwa's execution opened a new chapter of Nigerian history. Previously, the demand for Nigeria's oil meant that Western governments would pay lip service to democracy but stop short of concrete punitive measures such as economic sanctions or the freezing of foreign assets. After Saro-Wiwa's execution, however, Nigeria was suspended from the British Commonwealth, foreign ambassadors were recalled from Lagos and Abuja, and the Abacha administration was roundly condemned by organizations such as Amnesty International and the International Commission of Jurists. Now a pariah in the world community, Nigeria gained an reputation as a nation of criminals and an unsafe place to conduct business. It was reportedly the transit point for 50 percent of American-bound heroin, as well as the hatching ground for innumerable international scams.[23] Domestically, morale was at an unprecedented low and frustration at an all-time high.

Fela maintained a low profile at the Shrine as the country slipped deeper and deeper into political chaos. While he predictably gloated over the misfortunes of Abiola (ridiculing his physical appearance on "Underground System"), he was in fact deeply troubled that his arch-nemesis was being hailed as a heroic icon of democracy. As his daughter Yeni recalled, "Fela became very depressed. He was very upset that everyone was going to vote for Abiola—Fela had been attacking him for his corruption for years. They made Abiola a hero because he was supposedly a democratically-elected civilian, and after this it seemed to Fela that everything he had worked for was now being ignored."[24]

Possibly because of this, Fela never directly challenged General Abacha for his persecution of Abiola, and when asked his opinion on the state of his nation in 1996, he avoided local specifics while offering a confounding and dispirited assessment of his own career:

> Bill Clinton and the American government will shout to us that "democracy is the right thing to do." But they themselves are not democratic at all . . . If the President is also the supreme commander of the armed forces, as it is in the U.S., then it is a military government. It's just that they are covering up with some tricks, I call it DEMOCRAZY. . . . We have our own commander here, Sani Abacha, who also happens to be a president. What's the difference? It's just that one is wearing uniform and the other is not, that is the only fucking difference because without the soldiers, the guns, and the violence they cannot keep it going. . . . Then you see the whole picture, you say "Wow! All the time I was fighting for the struggle of the people I was only fighting for the white man." That's what it all amounts to![25]

If Fela was muted in his criticisms of Abacha, the songs he continued to compose and sing nightly at the Shrine were indictments of a type no longer tolerated. At his outdoor beach and stadium concerts in Lagos, he led audiences in thundering choruses of "Ole!" (Thief!) as he sung the names of each postindependence head of state on "Chop and Clean Mouth Like Nothing Happened, Na New Name for Stealing." Those who felt Fela's message was only for the "area boys" and "street girls" of Ikeja were surprised by his sold-out show in March 1997 at the MUSON Center—a venue operated by the Musical Society of Nigeria and usually reserved for musicians playing Western art music and its Nigerian variants. The audience, comprised mainly of elites who could afford the unusually high ticket price, seemed wholly receptive to Fela's message despite his "foul expressions," as one reporter noted.[26] And if the much-reported plight of the Ogoni people was largely and mistakenly regarded as a mere "regional" or "ethnic" problem by the majority of Nigerians (including those in Lagos)—who felt oil revenues were crucial to stability and who, having heard only the official version of events, concluded that activists such as Saro-Wiwa were mere troublemakers with personal agendas[27]—Fela adopted a different position in his unrecorded "Government of Crooks":

All of us know our country
Plenty-plenty oil-e dey
Plenty things dey for Africa
Petroleum is one of them
All di places that get di oil-o
Now oil pollution for di place
All the farms done soak with oil-o
All the villages don catch disease
Money done spoil di oil area
But some people inside government
Dem don become billionaires
Billionaires on top of oil-o
and underhanded crookedness . . .

All of us know our country
There is plenty of oil
Plenty of resources in Africa
Petroleum is one of them
All the places where oil lies
Are spoiled with pollution
The farms are soaked by oil spills
The villages are rife with disease
Money has ruined the oil areas
But some people in government
Have become billionaires
From oil wealth
and underhanded crookedness . . .

In the unrecorded "Chop and Clean Mouth Like Nothing Happened, Na New Name for Stealing," Fela sang as a tortured modern griot—recounting not the glorious deeds of national heroes, but rather the villainy of their progressive routing of the country's resources, culminating in the country's forced acquiescence to the demands of the IMF and its controversial programs:

FELA: Look how they slap our face for Africa

CHORUS: Dem go gbam-gbam! (imitates slapping sound)

FELA: Balewa carry right side dey beat them
Gowon and Obasanjo carry left side dey beat them
Shagari beat us for our heads
Buhari and Idiagbon beat us for our yansch
Babangida beat us for our necks . . .

Balewa come chop, dem shoot am-o
Now bye-bye o di gbere-o, him time don come-o

Gowon chop and clean mouth-o,

like nothing happen-o, he find him way-o

FELA: Look how they slap our faces in Africa

CHORUS: They go gbam-gbam! (imitates slapping sound)

FELA: Balewa beat us on our right side
Gowon and Obasanjo beat us on our left side
Shagari beat us on our heads
Buhari and Idiagbon beat us on our behinds
Babangida beat us on our necks . . .

Balewa came and ate, they shot him
Bye-bye, rest in peace, his time came . . .

Gowon came and ate and wiped his mouth,
like nothing happened, and found his way . . .

Murtala come, him don try-o	Murtala came and tried
dem shoot am-o, now bye bye o di	They shot him, bye-bye, rest in
gbere-o	peace
Obasanjo chop and clean mouth-o,	Obasanjo ate and wiped his mouth
like nothing happen-o, he find	like nothing happened, he found
him way-o	his way
Buhari come, Idiagbon come-o Dem	Buhari and Idiagbon ate and wiped
chop and clean mouth, like nothing	their mouths, like nothing
happen-o,	happened,
dem find dem way . . .	they found their way . . .
Babangida come with new invention	Babangida came with a new
	invention—
na computerized style of stealing	a computerized style of stealing

Even more astonishing in its forthrightness, the unrecorded "Movement Against Second Slavery" continues the antimilitary theme while vilifying specific politicians at the highest levels of government. Since 1989, Fela had articulated his theme of "second slavery," in which he interpreted contemporary African leaders who ruled by force and mortgaged their countries' futures to the West as reincarnations of tribal chiefs who colluded with Europeans during the era of the slave trade. In Nigeria, the interplay of political, ethnic, and religious tensions, as manipulated by those in power, frequently pit the predominantly Muslim Hausa-Fulani north against the predominantly Christian/traditionalist Yoruba and Igbo south. The fact that seven of the country's eleven postindependence presidents have been northerners makes the issue more explosive, with southern Nigerians long resentful of this power imbalance. In reality, this oversimplified understanding of the situation fails to account for the class-based collusion of a small number of power monopolists across religious, regional, and ethnic lines.[28] But simmering tensions were nevertheless intensified under Babangida as a result of Nigeria's hotly debated drift toward the international Muslim community, the dominance of the northern-based "Kaduna Mafia," and the administration's laissez-faire (some would even say encouraging) attitude toward a resurgence of ethnic strife and the types of lynchings and pogroms that had preceded the Civil War.[29] In fact, in Wole Soyinka's analysis, the Abacha government's campaign of terror against the residents of Ogoniland (conducted mainly by ethnically hostile soldiers shipped in from the North) may have represented the first Nigerian experiments with "ethnic cleansing" and a more general military subjugation of the more educated and politically sophisticated regions of southern Nigeria.[30]

Fela's "M.A.S.S." is rife with many of the most explosive tensions of the Nigerian body politic. Overall, he seems intent on thoroughly condemning the country's Muslim leadership, regardless of ethnicity. Even in the context of his other work, "M.A.S.S." is in all likelihood totally unique throughout Africa for its name-calling vilification of the country's most powerful figures. The song is a virtual compendium of Fela's ideological and rhetorical styles—encompassing his Pan-Africanist, anti-Christian/Muslim, and antimilitary stances; his derisive rhetoric; his personal experiences; and his later tendency to analyze sociopolitical phenomena in terms of his mystical beliefs:

FELA: Wetin this government dey do, no be for talk—Na for cry-o

CHORUS: Ye, ye, ye (imitation of crying sound)

FELA: Our government go sell us away
Selling the continent to make us slaves again
Dem come go Europe, white man wey dey for west, bring am come-o

Bringing the religion Christianity to go chop us away
Dem go Arabia, white man wey dey for east,
Bring am come-o
Bringing the religion Islam to dey chop us away
Islam and Christianity bring wars to Africa
To this-e continent
In the center of the world
Dem go bring confusion
To the center of the world
Wetin dis government dey do no be for talk
Na for cry-o
Time don reach for us to call alhajis so . . .
I don travel many places
This the first time I don hear about

I never hear "alhaji" as title

Only in the country Nigeria
You hear somebody be alhaji
"Alhaji so-so-and-so . . ."

FELA: We cannot talk about what these governments do—we can only cry

CHORUS: Ye, ye, ye (imitation of crying sound)

FELA: Our governments are selling us away
Selling the continent to make us slaves again
They go to Europe, home of the western white man, and bring them back here
Bringing Christianity to eat us up

They go to Arabia, home of the eastern white man
Bring them back here
Bringing the religion Islam to eat us up
Islam and Christianity bring wars to Africa
To this continent
In the center of the world
They bring confusion
To the center of the world
We cannot talk about what these governments do,
we can only cry
It is time for us to call the "alhajis" . . .
I have traveled many places
This is the first time I hear of such a thing
I have never heard of (the religious title) "alhaji" as a social title
Only in Nigeria
Do you hear of alhajis
"Alhaji so-so-and-so . . ."

Anywhere you travel go
And you hear somebody "Alhaji"

He go be Nigerian man-o
Brothers, come and hear this one:
"Alhaji" na Arabic language
The meaning of "alhaji" na
"stranger" . . .

Anywhere you travel
When you hear of someone named
"Alhaji . . ."
He is a Nigerian man
Brother, come and hear this:
"Alhaji" is an Arabic word
The meaning of "alhaji" is
"stranger" . . .

FELA: Alhaji Umaru Dikko[31]

CHORUS: Stranger Umaru Dikko!

FELA: Alhaji Dasuki[32]

CHORUS: Stranger Dasuki!

FELA: Alhaji Mohammedu Gambo[33]

CHORUS: Stranger Mohammedu Gambo!

FELA: Alhaji Mohammedu Buhari[34]

CHORUS: Stranger Mohammedu Buhari!

FELA: Alhaji Moshood Abiola[35]

CHORUS: Stranger Moshood Abiola!

FELA: Alhaji Tunde Idiagbon[36]

CHORUS: Stranger Tunde Idiagbon!

FELA: Alhaji Sani Abacha[37]

CHORUS: Stranger Sani Abacha!

FELA: Alhaji Babangida[38]

CHORUS: Stranger Babangida!

FELA: Alhaji Raji Rasaki[39]

CHORUS: Stranger Raji Rasaki!

FELA: Alhaji Abubakar Alhaji[40]

CHORUS: Stranger Abubakar Stranger!

FELA: Alhaji!

CHORUS: Stranger, Mohammed, stranger!

FELA: Alhaji!

CHORUS: Stranger Ibrahim, stranger!

FELA: Alhaji!

FELA: This na revelation
Revelation of our ancestors
Offender must point at himself

Brothers and sisters hear me

FELA: This is a revelation
A revelation of our ancestors
The offender must point at himself
[i.e., from guilt]

Brothers and sisters hear me

| Mothers and fathers hear me | Mothers and fathers hear me |
| Na stranger dey rule our country | Strangers rule our country |

CHORUS: For inside police	*CHORUS:* Inside the police force
For inside air force	Inside the air force
For inside navy	Inside the navy
For inside government	Inside the government

| *FELA:* Dem dey control am! | *FELA:* They control them! |

"Fight to Finish"

It is unclear exactly how Fela managed to flourish so long under Abacha's rule. Certainly, the goodwill that existed toward the Ransome-Kuti family in some quarters had run dry—Abacha was detaining, arresting, imprisoning, exiling, and even murdering Nigerians of the highest distinction at an unprecedented rate. But he may have been reluctant to publicly persecute a dissident who—much more than Soyinka or Saro-Wiwa—held a special place in many Nigerians' hearts despite his eccentricities. Or he may simply have felt Fela was no longer a substantial threat since he was reportedly in poor health after decades of committed hard living and was no longer ruling the record charts.

But with Lagos the major stronghold of anti-Abacha and antimilitary sentiment, Fela's musical manifestos showing no signs of abating, and the Shrine still drawing capacity crowds, Abacha scrambled to shore up his local and international reputation by any means at his disposal in the wake of the Ogoni executions. He cunningly rode the crest of public euphoria when Nigeria's Golden Eagles won the World Cup in soccer in 1996, sent in the bulk of peacekeeping troops to resolve civil conflict (ironically, the result of another military coup) in Sierra Leone, and helped negotiate a peace settlement ending six years of civil war in Liberia. At home, he continued to persecute dissident voices while embarking on a transition program that supposedly had him relinquishing power to a democratically elected civilian government in late 1998.

But Abacha's strategy seemed most curious in February 1996 when—claiming Fela was unleashing a "reign of terror" on the nation's youth—his National Drug Law Enforcement Agency (NDLEA), led by Major-General Musa Bamaiyi, arrested the singer on drug charges, remanded him to "counseling" for his marijuana use, and planted drug-squad soldiers in the Shrine to ensure that no more young people were induced to smoke marijuana. Explained as part of Bamaiyi's "Operation Burn the Weeds,"[41] this thinly disguised attempt at surveillance and intimidation was a public relations disaster, as throughout 1996 the public was treated to the spectacle of the Nigerian government, some of whose highest-placed officials have been long implicated in the world heroin trade, persecuting a fifty-seven-year-old musician for smoking marijuana while the country was being officially declared the world's most corrupt nation.[42]

During the late 1980s, Nigeria had in fact grown into one of the world's leading transit points for heroin and other hard drugs. The rapid development of some

Lagos areas (such as the notorious Allen Avenue and its environs in Ikeja) was widely acknowledged as having been primarily financed by the drug trade. This had consequences for Fela's organization, which, while ostensibly committed solely to marijuana smoking, was directly affected by the booming hard drug trade surrounding it in Ikeja. Many members of his entourage, including some of his wives, developed serious addictions to heroin (known locally as *gbana*) and crack by the 1990s.[43]

Fela was in and out of jail during 1996, and in the spring of 1997, when he reiterated his right to smoke marijuana in a nationally televised press conference (calling marijuana his "best friend" and claiming it was "a gift of the creator to Africans"[44]), the authorities moved in again. Fela was rearrested on drug charges and ordered to vacate the Shrine. Although he was soon released on bail, Fela refused to comply with the vacate order and continued to perform. In June, the authorities prepared to arrest him for contempt of court (it would have been approximately his two hundredth court appearance since 1974) as he was preparing for a rumored European concert tour. But by July, he lay ailing in his Ikeja home in the care of his elder sister Dolupo and daughter Yeni, having reportedly fallen seriously ill during his most recent detention, and refusing medical treatment from both Western and traditional physicians "on religious grounds." In late July, following reports that he was critically ill, Fela was moved to a private Lagos clinic by his brother Olikoye, who had returned to Nigeria from a World Health Organization assignment in the United States to attend to his younger brother, who was rumored to be suffering from AIDS-related illness.

> *Dem don devalue crude oil and cocoa. What I made them realize is that when you devalue the naira, you make African toto* [ass] *cheap. Maybe in the U.S., you will require 500 dollars to fuck. But here, ten dollars is enough. You see what I mean?*
>
> FELA *quoted in* UZOMAH 1997:38

With a thirty-year musical career in which political activism and social criticism were inextricably linked with a sense of the outrageous and the burlesque, it might be considered by turns ironic, prophetic, or fitting that Fela's last song was "C.S.A.S. (Condom Scallywag and Scatter)," a song of what one writer called "pure irresponsibility"[45] in which he began by complaining of the low prices (compared to women of other nationalities) fetched by Nigerian prostitutes in Europe,[46] continued by describing his vehement refusal of a woman's insistence that he use a condom, advised other men to never accept the use of condoms (it was "un-African"), and ended by simulating various sexual positions with his singers and dancers.[47] Far from admitting that he was a possible carrier of HIV or other sexually transmitted disease as a result of his rampantly promiscuous lifestyle, Fela claimed that AIDS was a "whiteman's disease" and refused to the end to be tested to determine the cause of the weight loss, persistent cough, and recurrent skin lesions that had afflicted him since the early 1990s.[48]

Fela had, however, begun to perform less frequently and had even abandoned his saxophone playing since mid-decade, due to an increasing lack of stamina. Lindsay Barrett described Fela's appearance as "skeletal" during his spring 1997 press conference, and Rachel Newsome reported on his final arrest, which sparked a public outcry when the public saw Fela's condition on national television: "Led out of his house in handcuffs on a charge of dealing, his frail figure in the last stages of serial AIDS-related infections, was an image just too emotive not to be canonised on the calendars and posters which appeared shortly afterwards. The police had not only failed to diminish his influence—they had provided a foil which reflected back Fela's semi-apostolic glory."[49]

In fact, articles speculating on the nature of his condition had appeared in the Nigerian press as early as 1992, and since the late 1980s, several false alarms had been raised concerning his alleged demise. Fela was reported to have suddenly died in 1987, to have slumped and died on a flight from London to Paris in 1990, and to have become fatally ill on several occasions during the early 1990s. Each time, as reporters and worried fans thronged the Murtala Mohammed Airport, the house on Gbemisola Street, or the Afrika Shrine, the Chief Priest would emerge smiling to disprove the doomsayers, recharged and ready to continue battle.

But on August 2, 1997, the musician who had given his fans so much joy through his sensual and sarcastic songs of suffering passed from this world and into the world of his ancestors, having lived through fifty-eight of modern Africa's most turbulent years. The immediate cause of death was given by his brother as heart failure, with the underlying cause a variety of AIDS-related complications. In the end, as his inheritance of the "Kuti" name had foreshadowed fifty-eight years earlier, Fela left this world on his own terms; he perished not at the hands of human beings so much as through his own resolute engineering.[50] Ten years prior to his demise, as his elder brother Olikoye (then Babangida's Minister of Health) repeatedly warned Nigerians that the scourge of AIDS was spreading through their nation at a rapid but unknowable rate, Fela told the *New Musical Express* that he did not believe he could be the victim of sexually transmitted illness.[51]

By the end of his life, then, Fela had become in some ways utterly triumphant and in others utterly defeated, and the legacy he bequeathed to the continent he loved so much was a dual legacy. On the one hand, he was "Abami Eda," an eccentric musical visionary who could live in this world as a virtual spirit being as a result of his musical heroism. On the other hand, having exhibited most of the classic symptoms of AIDS, and despite having two brothers in the forefront of the medical profession, he continued to proclaim the rejuvenating benefits of sex, sleeping with uncountable women while composing songs celebrating his refusal to practice responsible sex.

After all the religious and cultural justifications have been voiced, Africa's low position in the world economic and social order implies a hierarchy of oppression that is visited most harshly upon its women, and Fela, for all his courage, was ultimately a crucial link in this chain. In the final analysis, this link was probably a function of his own stubbornness. His dramatic progression from monogamous family man to pop-star playboy to outspoken hedonist was a direct result of the gradual opposition he met from the Nigerian state, and to whatever extent these were merely aspects of his personality at the beginning of his career, they evolved into hardened political strategies in the face of violent opposition. Later in his career, he was no longer a mere womanizer, but a political dissident who reiterated his right to sleep with as many women as he could, in order to dramatize his constructed self-image as an "African," as well as his right to do as he pleased regardless of the consequences.

By the end of his life, Fela's stubbornness moved him to challenge the force of death itself, despite the consequences for himself and those who shared their bodies with him. Femi Kuti claimed that it was Fela's nonstop consumption of marijuana that allowed him to bear the physical agony of all the beatings, but it is equally obvious that the women saved him, their bodies used to blunt the inevitable pain and paranoia that were by-products of Fela's chosen life path. What is most striking about all of the discussion surrounding the circumstances of Fela's death is the absense of a sense of empathy for these women's position. Ever since the 1978 communal wedding, Fela's wives had been viewed as a compromise to his own elite prestige, rather than as unequal partners in a relationship with a man who—despite being persecuted—continued to benefit in many ways from his privileged origins and star status. So while it remained unclear at the time of his death how many of his bedmates were fated to follow their leader, "Condom, Scallywag, and Scatter" and the circumstances of its creation tragically demonstrate that Fela's fusion of class advantage and female devaluation resulted in a morbid final scenario in which women of the Lagos underclass likely shared the ultimate price for his ideological linkage of hypersexualism, populism, and cultural revitalization.

Thus, "C.S.A.S."—either a final cry of bravado or a stubborn refusal to the end to alter a lifestyle that had in itself become an act of cultural resistance—became Fela's swan song. In retrospect it is clear that he was, in the larger picture, at least partly a victim of the enduring racist legacy that holds that people of African descent are constituted by their sexuality, as well as the monumental denial among some Africans that holds that AIDS is a "whiteman's disease" despite its decimation of black populations around Africa and elsewhere in the world. It was this tendency toward denial that motivated Dr. Ransome-Kuti, after much discussion within the family, to publicly disclose the cause of Fela's death, which he believed would honor his late brother's sense of honesty while potentially sparing the lives of untold millions of Nigerians. Fela was certainly not the first prominent Nigerian to die of AIDS, but in a country where causes of death are kept private as a matter of course, he was the first celebrity whose AIDS-related death was publicly acknowledged, and there was a sense that AIDS awareness in Nigeria had finally left the dark ages.[52]

As the news of Fela's death spread beyond Nigeria, tribute concerts, parties, television specials, and radio programs were organized in major cities around the globe to commemorate the passing of one of the century's great musicians. In Nigeria, sales of his music soared, condolences poured in to the Ransome-Kuti family from around the world, and Fela's music blared around the clock on radio and television stations that had banned it during his life.

Sun Re O

LAGOS, August 11—Entranced in a heady mixture of song, dance, and marijuana, thousands of fans paid an affectionate farewell Monday to Fela Anikulapo-Kuti, Nigeria's king of Afrobeat who died of AIDS on August 2. Dignitaries, politicians, students and diplomats filed past his glass and cane coffin as police controlled the well-behaved crowds. The crowds swayed and danced as bands played the songs which made his name across West Africa and in the wider world. The atmosphere became slightly more charged when students arrived in a convoy of buses chanting slogans in favor of the radical dead musician. Later, after Fela's corpse was taken away at the end of the ceremony, scores of marijuana users took over the square, smoking and hawking openly. Law enforcement agents did not react. Many were dancing to the lyrics of Fela's music bellowing out from loudspeakers.

Vanguard, *August 13, 1997*

"Brothers and sisters, we are gathered here today to pay our last respects to that great legend of Africa, Fela Anikulapo-Kuti." So announced Egypt 80 band-leader Lekan Animashaun on Monday, August 12, commencing a day of mourning on which Nigerians canceled prior commitments and payed their last respects to their departed countryman, whose body lay in state at the Tafewa Balewa Square in Lagos, the site of many of his most dramatic triumphs and tragedies. Here he had launched his political party in 1978; here he had been sentenced to a five-year prison term by military tribunal in 1984; and here he had given some of his most memorable concerts. Now, the music of several live bands, including Egypt 80 and Femi Kuti's Positive Force, filled the terraces, and the smell of Indian hemp filled the air, as hundreds of thousands of mourners patiently filed past under the harsh midday sun for a final view of the Chief Priest of the Shrine, who lay dressed in a colorful stage outfit inside a specially constructed glass-and-cane coffin, one last wrap of Indian hemp nestled between his fingers.

The Abacha government had nothing to do with the events commemorating Fela and even less to say publicly—the exceptions being the scores of military men who now claimed to the press that they never had a problem with Fela and that, in fact, the song "Zombie" was more popular inside their soliders' mess halls than anywhere else in the country.[53] Even so, the ceremony was reportedly the largest ever held in the Square, dwarfing even the state funerals given to national luminaries such as Obafemi Awolowo and Nnamidi Azikiwe. Foreign dignitaries on hand included representatives of the American, Chinese, French, and Italian governments, while local luminaries included evangelist and juju musician Ebenezer Obey, singer and PMAN president Christy Essien-Igbokwe, waka queen Salawa Abeni, Fela's old highlife competitor Geraldo Pino, a representative of the Oba Adedapo Tejuoso (the traditional ruler of Abeokuta), and Fela's Ghanaian business partner Faisal Helwani.

Following the lying-in-state ceremony, Fela took his last journey to the Afrika Shrine, in a caravan of cars that took seven hours to complete the half-hour journey from Lagos Island to Ikeja. All along the way, more than a million Lagosians thronged the funeral route to salute a musician who, in living "as an actor acting out a dream of himself,"[54] had passed much of his life among them as a virtual diety. Emotions were especially high as the caravan passed through the site of the old Kalakuta Republic (now the site of Funmilayo Anikulapo-Kuti Grammar School), where fans shed tears and held banners bidding their hero farewell.

The following afternoon, in a ceremony for family and friends that was thronged by thousands in the surrounding streets, Fela's body was lowered into a simple grave on the grounds of Kalakuta. At the time of his death, he had fathered seven known children—Femi, Yeni, Sola, Kunle, Motunrayo, Seun, and Omos-alewa—all of whom surrounded the grave as their father was laid to rest. Dr. Beko Ransome-Kuti was denied a day release from prison by the authorites, who feared his public appearance would result in a riot. And although her children were on hand, Fela's first wife Remi did not attend, declaring that she was grieving privately. In fact, while some of Fela's wives and consorts were in the house during his funeral, none were among the acknowledged mourners at his burial.[55]

Incredibly, more tragedy would afflict the Ransome-Kuti family in the weeks immediately following Fela's death; both his daughter Sola and his niece Frances Kuboye died in Lagos (of cancer and a heart ailment, respectively) within a month of his passing.

Despite the strongly divided opinions of Fela, the public reaction to his death was virtually unanimous. While his lifestyle was universally condemned, Fela had never wavered from his self-appointed role of calling attention to the sufferings of the common people. His musical talent could have had him ensconced in a life of fashionable exile in a foreign musical capital such as Paris, London, or Los Angeles; instead, he placed his entire career at the service of his people, and for this he died a Nigerian hero. The outpouring of emotion as Nigerians bade him farewell reflected the reality that in a country of 100 million people, he more than anyone else had dared sing and speak the truth to the country's rulers so directly. As one mourner told the *Vanguard* newspaper: "No president in the world could witness this kind of affection at his burial and it just goes to show what Fela really means for the people of this country."[56] At the heart of his chaotic, contentious, and contradictory lifestyle was an earnest and authentic search for an African cultural revitalization, a refusal to submit to mindless authority mindlessly, and one of the most irrepressible and profusely creative African spirits of the late twentieth century.

Conclusion:
"Look and Laugh"

"Suppose James Brown read Fanon?" Such was the rhetorical question tossed about during the late 1960s by the African-American poet/activist Larry Neal and his colleagues in the Black Arts Movement, as they pondered a means by which popular culture could function as a simultaneous vehicle for aesthetic pleasure, cultural awareness, and revolutionary consciousness.[1] Posed in reverse, the equation might ask, "Suppose Malcolm X heard E. T. Mensah?" or "Suppose Huey Newton heard Haruna Ishola?"[2] The potential cross-cultural combinations of music and pro-black ideology are endless. However stated, the equation is a good jumping-off point for assessing the breadth of Fela Anikulapo-Kuti's musical, political, and cultural mission. Should Fela's story be read as comedy? As tragedy? As heroic odyssey? Was he—as some claim—one who destroyed the greatness he had achieved, or one who was destroyed by adversaries threatened by his greatness? Was he another elite rebel who became obsessed with fighting the power, or another victim of the combined demons of drugs, tragedy, and excess multiplied exponentially by the extraordinary fame he achieved in his lifetime?

Two things are clear. Over three decades, Fela synthesized a unique musical language while also clearing—if only temporarily—a space for popular political dissent and a type of countercultural expression extremely rare in West African societies. And in the midst of recent political turmoil in Africa (Nigeria, Rwanda, Liberia, Sierra Leone, Somalia, Zaire), as well as a new cycle of pro-African cultural nationalism throughout the diaspora, Fela's political music holds a renewed relevance for Nigeria, the African continent, and the African diaspora.

Afrobeat as Postcolonial Art

Created within the turbulent Nigerian post-colony, Fela's work conforms closely to Fredric Jameson's interpretation of the "third-world artwork" as metaphor for the emergent nation-state.[3] Some might criticize Jameson's essay as ethnocentric in its reluctance to acknowledge the aesthetic dimensions of non-Western literature, but it is applicable to Fela's work for the simple reason that the latter consciously and explicitly used his art to address the condition of postcolonial Africa. The successive periods of Fela's career also conform remarkably closely to the "three stages of the native intellectual" advanced by Frantz Fanon in *Wretched of the Earth,* demonstrating Fela's roots in the struggles and symbols of the same nationalist period during which Fanon was writing.[4] In Fanon's schema, the work of the native intellectual is marked in its first phase by a strong identification with the worldview of the colonial master, usually following a period of education in the colonial center. The work of the second phase is a reaction to the first, during which the intellectual uncritically celebrates his native society rejecting anything associated with the colonizing culture. Finally, in the third phase, the native intellectual outgrows the romanticization of the previous phase, sharpening his critical apparatus and directing it toward his or her native society.

Making allowances for minor discrepancies and periods of overlap, Fela's work broadly conforms to Fanon's outline. The first phase is illustrated by his early career, in which he attempted to make a name for himself in Nigeria working self-consciously in the high-modernist modes of African-American jazz music, which he encountered during his student years in Britain. The second phase followed his politicization in America and is marked by his full embrace of popular music as a valid medium, and by songs such as "Buy Africa" or "Black Man's Cry," which celebrate the African nation and the black aesthetic. The third phase began after his 1974 imprisonment and especially took hold following the 1977 Kalakuta attack, and is reflected in works such as "Alagbon Close," "International Thief Thief," and "Overtake Don Overtake Overtake," which take a harshly critical look at the problems confronting contemporary Africa.

Substituting an alternate distinction offered by Fanon in *Wretched,* the period from 1958 (when he entered music school in England) through 1974 (the year of the first police raid on his home) might be thought of as Fela's *nationalist* period, during which he tended to see his work as part of the overall projects of nation-building and repairing the psychological damage of the colonial encounter. Fela's work after 1974 is best understood as *liberationist* in tone: it is ultimately concerned not with issues of national independence and solidarity, but with using a utopian vision of Africa (simultaneously premodern and postrevolutionary) to critique the contemporary problems of the postcolonial nation-state and act as a voice for its dispossessed. As time passed, in fact, Fela was increasingly loathe to identify himself as a "Nigerian," preferring to be called an *African.* In this he was clearly contesting the ideal of the nation-state—reflecting at once his embrace of Nkrumah's Pan-African ideal, the subversive dimensions of his "Afrotopian" vision, as well as disenchantment reflecting what Gayatri Chakravorty Spivak has called the failure of the nation-state model to speak to or change the condition of the underclass, or what Spivak calls the *subaltern.*[5]

In their self-conscious use of art as a tool for social criticism, many politically active African artists tend to have had some significant experience abroad (usually educational), often working in media considered to have had their genesis during the colonial era, such as film or literature.[6] In this respect, Fela's artistic evolution was closer in many ways to postcolonial writers and filmmakers such as Ngugi Wa Thiong'o, Wole Soyinka, and Ousmane Sembene than to other popular musicians. In fact, Fela shared much with Sembene in his loose application of Marxist ideas of class struggle, his liberationist approach, and his "neo-griot" goal of using his art to account for the true history of the masses. I am thinking especially of Sembene's critique of the Senegalese elite in his 1974 film *Xala*. It is no coincidence that this film was produced during the same period in which Fela offered "Colonial Mentality," "Mr. Grammartology-lisation-alism Is the Boss," and "Johnny Just Drop," covering the same topics. Both men critiqued African postcoloniality during a period in which the condition had become relatively well-defined, while their experiences abroad enabled them to view their cultures against the backdrop of planetary culture.

"Africa Man, Original": Fela, African Tradition, and Black Essentialism

Fela's most potent work reflects a period in which independent Africa's post-colonial dream of itself was ironically fueled by its accompanying chaos. While there were obvious problems, these could at least be proudly rationalized as *African,* as opposed to Western, problems. By the end of his life, however, this romanticization had worn thin for both Fela and his continent. He left this world on the ravaged wings of a disease he claimed could not affect black people, even as some of his worst prophecies were fulfilling themselves around the African continent. Thus, to clarify the nature of Fela's contribution, we need to deconstruct the essentialism that often led him to emphasize a simplistic notion of *tradition* at the expense of a true understanding of the dynamics shaping his art.

The first such deconstruction concerns class, which needs to be considered in order to understand Fela's mission as an abuse singer in Nigerian society. Spivak suggests that one must deconstruct one's own class privilege in order to function effectively as a voice of the disempowered,[7] and however haphazardly, Fela accomplished this. As affluent as he was during the 1970s, he spent the remainder of his career under financial stress, due mainly to his refusal to compromise his music in conformity with prevailing notions of artists and their role in society (although some have also been highly critical of his handling of his financial affairs). Fela's mixture of abuse, profanity, and social deviance was already a hard package for many Nigerians to swallow even during the height of his popularity in the mid-1970s. After 1977, when he largely abandoned his satiric social critiques for explicit political diatribes, he effectively consigned his music to an enforced subcultural location.

Despite this, Fela's emphasis on tradition continued to obscure the hegemonic implications of his privileged origins. These origins were most tellingly reflected in the fact that he could express such overt disrespect toward people who were his class inferiors, despite how much wealth and power they eventually achieved in society as soldiers, politicians, praise singers, and the like. The specifically hegemonic aspects of this, on the other hand, were most obvious in his devaluation of women and his treatment of his band members. His rise to notoriety was in some ways crucially predicated upon the highly visible role women of the Lagos underclass played in his organization as his wives, lovers, dancers, and singers, and his maintenance of that fame was built upon a similar relationship with his musicians. That Fela's relationship with his musicians conformed to a cultural pattern of exploitative bandleading was summarized in one local musician's comments to Steve Waidor-Pregbagha of *Source* shortly after his death:

> You can assess somebody by the people around him. For instance, Sunny Ade's congaist has his own personal house and rides a Mercedes-Benz car. Onyeka has produced some of the biggest stars in the country like Mike Okri, Chris Hanen, Stella Yamah, Ceceil Omohinmi. But I can not pinpoint what Fela did for his band boys before he died. Music made Fela what he is, but he gave nothing back to it. Fela has no single investment, not even a recording studio or a demo studio. It is sad. Now that he is gone, his band boys are confused.[8]

Former PMAN (Nigerian Musicians Union) president Eppi Fanio echoed these sentiments in the context of Fela's impact on aspiring Nigerian musicians:

> Apparently, his ego got the better of him. . . . Young musicians learning the ropes of the trade looked up to Fela to lead them to organize a union of musicians, to encourage them and educate them. They were disappointed. Fela was all for himself and all those aspiring musicians were left to the vicissitudes and uncertainty of the emerging music industry.[9]

Not all of Fela's musicians agreed with this assessment. His flugelhornist Steven Ukem told Ohi Alegbe, "Even though there's no money, the music is the thing that keeps me going. . . . Nobody can pay musicians in Nigeria. When Nigeria gets better, Fela would be richer." Tenor saxophonist Y. S. Akinibosun, who repairs wind instruments and drives a cab in his spare time, concurred and told Alegbe, "Only thieves pretend to depend on salaries today in Nigeria."[10] When class background, education, and economic advantage are factored in, it becomes apparent that Fela, despite his rhetoric, ultimately held some of the same disregard that African elites as a class hold for the underprivileged masses upon whose work and suffering their advancement is largely based.

Another instance in which the romanticization of tradition clouded important distinctions was Fela's embrace of traditional African religion. Fela dismissed Christianity for its complicity in colonial domination, but he was equally suspicious of traditional religion in its organized forms, which he viewed as irreversibly corrupted by colonialism. Nonetheless, Fela felt the need over time to align himself with traditional religion—mainly for reasons of self-authentication and psychological rejuvenation—and he resolved this contradiction through a highly personalized, idiosyncratic participation in traditional religion centering on the deployment of protective magical power. While this is understandable in light of his personal tragedies and the ever-present threat of government violence, it also led him to resolve social problems in unusual ways, such as his mystical interpretations of political events. During the last decade of his life, for example, Fela often discussed Africa's problems as the result of a ongoing collaboration between opportunistic, capitalist Europeans and corrupt African rulers, but metaphorized this in terms of an historical, supernatural conspiracy between African and European "gods" or "wizards."[11] The ultimate triumph of good over evil thus rested in the dispensation of the "African ancestors." In a symbolic sense, such an interpretation is plausible, in light of the stupendous disparities of wealth within Africa, and between Africa and the Western world. With their jetliners that soar through the sky to foreign capitals, luxury automobiles that navigate urban squalor in air-conditioned splendor, and foreign bank accounts that equal the annual gross national products of some small nations, the Nigerian elites' economic power and privilege certainly seem divinely omnipotent in their top-down preconditioning of millions of lesser lives. Fela's use of such rhetoric can be seen against a historical backdrop of African nationalist movements such as those waged in Kenya and Zimbabwe where, as Karin Barber notes, revolutionary songs "not only cite mythical ancestors as the guarantors of the justice of their cause, exhorting the people to cleave to their own traditional ways and cast off the imposed cultural values of the colonialist; they also state that the present struggle was foreseen by 19th century prophets, now reincarnated in present-day spiritual leaders: tradition has thus already spoken in the combatants' favor and guaranteed their victory."[12]

In the end it seems that despite his suspicion of religion, Fela was content to resolve the issue through the substitution of idealized African deities for their colonial Western counterparts. As Iyorchia Ayu notes, Fela "poses the religious question as a struggle between foreign gods and the African gods, instead of pushing for a materialist analysis of *all* religions, including the so-called traditional African religions."[13]

Fela's emphasis on tradition obscured the degree to which his life and work were firmly rooted in modern, urban life. While he advocated the development of an "African science" rooted in traditional practices, he did not reconcile this with his own acceptance of selected modern Western technology (such as electric musical instruments), or the broader implications of such choices in the transformation of African society.[14] In spite of his advocacy of tradition, Fela maintained a distinctly modern, thoroughly urban orientation in his own music and lifestyle, which had no functional connection to traditional performance contexts or rural life. Coming from a colonial African family that was fairly distant from—and occasionally hostile to—traditional culture, his later constructed relationship to that culture was highly self-conscious and, in conformity with elite patterns of appropriating traditional symbols in the construction of a national culture, also highly ambivalent.

The emphasis on tradition also led Fela to articulate a simplistic vision of African history. For example, the lyrics of "Gentleman" and "Why Black Man Dey Suffer" present an idyllic image of a pure, "original" Africa that remained harmonious and unsullied until the arrival of the European. Such a conception fails to account for the preexisting social and political divisions the colonialists were so able to exploit, as well as the continuous processes of change and outside influence that inform all cultures. Ironically, Fela offered in songs like "Gentleman" a take on African identity in which only certain types of dress, eating habits, and political engagement could be defined as authentically "African." In such moments, his insistence on an essentialized point of cultural reference lacked the subtlety and complexity of other syncretic practices found throughout contemporary African and diasporic culture, marked by the synthesis of new and potent African forms from a diverse mixture of local and foreign elements. Such a lack of subtlety is ultimately disempowering in its truncation of possibilities available to potentially imaginative and resourceful people. It is also contradicted by the richness of Fela's own music. As much as colonialism wrought havoc on African cultures, it also provided an opportunity for certain types of new cultural forms, and Fela's work typifies this encounter. In fact, it is rarely mentioned that his personal family history itself strongly reflected the various historical displacements of colonialism, the slave trade, and the inter-Yoruba wars of the nineteenth century. These factors, far from rooting him in a traditional worldview, were crucial in his formation of a unique and often dissenting social vision.

Fela's idea of "traditional" Africa functioned more as an idealized, "other-worldly narrative" similar to the cosmic narratives of musicians like George Clinton and Sun Ra,[15] as well as the terrestrial black utopian narratives of Afrocentrists and Rastafarians—reflecting contemporary sociopolitical alienation and the yearning for a better world, more than it concretely depicts the circumstances of precolonial Africa.

"Black Man's Cry"

Fela's emphasis on tradition also obscured the degree to which his work was rooted in contemporary processes of cross-cultural interchange. Clearly, his Western education and travel were crucial to his development, regardless of how much elements drawn from these experiences would later be refashioned as tools to combat Western economic and cultural hegemony.[16] As a dissident singer, for example, he relied on the multinational music industry throughout his career; considering his political stance, social image, and musical message, it would have been virtually impossible for him to rely on traditional patronage networks for support. His rise as a Pan-African musical superstar, as well as the emergence of an accompanying subculture, owed much to the expansion of the Western music industry throughout Africa and its stimulation of urban African youth cultures. His credibility as a social spokesperson and political dissident was also helped by his international popularity; international audiences were sometimes less critical of the elements of

Fela's personality with which native listeners took issue. In fact, these elements—Fela as polygamist, rebel, dissident, herbsman—formed the cornerstones of his marketed image in the West, much as they had for reggae musicians somewhat earlier.

African-American culture figures crucially among the foreign cultural elements informing Fela's work and radical vision, and his work provides a continuously interesting look at the way he digested and transmuted these influences. Fela's vision crystallized in an era in which black people from Africa, the Caribbean, and the Americas were forming unprecedented political, cultural, artistic, and personal alliances. The 1950s and 1960s were an era of nationalism in Africa and the Caribbean and civil rights in America. These movements paved the way for what might be called the internationalization of black power during the late 1960s and 1970s—a brief moment in which counterhegemonic protest in these places shared a rhetoric derived from the civil rights and postcolonial struggles.[17] Working within these historical circumstances, Fela promoted an "African" tradition that was actually a composite of various African, diasporic, and non-African elements. In so doing, he demonstrated what Paul Gilroy has identified as "the circulation and mutation of music across the black Atlantic [which] explodes the dualistic structure which puts Africa, authenticity, purity, and origin in crude opposition to the Americas, hybridity, creolisation, and rootlessness."[18] To state it another way, the African elements in afrobeat have been fashioned within an ongoing cross-cultural interaction between Africa and the diaspora, which has influenced the articulation of their "Africanity." Just as the rediscovery of African culture provided African-Americans with an ideological tool with which to dislodge centuries of deeply ingrained white supremacy, Fela's "rebirth" in African-American culture of the late 1960s provided him with the tools with which to interpret the absurdities of slavery, colonialism, postcolonialism, and neocolonialism. Michele Wallace sees the history of African-American counterculturalism as a catalyst for other such impulses around the world,

> not so much by its considerable political activity, but precisely by its counter-culture. While this "minor" culture may be difficult to link directly to political protest, it was always clearly formed in the spirit of subverting a majority culture that tried to choke it at the root. Precisely in its sex, drugs, dance, music, and style, it kept the record of its discontents accurately and well. Perhaps this counter-culture is the site where mainstream culture is most forcefully challenged, even as "revolutions" come and go.[19]

In the broadest musical sense, the diasporic art form of jazz, encompassing composition, improvisation, and folk-derived rhythms, enabled Fela to formulate a conception within which the African "high," "folk," and "popular" could merge. Instrumentally, techniques like modalism, ensemble stratification, and hocketing all clearly had their roots in traditional West African music, but their presence in Fela's music owes equally to their articulations in the music of African-American musicians such as John Coltrane and James Brown. Fela was clearly drawing on a range of references, symbols, and social circumstances similar to those of influential African-American performers who had conceptual breakthroughs in the same historical moment. With its acerbic organ, blaring big-band horn section, atonal fanfares, neo-Egyptian symbology, and occult overtones, for example, Fela's Egypt 80 music offered a sound and mood at times very similar to the more African-influenced work of Sun Ra's Arkestra of the 1960s and 1970s,[20] while his epic Afro-funk grooves, political commentary, druggy aura, foregrounded eroticism, semi-anarchist philosophy, and communal enterprise closely paralleled George Clinton's P-Funk collective. Even on the level of album cover art, one cannot escape the close connection between Ghariokwu Lemi's lurid caricatures of contemporary Nigeria and Funkadelic album cover artist Pedro Bell's warped cartoon ghettoscapes.

In terms of the rhetoric infusing his music, Fela's voice reflected the influence of what Gilroy has described as a "metaphysics of blackness," largely developed in the African diaspora (especially Afro-America) and characterized by a foregrounding of contentious gender dynamics, radical excavations and reformulations of black history, a confrontational approach to political activism, and an emphasis on "blackness" as a signifier for (Pan-)African identity.[21] His style of derisive criticism, while rooted in West African traditions of derisive humor, was strongly influenced by the political rhetoric and vernacular traditions of Afro-America. Fela applied this African-American-derived model of criticism (based on an oppositional racial dynamic) to his own communal West African society, in which individual success is seen as ultimately intertwined with the community's success, and gestures of respect—not abuse—predominate in social interactions.

A common criticism in Nigeria was that Fela "sings for himself," and this demonstrates his singularity of vision in a music culture in which a song's message is usually secondary to its function as an agent of social cohesion. In most Yoruba styles, music is often as cognitive as it is aesthetic, with this cognition occurring on at least three levels—lyrics, language-based drumming, and music. This particular mode of complexity is absent from Fela's music, which grafts explicit political commentary onto a musical foundation of highlife, jazz, and funk. The resulting directness alienated some African listeners, especially after the 1977 Kalakuta attack, when the focus of Fela's music shifted dramatically from humorous social lampoon to direct (and occasionally embittered) political critique.

Fela's adoption of pidgin English as a medium of urban African populist dissent gained a potent, cosmopolitan resonance through his fusion of African-American slang. In its mixture of urban African sensibility, political fervor, and jazz parlance, his 1982 biographical collaboration with Carlos Moore, *Fela, Fela: This Bitch of a Life* (1982), fuses expressive sensibilities such as those found in the autobiographies of Malcolm X and Miles Davis with his own voice. The high-profile use of marijuana, crucial to Fela's rebellious image, has strong roots in his experience of American youth culture of the 1960s, in which it was an important part of musical experience and countercultural protest, and as in the psychedelic soundscapes of American music of the 1970s, it is an important component of the aura surrounding much of his work. With its emphasis on ideology, revisionist black history, and art as a vehicle for mass mobilization, Fela's Kalakuta subculture (especially during the 1970s) also paralleled politicized African-American artists' collectives such as the Black Arts Movement. Thus, it is no coincidence that the African-American artists who visited Nigeria in 1977 gravitated to Fela's Shrine instead of the traditional fare offered by the Nigerian government during FESTAC.

It is also interesting to note that Fela's transformative spiritual vision of 1981 shared a number of political, cultural, and religious themes with the ideas of revisionist Egyptologists, Afrocentrists, and African scholars such as Dr. Ben-Jochanan, George James, Martin Bernal, Molefi Kete Asante, and Cheikh Anta Diop—all of whom variously assert a critical black African component of classical Egyptian civilization, an Egyptian genesis for West African cultural traditions, and/or a significant African contribution to the development of Western civilization. To the extent that Fela conformed to such a cultural-historical vision, he was adopting an inherently contradictory position. On the one hand, it serves to counteract the racist, colonial notion that Africans are jungle-bound savages fit only for the crudest forms of physical existence and incapable of fashioning a "higher" civilization. On the other hand, its goal of legitimizing African culture through comparison to historically "great" civilizations reflects the hegemony of a Western notion of "civilization" encompassing imperialist military empires, institutionalized religion, and colossal monuments—most of which stand in stark contrast to the agrarian, relatively egalitarian organization of many traditional West African societies.

Ex-president Obasanjo once famously accused Fela of destroying the lives of Nigerian youth; Fela predictably responded that Obasanjo had destroyed the lives of an entire nation. In this light, one final parallel with African-American culture may ultimately prove most insightful. Through the lens of popular culture, one finds many similarities between Fela's odyssey and the "blaxploitation" films created primarily for African-American audiences in the 1970s. Films like *Shaft* and *Superfly* depict black heroes working within a corrupt and racist system, and against a crime-ridden urban backdrop. Infused with an abundance of sex, drugs, mysticism, violence, vague politics, and power struggles, these films also feature some of the most innovative popular music of the era, a strong factor in their current revival. These films were created in the wake of the real-life black superheroes of the time—Kwame Nkrumah, Patrice Lumumba, Muhammad Ali, Malcolm X, Angela Davis, the Black Panthers—as well as musical superheroes like James Brown, Miles Davis, and John Coltrane, and could not have existed without the emergence of these avatars of black power in the real world.

Fela's real-life odyssey as the "Black President," played out against an urban African nightmare as squalid as anything John Shaft or Superfly ever had to maneuver through, makes for the ultimate blaxploitation flick. The similarities are not surprising, since Fela experienced his artistic epiphany in Afro-America at the precise historical moment that these images were forming. Clearly, he was drawing on the same references that formed the substance (and soundtracks) of authentic revolution on the one hand, and its fictionalized, cinematic representation on the other: images of a hip and politicized black superman/woman fighting "the system"—whether comprador/military black or colonialist/slavemaster white—to a neo-African beat.

Were the blaxploitation films simply a pop culture projection of newly consolidated black power? As Cedric Robinson notes, one long-term effect of these films' popularity was to blunt black political advancement by appropriating the aura of contemporary liberation struggles and trivializing it into a cinematic celebration of drugs, gangsterism, and other urban sociopathologies.[22] Similarly, Fela's emergence as an African blaxploitation hero parallels the problematics of the blaxploitation ideal. In the same way that liberation struggles became conflated with criminality in blaxploitation cinema, Fela's message of African empowerment became increasingly intertwined with dominant racist stereotypes of the African as vulgar, intoxicated, primitive, hypersexualized, and indigenous mystic.

Just as blaxploitation's conflation of black power struggles with criminality may have led to a misunderstanding of the impulse for African-American liberation among some Africans, the perception of Fela as a social deviant held political consequences. The anti-Fela position most frequently voiced holds that he "was a complete nuisance who had no respect for the rule of law or anybody else, including himself. He contributed a lot to the current state of absolute moral decadence among the youths in Nigeria's urban centers."[23] A more traditional Yoruba aphorism holds that "one is not fit to rule a nation if one's own home is not in order," and Fela's eccentric behavior compromised his credibility as a social spokesman and political contender. Waterman noted that "most urban Yoruba dismiss Fela and his ideological mix . . . because of his deviant public image. He 'shaks' (smokes marijuana), takes advantage of young migrant women from the village, defies constituted authority, and engages in explicit abusive language (*yabis*). A typical comment is 'there is truth in what he sings, but he is not responsible.' "[24]

The relationships among creative subcultures, politicized creativity, and political action become especially complex when the issue of mind-altering substances is factored in. Fela was never known to engage in anything other than marijuana smoking. While there is certainly a tremendous difference between this and the types of chemically induced nightmares associated with drug-saturated urban areas of the United States, it is still open to question how well Fela's explicit advocacy of marijuana smoking served his stated mission. Marijuana can create a space for creativity and community, as well as a means of informal subsistence for those marginalized in the greater economic order, but it had three drawbacks in Fela's case: its use was not consistent with the clear thinking required for the political program he advocated; it compromised his credibility as a social and political critic; and, most crucially, it was an illegal activity that gave the authorities an easy pretext for harassing him. More generally, it is open to question whether some aspects of Fela's lifestyle served to refute or confirm prevailing negative stereotypes of Africans and people of African descent in general, whether his wholesale rejection of Western education enabled or disabled Africa's ability to compete within an increasingly linked cultural landscape, and how the Nigerian youth most influenced by his message were able to use his influence to negotiate the challenges of modern society.[25] For example, although Fela spoke out against hard drugs such as heroin and crack and banned them from the Shrine, some members of his entourage nevertheless developed serious addictions to these substances.[26] One longtime fan said:

> Fela was one of those people who felt like the thieves, the prostitutes, and all those types of people were the "masses," and I don't think that's necessarily true. I think he could have let them know that no person had to be a thief, prostitute, or drug addict in our society. But in a way it was almost like he was encouraging their lifestyle. That's why I think he basically just wanted to rebel, because being from his type of background, he could have gone in a different direction. If he didn't want people studying in the white man's colonial way, he could have funded some alternative schools or something, set up some scholarships, especially back when he had a lot of money. Or at least he could have set up something for all those girls so they could have some education and a future for themselves. But after the government burnt his house and all that in 1977, it was like there was no turning back for him. It was just anti-establishment from that point on.[27]

Ultimately, Fela's essentialist statements about African culture should not be taken strictly at face value, but rather interpreted in the context of a strategic essentialism serving specific symbolic and psychological functions. His effort to find a fundamentally *black* solution to a range of complex problems was similar to other strategies of cultural affirmation—including Aime Cesaire and Leopold Senghor's "Negritude," Kwame Nkrumah's "African Personality," revisionist Egyptology, and Afrocentricity—that have sought to reverse the psychological damage wrought by colonialism and slavery through the inversion of racist Western assumptions and an affirmation of things black.

Despite its cross-cultural influences, Fela's work is powerfully consistent with several traditionally African models of music-making. His compositional rigor enabled him to consciously refashion a number of Pan-African musical and cultural elements to evoke a very traditional musical mood. Functionally, the afrobeat style is fundamentally African in its oppositional political stance, which privileges the interests of dispossessed African masses of over those of neocolonial Western governments, multinational corporations, and the local comprador elite. It is fundamentally African in its deft manipulation of the derisive rhetorical modes that inform most of Fela's song lyrics, as well as in the communal social setting in which it operated. It is also characteristically African in its musical construction, as Fela drew extensively upon traditional African musical styles as a source of compositional and conceptual inspiration—although it has not always been clear exactly *which* African musical traditions he drew upon.[28] But the potency of all these elements in combination may explain why Fela was consistently awarded top honors in the Nigerian Musicians' Union's (PMAN) incredibly vague "Afro Music" category, even though *all* the categories are ostensibly concerned with music produced in Africa by African musicians; the honor acknowledged the musical sound, political commitment, and cultural resonance of Fela's afrobeat.

There is also a strain of Fela's work that might be called fundamentally Yoruba in nature. Despite his insistence on Pan-African culture, most of the cultural symbols that enliven his work are Yoruba in origin. There were exceptions to this in his work of the 1970s, into which he integrated Ashanti aphorisms ("Fefe Na Efe") or Pan-Anglophone West African slang ("Shenshema"). But for the most part, when Fela chanted the names of mythical African figures such as Oranyan, Orompoto, or Orunmila in his songs, he was drawing not on the symbols of the entire continent, but those of his native Yoruba culture.[29] Toward the end of his life, he was even given to claiming that the Yoruba language was spoken in the spirit world; that it was encoded into other languages; and that he was capable of decoding the hidden Yoruba meanings behind the utterances of world political and religious leaders. And it is somehow difficult to imagine Fela fashioning his own parallel universe in other Nigerian cities such as Kano, Benin, or Onitsha as thoroughly as he did in Yoruba-dominated Lagos.

On a more philosophical level, Fela plumbed the depths of Nigerian society to fashion a contemporary tragic vision within a musical mood of pathos, in the process conforming deeply to mythopoetic tendencies in traditional Yoruba oral literature. Wole Soyinka defined tragedy in traditional Yoruba myth as "the anguish of [cosmic] severance, the fragmentation of essence from self,"[30] while Karin Barber noted a prevalent mood of pathos in highlife lyrics, seeing them as ultimately reflecting "all the ills characteristic of a society undergoing rapid urbanization."[31] Fela's project of cultural revitalization certainly aimed to reintegrate the African cultural psyche with what he considered its cosmic essence, and the most intractable worldly problems are often articulated in his work in terms of the supernatural. With what Gabriel Gbadamosi has called "the ghoulish dynamism of Nigerians," he explored his country's "traumatic self-image forming out of the collision of disparate influences"[32] with his sarcastic, trenchant imagery of political infighting ("Noise for Vendor Mouth"), civil confusion ("Confusion"), aimlessness ("Perambulator"), deprivation ("Original Sufferhead"), indignity ("Power Show"), cultural alienation ("Gentleman"), military domination ("Overtake Don Overtake Overtake"), and decay ("Confusion Break Bone")—immeasurably reinforced by the mocking and heavily traditional tone of his chorus singers. Fela's embrace of tragedy was not resigned or hopeless; rather, it reflected a characteristically Yoruba philosophy of tragedy (often conceived of as a transitional state essential to cosmic and social realignment) as well as a more worldly sense of ultimate revolutionary triumph.[33]

Political Music

Fela is mainly a hero to the young people. The older people think he's crazy. But everyone loves his music. Sometimes you can even catch the old people dancing to his music, if they think no one's around. But as

soon as someone walks in, they will stop and scowl and say "What
nonsense is this Fela singing about now?" But all the while they are really
loving the beats! They may not agree with the way he conducts himself,
but anywhere he goes in the country, people will hail him as if he's the
president. . . . They know he's stood up for what he believes in, and said
things that not too many people have had the courage to say—not only in
Nigeria, but all around Africa.

> YOMI GBOLAGUNTE, *interview with author, December 1992*

Having developed primarily as an aesthetic—as opposed to political—thinker,
Fela advanced an idealistic, utopian vision that was ultimately unsuited for politics, with its constant compromise and shifting alliances. He consistently derided
governmental agencies and dismissed the political process and most other institutions of a modern nation-state. He was also often uncritical in his blanket praise
of leaders such as Nkrumah and Idi Amin. Discussing his vision of governance in
1986, his comments were decidedly more musical than political: "I want to go
everywhere and play my music. I want to make people happy. Imagine the president playing music to announce budgets and policies. I want to preach spiritual
and political changes."[34]

Fela never articulated a specific political model or concrete ideology of governance, often seeming to vacillate between ideologies. To a question about the
American business presence in Nigeria in 1986, for example, he responded: "I
won't stand against American commerce, since I am in favor of the freedom of
undertaking. An American business would be able to open a firm like any African
would do, but only if there is a mutual respect and shared benefit."[35] On another
occasion in 1989, he prevailed upon then-president Ibrahim Babangida following
the military's cancellation of his scheduled concert in Abeokuta: "If you are seriously looking for an alternative solution to the challenges of our time, please turn
to the reports of the FESTAC Colloquium and the Political Bureau, where the
African people's have opted for socialism."[36]

Whether or not these two comments taken together reflect a nascent social-
democratic vision for Africa, one must also wonder whether Fela's ideological
ambivalence (or reticence) results from a realistic appraisal of the Nigerian government's close, oil-based relationships with the major Western powers, as well as
the fates that have befallen other African postcolonial revolutionaries. As Randall
Grass noted in a 1986 profile, "politics" to Fela ultimately represented a desire to
empower the masses so that they might lead dignified lives and attain life's basic
necessities, rather than any real desire to participate in the political process.[37]

One consequence of the extreme reaction of the Nigerian authorities is that
Fela's struggle gained as much credibility and momentum from what happened *to*
him as it did from what he actually accomplished politically. Like James Brown, his
most potent work tended to function simultaneously as a critical appraisal of society and a running commentary on his personal odyssey; and, like many traditional
African abuse singers, his derision was simultaneously aimed at those who committed wrongdoings against him as well as against the larger society. His ideolog-

ical development, as well as his flirtation with politics, should be viewed with this in mind. His political aspirations and ideological evolution also partially reflected his response to periodic state-sponsored violence against him. For example, his consistent opposition to military rule was understandable in light of his travails, but not always shared by the majority of Nigerians who remember the rampant corruption of the Shagari years and have (until recently) grudgingly accepted the military as the more disciplined and easily identifiable of two ruling evils.

A close examination of Fela's subculture reveals a vague anarchism ultimately opposed to *all* forms of authority, hierarchy, and official organization (the exception being that which Fela exercised within his personal sphere). As Jack Kilby noted, it seemed highly unlikely that Fela would ever find an African government of which he thoroughly approved,[38] and some, like Iyorchia Ayu, have interpreted this as an uncritical nihilism counterproductive to Fela's ultimate aims.[39] But it is also important to note that this philosophical anarchy served an ironic and organic function in Fela's art, since as much as he decried the civil disorganization of Nigeria, he also thrived on the energy it generated. In Nigeria, the adaptive creativity required to negotiate the traumatic process of rapid urbanization has fused with the traditionally syncretic, urban culture of the Yoruba, resulting in a profusion of "artistic" and "nonartistic" creativity with wide cultural, creative, intellectual, and political implications. Karin Barber observed during her stay in Nigeria:

> The frustration and rage of ordinary people at the blandly distracting rhetoric of their rulers sometimes boils up so high that even outsiders can see it. During and after the scandalous elections of 1983 in Nigeria, a satirical song by Wole Soyinka became so popular that it could be heard all day long on every Southern taxi driver's cassette player. This song . . . mocked all the populist slogans and meaningless panaceas of the last ten years. More usually, however, people's disillusion and resentment is expressed in a more subterranean manner, in the form of jokes, catchphrases, and anecdotes that circulate with great rapidity and undergo many phases of elaboration while they are in vogue. . . . Songs, jokes, and anecdotes may be the principal channel of communication for people who are denied access to the official media.[40]

Thus, despite Fela's distance from mainstream Yoruba political sensibilities, his work was rooted firmly within both traditional and contemporary social dynamics, conforming closely to peculiarly Yoruba modes of public, communal creativity and criticism. The creative anarchy of the afrobeat subculture was a reflection of the larger society within which it existed.

Elsewhere in Africa, some of Fela's musical colleagues have occasionally offered political commentary in their work—and have experienced varying degrees of reprisal. Zimbabwean singer/guitarist Thomas Mapfumo, whose music was a crucial political factor in the months leading up to Zimbabwe's 1980 independence, was imprisoned for three months as the Rhodesian government attempted to censor his popular antigovernment songs. In the early 1970s, singer Franklin Boukaka composed political songs critical of his government and society, before mysteriously perishing during a coup in his native Congo Republic. Singer Miriam Makeba had her South African citizenship revoked and received constant death threats as a result of her expatriate career singing and campaigning against apartheid. In Zaire, bandleader Franco and his entire forty-piece band spent two months in prison in 1979 after releasing a series of ostensibly obscene songs that followed an earlier series containing thinly veiled barbs at government officials and policies.[41] Fela's countryman Majek Fashek has chosen to sing his political reggae in exile, from a base in the United States. And South African protest singer Mzwakhe Mbuli, popularly known as the "People's Poet," was recently sentenced to thirteen years in prison by the Mandela administration as a result of his threats to expose government corruption.[42]

While these artists have suffered various repercussions for their occasional forays into political content, few have suffered as much for their opinions as did Fela—nor have they devoted an entire genre or career to political art, or attempted direct involvement in their country's political process (Boukaka is the exception). Fela's afrobeat was the only genre exclusively devoted to abusive humor, explicit political criticism, and critical exploration of the African postcolonial condition. Even on the purely instrumental level, the inherently optimistic, cooperative quality that characterizes much sub-Saharan African music (especially many of the pleasantries offered via the "world music" production aesthetic) begs the question of whether this music can ever be a vehicle for explicit political dissent.[43] Postwar Western art music, "free jazz" in America of the 1960s, punk rock in England of the 1970s, and the "noise" rock bands of the 1980s and 1990s all communicate an undeniable spirit of anger and alienation resulting from concrete sociopolitical circumstances. But until another African artist produces a similar sonic assault, Fela's music—with its blaring horns, disdainful attitude, and free-jazz interludes—may be the closest West African music gets to a sonic representation of dissent.

Fela's Musical Legacy

Afrobeat music represented two distinct achievements. The first was music as cultural intervention—Fela delved deeply into his native music culture to fashion a strongly indigenized popular style that countered the pervasive influence of foreign styles. Its second achievement was the creation of an "African funk" that, while strongly rooted in African-American music, transferred the counterhegemonic energy of that music into an African context, making politics accessible to alienated masses[44] and clearing a subcultural space for a type of explicit dissent extremely rare in African societies.

As the smoke of the initial "world-beat" explosion cleared during the 1990s and the older generation of African popular musicians was augmented by a younger generation, Fela emerged as an elder statesman of African music. A survey of artists who have directly or indirectly drawn on his work demonstrates his wide influence. Fela has been praised and acknowledged by some of the most influential musicians of recent decades, including Stevie Wonder, David Byrne, Jaco Pastorius, Afrika Bambaataa, Brian Eno, reggae production duo Sly Dunbar and Robbie Shakespeare, Paul McCartney, and a number of emerging producers of electronic dance music. In his 1989 autobiography, trumpeter Miles Davis—responsible for a number of crucial stylistic interventions in modern music—suggested Fela's music as an important reference point for future directions in world music.[45]

It remains to be seen whether younger practitioners will adapt the afrobeat style to subsequent generations, or whether it was a brief historical episode fueled by a charismatic individual and a particular set of economic, social, and political circumstances. One of the miracles of Fela's career was that he was able to keep his large bands active over three tumultuous decades. But because he centered his organization around his personal charisma, it has been difficult for musicians to use a tenure with his band as an apprenticeship to a greater public profile, as have other musicians such as Zairean guitarist Diblo Dibala, Senegalese guitarist Barthelemy Atisso, or Guinean guitarist Sekou Diabate. Talented Afrika 70 or Egypt 80 soloists such as Tony Allen, Y. S. Akinibosun, and others have generally not consolidated the experience into viable leadership roles on their own.

In recent years, a number of musicians have nevertheless experimented with elements of the afrobeat style. Since leaving Egypt 80 in 1986, Fela's eldest son Femi has emerged as the genre's main exponent, continuing to explore his father's musical direction and political concerns on four albums with his Positive Force Band. Rejecting his father's image as a social rebel while continuing the legacy of political music, Femi has cultivated an image as a clean-living, responsible musician while, like Ziggy Marley, working largely within the musical and rhetorical models established by his father. He told Ron Sakolsky:

> Nobody wanted to give me a chance, because I was Fela's son. They said I must do exactly what my father is doing. They thought that if I was going to take over playing afrobeat, I must smoke grass, have a lot of women around me, and if I'm not going to do all that, I can't be Fela's replacement. I said "Look, I don't intend to be Fela's replacement. I'm going completely different from where he's going. I must find my own life."[46]

Stylistically, Femi's afrobeat is marked by shorter songs, quicker tempos, and a denser, almost frantic arranging style than most of Fela's later music. Containing complex arrangements and occasional odd time signatures (one song is based upon a 5/4 afrobeat pattern), Femi's music clearly requires advanced instrumental skill, and the main criticism that has been leveled at his work to date by Nigerian listeners is that it is too frantic or busy, and that he "needs to settle down." Ironically, these are similar to the criticisms of his father's dense music during his Koola

Lobitos years. In style and theme, Femi's music betrays the influence of the music he played with his father while a member of Egypt 80 (1979–1986), blended with the influence of African-American styles such as hip-hop and electro-funk. Femi has also taken a different approach to marketing his music—several tracks from his 1999 CD *Shoki Shoki* remixed by leading electronica producers and aimed at various non-African audiences. In recent years, Femi and the Positive Force Band have built a loyal audience of their own, holding down the Sunday Jump at the Shrine and releasing music on Fela's Kalakuta label, as well as European and American labels. They have also toured Europe, headlining the 1990 WOMAD Festival, and they have a particularly strong following in France. In the summer of 1995 they released their first U.S. recording on Motown and performed as part of the traveling Africa Fete festival, giving their first U.S. performances to favorable reviews. By 1999, when Femi and the Positive Force Band returned for their second U.S. tour in the midst of renewed interest in his father's music, it was clear that their hard work had begun to pay serious dividends. Catching their doubters and detractors completely off guard, the band played a tight, blistering set that thrilled the audience and indicated the potentially powerful blend of afrobeat with hip-hop, funk, and other contemporary genres.

Femi distinguished his own brand of afrobeat from his father's in 1996:

> My music is more direct, more to the point. My father plays a number for about an hour now, his music is very relaxed. His music is more spiritual, I think. . . . Because I want to play music as well as make money, I will not play a number for that amount of time. I can understand the European mind, or the Western mind. They don't want to spend an hour trying to decide whether they like this number or not. Whereas the African man, he's ready to digest it for an hour, listen to the same rhythm. They believe the longer it is, the better it is for them.[47]

Following Femi's lead is a school of emerging Nigerian musicians including Lagbaja (Bisade Ologunde), Kola Ogunkoya, and Funsho Ogundipe, who have been influenced by afrobeat as well as jazz and various local and diasporic popular forms.

After leaving Afrika 70, master set drummer Tony Allen also released a number of LPs during the 1980s, including *No Discrimination* (1980) *N.E.P.A.* (1985), and *Afrobeat Express* (1989), which continue the afrobeat style he perfected with Fela. Textually, these albums explore moral and social themes while eschewing Fela's confrontational style. Aside from his brief collaborations with Sunny Ade on *Aura* and expatriate Zairean guitarist Ray Lema, Allen has kept a lower profile since his Afrika 70 days, moving between Africa and Europe. In late 1997, he was working on a "Funky Juju" project in France with former Parliament/Funkadelic vocalist Gary Cooper.

Other African artists referencing afrobeat have generally taken instrumental elements of the music and divorced them from Fela's political content. Most visibly, a number of juju musicians have integrated elements of afrobeat into their repertoire, and today it is rare that a well-known juju group does not include seg-ments of minor-key afrobeat-derived music in their performances. Best known among these are musicians like Sunny Ade, Ebenezer Obey, Dele Abiodun, and Segun Adewale. Along with Abiodun (whose *Confrontation* EP contains two lengthy tracks of pure afrobeat), Ade's adoption of afrobeat style (discussed in Chapter 6) is the most direct, while Obey's borrowings tend to be more compati-ble with traditional juju practice.

Sonny Okosun—one of Fela's most consistently supportive colleagues in Nige-ria—has occasionally experimented with afrobeat, most prominently on his *Papa's Land* LP. Ghanaian highlife singer Naa Ampadu experimented with a highlife-afrobeat fusion in his "Afro-hili" style.[48] The afrobeat influence can also be felt in the music of Hugh Masekela, who often features Fela's "Lady" in his concerts, and who drew heavily upon afrobeat in his work with Ghana's Hedzolleh Soundz. Fela's former musical and business associate Oluko Imo's 1988 release, *Oduduwa,* fea-tures Imo singing his "Were Oju Le" ("Their Eyes Are Getting Red,") over a late Afrika 70 instrumental track. Camerounian percussionist Brice Wassy, former musical director for Salif Keita, recorded a CD of Afro-fusion called *Shrine Dance,* inspired by his visits to the Afrika Shrine. The Paris-based group Ghetto Blaster, formed by ex–Egypt 80 percussionists Nicholas Avom and Udoh Essiet, released an album in the mid-1980s in what might be called a "club-afrobeat" style, while Nigerian singer Ephraim Nzeka has recorded an entire album of Fela's compositions entitled *Ephraim Sings Fela.* Recorded in Paris with a mixture of African and French studio musicians, both of these projects offer afrobeat with a polished, European dance music aesthetic, hinting at what Fela's music might have sounded like had he capit-ulated to the demands of his successive Western promoters.

Outside Africa, musicians have referenced afrobeat more symbolically. An afrobeat-inspired tenor guitar figure propels Bob Marley's "Could You Be Loved," composed after his brief trip to Africa in 1980. The oft-debated influence of afrobeat on James Brown's music seems evident in a number of compositions recorded after the latter's Nigerian trip, most notably on the JB's "Hot Pants Road" (1971). Afrobeat's particular influence on bassist Bootsy Collins may be detected in his 1980 piece with the group Sweat Band, titled "Jamaica," as well as in his 1976 composition "Stretchin' Out (In a Rubber Band)," which he says was inspired by music he heard during his Nigerian trip with Brown in 1970.[49] Later in the decade, Collins's P-Funk mentor George Clinton would pay homage to Fela in his 1983 song "Nubian Nut," which incorporates chorus lines from "Mr. Follow Follow."

Fela's afrobeat has also often served as a conceptual bridge for African-Amer-ican jazz musicians investigating the music of Africa. Alfred "Pee Wee" Ellis, who arranged much of James Brown's most innovative music, waxed favorably on Fela's music in a music magazine "blindfold test" and went on to contribute wind arrangements for the Malian neotraditional vocalist Oumou Sangare on her *Worotan* CD.[50] Along with his former James Brown bandmates Fred Wesley, David Matthews, and St. Clair Pinckney, Ellis also composed a 1996 homage to Africa as motherland titled "Africa, Center of the World," evoking themes similar to those in Fela's 1980 piece of the same name.[51] Soul-jazz vibraphonist Roy Ayers toured

Nigeria and recorded with Fela in 1980, and made several guest appearances with Egypt 80 in the United States.[52] Some of his 1980s performances contained derivations of Fela's music; one video shows him influenced by Fela's stage manner while his band plays an instrumental version of "International Thief Thief."[53] The Art Ensemble of Chicago, featuring Fela's friend and guest trumpeter Lester Bowie, recorded a version of "Zombie" on its 1987 release *Ancient to the Future,* and Bowie often sat in with Egypt 80 in the United States as a guest soloist. Saxophonist Branford Marsalis is seen sporting a "Free Fela" t-shirt in Spike Lee's film *School Daze,* and his collaborative hip-hop project *Buckshot Le Fonque* (1994) includes samples of Fela's "Beasts of No Nation." Trombonist Steve Turre's *Rhythm Within* (1994) includes music he says was inspired by Fela. In a similar musical vein, the eclectic fusion group Hotel X included an instrumental version of "Black Man's Cry" on its 1995 recording *Ladders.*

Based as much in African-American as African music, Fela's work will probably receive a full reappraisal when political and cultural developments stimulate a resurgence of Pan-African cultural sentiments similar to the period in which he originally developed his style. In the meantime, however, the music of the 1970s has been undergoing a major comeback as digital fodder for sampling among studio-based musicians (i.e., those practicing in hip-hop, jungle, house, acid jazz, or similar styles) on both sides of the Atlantic, as well as through retro tastes that seek the music out in its original form. Acid jazz, in particular, has stimulated a revival of the brand of 1960s and 1970s fusion music that coupled jazz-based arrangements with funk rhythms, performed by groups such as Earth, Wind, and Fire, Tower of Power, War, and Kool and the Gang. Saxophonist Houston Person's jazz-funk reworking of Fela's "I No Get Eye for Back" was released on a 1995 compilation celebrating the roots of acid jazz, and placing Fela's music in this context might mark the beginning of such a revisionist trend. A British review of his 1992 *Underground System* LP thus proclaimed:

> Fela Kuti's music was once seen as the apex of progressive, exciting African music; then abruptly, he became yesterday's man. Overdue for reappraisal, Fela helps the process with a strong album, an urgent return to form, taken at a faster lick than usual and with more thump and bass in the bottom and clarity at the top than ever before. . . . If you listen to George Clinton, Sun Ra, or trance-techno, but dismiss Fela as a sexist megalomaniac, then *Underground System* could tip you off your fence.[54]

In fact, electronica producers do seem to be gradually engaging with Fela's work. The Masters at Work team remixed "Expensive Shit" in 1998; "jungle" producers cite his work as an inspiration; and snippets of afrobeat are gradually beginning to show up as hip-hop samples.

One overlooked aspect of Fela's musical legacy is the indirect contribution it could make to the evolution of African "art" music. Although his music operated strictly within the sphere of popular music, and he was dismissive of more consciously westernized African composers, Fela's work nevertheless offers deep structural insights into the fusion of African and Western traditions and materials, and his body of work will likely nourish the future development of African art music.

"An Era of Bliss, Folly, and Sorrow"

This body of work is increasingly relevant in light of contemporary political and cultural developments in Africa and the diaspora. The idea of transnational alliance in Africa, considered outmoded and unrealistic during the 1970s and 1980s, has regained currency in light of the European Economic Community and could be relevant for African nation-states in increasingly dire political and economic straits.[55] At the same time, Africa has reemerged among African-Americans as a symbol of cultural affirmation during a period of increasing social conservatism and ethnic polarization. In such a historical moment, Fela's story could offer perspective on race and class, on both sides of the Atlantic. Just as Bob Marley, invoking the diasporic legacy of Garveyite Pan-Africanism, sang in "Africa Unite" that the political liberation of diasporic Africans depends on unity in Africa, Fela—as much as he drew on the same Egyptian-inspired cultural narratives that fuel Afrocentrism—forces the Afrocentrists to understand Pan-Africanism in light of the concrete struggles of contemporary Africa, as opposed to the imagined cultural utopia of ancient Nile Valley civilizations. More than anything, his work would force them to confront the reality of black-on-black oppression on the continent, as well as the class reality that any "great" empire (e.g., dynastic Egypt, colonial Europe, and the United States of America, as well as oil-boom Nigeria) is invariably built upon a solid foundation of human suffering and exploitation. And on the broadest level, Fela is typical of artists worldwide who emerge during periods of rapid industrialization, bemoaning the loss of traditional ways of life, economic segregation, and agitating against the forming upper classes.

Current political developments seem to indicate that Nigeria is at a critical historical crossroads. As the population doubles every twenty-two years, oil revenues decline, and environmental stressors become more acute, political rule is likely to become, if anything, harsher. In such a climate, the government will likely have to deal with problems incomparably more difficult than an eccentric musician composing sarcastic songs. In this context, Fela's odyssey will likely be fondly remembered as an episode that, while it accurately forecasted the future problems resulting from the corruption of Nigeria's leadership during the country's economic heyday, is inextricably linked to the halcyon days of that period. It was in recognition of this that the *Accra Daily Graphic* poignantly evoked Fela's passing as "the death of the era of bliss, folly, and sorrow."[56] Possibly in anticipation, Fela in his last phase seemed content to comment sardonically from the political sidelines through his songs. As he told a reporter in 1986: "I have opened the eyes of the people to oppression in our continent. The people know I did it. I'm honest and consistent. That's enough."[57]

Appendix: Koola Lobitos, Nigeria 70, Afrika 70, and Egypt 80 Personnel

Chorus Singers

Yemi Abegunde; Bimbo Adelanwa; Bola Adeniyi; Tejumade Anikulapo-Kuti; Alake Anikulapo-Kuti; Fehintola Anikulapo-Kuti; Folake Anikulapo-Kuti; Ihase Anikulapo-Kuti; Kevwe Anikulapo-Kuti; Owowunmi Anikulapo-Kuti; Remi Anikulapo-Kuti; Tokunbo Anikulapo-Kuti; Akosua Asiedu; Ronke Edason; Chioma Elosiuba; Ronke Emiko; Suru Eriomla; Felicia Idonije; Shade Komolafe; Ngozi Nwafor; Folake Oladeinde; Folake Oladejo; Bola Olaniyi; Kemi Omitola; Omolola Osaeti; Emaruagheru Osawe; Bose Osuhor; Shade Shehindemi; Oma Umude; Echa Ushie; Itohan Wochiren

Trumpeters/Flugelhornists

Eddie Aroyewu; Lester Bowie; Ehimua Ermest; Eddie Fayehun; Olu-Otenioro Ifayehun; Tony Njoku; Oye Shobowale; Nwokoma (Stephen) Ukem; Tunde Williams

Trombonist

Fesobi Olawaiye

Saxophonists

Oyinade Adeniran; Yinusa Akinibosun; Femi Anikulapo-Kuti; Lanrewaju Anikulapo-Kuti; Lekan Animashaun; Tex Becks; Ajayi Bodunrin; Igo (Okwechime) Chico; Rilwan (Showboy) Fagbemi; Suleiman Musa; Isaac Olasugba; Kola (Acheampong) Oni; Mukoro (Victor) Owieh; Christoper Uwaifor

Guitarists

Don Amechi; Peter Animashaun; Chukwudi Aroga; Leke Benson; Tunde Brown; Segun Edo; Emeke Elenda; Keji Ifarunmi; Clifford Itoje; Kunle Jatuasu; Kiala; Oghene Kologbo; Opoku Kwaku; Fred Lawal; Itam Mann; Mardo Martino; Bala Roger M'bala; David Obayendo; Soji Odurogbe; Yomi Ogundipe; Okalue (Laspalmer) Ojeah; Festus Okotie; Alex Oparah; Dele Osho; Yinka Roberts; Tutu Shoronmu; Adegoke Solomon; Turbo Tamuno; Victor Tieku

Bass Guitarists

Franco Aboddy; Herman Menimade Addo; Idowu Adewale; Rotimi Afariogun; Jonas Anyakor; Nweke Atifoh; George Mark Bruce; Ukweku Charles; Maurice Ekpo; Kalanky Jallo Clement; Seyi Cole; Victor Ebreneyin; Emmanuel Edoube; Felix Jones; Emmanuel Ngomalio; Ojo Okeji; Femi Oladegunwa; Owona

Pianists

Wole Bucknor; Emoghene Efe; Keji Hamilton; Durotimi Ikujenyo; Sid Moss; Dele Soshinmi

Drummers (Drum Set)

Adebiyi Ajayi; Tony (Oladipo Alabi) Allen; Ogbona Alphonso; Masefwe Anam; Nicholas Avom; Ginger Baker; John Bull; Francis Foster; Ola (Benjamin) Ijagun; Bayo Martins; Atiba Tiamiyu

Conga Players

Shina Abiodun; Nicholas Addo; Ajayi Adebiyi; Popoola Awodoye; Easy Adio; Kwame Bako; Moses Emmanuel; Benjamin Ijagun; Okon Iyang; Friday Jumbo; Henry (Oladeinde) Kofi; Daniel Akwesi Korranteng; Obeatta Michael; Dele Olayinka; Kola Olasanya; Nwale Omabuwa; Dele Osho; Essiet Udoh

Shekere/Maracas

Ajimere Issesele; George Kassim; Fosibor Okafor; Fesobi Olawaye; Isaac (Babajide) Olaleye; Dele Olayinka; Wale Toriola

Sticks/Clefs

Ayoola (James) Abayomi; Lamptey Addo; Alele Adama; Oghene Ogbeni; Taiwo Ojomo; Mosa Okome; Wale Toriola

Dancers

Nosa Awayo; Aduni Anikulapo-Kuti; Funmilayo Anikulapo-Kuti; Najite Anikulapo-Kuti; Omolara Anikulapo-Kuti; Serwa Asiedu; Pulcherie Hoga; Dele Johnson; Jumoke Osunla; Kehinde Umokoro

Artists/Photographers

Babatunde Okanlawon Banjoko; Ajao Bello; Frances Kuboye; Tunde Kuboye; Ghariokwu Lemi; Boniface Okafor; Remi Olowookere; Maxoh-Max-Alex; Tunde Orimogunje; Femi Bankole Osunla

Notes

Notes to Chapter 1

1. "Pansa Pansa" has since been released on the *Underground System* LP (see the Discography).
2. See Johnson 1921, Part II.
3. See Moore 1982, chapter 22: "Men, God, and Spirits."
4. Fela quoted in Darnton 1977:23.
5. For a comprehensive explanation of Yoruba religion, see Idowu 1962. Drewal 1989 provides a comprehensive survey of traditional Yoruba plastic arts, while Beier 1968 discusses more contemporary developments in the visual and plastic arts.
6. Smith 1988:9.
7. In December 1991, the administrative capital of Nigeria was officially moved to Abuja, located in Bauchi State in the central region of the country.
8. More detailed description of these genres will be given in chapter 2.
9. See Graham 1992:29 for a listing of Nigerian art music composers.
10. See, e.g., Euba 1988, chapter 4, for a discussion of the music of Yoruba composer Ayo Bankole.
11. See Waterman 1990:22 for a discussion of this tendency.
12. Fela's claim to be the sole originator of afrobeat has been contested by another Nigerian musician, Orlando Julius ("O. J.") Ekemode, whose music and claims are discussed in chapter 3.
13. For a detailed analysis of this process, see Waterman 1990, especially chapter 7: "Juju Music and Inequality." It is difficult to overstate the degree to which my work is indebted to Waterman's comprehensive analysis of Yoruba popular music traditions, social dynamics, and material relations.
14. Hadjor 1992:81 defines "comprador" as a "local merchant performing the function of a middleman between foreign producers and the local market."
15. See Noble 1993.
16. See Collins 1992:32.
17. Barber 1987:30.
18. My main sources for information about Mrs. Ransome-Kuti's life and activities are two profile articles by Cheryl Johnson-Odim (1986, 1995), and Nina Mba's 1982 book *Nigerian Women Mobilized*. The work of both authors was later combined into a full-length biography of Funmilayo Ransome-Kuti entitled *For Women and the Nation* (1997).

Notes to Chapter 2

1. Smith 1988:8.
2. See Idowu 1962 for a comprehensive summary of Yoruba religion.

3. The construction of modern pan-Yoruba ethnic identity is discussed in Smith 1988, chapter 12, "On The Threshold of Nigeria."

4. The historical kingdom of Benin, located in what is now Bendel State of south-central Nigeria, should not be confused with the later nation-state of the same name, which replaced its French colonial name Dahomey with the name of the historical kingdom in 1976.

5. British colonial rule in Nigeria was implemented in three phases. Lagos Island was annexed and colonized by the British in 1861. A protectorate agreement signed in 1900 designated the modern geographic boundaries and brought the entire region under British control as two separate administrative regions, Northern Nigeria and Southern Nigeria. These two protectorates were unified into the British colony called Nigeria in 1914, a name retained after independence from Britain in 1960.

6. See Johnson 1921:296.

7. From its founding in 1788, the British colony of Sierra Leone was a center for slaves repatriated by British antislaving patrols on the West African coast. It also grew into a center for education in West Africa; Fourah Bay College, located in the capital city of Freetown, was closely affiliated with Durham University in England from 1876. Many graduates of this school—including Fela's father, Reverend I.O. Ransome-Kuti—went on to establish institutions of higher learning throughout West Africa.

8. Forde 1951:3.

9. "Another Disruption in Egba Politics?" *Daily Service,* January 31, 1946.

10. My main sources of Yoruba history are Johnson 1921 and Smith 1988.

11. One child, Hildegard, died shortly after birth in 1937.

12. Accounts of Fela's childhood are drawn mainly from Moore 1982 and Idowu 1986. Accounts of his parents' professional activities are drawn primarily from Johnson-Odim/Mba 1997.

13. Soyinka's *Ake: Years of Childhood* (1981), an autobiographical account of his childhood in Abeokuta, provides a richly detailed account of the activities in and around the Ransome-Kuti family compound during the late 1940s and early 1950s.

14. Fela quoted in Udenwa 1986:B8.

15. Femi Oyewole quoted in Oroh 1988:18.

16. Delano 1942:7.

17. Ibid.

18. Ibid, 8.

19. Fela quoted in Idowu 1986:15.

20. Fela quoted in Moore 1982:36–39.

21. Fela quoted in Idowu 1986:15.

22. Fela quoted in Moore 1982:36.

23. Moore 1982:31.

24. I have not been able to locate information on these recordings.

25. Fela quoted in Idowu 1986:14.

26. Soyinka 1981:176.

27. For more detailed discussions of Yoruba masquerades and their musical accompaniment, see Euba 1988, Thompson 1974, and Drewal 1992.

28. The Ogboni are Abeokuta's traditional ruling council of male elders.

29. Recounted by Beko Ransome-Kuti in Oroh 1988:18.

30. Olufemi Olodumosi quoted in Oroh 1988:18.

31. Barrett 1997:1331.

32. For the purpose of either foreshadowing events or to provide Fela's running commentary on various public events as they unfolded, I have excerpted his comments from "Chief Priest Say," the classified column he ran in various Lagos newspapers during the 1970s and 1980s, at various points throughout the text.

33. Fela quoted in Moore 1982:38.

34. See ibid., 31.

35. Soyinka 1981:9.

36. "Portrait: The Ransome-Kutis of Abeokuta," *West Africa,* May 12, 1951, p. 413.

37. Fela quoted in Moore 1982:42.

38. Christened Frances Abigail Funmilayo, Mrs. Kuti dropped Frances Abigail from her name as a result of the racism she experienced during her period abroad (Johnson 1986:237). She also later dropped her late husband's English "Ransome" from her name, replacing it with the Yoruba "Anikulapo." This move was a statement of solidarity with Fela, who had replaced his own "Ransome" with "Anikulapo" in 1975.
39. Johnson 1986:247.
40. Mba 1982:151.
41. "10,000 Egba Women Led by Mrs. Kuti Demonstrate against Women's Taxation," *Daily Service,* December 1, 1947, p. 1.
42. "Police Run Helter-Skelter to Untie a Tax Tangle," *West African Pilot,* December 12, 1947, p. 2. Afin is the residence of the Alake.
43. Fela quoted in Moore 1982:44.
44. These lyrics are quoted from Mba 1982, chapter 5.
45. See Johnson 1976:251.
46. The NWU actually represented the expansion of a preexisting organization—Abeokuta Women's Union (AWU)—from local to national activity.
47. Mrs. Kuti also visited Poland, Yugoslavia, and East Germany.
48. Nkrumah was a college student in the American south during the 1940s. His autobiography is presented in *Ghana: The Autobiography of Kwame Nkrumah* (1957), while his political philosophy is presented in *Africa Must Unite* (1959).
49. Fela quoted in Moore 1982:46.
50. See Fela's comments in "Fela, Black People's Singing Champion They Could Not Gag," *African Concord,* October 28–November 3, 1988, p. 10.
51. The dispute between Funmilayo Ransome-Kuti and Azikiwe is discussed in detail in Mba 1982, chapter 8.
52. Johnson and Mba 1997:173.
53. This is discussed in Mba 1982:288.
54. Odunfa 1968:10.
55. Differences on the issues of nationalism and transnationalism led to disagreements between President Nkrumah and the three regional leaders (Azikiwe, Awolowo, Bello) of soon-to-be independent Nigeria (Ajala 1974:13).
56. For example, see Funmilayo Kuti's comments regarding the American nuclear offensive against Japan in Soyinka's *Ake.*
57. See his comments in Moore 1982:49.
58. Fela quoted in Idowu 1986:17.
59. The Kru are an ethnic group of coastal Liberia. Historically sailors, they established a number of settlements along the West African coast that became important sites for the dissemination of palmwine guitar (see Collins 1985, chapter 2).
60. See Segun Bucknor's comments in Collins 1992, chapter 3.
61. Olaiya quoted in Uhakheme 1997:14.
62. Fela quoted in "I Write Music to Correct Evils," *African Concord,* October 28–November 3, 1988, p. 10.
63. Tannenbaum 1985:23.
64. May 1983:15.
65. Fela quoted in Moore 1982:61.
66. Stapleton and May (1987) provide a historical overview of the African music industry in the section entitled "Industry and Diaspora."
67. Fela in Udenwa 1986:B8.

Notes to Chapter 3

1. Fela quoted in "I Write Music to Correct Evils," *African Concord,* October 28–November 3, 1988, p. 11.
2. Sowande and Nketia preceded Fela as Trinity students (see Hall 1997).
3. The information on African art music in this section is primarily drawn from Euba 1988, chapter 4.

4. See Graham 1988:53.

5. Fela quoted in Collins 1985:119.

6. See Tannenbaum 1985 for Fela's early influences, and Collins 1987 and 1992 for an account of Armstrong's trip to Ghana in 1956.

7. Barrett 1997:1332.

8. Braimah quoted in Moore 1982:57–58.

9. See Stewart 1992:64.

10. Fela quoted in Watrous 1989.

11. See Collins 1987 for a discussion of this.

12. The development of Mailo Jazz is discussed in Nunley 1987, chapter 7.

13. Yomi Gbolagunte, interview with author, December 1992. Originally from Surulere in Lagos, and holding a degree in dramatic arts from the University of Ife, Abayomi Gbolagunte is a saxophonist, poet, and self-described "cultural scientist" who was a regular visitor to Fela's Afrika Shrine between 1972 and 1985, and a regular attendant of his international concerts thereafter. He currently lives and works in the United States.

14. Examples include Coltrane's *Dakar* album and his song "Tunji."

15. Fela quoted in Tannenbaum 1985:23.

16. Idonije 1999.

17. Fela quoted in Idowu 1986:26.

18. Fela quoted in *Teacher Don't Teach Me Nonsense* (video), 1987.

19. Fela quoted in Moore 1982:62.

20. The African nations gaining their independence between 1958 and 1963 were Benin (1960), Botswana (1962), Cameroun (1961), Central African Republic (1960), Chad (1960), Republic of the Congo (1960), Gabon (1960), Guinea (1960), Ivory Coast (1960), Kenya (1963), Madagascar (1960), Mali (1960), Mauritania (1960), Niger (1960), Nigeria (1960), Rwanda (1962), Senegal (1960), Sierra Leone (1961), Somalia (1960), Tanzania (1961), Togo (1960), Uganda (1962), Burkina Faso (1960), and Zaire (1960).

21. Fela quoted in "I Write Music to Correct Evils," *African Concord,* October 28–November 3, 1988, p. 11.

22. Oliver 1990:96.

23. Soyinka 1988:260.

24. See Braimah's comments in Moore 1982:58.

25. Hall 1997:1336.

26. Fela quoted in "I Write Music to Correct Evils," *African Concord,* October 28–November 3, 1988, p. 11.

27. Ibid.

28. Remi Anikulapo-Kuti quoted in Moore 1982:170.

29. See Senghor's essay "Negritude: A Humanism of the Twentieth Century," included in Cartey and Kilson 1970. The term itself was actually coined by Aimé Cesaire in his poem "Cahier d'un Pays Natal (Return to My Native Land)."

30. See Angelou's 1986 book, *All God's Children Need Travelling Shoes.* Also see the recollections of Leslie Alexander Lacy in *Black Homeland, Black Diaspora.*

31. The term "Saro" is actually a corruption of "Sierra Leone."

32. Waterman 1990:50. See chapter 2 for a discussion of the Jolly Orchestra and the Lagos Saro community.

33. Stapleton and May 1987:297.

34. Guy Warren, "The Talking Drum Looks Ahead," from his LP *Themes for African Sounds* (1958).

35. Roach quoted in Collins 1992:290. See chapter 27, "The Original African Cross-Overs," for an overview of Ghanaba's work through 1992.

36. Segun Bucknor quoted in Collins 1985:136–37.

37. Recounted in Idonije 1997:19.

38. Idonije quoted in Oladinni 1997:48.

39. As discussed in Euba 1988:90–91.

40. Idonije 1997:19.

41. Idonije 1999.

42. Sola Odunfa quoted in "Lucky Lobitos Get Thirteen-Week Contract," *Daily Express,* March 30, 1965, p. 5.
43. Fela quoted in Stewart 1992:117.
44. A detailed account of the Lagos highlife scene during the 1960s is provided in Collins 1985.
45. Idonije 1997:19; 1999.
46. Fela quoted in Moore 1982:73.
47. Tony Allen quoted in Smith 1985:17.
48. Collins 1992:77.
49. Odunfa 1965:5.
50. The Ga language, used by Fela in his song "Oritshe," is spoken in the Greater Accra District of Ghana.
51. Lafiaji is a neighborhood of Lagos.
52. See Collins and Richards 1982:116.
53. The term "shout chorus" is generally used in jazz to indicate the climactic section of a horn arrangement.
54. Charles Keil cited in Waterman 1990:253.
55. Allen quoted in Stapleton and May 1987:70.
56. Joni Haastrup quoted in Stewart 1992:118.
57. Ajayi-Thomas 1992:119–20.
58. Fela quoted in Moore 1982:73.
59. Fela quoted in Darnton 1977:12.
60. Fela quoted in Idowu 1986:28.
61. Faisal Helwani quoted in Collins 1985:124.
62. Niven 1970 and Jacobs 1987 provide contemporary and historical accounts, respectively, of the Biafran conflict.
63. See Keil, cited in Waterman 1990:112.
64. Fela quoted in Dorgu 1968b:10.
65. See Okosuns, quoted in Stewart 1992:124.
66. Chernoff 1979:115.
67. Wilson 1974:21.
68. The early Latin-jazz experiments from the 1940s paired virtuoso jazz improvisers like Charlie Parker and Dizzy Gillespie with Cuban arrangers like Machito and Mario Bauza, and Cuban percussionists like Chano Pozo.
69. Alfred Ellis, interview with author, January 1993, New York City.
70. Davis quoted in Guralnick 1986:243.
71. For an overview of the boogaloo, see Roberts 1979.
72. For other examples of African-American music invested with new philosophical meanings by West African listeners, see Chernoff 1979:73–74.
73. Dorgu 1968a:3.
74. Timesgirl Cleopatra 1969:4.
75. Obatala 1971:8–12.
76. Ibid.
77. For accounts of Nkrumah's last days, see his *Dark Days in Ghana* (1970) and Milne 1990.
78. Apart from a personal trip to Abidjan, Ivory Coast, in early 1968, Brown first toured West Africa in late 1970. The "Soul-to-Soul" Festival, featuring a number of popular American performers including Roberta Flack, the Staple Singers, Carlos Santana, and Wilson Pickett, took place in Accra in 1971.
79. Fela quoted in Stewart 1991:65–66.
80. Dorgu 1969b.
81. "Soul Brother Number One" was the most popular nickname given to James Brown during the late 1960s, succeeding the previous "Mr. Dynamite."
82. Haastrup quoted in Stewart 1991:108.
83. Griot 1970.
84. Fela quoted in Moore 1982:74–75.
85. For further information and listening, see *Money No Be Sand* (Original Music 031), a compilation of early "Afro-Soul" experiments.

86. Fela quoted in Stewart 1992:118.
87. Fela quoted in Dorgu 1968e.
88. See Waterman 1990:17.
89. Saxophonist/bandleader O. J. Ekemode, a Nigerian musician currently living in the United States, contests Fela's claim of inventing the afrobeat style. Ekemode recounted Fela's visits to his mid-1960s shows in Ibadan to Gary Stewart (1992): "[Fela] always stand near the stage with his trumpet . . . and just play along. So by that time I really like the way he played trumpet. I always go and pull him on the stage to play. [In those days] he was playing jazz. And later he found out he has to come back to his roots before he can be known. And already we [Ekemode's group] were there" (101–2).

    Fela responded to Ekemode's claim: : "It doesn't bother me, because I think I've left something for them to investigate and try to do the best they can. But I think I've gone past that. . . . I've gone into [a] more serious kind of thing now" (102).

    I have not been able to obtain any of Ekemode's 1960s recordings. However, the stylistic blend on his 1985 release *Dance Afro-Beat* seems inspired by a variety of contemporary Nigerian styles, including highlife, juju, and Fela's afrobeat, and seems very different than his descriptions of his own mid-1960s style.
90. *Abiara* is a Yoruba word designating a child born shortly after the death of its father. Such a child is reputed to possess supernatural powers.
91. Fela quoted in Stapleton and May 1987:65.
92. Dorgu 1968a:4.
93. Fela quoted in ""Now, the Rebel Is Angry." *Daily Times,* May 6, 1969, p. 5.
94. See, for example, the Stones' "Sympathy for the Devil," and Davis's *Bitches Brew.*
95. Fela quoted in "U.S. Date for Fela," *Daily Times,* June 19, 1969, p. 4.
96. Fela quoted in Darnton 1977:12.
97. Fela quoted in Idowu 1986:34.
98. This incident recounted in ibid., 35.
99. Many details of Koola Lobitos's U.S. trip are related by Fela in Dorgu 1970.
100. Fela quoted in Idowu 1986:36.
101. Fela quoted in Oroh 1988:21.
102. Fela quoted in Moore 1982:85.
103. Ibid.
104. The political philosophies of many free-jazz musicians are discussed in Kofsky 1970 and Wilmer 1977.
105. See the introduction to Wilmer 1977.
106. Fela quoted in Tannenbaum 1985:23. This is evident is such works as Davis's *Kind of Blue* and Coltrane's *Coltrane at Birdland.*
107. Sandra (Smith) Isadore, interview with author, February 1999.
108. Fela quoted in Darnton 1977c:12.
109. Fela quoted in Moore 1982:88–89.
110. See ibid., 88.
111. See Nketia 1974:159 for a general discussion of modalism in African music; and Euba 1967 for a discussion of modalism in Yoruba music.
112. Examples include Henderson's *Power to the People,* Shorter's *Speak No Evil,* and Tyner's *Tender Moments.*
113. Barrett 1997:1332.
114. Fela quoted in "I Write Music to Correct Evils," *African Concord,* October 28–November 3, 1988, p. 12.

Notes to Chapter 4

1. Biafran War statistics are taken from Jacobs 1987.
2. Oil and economic statistics are taken from Kirk-Greene 1981.
3. See Stapleton and May 1987, part III, for an overview of the African recording industry.

4. Ibid., especially 275–78.

5. The compact disc compilations *Money No Be Sand* (Original Music, 1995) and *Africa Funk* (Harmless, 1999) contain examples of the late 1960s/early 1970s fusion of highlife and rock music.

6. See Morgan 1970b. Among others, the Clusters, the Assembly, and the Combos underwent significant personnel changes during 1969–1970.

7. Dorgu 1969c:3.

8. Morgan 1970a:8. The songs Morgan cites were all originally recorded by Brown on his 1969 LP *It's a Mother*.

9. "Summit Planned for Afro-Beat Musicians," *Daily Times,* October 28, 1970, p. 12.

10. "Blackism" is a term Fela adopted, and which became closely associated with him, but it was used quite generally among Nigerian students, artists, and intellectuals of the early 1970s to describe the country's emergent form of cultural nationalism. It was, like Nkrumah's "African Personality" or Senghor's "Negritude," a means of exploring the "essence" of African identity. The emphasis on "blackness" demonstrates the extent to which Nigeria was absorbing the influence of African-American formulations of racial identity.

11. This incident is recounted in Idowu 1986:39.

12. See ""Nigeria 70 to Release Afro-Beat Discs," *Daily Times,* June 3, 1970, p. 10.

13. Fela quoted in Watrous 1989:39.

14. See Okpewho 1992, chapter 6.

15. Ibid.

16. Labinjoh 1982:127.

17. See ibid.

18. "After the Fair Was Over," *West Africa,* March 6–12, 1971, p. 269.

19. "Summit Planned for Afro-Beat Musicians," *Daily Times,* October 28, 1970, p. 16.

20. "Welcome Lumumba," *Daily Times,* May 20, 1970, p. 8. See Moore 1982, chapter 3, for Fela's later feelings regarding "Viva Nigeria."

21. See Hall 1997:1336.

22. "People," *West Africa,* August 31, 1971.

23. "Summit Planned for Afro-Beat Musicians," *Daily Times,* October 28, 1970, p. 12.

24. "The Gypsy Look," *Daily Times,* July 18, 1970, p. 3.

25. "Bandleaders' Row," *Daily Times,* October 25, 1970, p. 6.

26. Yomi Gbolagunte, interview with author, December 1992.

27. See "People," *West Africa,* August 31, 1971.

28. Allen quoted in Stapleton and May 1987:70.

29. James Brown's rhythm guitarists during this period were Phelps Collins, Alphonso Kellum, Hearlon Martin, and Jimmy Nolen. Nolen is credited with innovating the widely imitated "chicken scratch" rhythm guitar style. "Blackman's Cry" and "J'ehin J'ehin" are two early examples of the "chicken scratch" technique adapted to the afrobeat style.

30. For an example of Fela's folk sources, listen to his piano solo on "Movement of the People No. 1," based on the Yoruba children's song that begins "Jiga Ni Balogun . . ." ("The jigger is the war-general"). For comparison with Jones's organ style, listen to the track "Boot-Leg" from *The Very Best of Booker T. & the MG's.* A comparison with James Brown's keyboard style demonstrates striking similarities in terms of both solo lines and "comping." Although Brown was not a trained keyboardist, the fact that he was a dominant influence on Fela's afrobeat conception implies that the two would negotiate the rhythm section underpinning in a similar way. Compare Brown's contemporaneous solo work on "Lowdown Popcorn" (1969), "Ain't It Funky Now" (1970), and "Funky Drummer" (1970).

31. The dispute between the two men has been variously attributed to money disputes, ideological differences, and Chico's reputed alcoholism. See Fairfax 1993:259 and Barrett 1997:1333.

32. *Daily Times,* September 19, 1970, p. 18.

33. Recounted by Fela in the video *Fela Live.*

34. See Fela quoted in Moore 1982:112.

35. Quoted in Labinjoh 1982:127.

36. For example, see "Singer Sandra Isn't Just a Screaming Political Extremist," *Daily Times,* October 13, 1970, p. 11.
37. "Police Seize Passport of Mrs. Kuti," *Daily Times,* October 22, 1970, p. 7.
38. Yomi Gbolagunte, interview with author, December 1992.
39. See, for example, "Soul: The Phenomenon of James Brown," *Daily Times,* August 16, 1970; or "What Power Means to the Black Man," *Daily Times,* October 9, 1970, p. 7. Not all African listeners were so enamored of Brown. Some characterized his performances as "poor" (Adeyemi-Osuma 1972:15) and others called him "definitely less a singer than a gymnastic entertainer" (Odunfa 1970:24). On the occasion of Brown's later performance in Zaire, local superstar Franco derided the jerkiness of Brown's dance style, remarking that he danced "like a monkey," and criticized Brown's lack of acknowledgment of Zairean musicians and of his African musical roots in general. (Ewens 1995:114).
40. See "Musicians to Receive Brown," *Daily Times,* November 26, 1970.
41. "Meeting of Two Rulers," *Daily Times,* November 30, 1970, p. 15. 11/30/70:15.
42. "Soul or Highlife—Both!" *Daily Times,* June 9, 1971, p. 13.
43. Both this quote and the "African James Brown" remark are taken from Brown and Tucker 1986:221.
44. Collins quoted in Watson 1997:46.
45. Allen quoted in Smith 1984:16.
46. Compare the original versions of these songs (all contained on the 1996 compilation *Foundations of Funk*) with their live arrangements on the 1971 concert recordings *Love Power Peace* and *Revolution of the Mind.*
47. "People," *West Africa,* February 13–19, 1971.
48. Fela quoted in Oroh 1988:22.
49. Regarding the challenge to soul music's popularity, see Adeyemi-Osuma 1972.
50. "Birth of a New Sound," *Daily Times,* July 29, 1970, p. 11.
51. "New Look, Fela in Animal Skin Attire," *Daily Times,* May 23, 1971, p. 11.
52. This information is taken from the liner notes to *Fela's London Scene* (Sterns CD 3007).
53. Baker appears as a guest drummer on *Fela Ransome-Kuti and the Africa 70 Live with Ginger Baker* and *Why Black Man Dey Suffer* and is listed as producer on *He Miss Road.*
54. Waterman 1990:83–84.
55. See Stapleton and May 1987:17.
56. Fela in Stewart 1993:121.
57. Olakunle Tejuoso, interview with author, December 1992.
58. Okpewho (1992:74) calls this practice of bending accents or adding syllables "marking time."
59. Fela quoted in Oroh 1988:22.
60. See the introduction to Gurnah 1993.
61. Achebe 1975:91–103.
62. For example, listen to "Let a Man Come In and Do the Popcorn," "Soul Power," and "Get Up, Get Into It, Get Involved," all of which are built upon the same rhythm pattern.
63. See Gilroy 1993a:105–6 for an interesting discussion of the cultural implications of twelve-inch format and technology.
64. Fela quoted in Idowu 1986:37.
65. See Barrett 1997:1333.
66. I am here drawing on a point raised by Paul Gilroy in his essay "Living Memory and the Slave Sublime" (Gilroy 1993:187–223).
67. Randall Grass has observed that the atmosphere at the Shrine resembled a religious ceremony (Grass 1982:26).
68. Fela quoted in Sweeney 1992.
69. See Santoro 1987:52.
70. Darnton 1977:11.
71. This is a composite listing of the most stable members of Africa 70 throughout the 1970s. For a listing of all Africa 70 personnel, see the Appendix.
72. "New Afro-Beat Tune Is on the Way Up," *Daily Times,* December 30, 1970, p. 10.
73. Masekela quoted in liner notes to his 1993 LP *Hope.*

74. Lester Bowie quoted in Tannenbaum 1985:26. Bowie appears as guest trumpet soloist on *Perambulator, I Go Shout Plenty, Sorrow, Tears, and Blood, Fear Not For Man,* and *No Agreement.*
75. This incident is recounted in Blake 1981:192. The song "Band on the Run" recounts the Lagos experiences of McCartney and his band members.
76. Fela quoted in Stewart 1992:84.
77. Yomi Gbolagunte, interview with author, December 1992.
78. Collins 1985:116.
79. Fela quoted in Snowden 1984:14.
80. See Waterman 1990:154–65.
81. Fairfax 1993:267.
82. Tannenbaum 1985:28.
83. This building was actually the property of Fela's mother.
84. Hernton and Turner 1977:88.
85. Collins 1992:81.
86. For example, see Darnton 1977c.
87. Fela quoted in Oroh 1988:20.
88. McLane 1986:73.
89. See, for example, Achebe's *Things Fall Apart* and Ayi Kwei Armah's *Two Thousand Seasons.*
90. See, for example, Cyprian Ekwensi's *Jagua Nana.*
91. Much of Wole Soyinka's work, which uses the images and poetry associated with traditional Yoruba orishas to discuss contemporary life, reflects this endeavor.
92. See, for example, Allen 1972.
93. See the introduction to Robinson and Berger 1986.
94. Fela quoted in Grass 1986b:65.
95. See Oduyoye 1995:105.
96. See chapter 2 above.
97. Odunfa 1968:10.
98. Stewart 1992:4.
99. See Malcolm X (with Haley) 1965, chapter 17.
100. Malcolm X quoted in Sales 1994:151.
101. See Hernton and Turner 1977:88.
102. See Goldman 1980.
103. See Ayu 1985:38–39.
104. Dolupo Ransome-Kuti quoted in Johnson and Mba 1997:51.
105. Gilroy 1993b:7.
106. See Stapleton and May 1987:17 for a discussion of this role of the urban African musician.
107. See Gabriel Gbadamosi's analysis of *The Road* in Gurnah 1993.

Notes to Chapter 5

1. "Africa's Richest Nightmare," *Punch,* November 28, 1982, p. 16.
2. The first National Develpment Plan had been issued by the Balewa government in 1962.
3. Bonuola 1975.
4. Ibid., p. 14.
5. Odiari 1976.
6. See the section "Asceticism and the Redistributive Imperative" in chapter 2 of Belasco 1980 for a discussion of this process among the Yoruba.
7. Ibid.
8. Waterman (1990) reports that "at any large ceremony a human penumbra surrounds the core of celebrants and musicians. Unemployed or part-time wage workers, small-scale artisans and petty hawkers, and beggars are allowed to gather around the edge's of the hosts's compound, and to partake of the food, drinks, and gifts circulated among invited participants" (177).
9. Figures in this paragraph are taken from Kirk-Greene and Rimmer 1981, chapter 5.

10. See "Africa's Richest Nightmare," *Punch,* November 18, 1982, p. 16.
11. For a more concise definition of the term, see Waterman 1990:170–71.
12. Ibid.
13. Ibid.
14. See "Deaths We Can Avoid," *Daily Times,* May 31, 1976, p. 3.
15. The member states of ECOWAS at its formation were Benin, Burkina Faso, Cape Verde, Gambia, Ghana, Guinea, Guinea-Bissau, Ivory Coast, Liberia, Mali, Mauritania, Niger, Nigeria, Senegal, Sierra Leone, and Togo (Stacy and McIlvaine 1982:xi).
16. Bonuola 1975.
17. For example, during my visit to Nigeria in the spring of 1992, Fela told me that he had recently been visited at home by the daughter of then-president Ibrahim Babangida.
18. Collins 1992:69.
19. Moore and Kamara 1981:66.
20. Collins 1992:69.
21. Among the Mande of Mali, the epic of *Son-Jara* is a well-known example of this type of poetry.
22. See Leymarie 1978 or Hale 1998 for a comprehensive study of griots.
23. For the relationship of Yoruba kings to Oduduwa, their mythical cultural progenitor, see Pemberton and Afolayan 1996.
24. See Drewal 1989 for a comprehensive overview of Yoruba plastic arts.
25. See Waterman 1990:88–89.
26. Stewart 1992:74–75.
27. For example, see Niji Akanni's (1990) discussion of the Yoruba Alarinjo tradition in his eulogy for Herbert Ogunde.
28. For a discussion of the social status of griots, see Leymarie 1978, chapter 5.
29. See Agovi's essay "Politics of Governance in Nzema 'Avudwene' Songs," in Furniss and Gunner 1995:48.
30. See Adedeji 1964:62.
31. See Okpewho 1992, chapter 6.
32. Agovi, "Politics of Governance," 60.
33. Ibid, 49.
34. Okpewho 1992:148–49.
35. Keil 1979:152.
36. This is an important subtheme in both Leymarie 1978 and Waterman 1990.
37. See Keil 1979:113.
38. Ibid., chapter 3.
39. Adedeji 1964:65.
40. Ibid, 64.
41. Ibid.
42. Ibid, 67.
43. Ibid.
44. Ibid, 71.
45. See Waterman 1990:22.
46. Ewens 1994:180.
47. "Bandits Halt Sunny Ade at Varsity Dance," *Daily Times,* January 18, 1976, p. 29.
48. Fela quoted in Fara 1986:45.
49. See Akanni 1990:33.
50. Fairfax 1993:375.
51. Fela quoted in Moore 1982:156.
52. Abudah 1982.
53. Waterman 1990:22. It is likely that Acheampong's antagonistic relationship with activist students in Ghana may have also caused Fela to view him in an unfavorable light.
54. For example, see Funmilayo Kuti's comments in "Kalakuta Incident—Fela's Mother Says It Was Shameful," *Daily Times,* April 26, 1977, p. 32.

55. Collins and Richards 1989:41.
56. See "Hemp Earns Drummer 10 Years in Jail," *Daily Times,* March 7, 1975, p. 3; "Hemp: Councillor Jailed 10 Years," *Daily Times,* March 20, 1975, p. 8; "Girl, 20, Jailed 10 Years for Hemp," *Daily Times,* March 25, p. 2.
57. One survey suggested that one in ten secondary school students had smoked marijuana. See "One out of 10 Pupils Takes Drugs," *Daily Times,* August 27, 1975.
58. These women are profiled in Moore 1982, chapter 19.
59. "Fela Out Again with a Bang." *Daily Times,* March 24, 1972, p. 10.
60. For a contrasting example, see Gary Stewart's profile of Kanda Bongo Man (Stewart 1992:8).
61. Collins 1992:72.
62. Sgt. Yunusa Irekpita Ibrahim, letter to *Daily Times,* August 6, 1977, p. 3.
63. Labinjoh 1982:133.
64. Waterman 1990:96.
65. For a discussion of this style, see Ewens 1991:103 or Waterman 1990:96–97.
66. Labinjoh 1982:133. Parts of this essay recount time spent at Fela's compounds during the mid and late 1970s.
67. See Nelson Tackie's recollections in Bergman 1985:65.
68. Moore and Kamara 1981:67.
69. Yomi Gbolagunte, personal communication, July 1995.
70. Such public disorder is uncharacteristic of the highly decorum-conscious Yoruba. Babatunde Lawal (1996:270) cites Victor Turner's idea of "symbolic inversion" to describe the reversal of behaviors that often accompanies Egungun and Gelede masquerades.
71. Nunley 1988 offers an introductory summary of the Freetown masquerade societies.
72. Ibid., 121.
73. Labinjoh 1982:133.
74. Okri 1992:3093.
75. Yomi Gbolagunte, interview with author, December 1992.
76. Idowu 1986:42.
77. Fela quoted in ibid.
78. "Indian Hemp Found in Fela's House," *Daily Times,* May 2, 1974, p. 1.
79. Recounted by Fela in Moore 1982:127.
80. Fela quoted in ibid., 119–20.
81. "Fela Freed of Hemp Charge," *Daily Times,* November 28, 1974, p. 28.
82. Grass 1982:74.
83. For example, see the cover of the *Shuffering and Shmiling* LP.
84. See Fela's comments in Moore 1982:250.
85. Johnson and Mba 1997:168.
86. Fela in Collins 1985:120. According to Lindsay Barrett, "Kalakuta" was reportedly christened in a linguistic corruption of the notorious Black Hole of Calcutta.
87. "Research into African Medicine Urged," *Daily Times,* March 22, 1975, p. 13.
88. Fela recounts this incident in Ayodeji 1982b.
89. Obideyi 1977b.
90. Collins 1985:115.
91. See the editorial "Peace and the Public," *Daily Times,* November 29, 1974, p. 3.
92. Birnbaum 1977:36.
93. "Students Demand Return to Civilian Rule," *Daily Times,* April 25, 1975, p. 3.
94. Kirk-Greene and Rimmer 1981:12. For the public debate about these executions, see "Should Corrupt Public Officials Be Executed?" *Daily Times,* December 21, 1975, p. 12.
95. See Darnton 1977c:24. For the ideological position of the subsequent (Obasanjo) regime, see Chief of Staff Shehu Yar'Adua's comments in "Yar' Adua on Government's Political Programme: No Ideology," *Daily Times,* July 30, 1976, p. 1.
96. See, for example, Peter Ekwunife, "An Ideology Called Ramatism," *Daily Times,* March 6, 1976.
97. See Willy Bozimo, "Nigeria's Antiquities Abroad," *Daily Times,* August 23, 1976, p. 7.

98. Fela openly admired Amin until the brutality of the latter's regime became public knowledge in 1979, and in fact composed "Who No Know Go Know" (1975) partly in praise of the Ugandan leader. Despite Amin's subsequent disgrace, Fela praised him once again on "Underground System" (1992).
99. "Big Blow to I.O.C.," *Daily Times,* July 19, 1976, p. 32.
100. "A Necessary Postponement," *Daily Times,* April 12, 1976, p. 3.
101. For example, see "Chief Priest Say," *Daily Times,* September 5, 1975.
102. Fela quoted in Collins 1985:120.
103. It was later claimed that Mohammed died with less than ten naira in his bank account. See Tunde Obadina and Olusoji Akinrade's interview with Chief M. K. O. Abiola, "The Man Who Would Be King" in *Punch,* May 5, 1982.
104. "Why the Coup Was Planned," *Daily Times,* February 19, 1976, p. 32.
105. "Embassy Stormed," *Daily Times,* February 18, 1976.
106. Fela responded to Mohammed's assassination via his classified ad in the *Daily Times:* "Our country must have a definite revolutionary ideology to progress (e.g. Nkrumahism), otherwise we shall never have a stable country. We shall always be losing our valuable properties, and our good leaders, too. . . . Let's all think and unite" (March 24, 1976, p. 14).
107. Bozimo 1976a.
108. "Yusuf Takes the Oath," *Daily Times,* August 6, 1975, p. 1.
109. See Moore 1982:142–43.
110. The image of the *agbepo*–the worker who carts human waste by night–is recurrent in Fela's lyrics, used to symbolize Africa's subordinate economic and political position in the world.
111. Yomi Gbolagunte, interview with author, December 1992.
112. See Falola and Ihonvbere 1985, chapter 5.
113. FESTAC figures are from Kirk-Greene and Rimmer 1981:12–13; information on the construction of the national theater from Bozimo 1976b.
114. "Liberation Movements to Take Part in FESTAC," *Daily Times,* August 20, 1976, p. 9.
115. For the government's version of this conflict, see Okutubo1976; for Fela's side, see "Why I Quit FESTAC Panel," *Daily Times,* October 19, 1976, p. 32.
116. Highet 1977:26.
117. See, for example, the comments of Chief Obafemi Awolowo, which encapsulate both of the general anti-FESTAC sentiments: "Asked for his views on the impending Black Arts Festival (FESTAC), Chief Awolowo said: 'I don't know what the country stands to achieve by the cultural jamboree.' In his view, it is '. . . unnecessary for the nation to revive every primitive culture for the nation to see.' He said it would look as if 'we want to go backward simply because we don't know how to go forward.' As for the white race, Chief Awolowo said 'They are interested in watching us demonstrate our primitivity. What is necessary now is that we should continue to improve in technological know-how and not to be showing the world how primitive we are.' In his opinion, the multi-million naira meant for FESTAC should be diverted to equipping our laboratories, expanding our educational facilities, improving agriculture, health, and veterinary services" ("So Far, So Wonderful," *Daily Times,* December 7, 1975, p. 1).
118. On Guinea, see "Toure Attacks Festival of Arts," *Daily Times,* April 15, 1975; on Senegal, see "Senegal Gets a Tick Off," *Daily Times,* July 7, 1976.
119. "Enahoro Quizzed," *Daily Times,* June 8, 1976, p. 1.
120. Hall 1997:1336.
121. See, for example, "Traffic Control and the Liberty of the Individual: The Horsewhip Recipe Reconsidered," in *Daily Times,* November 13, 1976, p. 7.
122. "Stevie Wonder in Lagos with a Bang," *Daily Times,* February 7, 1977, p. 3.
123. Highet 1977:36.
124. For example, see letters to the *Daily Times,* October 30, 1976, and November 20, 1976, criticizing Fela's withdrawal from the festival.
125. See Tony Amadi, "Marketing Afrobeat Abroad," *Daily Times,* August 26, 1976, p. 27.
126. See Derin Ogundipe's recollections in *Guardian,* August 13, 1997, p. 31.

127. The pamphlets were titled "Y.A.P. News"—the title was simultaneously the organization's acronym and a play on the word "yab" (after yabis), for the abusive antigovernment rhetoric they contained.
128. Aderinola 1976.
129. Fairfax 1993:285.
130. Fela quoted in Darnton 1977:23.
131. Hernton and Turner 1977:88.
132. Odunaike 1977:24.
133. "Fela's Own Story," *Daily Times,* March 16, 1977, p. 28.
134. "How Sheri Died," *Daily Times,* March 12, 1977, p. 3.
135. "Soldiers Beat Up Editor," *Daily Times,* January 22, 1977, p. 2.
136. See Rufai Ibrahim, "Military-Civilian Clashes," *Daily Times,* September 28, 1977.
137. "Fela's Modest Triumph," *Punch,* January 30, 1979, p. 1.
138. "Government Acquires Fela's House," *Daily Times,* April 29, 1977, p. 1.
139. Ibid.
140. Emmanuel Iwuala, letter to *Daily Times,* October 7, 1977, p. 13.
141. *Daily Express,* April 30, 1977, as excerpted in Fairfax 1993:323.
142. See Goldman 1980 for a brief profile of Kwesi Yoppee.
143. See Collins 1992:82. Also see Collins 1998 for a diary of the filming.
144. Yomi Gbolagunte, interview with author, December 1992.
145. See, for example, "Fela and His Wives," *Daily Times,* February 22, 1978, p. 26.
146. See Collins 1998.
147. Fela quoted in Molokwu 1987.
148. Ward 1937:27.
149. Ibid., 34.
150. Ibid., 46.
151. The components of a traditional Yoruba marriage are discussed in Ward 1937, from which all of the following examples are taken.
152. Bisi Adebiyi, letter to the *Daily Times,* March 18, 1978, p. 13.
153. Fela quoted in Maduneme and Akindele 1978.
154. See, for example, portions of Achebe's *Man of the People,* Armah's *Fragments,* or Omotoso's *The Edifice.* Relationships of this type are also explored in detail in Jenkins 1975, chapter 6.
155. Fela paraphrased in Maduneme and Akindele 1978.
156. Ezenekwe 1978.
157. Omosanya 1978.
158. "Fela's Mum Is Ill," *Daily Times,* February 16, 1978, p. 15.
159. "Mrs. Kuti: A Freedom Fighter—Obasanjo," *Daily Times,* April 15, 1978, p. 5.
160. See "School's Take-Over: Delay in Payment of Dues Deplored," *Daily Times,* August 20, 1976, p. 14.
161. Fela discussed the circumstances surrounding these recordings in a 1986 interview with Lister Hewan-Lowe, *WUSB Program Guide,* Fall 1986.
162. Fela and Decca both present their respective positions on this dispute in *Punch,* September 2, 1978, pp. 6–9.
163. For a brief biography of Abiola, see "Social Democrat Takes Lead in Nigerian Vote," *New York Times,* June 15, 1993; and Iloegbunam 1998.
164. Although he would later support Abiola's presidential aspirations, Wole Soyinka vehemently criticized Abiola in his article "The True Meaning of Ake," *Punch,* January 8, 1982, p. 5.
165. Fela 1976a, 1982.
166. H. S. Bwala, letter to *Punch,* December 28, 1979, p. 4.
167. C. N. Ofili, " 'Suffering and Smiling'—Do You Dance to Mock Yourself?" letter to *Punch,* June 9, 1979, p. 4.
168. Debekeme 1978.
169. Fairfax 1993:358.

170. Allen quoted in Smith 1984:17.
171. Barrett 1997:1335.
172. Kirk-Greene and Rimmer 1981:88.
173. Yomi Gbolagunte, interview with author, December 1992.

Notes to Chapter 6

1. See Achebe 1983:60.
2. Teniola 1978.
3. This figure is cited by Femi Kuti in Sakolsky 1996:44.
4. See Idowu 1986, chapter 8.
5. Adesina 1997:1330.
6. Okri 1982:3093.
7. Teniola 1978.
8. The major points of the M.O.P. manifesto are discussed in Ogunsanwo 1978.
9. Adelokiki 1978a.
10. Ogunsanwo 1978.
11. Ogunnaike 1978.
12. Tialobi 1978.
13. Adelokiki 1978b.
14. C. N. Ofili, letter to *Punch,* June 9, 1979, p. 4.
15. Arogundade 1979b:8.
16. Fela quoted in Haastrup 1979:7.
17. Some of Fela's earlier releases conform to this format. These are: *Confusion* (1975), *Johnny Just Drop* (1977), *Shuffering and Shmiling* (1978), and *Vagabonds in Power* (1979).
18. Fela quoted in Arogundade 1979d:11.
19. Beko Ransome-Kuti quoted in Gesinde 1981:12.
20. The main set drummers who succeeded Tony Allen during the early 1980s were Nicholas Avom, Masefswe Anam, and Benjamin Ijagun.
21. Fela quoted in Arogundade 1979d:11.
22. "Afrika Shrine," classified advertisement from *Punch,* August 25, 1979, p. 12.
23. Ibid.
24. Fela quoted in Barber 1983:36.
25. Fela quoted in Stewart 1992:120. The city of Ile-Ife, located approximately 150 miles north of Lagos, is considered the spiritual, cultural, and historical center of Yorubaland.
26. See Brown 1986. Historical accounts actually indicate that Park's first West African expedition took place in 1795 (Lupton 1979:40).
27. See Kilby 1983.
28. Stewart, 1992:115.
29. Yoruba legend maintains that Oranyan was the seventh son of Oduduwa, progenitor of the Yoruba people; Oranyan also founded and presided over the Oyo Yorubas (Johnson 1921:8). It is said that at the end of his life, this king metamorphosed into a granite obelisk (Opa Oranyan), which today stands in the city of Ile-Ife. Orompoto was a historical king of the Oyo Igboho court, founded during a period (the precise years are unclear) in which the seat of Yoruba power was exiled from the ancient capital of Old Oyo (ibid., 161–62). (Oranmiyan is a variation on Oranyan.)
30. For example, see Drewal 1988 for a discussion of Mami Wata worship in West Africa.
31. Waterman, 1990:86.
32. Fela quoted in Snowden 1984:13.
33. Ayodeji 1981:6.
34. "Fela, Afrika Shrine Presents Professor Addaie," classified advertisement from *Punch,* May 5, 1981, p. 10.
35. Waterman 1990:65.
36. See Ewens 1995:122–25.

37. Ibid., 41–42.
38. Ayu 1985:35.
39. Fairfax, 1993:378.
40. In the final verse, Fela sings: "Dem bring rabbit, dem bring egg, spirit catch dem, dem dey fuck, dem dey scream, dem dey shout"; these are apparent references to spirit possession and malevolent use of witchcraft.
41. Stewart 1992:115.
42. Femi Anikulapo-Kuti quoted in Newsome 1999.
43. Aridegbe 1979.
44. Fairfax, 1993:359.
45. "Fela Threat on Abiola," *Punch,* January 19, 1980, p. 1.
46. "Faeces Dumped at Abiola's Gate," *Punch,* January 26, 1980, p. 1.
47. This was one of several incidents in which Fela used luxury vehicles for such purposes.
48. Niyi Odutola, letter to *Punch,* May 29, 1982, p. 8.
49. This incident is recounted in Goldman 1980.
50. Salisu 1979.
51. See Amadi 1976 and Darnton 1976, 1977a, 1977b, 1977c.
52. Both of these reviews are cited in Idowu 1986:68.
53. Manuel 1988:76.
54. This observation is made in Barrett 1981.
55. Ibid.
56. Bob Marley died in Miami, Florida, on May 11, 1981.
57. Barrett 1981.
58. See Fairfax 1993:385 and Barrett 1997:1335.
59. Fela's decision was rooted in a common African belief that a large entourage is a reflection of a person's importance; for Fela, projecting his stature was just as important as maximizing profits. This was clearly not an attractive proposition for a promoter or businessman, although it does seem to have achieved Fela's desired effect. One European observer noted: "Fela Kuti . . . took quarters in the Hotel Plaza with his entourage and twenty-seven wives, residing on two floors in the manner of one who knows he has become a political factor in his home country, Nigeria. . . . He also found out that the Nigerian Army had taken the opportunity of his European trip to destroy his burnt house. . . . Who is saying that this man is no political factor?" (Holger Krussman, quoted in Idowu 1986).
60. Watts 1984:54.
61. The security branch of the Nigerian government, similar to the Central Intelligence Agency (CIA) in the United States.
62. Fela quoted in Stewart 1992:121.
63. Cited in Rumsey 1985:11.
64. Ibid.
65. Tate 1992:60.
66. Igiehon quoted in Uhakheme 1997b:19.
67. King Sunny Ade, interview with author, August 1992.
68. Allen quoted in Smith 1984:17.
69. Milkowski 1983:50.
70. Tate 1992:58.
71. Arogundade 1980a:9.
72. Ade quoted in Arogundade 1980b.
73. Pye 1983:20.
74. Ayodeji 1982a.
75. Abudah 1982.
76. Agbenika 1981.
77. Famuyibo 1981.
78. Awogbemi and Adelokiki 1981.

79. Shoyombo and Edun 1983.
80. This claim was made most notably by the Yoruba educator Tai Solarin (see Ette 1994).
81. Babatunde 1982.
82. Akiyode 1980.
83. Recounted in Goldman 1980:6.
84. Fela in Highet 1989:42.
85. Interview with Usman Abudah in *Punch,* May 16, 1982, p. 19.
86. Fela quoted in Bergman 1985:68.
87. Ayodeji 1984:8.
88. See Imbert's recollections in Rumsey 1986.
89. May 1983:14.
90. Built in 1969, the Kainji Dam on the Niger River was the first hydroelectric power project in Nigeria.
91. Stephens 1986:31.
92. Tannenbaum 1985:28. The reference is to organist Booker T. Jones, of the 1960s Stax soul group Booker T. and the MG's.
93. Barber 1984.
94. In addition to Fela (on soprano sax), the improvising of Animashaun and Femi Kuti can be heard on *Live in Amsterdam.* Y. S. Akinibosun can be seen on the videotape *Fela Live,* as well as several Egypt 80 recordings from the late 1980s, including "Overtake Don Overtake Overtake," "Beasts of No Nation," "Teacher Don't Teach Me Nonsense," and "Underground System."
95. Ayodeji 1984.
96. Barber 1984:59.
97. Steffens 1984.
98. Cited in Howe 1986.
99. A detailed description of one such performance—including the Professor's "kill-and-wake" presentation—is given in Goldman 1981.
100. Sinker 1986:77.
101. White 1978:301.
102. Amore 1984:8.
103. Uzoukwu 1984:1.
104. Ayu 1985:38–39.
105. "The Amazing and Perilous Odyssey of Fela Anikulapo-Kuti," *Revolutionary Worker,* May 15, 1985, p. 46.
106. See Femi Kuti's comments in Ibeji 1984.
107. Justice Okoro-Idogu later denied that such an exchange had taken place. See "Living Without the Bench," *African Guardian,* January 16, 1989, p. 8.
108. Fela quoted in Brown 1986:29.
109. Fela quoted in Fara 1986:44.
110. Fela quoted in Idowu 1986:186.
111. Femi Anikulapo-Kuti quoted in Adesina 1988:27.
112. See Femi's recollections in Sakolsky 1996:42.
113. Femi Anikulapo-Kuti quoted in Sementari 1997:41.
114. Fela quoted in Oroh 1988:23.
115. Fela quoted in "Fela, Black People's Singing Champion They Could Not Gag," *African Concord,* October 28–November 3, p. 11.
116. Fadugba 1979a:7.
117. Fela quoted in Molokwu 1987.
118. Fela quoted in Rumsey 1986.
119. Laswell quoted in Reese 1986:88.
120. Bovell quoted in Van Pelt 1997:55.
121. Fela quoted in Udenwa 1986:B8.
122. Okwechime 1986a:38.

123. The *gbedu* is associated with the Ogboni society of male elders in Abeokuta.
124. From *Liberation,* 1986.
125. Stephens 1987:30–31.
126. Ibid.
127. See "Expensive Publicity," *African Guardian,* January 22, 1987, p. 33.
128. Fela quoted in Oroh 1988:22.
129. Chernoff 1985:15.
130. Stewart 1992:117.
131. Niyi Odutola, in letter to *Punch,* May 29, 1982, p. 8.
132. See the cover of *Overtake Don Overtake Overtake* (1989).
133. Okwechime 1986b:39.
134. See Ajala 1973, Part Three: "The Case against Pan-Africanism."
135. This idea is fundamental to Gilroy's essay "Black Music and the Politics of Authenticity" (in Gilroy 1993a), upon which I am drawing throughout this section.
136. In fact, Africans living in the West were a frequent target of Fela's sarcasm; on "Gimme Shit, I Give You Shit" (1983), for example, he compared Africans struggling to survive in the West with Europeans living in affluence in Africa.
137. Differences in personal style notwithstanding, Fela's position on the relation of Islam to black culture is actually quite similar to the position taken by Asante (1988, chapter 1).
138. Actually, at this concert, Fela was more successful than any of the others in communicating the complex messages of his latest songs to a fully attentive and appreciative audience.
139. Ade Thomas, interview with author, Lagos, March 1992.
140. Akpederi 1987:28.
141. Stein 1997:23.
142. Fela quoted in Stewart 1992:117.

Notes to Chapter 7

1. See, for example, the introduction to Soyinka 1996.
2. Ihonvbere 1994:1.
3. Ibid., 119.
4. Ibid.
5. See Othman 1989.
6. Ihonvbere 1994:194.
7. Ibid., 201.
8. Fela quoted in Stewart 1992:119.
9. Fela quoted in "Fela, This Life at 55," *West Africa,* November 8–14, 1993, p. 2023.
10. See "Cry Freedom," *African Guardian,* July 13, 1992.
11. Fela quoted in Brown 1986:34.
12. Ihonvbere, 1994:97.
13. See promoter Keith Wilson's comments in Adeniyi-Jones 1988:34.
14. Nwaobi 1990:33.
15. Ibid.
16. See Ihonvbere 1997:50.
17. See, for example, Sankure 1993.
18. See "Hit Parade of Stashed Away Fortunes of African Dictators," *Evenement du Jeudi,* May 22–28, 1997.
19. Noble 1993:2.
20. See Saro-Wiwa 1992.
21. Ibid., 22.
22. See Rieff 1997.
23. Ibid., 39.
24. Newsome 1999.

25. Fela quoted in Jones 1996:57.
26. Uzomah 1997a:36.
27. Rieff 1997:38.
28. Soyinka 1996:6–8.
29. See Ihonvbere 1997:23.
30. Soyinka 1996:6.
31. Former minister of transport in the Shagari regime, Dikko fled to England after reportedly amassing over 200 million naira through corrupt business dealings. He later became the focal point of a diplomatic standoff between Nigeria and England, which refused to extradite Dikko to stand trial in Nigeria.
32. Sultan of Sokoto, northern Muslim religious leader.
33. Inspector General of Police, early to mid-1980s.
34. General Mohammedu Buhari, commander-in-chief of military government, 1984–1985.
35. Wealthy businessman and chairman of Decca Records Nigeria and I.T.T. Nigeria who became president-elect in annulled civilian elections of 1993 and was imprisoned for treason by General Sani Abacha in 1994.
36. Head of National Security Organization under Buhari.
37. Former military chief of staff under Babangida who became president in the military coup that overthrew Shonekan government in 1993.
38. President of military government, 1985–1993.
39. Governor of Lagos State, 1980s.
40. Sarduana of Sokoto, northern Muslim religious leader.
41. See Olowo 1998 for a profile of Bamaiyi and the NDLEA's antidrug efforts.
42. Crossette 1997:3. This declaration was made by the International Commission of Jurists.
43. See Barrett 1998:40.
44. Uzomah 1997:38.
45. Jones 1996:58.
46. This was actually a topic of discussion in the international African press. See, for example, "Hard Times for African Prostitutes in Europe," *New African,* February 1998.
47. Waidor-Pregbagha 1997:44.
48. Kunle Solana queried Fela on the state of his health in 1992 for *Poise* magazine: "Does Fela have the dreaded *Acquired Immune Deficiency Syndrome,* otherwise known as AIDS? This is the question on everyone's lips. . . . Some are already becoming uncomfortable because they believe that AIDS symptoms are already manifesting in his body. *Poise* magazine does not believe in rumours. So, the only 'Abami Eda' in the world's music industry was confronted. In his usual style, Fela yabs his critics: 'I no know the thing called AIDS. AIDS na oyinbo [white man] sickness, na their wahala [problem] be that. . . . I don't believe in AIDS, so you can't test me for AIDS. I will resist any attempt to test me for AIDS' " (Solana 1992).

    Fela also offered a number of novel explanations for his various maladies. In an interview with Thomas Peretu for *Lagos Weekend,* he explained the skin rashes that had been the subject of much press speculation during 1991–1992: "Afro-Beat King, Fela Anikulapo-Kuti has revealed that the rashes on his skin first appeared about four years ago: 'These rashes no be ordinary rashes. They are spiritual. They have a purpose. What people do not know is that I am changing skin, and it takes about five years to do that. The rashes will go off on December 31 when they will have completed five years. My new skin will appear on January 1, 1992' " (Peretu 1991).
49. Newsome 1999.
50. The name *Kuti* translates roughly from Yoruba as "He who cannot be killed by human entity."
51. See Fela's comments in Brown 1986:34. Along with his first cousin, Dr. Femi Soyinka, Dr. Ransome-Kuti had been in the forefront of AIDS awareness efforts in Africa since the mid-1980s.
52. The reaction among Fela's inner circle was not quite as unanimous. Femi Kuti initially spoke against the use of condoms in an interview (Ibe and Silas 1997:28) and told another interviewer that although he could not consider himself monogamous, he was not planning to get tested for HIV (Ayorinde 1997:1). But he had apparently changed his position two years later, telling the *New*

York Times's David Hecht, "If you don't adapt, you die" (Hecht 1992:E2). When Dr. Ransome-Kuti advised the members of Fela's former harem that they should get tested, many protested, ridiculing the plea and claiming that if they were in fact carriers of the virus, they would deliberately spread it to other partners (Waidor-Pregbagha 1997:43). Others refused to believe that Fela's death was AIDS-related; instead, they claimed, he had been killed by a slow-acting poison injected by the NDLEA during his last incarceration.

53. See, for example, "Fela Attempted to Join the Army," *Guardian,* August 13, 1997, p. 1.
54. Okri 1992:3094.
55. Sotunde 1997:3.
56. Bose Ladipo quoted in Anaba 1997.

Notes to Chapter 8

1. Neal 1987:18.
2. Actually, Malcolm X did encounter a highlife band at a 1964 reception given in his honor by expatriate African-Americans living in Ghana. The results were not particularly remarkable—by all accounts he dismissed the lighthearted music and delivered a sobering speech on the plight of African-Americans (Angelou 1986:133–34). Had he delivered his speech to the musical backing, however, those in attendance might have witnessed the first afrobeat song.
3. See Jameson 1986.
4. See Fanon 1963:222–23.
5. See Spivak 1985.
6. See Diawara 1992, especially "Anglophone African Production" and "The Artist as Leader of the Revolution."
7. Ibid., 120.
8. Reggae musician "Sweetman" quoted in Waidor-Pregbagha 1997:42.
9. Fannio 1998.
10. Alegbe and Ojudu 1988: 35.
11. See Stewart 1992:115.
12. Barber 1987:22–23.
13. Ayu 1985:35.
14. See Grass 1986a:143 for a discussion of this point.
15. I am drawing here on ideas expressed by John Corbett in his essay "Brothers from Another Planet" (from Corbett 1994).
16. For a comprehensive discussion of this type of cultural process, see Comaroff and Comaroff 1991, which examines the black South African appropriation and redeployment of European cultural symbols in the contest of European (and later white South African) political control.
17. See Timothy McCartney's "What Is the Relevance of Black Power to the Bahamas?" or Locksley Edmondson's "The Internationalization of Black Power," both in Coombs 1974.
18. Gilroy 1993a:199.
19. Wallace 1990:195.
20. For example, Sun Ra's *Horizon* (El Saturn 1217718), *Live at Montreux* (Inner City IC 1039), or *Strange Celestial Road* (Rounder 3035).
21. This is a consistent theme throughout Gilroy's work; see, for example, Gilroy1993a, chapter 6.
22. See Robinson 1998.
23. Posting to www.soc.culture.nigeria, July 28, 1998.
24. Waterman 1990:226.
25. This was evidently a point of conflict within the Ransome-Kuti family. John Collins reported: "One day, when I was teaching Fela's children some science at [Funmilayo Ransome-Kuti's] house in Abeokuta, Fela burst into the room and told me to stop, accusing me of teaching his children colonial mentality. His mother blasted him for this and told Fela she wanted her grand-children educated even if he didn't and told him to leave the room; he left" (Collins 1992:82).
26. Barrett 1997:1335.

27. Yomi Gbolagunte, personal communication, May 1, 1996.
28. I discovered one exception to this during my visit to Nigeria in 1992, when Fela danced an *apala* step to his song "Government Chicken Boy," a song built on a rhythm pattern used frequently by the late neotraditional musician Haruna Ishola.
29. This point is also made in Ayu 1985:34.
30. Soyinka 1976:140–60.
31. Barber 1987:37.
32. Both quotes are taken from Gbadamosi's discussion of Wole Soyinka in Gurnah 1993.
33. In his essay "The Fourth Stage," Soyinka has discussed this use of tragedy as it exists in the traditional Yoruba dramas related for the *orisa* Ogun (in Soyinka 1976). See also Gabriel Gbadamosi's essay on Soyinka in Gurnah 1993).
34. Fela quoted in Brown 1986:29.
35. Fela quoted in Fara 1986:45.
36. From open letter to President Ibrahim Babangida, April 1989.
37. Grass 1986a:142.
38. Kilby 1985b:2311.
39. See Ayu 1985:35.
40. Barber 1987:3.
41. See Ewens 1994:166.
42. See Flynn 1999.
43. Toop (1997a:74) explores this question.
44. Karin Barber has discussed the manner by which West African popular music—often a primary medium of public communication—provides notions on how to understand politics (Barber et al. 1987:2).
45. Davis 1989:393.
46. Femi Kuti quoted in Sakolsky 1996:43.
47. Ibid.
48. See Collins 1992:151.
49. See Collins's comments in the notes to his 1994 release *Back in the Day: The Best of Bootsy.*
50. See Ellis's remarks in Sinker 1993.
51. Included on the 1996 LP *This Is Rare Groove!* by J-Funk Express.
52. The 1980 LP *Music of Many Colors* features Fela and Ayers performing together. Ayers also appeared as a guest soloist in Fela's 1986 and 1991 concerts in New York City.
53. See the video *Fela and Roy Ayers: Africa '79.*
54. Toop 1993:57.
55. Ndibe 1995 examines the various resurgent currents of Pan-Africanism.
56. See *West Africa,* August 18–24, 1997, p. 1326.
57. Fela quoted in "Radical with a Cause," *West Africa,* February 20, 1989.

Bibliography

In my construction of a chronological narrative of Fela's life, I have drawn on a number of books, periodicals, newspapers, and journals that reported on him and his work. With the exception of Nigerian newspapers, this book relies mainly on materials published since 1977; prior to that, Fela did not have extensive contact with the Western media. For the early biographical data on his life, especially in the second chapter, I am strongly indebted to two previous publications: Carlos Moore's *Fela: This Bitch of a Life* (1982), and M. K. Idowu's *Fela: Why Blackman Carry Shit* (1986). My work also draws on the accounts of John Collins (1985, 1992) for close portraits of Fela at the height of his popularity in the 1970s. For Nigerian accounts of his later activities, I have relied on a variety of Nigerian weekly news magazines and specific newspaper reporters who covered the phases of his career, especially Fola Arogundade, Oladipo Ayodeji, Lindsay Barrett, Victor Dorgu, Mac Morgan, Okey Ndibe, John Nwaobi, and Chuzzy Udenwa, among others. A number of insightful profiles appeared in Western periodicals, including May 1977, 1983; Darnton 1977; Hernton and Turner 1978; Goldman 1980; Barrett 1981, 1997; Moore and Kamara 1981; Grass 1986a; and an unattributed 1985 profile in *Revolutionary Worker*. The African newspapers cited in the text (*Daily Times, African Guardian, Newswatch,* etc.) are published in Lagos, except for *Punch,* which is published in Ikeja and Lagos.

Publications

Abudah, Usman. 1982. "Fela . . . An Unpredictable Nigerian Living Legend." *Punch,* May 16, 1982, p. 19.
Achebe, Chinua. 1975. *Morning Yet on Creation Day.* New York: Anchor Press/Doubleday.
———. 1983. *The Trouble with Nigeria.* London: Heinemann.
———. 1987. *Anthills of the Savannah.* New York: Anchor.
Adedeji, Joel. 1967. "Form and Function of Satire in Yoruba Drama." *Odu* 4, no. 1:61–72.
Adeleke, Segun. 1988. "The Fire Still Burns." *Newswatch,* October 24, pp. 54–55.
———. 1990. "The Fire Still Burns." *Newswatch,* January 15, p. 43.
Adelokiki, Soji. 1978a. "MOP Promises Democratic Government." *Punch,* December 22, p. 7.
———. 1978b. "No MOP, No Election—Fela." *Punch,* December 28, p. 1.
Adeniyi-Jones, Jide. 1988. "Reggae Splashes Africa." *African Guardian,* March 14, p. 34.

Aderinola, Dapo. 1976. "Fela for Politics." *Daily Times* (Lagos), September 17, p. 40.

Adesina, Debo. 1988. "From Mission to Shrine." *African Guardian,* October 17, pp. 26–27.

Adesina, Kola. 1997. "Olufela Anikulapo-Kuti (1938–1997)." *West Africa,* August 19–24, pp.1330–31.

Adeyemi-Osuma, Kofo. 1972. "Towards Musical Revolution in Nigeria." *Daily Times,* February 6, p. 15.

Agbenika, Joshua. 1981. "Four Uni-Ife Students Killed." *Punch,* June 9, p. 1.

Ajala, Adekunle. 1973. *Pan-Africanism.* New York: St. Martin's Press.

Ajayi, Dapo. 1970. "Blackism." *Daily Times,* October 11, p. 7.

Akanni, Niji. 1990. "Last Curtain Call." *African Guardian,* April 16, pp. 32–33.

Akiyode, Toye. 1980. "Fela, Awojobi Rebuked." *Punch,* August 10, p. 1.

Akpederi, John. 1987. "Making a Volte Face." *African Guardian,* January 22, p. 28.

Alabi, Pade. 1969. "Cold Sweat!" *Sunday Times,* March 9, p. 3.

Alaka, Tunde. 1969. "Why the Savage Punishment for Hemp Smokers?" *Daily Times,* January 11, p. 5.

Alegbe, Ohi, with Richard Mofe-Danfo. 1989. "Femi's Fine Fury." *African Concord,* May 1, p. 33.

Alegbe, Ohi, and Babafemi Ojudu. 1988a. "I Won't Fight Another Generation." *African Concord,* October 24, pp. 22–23.

———. 1988b. "The Egypt 80 Band." *African Concord,* October 24, pp. 34–35.

Allen, Chris, with J. Baxter, M. Radu, and K. Somerville. 1989. *Benin, the Congo, and Burkina Faso.* London: Pinter.

Amadi, Tony. 1971. "A Deep Cry from the Soul of a Blackman." *Daily Times,* March 3, 13.

———. 1976. "Marketing Afrobeat Abroad." *Daily Times,* August 26, p. 27.

Ambrose, Robert. 1997. "The Fallen Giant: Personal Reminiscences of Fela Kuti." *The Beat* 16, no. 5/6:53–59.

Amoda, Moyibi. 1970. "Soul: The Phenomenon of James Brown." *Daily Times,* August 16, pp. 4, 13.

Amore, Sola. 1984. "WAI–Yet Another Foolery?." *Punch,* April 17, p. 8.

Anaba, Eze. 1997. "Fela Goes Off in a Blaze of Glory." *Vanguard,* August 13, p. 2.

Angelou, Maya. 1986. *All God's Children Need Travellin' Shoes.* New York: Random House.

Anikulapo-Kuti, Fela. 1975. "Chief Priest Say: Kalakuta government does not force people . . ." Classified ad from *Daily Times,* August 9, p. 14.

———. 1976a. "Chief Priest Say: If expenses of 80,000 pilgrims . . ." Classified ad from *Daily Times,* January 1, p. 24.

———. 1976b. "Chief Priest Say: Tell the man with the gun . . ." Classified ad from *Daily Times,* March 13, p. 14.

———. 1980. "Chief Priest Say: If you get enemy for town . . ." Classified ad from *Punch,* February 24, p. 13.

———. 1981. "Chief Priest Say: :Let us laugh at our traditional rulers . . ." Classified ad from *Punch,* January 17, p. 13.

———. 1982. "Chief Priest Say: For pope country . . ." Classified ad from *Punch,* February 26, p. 19.

Appiah, Kwame Anthony. 1992. *In My Father's House: Africa in the Philosophy of Culture.* New York: Oxford

Apter, Andrew. 1996. "The Pan-African Nation: Oil-Money and the Spectacle of Culture in Nigeria." *Public Culture* 8:441–66.

Aridegbe, Ademola. 1979. "Fela Charged to Court, 56 Others Arraigned." *Punch,* October 3, p. 1.

Armah, Ayi Kwei. 1968. *The Beautyful Ones Are Not Yet Born.* London: Heinemann.

———. 1971. *Fragments.* New York: Collier.

Arogundade, Fola. 1979a. "Why I'm No Longer Guy Warren." *Punch,* May 12, p. 8.

———. 1979b. "Fela Is as Good as New." *Punch,* June 9, p. 8.

———. 1979c. "Bravo Fela and Congrats!" *Punch,* September 1, p. 8.

———. 1979d. "How Fela Creates His Music." *Punch,* September 23, p. 11.

———. 1979e. "Fela Conquers the Theatre." *Punch,* November 12, p. 1.

———. 1980a. "Christianity Is Obey's New Way of Life," *Punch,* July 12, p. 9.

———. 1980b. "Sunny to Be Ordained an Apostle." *Punch,* October 18, p. 9.

Asante, Molefi Kete. 1988. *Afrocentricity.* Trenton, N.J.: Africa World Press.

Asante-Darko, Nimrod, with Sjaak Van Der Geest. 1983. "Male Chauvinism: Men and Women in Ghanaian Highlife Songs." In *Female and Male in West Africa,* ed. Christine Oppong. London: George Allen and Unwin.

Assante, Ernesto. 1988. "La Rabbia di Fela Kuti." *La Repubblica,* November 18.

Awogbemi, Bayo, and Soji Adelokiki. 1981. "Health Ministry Is Broke." *Punch,* August 5, p. 1.

Ayodeji, Oladipo (Ladi). 1981. "Ghanaian Spiritualists in 'Kill-and-Wake' Show." *Punch,* April 24, p. 6.

———. 1982a. "Fela: There's Jamming in All Fronts." *Punch,* May 1, p. 9.

———. 1982b. "Fela: Countering the Status Quo." *Punch,* May 15, p. 9.

———. 1984. "An Expensive Shit," *Punch,* May 19, p. 8.

Ayonote, Rotimi A. 1997. *Fela Anikulapo-Kuti, Africa's Greatest Musician: An Index to Sources of Information.* Ekpoma: Edo State University Institute of Education.

Ayorinde, Steve. 1997. "Son Ends Mourning, Rules Out AIDS Test." *Guardian,* August 13, p. 1.

Ayu, Iyorchia. 1985. *Creativity and Protest in Popular Culture: The Political Music of Fela Anikulapo-Kuti.* Ife: Nigerian Democratic Review.

Babatunde, Semiu. 1982. "Embargo on New Parties." *Punch,* August 10, p. 1.

Barber, Karin, ed., with Mary-Jo Arnoldi, Frederick Cooper, Donald Cosentino, and Bennetta Jules-Rosette. 1987. "Popular Arts in Africa." *African Studies Review* 30, no. 3 (September):1–331.

Barber, Lynden. 1983. "The Republic of Kuti." *Melody Maker,* December 3, pp.16, 36.

———. 1984. "Live in Amsterdam." *Melody Maker,* May 12, p. 59.

Barbooze, Sol. 1969. "Old Pop Hits Back on the Shelves." *Daily Times,* September 3, p. 7.

Barnes, Jake. 1994. "Invisible Jukebox: Roy Ayers." *Wire,* January, pp. 52–53.

Barrett, Lindsay. 1981. "Fela Conquers Europe." *West Africa,* April 6, pp. 729–31.

———. 1997. "Immortal Power, Musical Vision." *West Africa,* August 18–24, pp. 1331–36.

———. 1998. "Chronicle of a Life Foretold." *Wire,* March, pp. 34–40.

Bebey, Francis. 1975. *African Music: A People's Art.* Westport, Conn.: Lawrence Hill & Co.

Bender, Wolfgang. 1991. *Sweet Mother: Modern African Music.* Chicago: University of Chicago Press.

Ben-Jochanan, Yosef A. A. 1971. *Black Man of the Nile and His Family.* New York: Alkebu-Lan.

Bergman, Billy. 1985. *Goodtime Kings: Emergent African Pop.* New York: Quill.

Bernal, Martin. 1987. *Black Athena: The Afro-Asiatic Roots of Classical Civilization.* New Brunswick, N.J.: Rutgers University Press.

Birnbaum, Larry. 1977. "Zombie." *Downbeat,* June 15, p. 35.

Blake, John. 1981. *All You Needed Was Love: The Beatles after the Beatles.* New York: Perigee.

Block, Robert. 1999. " 'Soldier Go, Soldier Come' Is the Refrain for Jaded Nigerians." *Wall Street Journal,* February 24, p. A1–A6.

Boehm, Mike. 1989. "Nigerian Musician Sees Music as a Tool." *Los Angeles Times,* July.

Boggs, Vernon. 1992. *Salsiology: Afro-Cuban Music and the Evolution of Salsa in New York City.* New York: Excelsior.

Boi, Lei. 1965. "Nigerian Music Goes Modern." *Daily Express,* September 28, p. 4.

Bonuola, Lade. 1975. "The A.B.C. of the Floating Cement." *Daily Times,* October 26, p. 14.

Bozimo, Willy. 1976a. "Countdown on Festac '77." *Daily Times,* May 1, p. 16.

———. 1976b. "National Theatre: A Symbol of Our Cultural Awareness." *Daily Times,* September 30, p. 20.

Brackett, David. 1992. "James Brown's 'Superbad' and the Double-Voiced Utterance." *Popular Music* 11, no. 3.

Brown, Elaine. 1993. *A Taste of Power.* New York: Pantheon.

Brown, James, and Bruce Tucker. 1986. *James Brown: The Godfather of Soul.* New York: Macmillan.

Brown, Len. 1986. "The Great Pretender." *New Musical Express,* October 25, pp. 28, 29, 34.

Bwala, H. M. 1979. " 'Suffering and Smiling': Credit to a Great Musician." Letter published in *Punch,* December 28.

Carby, Hazel. 1998. *Race Men.* Cambridge: Harvard University Press.

Carducci, Joe. 1994. *Rock and the Pop Narcotic: Testament for the Electric Church.* Los Angeles: 2.13.61.

Cartey, Wilfred and Martin Kilson. 1970. *The Africa Reader: Independent Africa.* New York: Random House.

Charters, Samuel. 1981. *The Roots of the Blues: An African Search.* London: Marion Boyars.

Chernoff, John M.. 1979. *African Rhythm and African Sensibility.* Chicago: University of Chicago Press.

———. 1984. "The Artistic Challenge of African Music: Thoughts on the Absence of Drum Orchestras in Black American Music." *Black Music Research Journal,* Spring, pp. 1–19.

Cheyney, Tom. 1986. "Fela Is Free: Nigerian Bandleader Released from Prison." *Reggae and African Beat* 3:9, 48.

Chinwezu. 1988. *Voices from Twentieth Century Africa: Griots and Towncriers.* London: Faber and Faber.

Chukwuike, Longinus. 1986. "Fela Extra." *African Guardian Supplement,* April 27, p. B2.

Cleaver, Eldridge. 1967. *Soul on Ice.* New York: McGraw-Hill.

Clifford, James. 1988. *The Predicament of Culture.* Cambridge: Harvard University Press.

Collins, John. 1978. "Sixty Years of West African Popular Music." *West Africa,* October 16, pp. 2041–44.

———. 1985. *Musicmakers of West Africa.* Washington, D.C.: Three Continents Press.

———. 1987. "Jazz Feedback to Africa." *American Music,* Summer, pp. 176–93.

———. 1992. *West African Pop Roots.* Philadelphia: Temple University Press.

———. 1998. "Fela and the Black President Film." *Glendora Review* 2, no. 2:57–73.

Collins, John, and Paul Richards. 1982. "Popular Music in West Africa: Suggestions for an Interpretive Framework." In *Popular Music Perspectives*. Exeter: International Association for the Study of Popular Music.

———. 1989. "Popular Music in West Africa." In *World Music, Politics and Social Change,* edited by Simon Frith. Manchester, U.K.: Manchester University Press.

Comaroff, Jean, and John Comaroff. 1991. *Of Revelation and Revolution: Christianity, Colonialism and Consciousness in South Africa.* Chicago: University of Chicago Press.

Conrath, Phillippe. 1986a. "Fela, roi de l'arene." *Liberation,* October 13–September 14, pp. 34, 35.

———. 1986b. "Fela Descend Dans L'Arene." *Liberation,* September 11, p. 45.

Coombs, Orde, ed. 1974. *Is Massa Day Dead? Black Moods in the Caribbean.* New York: Anchor Books.

Corbett, John. 1994. *Extended Play: Sounding Off from John Cage to Dr. Funkenstein.* Durham, N.C.: Duke University Press.

Crossette, Barbara. 1997. "Survey Ranks Nigeria as Most Corrupt Nation." *New York Times,* August 3, p. 3.

Darnton, John. 1976. "Afrobeat, New Music with a New Message." *New York Times,* July 7, p. 42.

———. 1977a. "Nigerian Soldiers Burn Home of a Dissident Musician." *New York Times,* February 20, p. 3.

———. 1977b. "Nigeria Arrests, Then Expels the Times' West Africa Correspondent." *New York Times,* March 14, p. 3.

———. 1977c. "Nigeria's Dissident Superstar." *New York Times,* July 24, pp. 10–12, 22–24, 26, 28.

Davidson, Basil. 1989. *Black Star: A View of the Life and Times of Kwame Nkruma.* Boulder, Colo.: Westview Press.

———. 1992. *The Black Man's Burden: Africa and the Curse of the Nation State.* New York: Times Books.

Davis, Miles, with Quincy Troupe. 1990. *Miles: The Autobiography.* New York: Simon and Schuster.

Davis, Stephen. 1983. *Bob Marley.* Garden City, N.Y.: Doubleday.

Debekeme, Zee-Tei. 1978. "Kalakuta Falls." *Punch,* October 30, p. 1.

Delano, Isaac. 1942. *The Singing Minister of Nigeria.* London: United Society for Christian Literature.

Dennis, Ferdi. 1983. "London Greets a Musical Invasion." *West Africa,* December 19–26.

Denselow, Robin. 1997. "The Last Days of Fela Kuti." http://web.sn.apc.org/wmail/issues/970808

Diawara, Manthia. 1992a. *African Cinema: Politics and Culture.* Bloomington: Indiana University Press.

———. 1992b. "Afro-Kitsch." In *Black Popular Culture,* ed. Gina Dent. Seattle: Bay Press.

Diop, Cheikh Anta. 1974. *The African Origin of Civilization: Myth or Reality?* New York: Lawrence Hill & Co.

Dorgu, Victor. 1968a. "Boogaloo." *Daily Times,* February 4, p. 3.

———. 1968b. "Are the Youngsters Taking Over?" *Daily Times,* July 28, p. 10.

———. 1968c. "The Uhuru Touch." *Daily Times,* October 6, p. 10.

———. 1968d. "I Give Up Soul Music, Says Fela." *Daily Times,* August 4, p. 4.

———. 1968e. "Fela Drops Highlife." *Daily Times,* August 18, p. 6.

———. 1968f. "When Afro-Beat Meets Soul." *Daily Times,* September 1, p. 4.

———. 1969a. "Cold Sweat!" *Sunday Times,* March 9, p. 8.

———. 1969b. "Afro-Beat Gets a New Home." *Daily Times,* April 1, p. 5.

———. 1969c. "Soul Fever in the City." *Daily Times,* December 14, p. 3.

———. 1970. "To Hell and Back." *Daily Times,* April 5, p. 8.

Douglas, Mary. 1966. *Purity and Danger: An Analysis of the Concepts of Pollution and Taboo.* London: Routledge.

Drachler, Jacob. 1975. *Black Homeland, Black Diaspora.* Port Washington, N.Y.: Kennikat Press.

Drewal, Henry. 1988. "Performing the Other: Mami Wata Worship in West Africa." *Drama Review* 32, no. 2 (Summer):160–85.

———. 1989. *Yoruba: Nine Centuries of African Art and Thought.* New York: Center for African Art.

Ekpo, Eyo. 1982. *Art Treasures of Ancient Nigeria.* New York: Alfred A. Knopf.

Ekwensi, Cyprian. 1961. *Jagua Nana.* London: Heinemann.

Erlmann, Veit. 1991. *African Stars: Studies in Black South African Performance.* Chicago: University of Chicago Press.

Eshun, Kodwo. 1994. "Soundcheck: The 1969 Los Angeles Sessions." *Wire,* January, p. 78.

Ette, Mercy. 1994. "The Man Died." *Newswatch,* August 8, pp. 29–35.

Euba, Akin. 1967. "Islamic Musical Culture among the Yoruba: A Preliminary Survey." In *Essays on Music and History in Africa,* ed. Klaus Wachsman. Evanston, Ill.: Northwestern University Press.

———. 1988. *Essays on Music in Africa.* Bayreuth, Ger.: Iwalewa-Haus (University of Bayreuth).

Ewens, Graeme. 1991. *Africa Oye! A Celebration of African Music.* New York: Da Capo.

———. 1995. *Congo Colossus: The Life and Legacy of Franco and OK Jazz.* Norfolk, U.K.: Buku Press.

Ezenekwe, Arthur. 1978. "Fela Kicked Out of Ghana." *Daily Times*. March 3, 1978, p. 32.

Fadugba, Nick. 1979a. "Fela Flays *Times:* Defends His Music and Politics." *Daily Times,* September 29, p. 7.

———. 1979b. "Fela: I Wanted to Be Great." *Daily Times,* October 6, p. 12

Fairfax, Frank Thurmond, III. 1993. "Fela, the Afrobeat King: Popular Music and Cultural Revitalization in West Africa." Ph.D. dissertation, University of Michigan.

Falola, Toyin, ed. 1991. *Yoruba Historiography*. Madison: University of Wisconsin Press.

Falola, Toyin, and Julius Ihonvbere. 1985. *The Rise and Fall of Nigeria's Second Republic: 1979–1984*. London: Zed.

Famuyibo, Ranti. 1981. "How N55m FESTAC Money Evaporated." *Punch,* May 15, p. 2.

Fanio, Eppi. 1998. "Rethinking Fela." http://ntama.uni-mainz.de/~ntama/main/fanio/

Fanon, Frantz. 1963.*The Wretched of the Earth*. New York: Grove Press.

Fara, C.. 1986. "Fela Fete." *Telerama,* September 10, p. 44, 45.

———. 1992. "Fela: le grand retour." *Jeune Afrique,* November 19–25, p. 15.

Flynn, Dorothy. 1999. "Mzwakhe Mbuli: Hard Times Just Got Harder for South Africa's People's Poet." *The Beat* 18, no. 3:64–65.

Forde, Darryl. 1951. *The Yoruba-Speaking Peoples of South-Western Nigeria*. London: International African Institute.

Forrest, Tom. 1993. *Politics and Economic Development in Nigeria*. Boulder, Colo.: Westview Press.

Fosu-Mensah, Kwabena, et al. 1987. "Musical Activity in West Africa." *African Affairs,* April.

Francis, Miller. 1985. "Fela: The Struggle Continues." *Reggae and African Beat* 4, no. 6 (February): 12.

———. 1986. "Fela Speaks." *Southline,* September 3.

French, Howard W. 1998. "Dread Rules: An Unpopular Leader Leaves Nigerians Fearful and Divided." *New York Times,* June 9, p. A10.

Frith, Simon, ed. 1989. *World Music, Politics and Social Change*. Manchester, U.K.: Manchester University Press.

Frith, Simon, and Goodwin, Andrew, eds. 1990. *On Record: Rock, Pop and the Written Word*. New York: Pantheon

Furniss, Graham, and Liz Gunner, eds. 1995. *Power, Marginality, and African Oral Literature*. Cambridge: Cambridge University Press.

Gadjigo, Samba, with Ralph Faulkingham, Thomas Cassirer, and Reinhard Sander. 1993. *Ousmane Sembene: Dialogues with Critics and Writers*. Amherst, Mass.: Five Colleges.

Garafalo, Reebee. 1992. *Rockin' the Boat: Mass Music and Mass Movements*. Boston: South End Press.

Gates, Henry Louis. 1995. "Kernel of Light." *New Republic,* December 18, pp. 12, 13.

Geertz, Clifford. 1973. *Interpretation of Cultures*. New York: Basic Books.

Gilroy, Paul. 1993a. *The Black Atlantic: Modernity and Double Consciousness*. Cambridge: Harvard University Press.

———. 1993b. *Small Acts: Thoughts on the Politics of Black Cultures*. London: Serpent's Tail.

Goldman, Vivien. 1980. "The Rascal Republic Takes on the World." *New Musical Express,* October 18, pp. 6, 7, 8.

———. 1984. "Resurrection Shuffle." *New Musical Express,* January 14, p. 3.

Goodwill, Clayton. 1998. "Hard Times for African Prostitutes in Europe." *New African,* February, pp. 36–38.

Graham, Ronnie. 1988. *Da Capo Guide to Contemporary African Music*. New York: Da Capo.

———. 1992. *Stern's Guide to African Music, Volume 2*. London: Pluto.

Gramsci, Antonio. 1971. *Selections from the Prison Notebooks*. New York: International.

Grass, Randall F. 1982. "Bongoes and the Groovies: On the Road with a Nigerian Rock Band." *Musician,* October, pp. 70–74.

———. 1983. "Fela: Return of the Afrobeat Rebel." *Musician,* October, pp. 24, 26, 28, 30.

———. 1984. "Fela Anikulapo-Kuti: Still Suffering." *Reggae and African Beat,* December, p. 15.

———. 1985. "Fela: Rebel on Ice." *Spin,* May, pp. 37, 38, 39, 73.

———. 1986a. "Fela Anikulapo Kuti: The Art of an Afrobeat Rebel." *Drama Review,* Spring, pp. 131–48.

———. 1986b. "Fela Freed." *Spin,* July, pp. 63, 64, 65.

Griot. 1970. "Soul and Highlife." *West Africa,* April 18, p. 425.

Guralnick, Peter. 1986. *Sweet Soul Music: Rhythm-and-Blues and the Southern Dream of Freedom*. New York: Harper & Row.

Gurnah, Abdulrazak. 1993. *Essays on African Writing: An Evaluation*. Oxford: Heinemann.

Haastrup, Kehinde. 1979a. "Surulere Nightclub Goes Discotheque." *Punch,* June 3, p. 3.

———. 1979b. "Fela Preaches again at New Shrine." *Punch,* August 30, p. 8.

————. 1979c. "Fela: My Mama Lives." *Punch,* September 20, p. 7.

Hadjor, Kofi. 1992. *Dictionary of Third World Terms.* London: Penguin.

Hale, Thomas. 1998. *Griots and Griottes: Masters of Word and Music.* Bloomington: Indiana University Press.

Hall, Stuart. 1990. "Cultural Identity and Diaspora." In *Identity: Community, Culture, Difference,* ed. Jonathan Rutherford. London: Lawrence & Wishart.

Hall, Stuart, and Jefferson, Tony, eds. 1976. *Resistance through Rituals: Youth Subcultures in Postwar Britain.* London: Harper Collins Academic.

Harrington, Richard. 1986. "Fela Kuti and the Chords of Africa." *Washington Post,* November 7, pp. C1–C2.

Harrison, Daphne D. 1985. "Aesthetics and Social Aspects of Music in African Ritual Settings." In *More Than Drumming,* ed. Irene V. Jackson. Westport, Conn.: Greenwood Press.

Harvey, Steve, and Fareed Armaly. 1988. "Maceo Parker/Fred Wesley Interview." *Terminal Zone,* no. 1:21–30.

Hebdige, Dick. 1979. *Subculture: The Meaning of Style.* London: Routledge.

Hecht, David. 1999. "A Son Builds on His Father's Afro-Beat and Politics." *New York Times,* July 28, p. E2.

Hernton, Calvin, and Terisa Turner. 1978. "Music and Politics in Nigeria: Does Musician Fela Pose a Threat to the Nigerian Status Quo?" *Essence,* July, pp. 54, 79, 83–84, 86, 88, 91, 93–94.

Herszenhorn, David. 1997. "Fela, 58, Dissident Nigerian Musician, Dies." *New York Times,* August 4, p. D12.

Hewan-Lowe, Lister. 1986 "Fela Anikulapo-Kuti." *WUSB Program Guide* 3, no. 1 (Fall).

Highet, Juliet. 1977. "FESTAC." In *Traveller's Guide to Africa.* 2d ed. Letchworth, U.K.: Garden City Press.

————. 1989. "When Music Becomes a Weapon." *New African,* September, pp. 41–42.

Hilliard, David. 1993. *This Side of Glory.* New York: Little Brown.

Howe, John. 1986. "Fela . . . Rampant." *West Africa,* July 14, p. 1475.

Howe, Stephen. 1998. *Afrocentricity.* London: Verso.

Ibe, Paul, and Udo Silas. 1997. "I Don't Want to Be Another Fela." *THISDAY,* August 16, pp. 26–28.

Ibeji, Ikechi. 1984. "Egypt 80 Minus Fela for the Yankees." *Punch,* October 6, p. 8.

Ibironke, Dare. 1979. "Afrika Shrine Opens." *Punch,* August 28, p. s1.

Idemudia, Fidelis, and Elizabeth Abode. 1997. *The Death Funeral Ceremony of Fela Anikulapo-Kuti: A Bibliography.* Ekpoma: Edo State University Institute of Education.

Idika, Joe, and Steve Ajulo. 1997. "For Fela, Law and Order on Break for Two Days." *The Guardian,* August 14, p. 17.

Idonije, Benson. 1997. "Why Fela Went for the Military Interview." *The Guardian,* August 16, p. 19.

————. 1999. "Koola Lobitos . . . The Beauty of Melody." *The Guardian,* October 13.

Idowu, E. Bolaji. 1962. *Olodumare: God in Yoruba Belief.* London: Longmans.

Idowu, Mabinuori Kayode. 1986. *Fela: Why Blackman Carry Shit.* Ikeja, Nigeria: Opinion Media Limited.

Ihonvbere, Julius O. 1994. *Nigeria: The Politics of Adjustment and Democracy.* New Bruswick, N.J., and London: Transaction.

Iloegbunam, Chuks. 1998. "Abiola's Shock Death." *West Africa,* July 6–26, pp. 584–85.

Iorio, Paul. 1986. "Fela Vows Continued Opposition to Oppression." *Cashbox,* June.

Jacobs, Dan. 1987. *The Brutality of Nations.* New York: Alfred A. Knopf.

James, Darius. 1995. *That's Blaxploitation!* New York: St. Martin's Press.

Jameson, Fredric. 1986. "Third-World Literature in the Age of Multinational Capitalism." *Social Text* 4 (Fall): 65–88.

Jenkins, David. 1975. *Black Zion: Africa, Imagined and Real, As Seen by Today's Blacks.* New York: Harcourt Brace Jovanovich.

Jenkins, Ron. 1994. *Subversive Laughter: The Liberating Power of Comedy.* New York: Free Press.

Johnson, Rotimi. 1985. "The Language and Content of Nigerian Popular Music." In *Perspectives on African Music,* ed. Wolfgang Bender. Bayreuth, Ger.: African Studies Series.

Johnson-Odim, Cheryl. 1986. "Class and Gender: Yoruba Women in the Colonial Period." In *Women and Class in Africa,* ed. Claire Robertson and Iris Berger. New York: Africana.

————. 1995. "On Behalf of Women and the Nation." In *Expanding the Boundaries of Women's History,* ed. Cheryl Johnson-Odim and Margaret Strobel. Bloomington: Indiana University Press.

Johnson-Odim, Cheryl, and Nina Mba. 1997. *For Women and the Nation: Funmilayo Ransome-Kuti of Nigeria.* Urbana and Chicago: University of Illinois Press.

Johnson, Tom. 1989. *The Voice of New Music.* Netherlands: Het Apollohuis.

Johnson, Rev. Samuel. 1921. *History of the Yorubas.* Norfolk, U.K.: Lowe & Brydone Ltd.

Jones, Andrew. 1989. "I Fought the Law." *Montreal Mirror,* July 14.

Jones, Keziah. 1996. "Chief Priest." *True,* July–August, pp. 56–58.

Kaufman, Michael T. 1998. "Sani Abacha, 54, a Beacon of Brutality in an Era When Brutality Was Standard." *New York Times,* June 9, p. A10.

Keil, Charles. 1979. *Tiv Song.* Chicago: University of Chicago Press.

Kennedy, Jean. 1992. *New Currents, Ancient Rivers: Contemporary African Artists in a Generation of Change.* Washington, D.C.: Smithsonian Institution Press.

Kilby, Jack. 1983. "Fela Is Playing It Cool Now." *West Africa,* November 19–26, pp. 2934–36.

———. 1985a. "Master of Afrobeat." *West Africa,* January 28, p. 150.

———. 1985b. "His Own Worst Enemy." *West Africa,* November 4, p. 2311.

Kirk-Greene, Anthony, and Douglas Rimmer. 1981. *Nigeria since 1970: A Political and Economic Outline.* New York: Africana.

Kofsky, Frank. 1970. *Black Nationalism and the Revolution in Music.* New York: Pathfinder.

Kostakis, Peter. 1988. "Continental Drift and Pop." *Downbeat,* January, p. 26.

Kruse, Holly. 1993. "Subcultural Identity in Alternative Music Culture." *Popular Music* 12, no. 1:12–31.

Kuti, Fela Anikulapo. 1989. "Protest Over the Illegal Cancellation of My Concert at Abeokuta." Open letter to President Ibrahim Babangida. April 14.

Labinjoh, Justin. 1982. "Fela Anikulapo-Kuti: Protest Music and Social Processes in Nigeria." *Journal of Black Studies* 13, no. 1 (September): 119–35.

Lawal, Ayodele. 1999. "Fela's Estate Shared." http:/www.africanews.org

Lawal, Babatunde. 1996. *The Gelede Spectacle.* Seattle: University of Washington Press.

Leymarie, Isabelle. 1978. "The Role and Fucntions of the Griots among the Wolof of Senegal." Ph.D. dissertation, Columbia University.

Lupton, Kenneth. 1979. *Mungo Park: The African Traveler.* Oxford: Oxford University Press.

Maduneme, Alphonsus, and Laja Akindele. 1978. "Fela to Marry 27 Women." *Daily Times,* February 6, 1978, p. 40.

Malcolm X (with Alex Haley). 1965. *The Autobiography of Malcolm X.* New York: Grove Press.

———. 1989. *The Last Speeches.* New York: Pathfinder.

———. 1992. *February 1965: The Final Speeches.* New York: Pathfinder.

Manuel, Peter. 1988. *Popular Musics of the Non-Western World.* Oxford: Oxford University Press.

May, Chris. 1977. "Music Written in Blood: Fela Anikulapo-Kuti, the Afro-Rock Giant They Cannot Silence." *Black Music,* May 1977, pp. 22–25.

———. 1983. "Shuffering and Shmiling." *Black Music and Jazz Review,* November, pp. 14–16.

Mba, Nina Emma. 1982. *Nigerian Women Mobilized.* Berkeley: Institute of International Studies.

Mbachu, Dulue. 1989. "Fela's Growing Fellowship." *West Africa,* December 11–17, 2081.

McFadden, Robert. 1998. "Nigeria Dictator Dies after 5 Years of Ruthless Rule." *New York Times,* June 9, pp. A1, A10.

McLane, Daisann. 1986. "Power Show." *Village Voice,* November 25, pp. 73, 74.

Merriam, Alan. 1964. *The Anthropology of Music.* Evanston, Ill.: Northwestern University Press.

Milkowski, Bill. 1983. "Caught: King Sunny Ade." *Downbeat,* May, p. 50.

———. 1995. *Jaco: The Extraordinary and Tragic Life of Jaco Pastorius.* San Francisco: Miller Freeman Books.

Miller, Jim. 1985. "Rocking All the Way to Jail." *Newsweek,* July 15, p. 67.

Milne, June. 1990. *Nkrumah: The Conakry Years.* London: Panaf.

Molokwu, Azuka. 1989. "Fela Speaks on Music and Marriage." *African Connection,* July 28, 7–11. First appeared in *Punch,* November 1987.

Monson, Ingrid. 1999. "Riffs, Repetition, and Theories of Globalization." *Ethnomusicology* 34, no. 1:31–65

Moore, Carlos. 1982. *Fela, Fela: This Bitch of a Life.* London: Allison & Busby.

Moore, Carlos, with Sylviane Kamara. 1981. "Fela: La Musique, Mes Femmes, Et La C.I.A." *Jeune Afrique,* March 18, p. 65–73.

Moore, Gerald, ed. 1980. *Twelve African Writers.* Bloomington: Indiana University Press.

Morgan, Mac. 1969a. "A First for Fela." *Daily Times,* August 27, p. 9.

———. 1969b. "Has the Organ a Place in Juju Music?" *Daily Times,* October 22, p. 7.

———. 1970a. "Tunde the Night Bird Sings New Hit Successes." *Daily Times,* February 18, p. 8.

———. 1970b. "Split Is the Bane of Our Musicians." *Daily Times,* September 9, p. 10.

———. 1970c. "Fans Eagerly Await James Brown Shows." *Daily Times,* November 25, p. 12.

———. 1970d. "It Wasn't a Bad Year for Music." *Daily Times,* December 23, p. 13.

———. 1971a. "The Groups That Caused a Musical Revolution." *Daily Times,* March 10, p. 13.

————. 1971b. "A Rich Feast of Big Musical Events Ahead." *Daily Times,* March 24, p. 15.

————. 1971c. "Is This an Invasion of Entertainment by Women Artistes?." *Daily Times,* May 12, p. 11.

Mudimbe, V. Y. 1988. *The Invention of Africa: Gnosis, Philosophy, and the Order of Knowledge.* Bloomington: Indiana University Press.

Navarro, Mireya. 1994. "Politics with the Beat of the Bronx." *New York Times,* June 25, pp. 25, 29.

Neal, Larry. 1987. "The Social Background of the Black Arts Movement." *Black Scholar* 1, no. 1:19.

N'Djehoya, Blaise. 1986. "Le Fete A Fela." *Le Matin,* October 13.

Ndibe, Okey. 1988. "Madness As Virtue." *African Guardian,* October 17, p. 28.

————. 1995. "Movement for African Unity." *West Africa,* August 28–September 3, pp. 1353–55.

Newsome, Rachel. 1999. "Fela's Son Proves He's a Political Force Too." http:/www.mg.co.za/mg/news/99apr1/13apr-kuti.html

Nisenson, Eric. 1993. *Ascension: John Coltrane and His Quest.* New York: St. Martin's Press.

Niven, Sir Rex. 1970. *The War of Nigerian Unity.* Totowa, N.J.: Rowman & Littlefield.

Nketia, J. H. Kwabena. 1974. *The Music of Africa.* New York: Norton.

Nkrumah, Kwame. 1957. *Ghana: The Autobiography of Kwame Nkrumah.* London: Thomas Nelson & Sons.

————. 1963. *Africa Must Unite.* New York: International Publishers.

————. 1965. *Neo-Colonialism: The Last Stage of Capitalism.* New York: International.

————. 1968. *Dark Days in Ghana.* New York: New World Press.

————. 1970. *Class Struggle in Africa.* London: Panaf.

Nnite, Chukwujindu. 1977. "Carvers That Deserve a Handshake." *Daily Times,* January 20, p. 16.

Noble, Kenneth. 1993. "Nigerian Star Blames Politics for Murder Charge." *New York Times,* August 15, p. A2.

Nunley, John. 1987. *Moving with the Face of the Devil: Art and Politics in Urban West Africa.* Urbana: University of Illinois Press.

————. 1988. "Purity and Pollution in Freetown Masked Performance." *Drama Review* 32, no. 2 (Summer): 102–22.

Nwaobi, John. 1989. "Beauty and the Beast." *African Guardian,* May 15, p. 37.

————. 1990. "Taking On the Guns." *African Guardian,* January 1, p. 33.

Obadina, Tunde, with Olusoji Akinrade. 1982. "The Man Who Would Be King." *Punch,* May 5–7, pp. 12–13.

Obatala, J. K. 1971. "Soul Music in Africa: Has Charlie Got a Brand New Bag?" *Black Scholar* 20 (February): 8–12 .

Obideyi, Emmanuel. 1977a. "Doctor Gets Ten Years for Hemp." *Daily Times,* March 19, p. 32.

————. 1977b. "Fela Spent 17 Days in Hospital." *Daily Times,* February 10, p. 2.

Odiari, Felix. 1976. "Congestion Threatens Airport." *Daily Times,* January 31, p. 32.

Odunaike, Wole. 1977. "Why I Was Beaten Up." *Daily Times,* March 9, pp. 1, 24.

Odunfa, Sola. 1965. "Fela Infuses New Life into Highlife." *Daily Express,* September 23, p. 5.

————. 1968. "Mrs. Funmilayo Kuti, Crusader for Rights of Women." *Daily Times,* February 10, p. 5.

————. 1969. "How Do They Take Out Our Currency?." *Daily Times,* June 9, p. 5.

————. 1970a. "Screaming Sandra Isn't Just a Political Extremist." *Daily Times,* October 13, p. 11.

————. 1970b. " 'I Feel at Home in Lagos'–James Brown." *Daily Times,* November 30, pp. 1, 5.

————. 1970c. "Soul Power Thrills Lagos Crowds." *Daily Times,* December 2, p. 24.

Oduyoye, Mercy Amba. 1995. *Daughters of Anowa.* Maryknoll, N.Y.: Orbis Books.

Ofili, C. N. 1979. " 'Suffering and Smiling'–Do You Dance to Mock Yourself?" Letter Published in *Punch,* June 9, p. 4.

Ogunnaike, Bayo. 1978. "Fela Blasts the Press." *Punch,* December 9, p. 1.

Ogunsanwo, Femi. 1978. "More Food for the People, Says Hopeful Fela." *Daily Times,* December 23.

Okoruwa, Gloria, and Festus Ishiekwene. 1997. *The Death of Fela Anikulapo-Kuti, the Afro-Beat: A Bibliography.* Ekpoma: Edo State University Department of Library Science.

Okpalaeke, Declan, with Ebere Ahanihu, Remi-Edward Adebiyi, and Muyiwa Adeyemi. 1997. "Escorting the Legend Home." *The Guardian,* August 16, pp. 10–12.

Okpewho, Isidore. 1992. *African Oral Literature: Backgrounds, Character, and Continuity.* Bloomington: Indiana University Press.

Okri, Ben. 1982. "Living Legend." *West Africa,* November 29, pp. 3091–94.

Okutubo, Taiwo. 1976. "Why Fela Won't Serve." *Daily Times,* October 13, p. 1.

Okwechime, Ndubuisi. 1986a. "And the Music Played Again." *This Week,* September 22, pp. 36–38.

————. 1986b. "A Challenger for Daddy's Throne." *This Week,* September 22, p. 39.

Oladinni, Victor. 1997. "The Legend Lives On." *Tell,* August 18, pp. 48–49.

Olaniyan, Richard, ed. 1985. *Nigerian History and Culture.* Essex, U.K.: Longman's,

Olarunyomi, Sola. 1994. "The One Who Never Dies." *West Africa,* June 6–12, p. 1002.

Oliver, Paul, ed. 1990. *Black Music in Britain: Essays on the Afro-Asian Contribution to Popular Music.* Philadelphia: Open University Press.

Olowo, Bola. 1998. "The Drugs War." *West Africa,* February 16–22, pp. 228–29.

Omoifo, Ifi. 1989. "Living without the Bench." *African Guardian,* January 16, pp. 8–9.

Omosanya, Biodun. 1978. "Government Urged to Compensate Fela." *Daily Times,* February 11, 1978, p. 32.

Omotoso, Kole. 1971. *The Edifice.* London: Heinemann.

Onuorah, Madu. 1997. "Fela Attempted to Join the Army, Says Defence Spokesman." *The Guardian,* August 13, p. 1.

Oppong, Christine, ed. 1983. *Female and Male in West Africa.* London: Allen & Unwin.

Oroh, Abdul. 1988. "I'm Still Scratching the Surface." *African Guardian,* October 17, pp. 20–23.

Oroh, Abdul, with Debo Adesina, John Nwaobi, Dili Ojukwu Chinweoke Oluha, and Humphrey Bekaren. 1988. "Fela, Just Fela." *African Guardian,* October 17, pp. 17, 18, 24, 25, 26.

Othman, Shehu. 1997. "Power for Profit: Class, Corporatism, and Factionalism in the Military." In *Contemporary West African States,* ed. Donal O'Brien, John Dunn, and Richard Rathbone. Cambridge: Cambridge University Press.

Oumano, Elena. 1989. "Fela Honors James Brown at Apollo Benefit." *City Sun,* August 2–8, p. 19.

Oyelude, Dosu. 1970. "Nigerian Musicians on the War Path." *Daily Times,* October 18, pp. 3, 8.

Pareles, Jon. 1986a. "Fela Anikulapo-Kuti, Nigeria's Musical Activist." *New York Times,* November 7, p. C23.

———. 1986b. "Fela Anikulapo Kuti's Afrobeat." *New York Times,* November 10, p. C18.

———. 1991. "Fela Spreads the Word in Song and Sermon at the Apollo." *New York Times,* July 26, p. C17.

p'Bitek, Okot. 1969. *Song of Lawino: An African Lament.* New York: Meridian.

Peil, Margaret. 1991. *Lagos: The City Is the People.* Boston: G. K. Hall & Co.

Pemberton, John, and Funso Afolayan. 1996. *Yoruba Sacred Kingship.* Washington, D.C.: Smithsonian Institution Press.

Peretu, Thomas. 1991. "Fela Makes Love Three Hours Daily." *Lagos Weekend,* April 5, p. 1.

Pye, Ian. 1983. "Alive." *Melody Maker,* November 19, p. 20.

Radano, Ronald. 1993. *New Musical Figurations: Anthony Braxton's Cultural Critique.* Chicago: University of Chicago Press.

Reese, Jerome. 1986. "Bill Laswell." *Musician,* December, pp. 85–88, 112, 130.

Rieff, David. 1997. "The Threat of Death." *New Republic,* June 16, p. 33–41.

Roberts, John Storm. 1979. *The Latin Tinge: The Impact of Latin American Music on the United States.* London: Oxford.

Robinson, Cedric. 1983. *Black Marxism: The Making of the Black Radical Tradition.* London: Zed.

———. 1998. "Blaxploitation and the Misrepresentation of Liberation." *Race and Class* 40, no. 1 (July–September): 1–12.

Rodney, Walter. 1982. *How Europe Underdeveloped Africa.* Washington, D.C.: Howard University Press.

Romeo, Noemi. 1989. "L'Africa del grande Fela Kuti incanta i giovani torinesi." *Stampasera,* July 5, p. 4.

Rose, Cynthia. 1990. *Living in America: The Soul Saga of James Brown.* London: Serpent's Tale.

Rose, Tricia. 1994. *Black Noise: Rap Music and Black Culture in Contemporary America.* Hanover, N.H.: University Press of New England.

Rotibi, Bayo. 1977. "Boost to Nigeria's Ego." *Daily Times,* January 4, pp. 1, 5.

Rukari, Zeeky. 1968. "Lobitos Have a New Sound." *Sunday Times,* June 30, p. 11.

Rumsey, Spencer. 1986. "I Want Something for the World." *Ear,* June–July, pp. 10–12.

———. 1989. "The Beat of Dissent." *New York Newsday,* July 28, p. 2–3, 7.

Sakolsky, Ron. 1996. "Femi Kuti: The Positive Force." *The Beat* 15, no. 2:42– 45.

Salamon, Frank. 1991. "Africa as a Metaphor of Authenticity in Jazz." *Studies in Third World Societies* 46 (December):1–20.

Sales, William W. 1994. *From Civil Rights to Black Liberation: Malcolm X and the Organization of Afro-American Unity.* Boston: South End Press.

Salisu, Dale. 1979. "Lagos Night Life Is No Longer High." *Punch,* August 18, p. 9.

Sankure, Rotimi. 1993. "Fela's Song of Praise." *African Guardian,* January 25, p. 38.

Santoro, Gene. 1987. "Caught: Fela." *Downbeat,* March, p. 52.

Sanya, Paul. 1970. "What Power Means to the Black Man." *Daily Times,* October 9, p. 7.

Saro-Wiwa, Ken. 1989. *On a Darkling Plain: An Account of the Nigerian Civil War.* London: Saros International.

————. 1992 "Nigeria Is an Ungodly Society." *African Guardian,* October 5, p. 22.

————. 1995. *A Month and A Day: A Detention Diary.* New York: Penguin.

Sciolino, Elaine. 1998. "With Nigeria's Military Ruler Dead, Concern Is Voiced for the Fate of His Jailed Foe." *New York Times,* June 9, p. A10:

Semenitari, Ibim. 1997. "My Life with Fela." *Tell,* August 18, pp. 40–42.

Shoyombo, Yomi, and Tajudeen Edun. 1983. "2.2 Million Aliens out of Nigeria." *Punch,* March 25, p. 1.

Simpkins, Cuthbert. 1975. *Coltrane: A Biography.* Philadelphia: Herndon House.

Sinker, Mark. 1986. "Lagos Jumping" (concert review). *New Musical Express,* December.

————. 1993. "Invisible Jukebox: Pee Wee Ellis." *Wire,* September, pp. 44–45.

Slobin, Mark. 1993. *Subcultural Sounds: Micromusics of the West.* Hanover, N.H.: University Press of New England.

Small, Christopher. 1987. *Music of the Common Tongue: Survival and Celebration in African-American Music.* New York: Riverrun.

Smith, Jennifer B. 1999. *An International History of the Black Panther Party.* New York: Garland Publishing.

Smith, Robert S. 1988. *Kingdoms of the Yoruba.* Madison: University of Wisconsin Press.

Snowden, Don. 1984. "Fela's Last Phone Call." *The Beat,* December, pp. 12–14.

————. 1986. "Controversial Kuti: He's Philosopher, Rebel, and Passionate Musician." *Los Angeles Times,* November 12, pp. 1, 6.

Sotunde, Iyabo. 1997. "Wives Absent at Burial." *The Guardian,* August 13, p. 3.

Soyinka, Wole. 1965. *The Road.* London: Oxford University Press.

————. 1976. *Myth, Literature, and the African World.* Cambridge: Cambridge University Press.

————. 1981. *Ake: Years of Childhood.* London: Rex Collings Ltd.

————. 1988. *Art, Dialogue, and Outrage: Essays Literature and Culture.* Ibadan: New Horn Press.

————. 1995. *The Beatification of Area Boy.* London: Methuen.

————. 1996. *The Open Sore of a Continent.* London: Oxford University Press.

Sparks, Samantha. 1986. "Fela on the Move." *West Africa,* November 24, pp. 2456–57.

Spivak, Gayatri Chakravorty. 1985. "Can the Subaltern Speak? Speculations on Widow Sacrifice." *Wedge,* Winter/Spring.

Stacy, Marilyn, and Karen McIlvaine. 1982. *ECOWAS: Select Readings, 1975–1981.* New York: African Development Information Association.

Standley, Fred, and Louis Pratt, eds. 1989. *Conversations with James Baldwin.* Jackson: University Press of Mississippi.

Stapleton, Chris, and Chris May. 1987. *African All-Stars: The Pop Music of a Continent.* London: Quartet.

Steffens, Roger. 1984. "Ras Rojah." *The Beat,* December, 39–41.

————. 1986a. "Fela: Revolution and Evolution." *Reggae Times,* May–June, pp. 8–9.

————. 1986b. "Free at Last: Now That the Nightmare Is Over, Fela Has a Dream." *Option,* September–October, pp. 26–29.

Stein, Rikki. 1997. "Black President." *Straight No Chaser,* no. 43 (Autumn): 20–25.

Stephens, Greg. 1987. "Fela in America: Black Culture Hero for the '80s?" *Reggae and African Beat,* January, pp. 30, 31, 49.

Stewart, Gary. 1992. *Breakout: Profiles in African Rhythm.* Chicago: University of Chicago Press.

Storey, John. 1993. *An Introductory Guide to Cultural Theory and Popular Culture.* Athens: University of Georgia Press.

Sweeney, Philip. 1992. "All Kinds of Freedom." *The Independent,* November 12.

Tannenbaum, Rob. 1985. "Fela Anikulapo-Kuti." *Musician,* May, pp. 23–30.

Tate, Greg. 1992. *Flyboy in the Buttermilk: Essays on Contemporary America.* New York: Simon & Schuster.

Teniola, Eric. 1978. "5 Parties Registered." *Daily Times,* December 23, p. 1.

Thomas, T. Ajayi. 1992. *History of Juju Music.* New York: Thomas.

Thompson, Robert Farris. 1974. *African Art in Motion.* Los Angeles: University of California Press.

————. 1983. *Flash of the Spirit: African and Afro-American Art and Philosophy.* New York: Random House.

Tialobi, Gordon. 1978. "Movement of the People Programme Made Easy." *Punch,* December 28, p. 1.

Timesgirl Cleopatra. 1969. "Say It Loud, I Hate Soul." *Daily Times,* May 11, p. 2.

Tomlinson, John. 1991. *Cultural Imperialism.* Baltimore: Johns Hopkins University Press.

Toop, David. 1993. "Sound Check: *Underground System.*" *Wire,* February, p. 57.

————. 1997a. "The Meaning of World Music." *Wire,* January, p. 74.

————. 1997b. "On Some Deaths in the Family." *Wire,* October, p. 90.

Tutuola, Amos. 1954. *My Life in the Bush of Ghosts.* New York: Grove Press

Udenwa, Chuzzy Onuora. 1985a. "Fela's Queens." *African Guardian Supplement,* October 13, pp. B1, B2, B4.

———. 1985b. "Toast to Fela at 47." *African Guardian Supplement,* October 13, p. B4

———. 1986a. "Fela: A Taste of Freedom." *African Guardian Supplement,* April 27, pp. B1, B2.

———. 1986b. "Fela Sacks Queen." *African Guardian Supplement,* June 13, p. 2.

———. 1986c. "Fela: Starting the Journey Afresh." *African Guardian Supplement,* August 24, p. B8.

———. 1988. "A Man of Three Sides." *African Guardian,* October 17, p. 23.

Uhakheme, Ozolua. 1997a. "When Fela Was with Me—Olaiya." *The Guardian,* August 16, p. 14.

———. 1997b. "He Was Bad for Business, Says Promoter." *The Guardian,* August 16, p. 19.

Ukpabi, Ijeoma. 1992. "A Life All Their Own." *African Guardian,* September 21, p. 41.

United States Department of State. 1992. *Post Report: Nigeria.* Washington, D.C.: U.S. Government Printing Office.

Uzoigwe, G. N. 1985. "European Partition and Conquest of Africa: An Overview." In *General History of Africa Volume 7: Africa under Colonial Domination,1880–1935,* ed. A. Adu Boachen. London: Heinemann.

Uzoma, Henry. 1997. "The Worlds of Fela." *Source,* August 18, pp. 34–40.

Uzoukwu, Alozie. 1984. "Musicians Urged to Exercise Caution." *Punch,* March 27, p. 1.

Van Pelt, Carter. 1997. "Fela Anikulapo-Kuti: Africaman Original." *The Beat* 5/6, no. 16:52–59.

Veal, Michael. 1994. "Music as a Weapon: The Political Music of Fela Anikulapo-Kuti." Master's thesis, Wesleyan University.

Vincent, Rickey. 1996. *Funk: The Music, The People, and the Rhythm of the One.* New York: St. Martin's Griffin.

Vogel, Susan. 1991. *Africa Explores: Twentieth Century African Art.* New York: Center for African Art.

Waidor-Pregbagha, Stevie. 1997. "And after Fela?" *Source,* August 18, pp. 42–45.

Wallace, Michele. 1990. *Invisibility Blues.* London: Verso.

Wallenstein, Barry. 1988. "In Words, Out of Music." *Wire,* June 1988, pp. 42–45.

Ward, Edward. 1937. *Marriage among the Yoruba.* Washington, D.C.: Catholic University of America.

Waterman, Christopher. 1990. *Juju: A Social History and Ethnography of an African Popular Music.* Chicago: University of Chicago Press.

Watrous, Peter. 1989. "Fela Offers a Mosaic of Music and Politics." *New York Times,* July 28, p. C10.

Watson, Ben. 1997. "Invisible Jukebox: Bootsy Collins." *Wire,* December, pp. 46–48.

Watts, Ian. 1984a. "Cross-Rhythms of Music and Politics." *Africa,* January, pp. 54–55.

———. 1984b. "The Man behind the Music." *Africa,* January, p. 55.

Weinstein, Norman. 1992. *A Night in Tunisia: Imaginings of Africa in Jazz.* Metuchen, N.J.: Scarecrow Press.

White, Timothy. 1978. *Catch a Fire: The Life of Bob Marley.* New York: Henry Holt.

Williams, Chancellor. 1987. *The Destruction of Black Civilization: Great Issues of a Race from 4500 BC to 2000 AD.* Chicago: Third World.

Williams, Raymond. 1977. *Marxism and Literature.* Oxford: Oxford University Press.

Wilmer, Valerie. 1977. *As Serious as Your Life: The Story of the New Jazz.* London: Serpent's Tail.

Wilson, Olly. 1974. "The Significance of the Relationship between African-American Music and West African Music." *Black Perspective in Music* 2 (Spring): 3–22.

Yamada, Paul. 1980s. "George Clinton Interview." *Terminal Zone,* no. 1:3–22.

Zefferi, Paolo. 1988. "Una Suite "Nera" Contro Il Potere." *Spettacoli,* November, p. 38.

Videos

Anikulapo-Kuti, Fela. 1991a. *Fela Live.* Shanachie 101.

———. 1991b. *Fela In Concert.* View Video Jazz Series 1305.

Anikulapo-Kuti, Fela, and Roy Ayers. 1987. *Fela and Roy Ayers: Africa '79.* Family One Productions 90140.

Various artists. 1988. *Konkombe: The Nigerian Pop Music Scene.* Shanachie 1201.

Interviews with Author

Sunny Ade, New Haven, Connecticut, August 1992.

Fela Anikulapo-Kuti, New York, July 1989.

Fela Anikulapo-Kuti, Lagos, Nigeria, March 1992.

John Collins, New Haven, Connecticut, February 2000.
Alfred "Pee Wee" Ellis, New York, November 1992.
Abayomi Gbolagunte, New York, December 1992.
Jay Hoggard, Middletown, Connecticut, July 1997.
Sandra Iszadore, Los Angeles, February 1999.
Akanbi Moses, New Haven, Connecticut, August 1992.
Julius Ndimbie, telephone interview, April 1993.
Maceo Parker, New York, November 1992.
Kate Rushin, Middletown, Connecticut, June 1996.
Olakunle Tejuoso, New York, December 1992.
Ade Thomas, Lagos, Nigeria, March 1992.

Discography

Compiled by Michael Veal
and Toshiya Endo

Recordings by Fela Anikulapo-Kuti (formerly Fela Ransome-Kuti)

With the Highlife Rakers

1960? *Fela Ransome-Kuti and His Highlife Rakers.* 7" UK. Melodisc 1532. Contains "Aigana" and "Fela's Special." (This recording was tracked down by Ray Templeton who has several Melodisc singles with higher label numbers, all of which have pre-1966 dates on the label. Therefore it is unlikely to have been released later than 1960.)

With Koola Lobitos

1963–1969. "Abiara," "Ajo," "Alagbara," "Araba's Delight," "Bonfo," "Egbin," "Eke," "Fere," "Great Kids," "Home Cooking," "Iya Mi O Se O," "Lagos Baby," "Laise, Lairo," "Mi O Mo," "My Baby Don Love Me," "Omuti Ti Se," "Onidodo," "Onifere," "Oritshe," "Se E Tunde," "Wa Dele," "Wakawaka," and "Yese Yese." (Recording information is unknown for these singles.)

1969? *Fela Ransome-Kuti and His Koola Lobitos Live at Afro-Spot.* Label information unknown. Contains "Everyday I Got My Blues," "Moti Gborokan," "Wakawaka," "Ako," "Ololufe," "Laise, Lairo."

With Nigeria 70

1969. *The '69 Los Angeles Sessions.* UK (1993): Stern's STCD3005. Contains "My Lady Frustration," "Viva Nigeria," "Obe," "Ako," "Witchcraft," "Wayo," "Lover," "Funky Horn," "Eko," and "This Is Sad."

1970. *Fela's London Scene.* Nigeria: EMI HNLX 5200; USA (1971): Editions Makossa M2399. Contains "J'ehin-J'ehin," "Egbe Mi O," "Who're You," "Buy Africa," and "Fight to Finish."

With Afrika 70

Early 1970s. "Ariya," "Beautiful Dancer," "Beggar's Song," "Black Man's Cry" (studio version), "Fogofogo," "Going In and Out," "Jeun 'K'oku," "Monday Morning in Lagos" (single version), "Shenshema." (Recording information is unknown for these singles.)

1971. *Fela Ransome Kuti and the Africa 70 Live with Ginger Baker.* EMI Zonophone SLRZ 1023. UK: Regal Zonophone SLRZ1023; France(1975): Pathe Marconi 062-04933. Contains "Let's Start," "Black Man's Cry," "Ye Ye De Smell" and "Egbe Mi O (Carry Me, I Want to Die)."

1971. *Why Black Man Dey Suffer* (with Ginger Baker). Unreleased on EMI. Released as African Songs Limited AS 0001. Contains "Why Black Man Dey Suffer" and "Ikoyi Mentality Versus Mushin Mentality."

1972. *Music of Fela–Roforofo Fight.* Nigeria: Jofabro Nigeria JILP001; USA (1975): Editions Makossa EM2307 and EM230. Contains "Roforofo Fight," "Trouble Sleep Yanga Wake Am," "Question Jam Answer," and "Go Slow."

1972. *Na Poi.* Nigeria: EMI HMV HNLX 5070. Contains "Na Poi (part 1)," "Na Poi (part 2)," and "You No Go Die Unless You Wan Die."

1972. *Open and Close.* Nigeria: EMI HNLX 5090; France (1975): Pathe Marconi 062-81957. Contains "Open and Close," "Swegbe and Pako," and "Gbagada Gbagada Gbogodo Gbogodo."

1972. *Shakara.* Nigeria: EMI 008N; USA (1974): Editions Makossa EM2305; France(1974): Pathe Marconi 062 82718; UK (1975): Creole CRLP501. Contains "Shakara Oloje" and "Lady."

1973. *Afrodisiac.* Nigeria: EMI 06281290; UK (1972): Regal Zonophone EMI 062 81290; France (1975): Pathe Marconi 062 81290. Contains "Alu Jon Jonki Jon," "Chop and Quench," "Eko Ile," and "Je'n Wi Temi."

1973. *Gentleman.* Nigeria: EMI NEMI 0009; France (1975): Pathe Marconi 2C 062 81960; UK (1979): Creole CRLP502. Contains "Gentleman," "Fefe Naa Efe," and "Igbe (Shit)."

1974. *Alagbon Close.* Nigeria: Jofabro Nigeria JILP1002; USA (1975): Editions Makossa EM2313. Contains "Alagbon Close" and "I No Get Eye for Back."

1975. *Confusion* [parts 1 and 2]. Nigeria: EMI NEMI 0004. Contains "Confusion" (instrumental) and "Confusion" (vocal).

1975. *Everything Scatter.* Nigeria: Phonogram Coconut PMLP1000; UK (1977): Creole CRLP509. Contains "Everything Scatter" and " Who No Know Go Know."

1975. *Expensive Shit.* Nigeria: Sound Workshop SWS1001; USA (1975): Editions Makossa EM2315. Contains "Expensive Shit" and "Water No Get Enemy."

1975. *Fela's Budget Special.* Nigeria: EMI HNLX 5081. Contains "Monday Morning in Lagos," "Shenshema," "Don't Gag Me," "Beggar's Song," "Alu Jon-Jon-Ki-Jon," and "Chop & Quench" (instrumental).

1975. *He Miss Road.* Produced by Ginger Baker. Nigeria: EMI 006N; France (1975): Pathe Marconi 052 81958; UK (1984): rereleased on Sterns 3008. Contains "He Miss Road," "Monday Morning in Lagos," and "He No Possible." The title of the track "He No Possible" was translated to English ("It's No Possible") for the Stern's release.

1975. *Noise for Vendor Mouth.* Nigeria: Afrobeat ABR011. Contains "Noise for Vendor Mouth" and "Mattress."

1976. *Again, Excuse O.* Nigeria: Coconut PMLP1002. Contains "Excuse-O" and "Mr. Grammartology-lisation-alism Is the Boss."

1976. *Before I Jump Like Monkey Give Me Banana.* Nigeria: Coconut PMLP1001. Contains "Monkey Banana" and "Sense Wiseness."

1976. *Ikoyi Blindness.* Nigeria: Africa Music LP AMILP001. Contains "Ikoyi Blindness" and "Gba Mi Leti Ki N'dolowo."

1976. *Kalakuta Show.* Nigeria: EMI suffix unknown; USA (1976): Editions Makossa M2320; UK (1976?): Creole CRLP 507A. Contains "Kalakuta Show" and "Don't Make Ganran Ganran."

1976. *No Bread.* Nigeria: Sound Workshop SWS1003; USA (1982): Editions Makossa EM2382 (*Unnecessary Begging*). Contains "No Bread" and "Unnecessary Begging."

1976. *Upside Down.* Nigeria: Decca Afrodisia DWAPS2005. Contains "Upside Down" and "Go Slow."

1976. *Yellow Fever.* Nigeria: Decca Afrodisia DWAPS 2004. Contains "Yellow Fever" and "Na Poi 75."

1976. *Zombie.* Nigeria: Coconut PMLP1003; UK (1977): Creole CRLP511. Contains "Zombie" and "Mr. Follow Follow"

1977. *Fear Not for Man.* Nigeria: Decca Afrodisia DWAPS 2035. Contains "Fear Not for Man" and "Palm-Wine Sound."

1977. *I Go Shout Plenty.* Nigeria: Unreleased as Decca Afrodisia DWAPS 2036. Contains "I Go Shout Plenty" and "Frustration of My Lady." ("I Go Shout Plenty" released in 1986 as Decca Afrodisia DWAPS 2251. "Frustration of My Lady" released in 1983 on Lagos International LIR6.)

1977. *Johnny Just Drop* [parts 1 and 2]. Nigeria: Decca Afrodisia DWAPS 2023. Contains "Johnny Just Drop" (instrumental and vocal)

1977. *No Agreement.* Nigeria: Decca Afrodisia DWAPS 2039; France(1977): Barclay 829 682-1. Contains "No Agreement" and "Dog Eat Dog."

1977. *Observation No Crime.* Nigeria: Unreleased as Decca Afrodisia DWAPS2037. Contains "Observation No Crime" and "Lady."

1977. *Opposite People.* Nigeria: Decca Afrodisia DWAPS 2026. Contains "Opposite People" and "Equalisation of Trouser and Pant."

1977. *Shuffering and Shmiling* . Nigeria: Coconut PMLP1005. Contains "Shuffering and Shmiling" (instrumental and vocal)

1977. *Sorrow, Tears and Blood.* Nigeria: Unreleased as Decca Afrodisia DWAPS2025; released as Kalakuta KK001-A. Contains "Sorrow, Tears and Blood" and "Colonial Mentality."

1977. *Stalemate.* Nigeria: Decca Afrodisia DWAPS 2033. Contains "Stalemate" and " African Message (Don't Worry About My Mouth-O)."

1977. *Why Black Man Dey Suffer.* Nigeria: Unreleased as Decca Afrodisia DWAPS 2036. Contains "Why Black Man Dey Suffer" and "Man." ("Why Black Man Dey Suffer" released in 1986 on Decca Afrodisia DWAPS 2251.)

1978. *Shuffering and Shmiling* [parts 1 and 2]. Phonogram Coconut PMLP 1005; Celluloid 6117.

1979. *I.T.T. (International Thief Thief)* [parts 1 and 2]. Nigeria: Kalakuta 002. Contains "I.T.T." (instrumental and vocal)

1979. *Unknown Soldier* [parts 1 and 2]. Nigeria: Phonodisk Skylark SKLP 003A. Contains "Unknown Soldier" (instrumental and vocal).

1979. *V.I.P. (Vagabonds in Power)* [parts 1 and 2]. Nigeria: Jofabro KILP 001; Kalakuta KILP001. Contains "Vagabonds in Power" (instrumental and vocal)

1980. *Authority Stealing.* Nigeria: Kalakuta [no suffix]. Contains "Authority Stealing" (instrumental and vocal).

1980. *Music of Many Colors* (with Roy Ayers). Nigeria: Phonodisk PHD003. Contains " Africa–Center of the World" and "Blacks Got to Be Free."

1981. *Coffin for Head of State.* Nigeria: Kalakuta KALP003. Contains "Coffin for Head of State" (instrumental and vocal).

1986. *I Go Shout Plenty.* Nigeria: Decca Afrodisia DWAPS 2251. Contains "I Go Shout Plenty" and "Why Black Man Dey Suffer" (second version).

With Egypt 80

1982. *Original Sufferhead.* Nigeria: Lagos International LIR 2; UK (1981): Arista SPART1177. Contains "Original Sufferhead" and "Power Show."

1983. *Perambulator.* Nigeria: Lagos International LIR 6. Contains "Perambulator" and "Frustration of My Lady" (see Decca DWAPS 2036).

1984. *Live in Amsterdam–Music Is the Weapon.* UK: EMI FELA2401293;US: Capitol STB 12359; Phillips PH 2000, 2002; Nigeria(1986): Polygram PH2000 and PH2002. Contains "Movement of the People No. 1," "Gimme Shit, I Give You Shit," and "Custom Check Point."

1985. *Army Arrangement* (original version) [parts 1 and 2]. USA: Celluloid 6115.

1985. *Army Arrangement* (remix). Produced by Fela and Bill Laswell. UK: Yaba-Celluloid 6109. Nigeria: Kalakuta K007. Contains remixes of "Army Arrangement," "Cross-Examination," and "Government Chicken Boy."

1986. *Teacher Don't Teach Me Nonsense* . Nigeria: Polygram Phillips PH2004; Mercury 422 833 525-1; France: Barclay 831325-1/ 831-362-1, 831-362-2 . Contains "Teacher Don't Teach Me Nonsense" (instrumental and vocal). (The Mercury and Barclay releases also contain "Look and Laugh"[instrumental and vocal].)

1989. *Beasts of No Nation.* Kalakuta 008. Shanachie 43070. Justine JU-UDR 360153. Contains "Beasts of No Nation" and "Just Like That." (The Justine release contains complete versions of both songs. The Kalakuta release contains the complete version of "Beasts." The Shanachie release contains the vocal half of "Beasts" and a complete version of "Just Like That" [see Kalakuta 011]).

1989. *Overtake Don Overtake Overtake.* Nigeria: Kalakuta K009. Contains "Overtake Don Overtake Overtake" (instrumental and vocal).

1990. *Confusion Break Bone.* Nigeria: Kalakuta K010. Contains "Confusion Break Bone" (instrumental and vocal).

1990. *Just Like That.* Nigeria: Kalakuta K011. Contains "Just Like That" and the vocal half of "Movement of the People Political Statement Number 1." (See EMI 2401293 for complete version)

1992. *Underground System.* Nigeria: Kalakuta KALP013; UK (1992): Sterns STCD1043. Contains "Underground System" and "Pansa Pansa."

Unrecorded/Unreleased Compositions

"Akunakuna, Senior Brother of Perambulator" (1980s)
"Bamaiyi" (1990s)
"Big Blind Country" (1980s)
"Chop and Clean Mouth Like Nothing Happened, Na New Name for Stealing" (1990s)
"Clear Road for Jagba Jagba" (1990s)
"Cock Dance" (1990s)
"Condom, Scallywag, and Scatter" (1990s)
"Country of Pain" (1980s)
"Football Government" (1970s)
"Government of Crooks" (1980s)
"Male" (1970s)
"Music Against Second Slavery" (1990s)
"Nigerian Natural Grass" (1970s)
"O.A.U." (1980s)
"Observation No Crime" (1970s)

Other Artists with Afrika 70 or Egypt 80

Allen, Tony. 1975. *Jealousy* (with Afrika 70). Nigeria: Sound Workshop SWS 1004. Contains "Jealousy" and "Hustler."
———. 1977. *Progress* (with Afrika 70). Nigeria: Coconut PMLP1004; Phonogram PMLP 1004. Contains "Progress" and "Afro Disco Beat."
———. 1979. *No Accommodation for Lagos* (with Afrika 70). Phonogram POLP 035. Contains "No Accommodation for Lagos" and "African Message."
Imo, Oluko. 1988. *Oduduwa* (with Afrika 70). Nigeria: Arigidi O1-7. Contains "Oduduwa" and "Were Oju Le."
Iszadore, Sandra Akanke. 1976. *Upside Down* (with Afrika 70). Decca Afrodisia DWAPS 2005.
Williams, Tunde. 1977. *Mr. Big Mouth* (with Afrika 70). Nigeria: Decca Afrodisia DWAPS2030. Contains "Mr. Big Mouth" and "The Beginning."

Recordings by Other Artists Cited in Text

Abiodun, Dele. 1985. *Adawa Super Sound.* Shanachie 43032.
Ade, King Sunny. 1976. *Synchro System–Movement.* African Songs Limited AS 26.
———. 1977. *Synchro Chapter 1.* Sunny Alade SALPS 7.
———. 1983. *Synchro Series.* Sunny Alade SALPS 37.
———. 1983. *Synchro System.* Mango Records MLPS 9737.
———. 1984. *Aura.* Island ILPM 9746.
———. 1986. *"O Ti To"* (*The Truth*). Sunny Alade SALPS 46.
Allen, Tony. 1979. *No Discrimination.* Shanu-Ola GSLP 1012.
———. 1985. *N.E.P.A.* (*Never Expect Power Always*). Celluloid/Moving Target MT 002.
Anikulapo-Kuti, Femi, and the Positive Force Band. 1989. *No Cause for Alarm.* Polygram.
———. 1991. *M.Y.O.B.* (*Mind Your Own Business*). Kalakuta 012.
———. 1995. *Femi Kuti.* Tabu 314530477-2.
———. 1999. *Shoki Shoki.* Barclay 559 035.
Art Ensemble of Chicago. 1987. *Ancient to the Future.* DIW 804.
Baker, Ginger. 1970s. *Stratavarious.* Polydor 2383 133.
Barker, Dave, and the Upsetters. 1996. *Prisoner of Love.* Trojan CDTBL 127.
Barrister, Alhaji (Chief) Sikiru Ayinde. 1980s. *Iwa.* Phonodisk SKOLP 018.

Barrister, Alhaji (Chief) Wasiu Ayinde. 1980s. *Ori.* Omo Aje OLPS 1331.

Beginning of the End. 1970. "Funky Nassau." Included on *Atlantic Rhythm and Blues Volume 7: 1969–1974.* Atlantic 7 81299-2.

Booker T. & the MG's. 1994. *The Very Best of Booker T. & the MG's.* Rhino R2 71738.

Brown, Chuck, and the Soul Searchers. 1986. *Live!* Future Sounds F0007.

Brown, James. 1969. *It's A Mother!* King KSD 1063.

———. 1971. *Revolution of the Mind.* Polydor 314 517 983-2.

———. 1986. *James Brown's Funky People.* Polydor 829 417-2.

———. 1988. *James Brown's Funky People, Part Two.* Polydor 835 857-2.

———. 1990. *Star Time.* Polygram 849-108-2.

———. 1992. *Love Power Peace–Live at the Olympia, Paris 1971.* Polydor 314 513 389-2.

———. 1993. *Soul Pride: The Instrumentals 1960–1969.* Polydor 314 517 845-2.

———. 1995. *Funky Good Time: The JB's Anthology.* Polydor 31452 7094-2

———. 1996. *Foundations of Funk: A Brand New Bag, 1964–1969.* Polydor 31453 11652-2.

———. 1996. *Funk Power 1970: A Brand New Thang.* Polydor 31453 1684 4/2.

Buckshot Le Fonque. 1994. *Buckshot Le Fonque.* Columbia CK 57323.

Byrne, David. 1981. *The Catherine Wheel.* Sire SIR M5S 3645.

Cardona, Milton. 1986. *Bembe.* American Clave 1004.

Clinton, George. 1983. *You Shouldn't Nuf ' Bit, Fish.* Capitol CDP 7 96357.

Collins, Bootsy. 1994. *Back in the Day: The Best of Bootsy.* Warner Bros. 2-26581.

Coltrane, John. 1962. *Live at the Village Vanguard.* MCA/Impulse MCAD 31936.

———. 1963. *Impressions.* Impulse AS 42.

Cymande. 1973. *Bra.* Janus J-215.

Davis, Miles. 1959. *Kind of Blue.* Columbia CK 40579.

———. 1969. *Bitches Brew.* Columbia G2K 40577.

DeSouza, Ignace. 1994. *Ignace DeSouza.* Original Music OMCD 026.

Dibango, Manu. 1973. *Soul Makossa.* Fiesta 51.199.

Ekemode, Orlando Julius. 1985. *Dance Afro-Beat.* Shanachie 43029.

Ellington, Duke. 1989. *The Great Paris Concert.* Atlantic 304-2.

Eno, Brian, and David Byrne. 1981. *My Life in the Bush of Ghosts.* Sire 6093-2.

Funkadelic. 1973. *Cosmic Slop.* Westbound.

Ghetto Blaster. 1987. *People.* Celluloid/Pipeline MT 012.

Hotel X. 1995. *Ladders.* SST CD 317.

Ilori, Solomon, and His Afro-Drum Ensemble. 1963. *African Highlife.* Blue Note BN 84136.

Ishola, Haruna. 1970s. *Oluwa Nikan Loba.* Star SRPS 37.

J-Funk Express. 1996. *This Is Rare Groove!* 99 Records 9026.

Jara, Victor. 1970s. *Victor Jara: An Unfinished Song.* Redwood Records RR 3300.

Kollington, Ayinla. 1980s. *Mo Tun De Pelu Ara.* Olumo KRLPS 1.

Les Meilleurs de la 1ere Biennale Artistic et Culturelle de la Jeunesse. 1970. *Orchestre Regional de Segou.* Editions du Ministere De L'Information BM 30 L 2601.

———. 1970. *Orchestre Regional de Mopti.* Editions du Ministere De L'Information BM 30 L 2602.

———. 1970. *Orchestre Regional de Sikasso.* Editions du Ministere De L'Information BM 30 L 2603.

———. 1970. *Orchestre Regional de Kayes.* Editions du Ministere De L'Information BM 30 L 2604.

———. 1970. *Rail Band de Bamako.* Editions du Ministere De L'Information BM 30 L 2605.

———. 1970. *Mali National Orchestra "A."* Editions du Ministere De L'Information BM 30 L 2606.

Maal, Baaba. 1991. *Baayo.* Mango 162 539 907-2.

Marley, Bob, and the Wailers. 1971. *Rasta Revolution.* Trojan CDTRD 406.

———. 1977. *Exodus.* Island ILPS 9498.

———. 1978. *Kaya.* Island ILPS 9517.

———. 1979. *Survival.* Island ILPS 9542.

———. 1981. *Reggae on Broadway.* DMD 291.

Masekela, Hugh. 1974. *Introducing Hedzoleh Soundz.* Blue Thumb BTS 62.

———. 1974. *I Am Not Afraid.* Blue Thumb BTS 6015.

————. 1975. *The Boy's Doin' It.* Casablanca NBLP 7017.

————. 1985. *Waiting for the Rain.* Jive/Afrika JL8-838.

————. 1993. *Hope.* Worldly/Triloka 7203-2.

Millie (Millicent Small). 1964. "My Boy Lollipop" Included on *Tougher Than Tough: The Story of Jamaican Music.* Island 162-539-935-2.

Nzeka, Ephraim Uzomechina. 1980s. *Ephraim Sings Fela.* Tabansi TRL 277.

Obey, Chief Commander Ebenezer, and His Inter-Reformers Band. 1976. *Operation Feed the Nation.* Obey WAPS 338.

Olatunji, Yusuf. 1960s. *Yusuf Olatunji, Volume 17.* Phonogram PL 6361050.

Omowura, Ayinla. 1970s. *Ayinla Omowura and His Apala Group.* EMI HNLX 5085.

Orchestra Baobab. 1993. *Bamba.* Stern's STC 3003.

Owoh, Orlando. 1995. *Dr. Ganja's Polytonality Blues.* Original Music OMCD 035.

Parliament. 1977. *Parliament Live: P-Funk Earth Tour.* Casablacnca 834 941-2.

Perry, Lee. 1989. *Open the Gate.* Trojan CDPRY2.

————. 1990. *Build the Ark.* Trojan CDPRY3.

————. 1990. *Public Jestering.* Attack ATLP 108.

Person, Houston. 1977. "I No Get Eye for Back." Included on *Move To the Groove: The Best of 1970s Jazz-Funk.* Verve 314 525 797-2.

Sangare, Oumou. 1991. *Moussolou/* World Circuit WCD 021.

————. 1996. *Worotan.* World Circuit 045.

Sun Ra and His Arkestra. 1970s. *Horizon.* El Saturn 1217718.

————. 1978. *Live at Montreux.* Inner City 1039.

————. 1980. *Strange Celestial Road.* Rounder 3035.

Sweat Band. 1980. *Sweat Band.* Uncle Jam JZ 36857.

Talking Heads. 1980. *Remain in Light.* Sire 6095-2.

Tosh, Peter. 1976. *Legalize It.* Columbia 34253.

————. 1977. *Equal Rights.* Columbia 34670.

Turre, Steve. 1995. *Rhythm Within.* Antilles 314 527 159-2.

Various artists. 1985. *Juju Roots.* Rounder 5017.

Various artists. 1990. *Giants of Danceband Highlife.* Original Music OMCD 011.

Various artists. 1992. *Heavy on the Highlife.* Original Music OMCD 012.

Various artists. 1993. *Azagas and Archibogs.* Original Music OMCD 014.

Various artists. 1995. *Money No Be Sand.* Original Music OMCD 031.

Various artists. 1998. *Africa Funk: The Original Sound of 1970s Funky Africa.* Harmless HURTCD016.

Warren, Guy. 1958. *Themes for African Drums.* RCA-Victor LSP-1864.

Wright, Charles, and the Watts 103rd Street Rhythm Band. 1995. *Express Yourself: The Best of Charles Wright and the Watts 103rd Street Rhythm Band.* Warner Bros. 4-45306.

Index

Names and Subjects

Songs

All songs by Fela Anikulapo-Kuti unless otherwise noted.